# THE OLD SOUTH

*The Founding of American Civilization*

# THE OLD SOUTH

## *The Founding of American Civilization*

By

### THOMAS JEFFERSON WERTENBAKER

*Edwards Professor of American History*
*Princeton University*

*ILLUSTRATED*

**COOPER SQUARE PUBLISHERS, INC.**
*New York · 1963*

# PREFACE

TO MILLIONS of Americans the South is a land of mystery. They think of it as the Solid South, a uniform section where rich tobacco and rice planters formerly held sway with their scores of slaves, wide fields and stately mansions, but now changing under the impetus of a new industrial life. But those who today motor over the Skyline Drive, or visit the quaint buildings of the restored Williamsburg, or view the Moravian section of Winston-Salem, or catch the charm of old Charleston, are surprised to find that much that they see does not fit into this pattern. If they pause long enough to study the history of the region they discover that the South is not and never has been uniform, that even in colonial days thousands of its people were not engaged in cultivating the great staple crops, that a very large percentage are and for centuries have been deeply religious, that the population is by no means entirely English in its origins, that there were formerly a large artisan class and a group of merchants whose activities vied with those of the famous traders of New England.

This volume is confined to the study of Maryland, Virginia, North Carolina and South Carolina, for the most part during the colonial and early national periods. There has been no attempt to give a complete social history of the Old South, but merely to develop such topics as best illustrate the forces which moulded its civilization. Political history, church history, the plantation system, slavery have been purposely neglected because historians have already devoted so much attention to them. For studies of the Southern Highlanders, the advance into the Carolina Piedmont, education and many other important topics space has been lacking. Architecture has been emphasized, not because it is of outstanding importance, but because it serves so admirably to illustrate the forces which created our civilization.

The author wishes to acknowledge his indebtedness to his two research assistants, Major Charles P. Stacey, of the Canadian Expeditionary Force, and Miss Jane Link, of Princeton, New Jersey. He also extends his thanks to Miss Katharine Brown of Norwich, Connecticut, for reading the manuscript. Grateful acknowledgment is made to the Rockefeller Foundation for generous financial aid through the Council of Humanities of Princeton University, and to the David H. McAlpin Research Fund of the Department of History, Princeton University, which enabled him to consult the Brock Collection of Virginia History in the Huntington Library, San Marino, California.

T. J. W.

# CONTENTS

PREFACE v

Chapter I. INTRODUCTION 1

Chapter II. INTELLECTUAL LIFE OF THE
TOBACCO ARISTOCRAT 19

Chapter III. MANOR HOUSE AND COTTAGE 71

Chapter IV. ADVANCE INTO PIEDMONT 118

Chapter V. TUCKAHOE AND COHEE 164

Chapter VI. THE ARTISAN AT WORK 220

Chapter VII. MANSIONS ON THE ASHLEY 271

Chapter VIII. THE GOOD EARTH 305

CONCLUSION 348

INDEX 353

# TEXT ILLUSTRATIONS

*Figure*                                                                      *Page*

1  Advertisement of Symes' Free School                                          25
   *From "The Virginia Gazette," March 12, 1752*

2  The Castle                                                                    77
   *Courtesy Virginia Historical Society*

3  The Raleigh Tavern                                                           98
   *From W. C. Langdon, "Everyday Things in American Life, 1607–1777"*

4  Advertisement of Crown Tavern                                               99
   *From "The Virginia Gazette," 1752*

5  Plans of Southern Mansions: Westover, Chase House and Miles
   Brewton House                                                              101
   *From Fiske Kimball, "Early American Domestic Architecture"*

6  Stairway at Westover                                                        102
   *From W. C. Langdon, "Everyday Things in American Life, 1607–1777"*

7  Iron gate, Westover                                                         103
   *From W. C. Langdon, "Everyday Things in American Life, 1607–1777"*

8  Four ways of taking tobacco to market                                       131
   *From William Tatham, "Essay on Tobacco," courtesy Colonial Williams-
   burg, Inc.*

9  Canal boats, Richmond, Va.                                                  133
   *Redrawn by E. G. Lutz from "Harpers Weekly"*

10 Virginia tobacco wharf                                                      135
   *From W. C. Langdon, "Everyday Things in American Life, 1607–1777"*

11 Tanning leather                                                             251
   *From Roger Burlingame, "March of the Iron Men"*

12 The Shoemaker                                                               253
   *From Roger Burlingame, "March of the Iron Men"*

# PLATES

*Plate*  *Facing Page*

1 Plan showing forms popular with southern colonial gardeners 48
*From "Gardens of Colony and State," by courtesy of the Garden Club of America*

2 Mount Vernon 49

3 Early Virginia Hunting Scene 80
*From "Hounds and Hunting Through the Ages," by Joseph Thomas, M.F.H. Courtesy Mrs. Chalmers Wood*

4 Announcement of the first appearance of the Hallams in America 80
*From "The Virginia Gazette" of August 28, 1752*

Mrs. Hallam as "Marianne" in "The Dramatist" 80
*From the Theatre Collection of the Harvard College Library*

5 Surrey House, Chiddingfold; Cottage at Cottenham, Cambridge 81

Adam Thoroughgood House, Princess Anne County, Virginia 81
*Courtesy Norfolk-Portsmouth Advertising Board*

6 English gambrel, Cambridge; Bacon's Castle, Surry County, Virginia 88

7 Moore House, Yorktown, showing Virginia gambrel 88

8 St. Luke's—rear 89
*Courtesy Historic American Building Survey, Library of Congress*

9 St. Luke's, Smithfield, Virginia 89
*Courtesy Historic American Building Survey, Library of Congress*

10 Wren Building, College of William and Mary 96
*From a photograph copyright Colonial Williamsburg, Inc.*

11 The Capitol, Williamsburg, Virginia 96
*From a photograph copyright Colonial Williamsburg, Inc.*

12 House of Burgesses, Capitol, Williamsburg, Virginia 97
*From a photograph copyright Colonial Williamsburg, Inc.*

## PLATES

*Plate*                                                     *Facing Page*

13 The General Court, Capitol, Williamsburg, Virginia          97
*From a photograph copyright Colonial Williamsburg, Inc.*

14 Eaton Hall and Garden                                       104

15 Palace from Garden                                          104
*From a photograph copyright Colonial Williamsburg, Inc.*

16 Tulip Hill, Anne Arundel County, Maryland                   105

17 Bruton Church, Williamsburg, Virginia                       108
*From a photograph copyright Colonial Williamsburg, Inc.*

18 Hammond House, Annapolis, Maryland                          108

19 Vawter's Church, Essex County, Virginia                     109

20 Christ Church, Alexandria, Virginia                         109
*Courtesy Historic American Building Survey, Library of Congress*

Pohick Church, Fairfax County, Virginia; Acquia Church,
near Fredericksburg, Virginia                                  109

21 The Lawn, University of Virginia                            112
*Courtesy Historic American Building Survey, Library of Congress*

22 Monticello, near Charlottesville, Virginia                  112
*Courtesy Historic American Building Survey, Library of Congress*

23 West Lawn, University of Virginia                           113
*Courtesy Historic American Building Survey, Library of Congress*

24 Wachovia Historical Society Museum, Winston-Salem; Mabry
Mill, Floyd County, Virginia; Barn, Jefferson County, West
Virginia; Log House, Catoctin, Frederick County, Maryland      176
*Courtesy Historic American Building Survey, Library of Congress*

25 Bethabara Moravian Church                                   177
*Courtesy Historic American Building Survey, Library of Congress*

26 Michael Brown House, Rowan County, North Carolina;
Moravian Clay Products, Winston-Salem                          177
*Courtesy Historic American Building Survey, Library of Congress*

27 Rose Hill, Frederick County, Maryland                       208
*Courtesy Historic American Building Survey, Library of Congress*

xii

## PLATES

*Plate*                                                               *Facing Page*

28 Wheatland, Jefferson County, West Virginia      208
*Courtesy Historic American Building Survey, Library of Congress*

29 Carpenter's Tools      209
*Courtesy Colonial Williamsburg, Inc.*

30 Almodington, Somerset County, Maryland      224
*Courtesy Metropolitan Museum of Art*

31 Marmion, King George County, Virginia      224
*Courtesy Metropolitan Museum of Art*

32 Grist Mill, New Kent County, Virginia      225
*Courtesy Historic American Building Survey, Library of Congress*

33 Virginia sawmill      225
*Courtesy Historic American Building Survey, Library of Congress*

34 Cooper's Tools      240
*Courtesy Colonial Williamsburg, Inc.*

35 Cabinetmaker's Tools      240
*Courtesy Colonial Williamsburg, Inc.*

36 Blacksmith's Tools      241
*Courtesy Colonial Williamsburg, Inc.*

37 Deane Shop and Forge, Williamsburg, Virginia      241
*Courtesy Colonial Williamsburg, Inc.*

38 Cobbler's Tools      256
*Courtesy Colonial Williamsburg, Inc.*

39 Shoemaker, Colonial Williamsburg      256

40 Barber Shop, Williamsburg, Virginia      257
*Courtesy Colonial Williamsburg, Inc.*

41 Interior of Barber Shop, Williamsburg, Virginia      257

42 Cabinet Making, Williamsburg, Virginia      272
*Courtesy Colonial Williamsburg, Inc.*

43 China Press, Charlottesville, Virginia      272

Corner Cupboard, Norfolk, Virginia      272
*Courtesy P. W. Yeatman, Princeton, N. J.*

*Plate*                                                                   *Facing Page*

44 Old view of Tradd Street, Charleston; Mathews House, 43 East
   Battery, Charleston                                                      273

45 Miles Brewton House, 27 King Street                                     273
    *Courtesy Historic American Building Survey, Library of Congress*

   Drayton Hall                                                          273

46 Mulberry Castle, near Charleston                                        284
    *From "Gardens of Colony and State," by courtesy of the Garden Club of
    America*

47 South Carolina Plantation Boat                                          284
    *Courtesy Charleston Museum*

48 Fireproof Building                                                      285
    *Courtesy Historic American Building Survey, Library of Congress*

   Nathaniel Russell House                                               285
    *Courtesy Pictorial Archives of Early American Architecture, Library of
    Congress*

49 Henry Manigault House, Charleston                                       285
    *Courtesy Pictorial Archives of Early American Architecture, Library of
    Congress*

50 George Edwards House                                                    296
    *Courtesy Pictorial Archives of Early American Architecture, Library of
    Congress*

51 Judge King House                                                        296
    *Courtesy Historic American Building Survey, Library of Congress*

   Doorway, showing influence of Adam Brothers                           296
    *Courtesy Pictorial Archives of Early American Architecture, Library of
    Congress*

52 St. Andrew's Church                                                     297

53 St. James', Goose Creek                                                 297

54 St. Philip's, Charleston                                               300

55 St. Michael's, Charleston                                              300
    *Courtesy Pictorial Archives of Early American Architecture, Library of
    Congress*

56 Wrought-Iron Work, Market Hall; Gate, Sussa House; Gateway, St. John's Lutheran Church; Nathaniel Russell House,
   Charleston                                                            301
    *Courtesy Pictorial Archives of Early American Architecture, Library of
    Congress*

# THE OLD SOUTH

*The Founding of American Civilization*

## Chapter I

## INTRODUCTION

THE chief inheritance of the old South was English. It was at Roanoke Island that the first English child was born in America; Jamestown witnessed the inauguration of the first representative assembly, that priceless boon of English liberty; in Virginia, Maryland and South Carolina the Anglican Church was established by law; local government in the South was patterned after English local government, education after English education, architecture after English architecture. The people, most of them, spoke English, read English books, wore English clothes, sat in English chairs and slept in English beds, were entertained at the theatre by English actors, cut their wood with English axes, ate out of English pewter dishes, celebrated the English holidays with old English customs, continued for generations to correspond with relatives in England. The people of the South were saddened and angered by the bombing of Westminster Abbey, for they love and revere this great cathedral in which so many of their ancestors worshipped long before Jamestown and Charleston were founded. They had even greater cause to grieve over the injury to Westminster Hall, that cradle of American as well as English liberty.

But the colonial South was by no means entirely English in its origins. The traveller who visited various parts of the region just prior to the Revolution would have been surprised at the number of foreigners, some scattered here and there among the English, others segregated in pockets of considerable size. In Virginia or at Charleston he would have met many persons whose names— Maury, Fontaine, Huger, Manigault—betrayed their French origin. At Norfolk he would have found scores of Scotch, whose crowded warehouses lining the banks of the Elizabeth, marked them as prosperous merchants. In western Maryland or at Strasburg in the Valley of Virginia or at Salem in North Carolina, he

I

would have encountered many Germans and Swiss, speaking their so-called Pennsylvania Dutch, clinging to their old faiths, customs and superstitions. Here he would have stumbled upon a group of Welsh, there his curiosity would have been stirred by a tiny Roman Catholic church with a congregation made up chiefly of Irish. Lexington, Virginia, he would have discovered, was as completely Scotch-Irish as though it were located in Ulster, while Mecklenburg County, in North Carolina, was the land of the Scotch Highlanders.

In Scotland for centuries the Highlanders, led by their clan chieftains, waged war on the lowlanders, their fierce raids leaving trails of ruined farms and burned houses. It was a strange fate which brought about a resumption of this struggle on the frontiers of far-off North Carolina. The Highland immigrants, with the advent of the Revolution, sided with George III and the mother country. Not so their neighbors, the Scotch-Irish, for they had left their homes in Ulster and come to America because of English discrimination against their Church and their industry. So when Cornwallis sent Captain Ferguson to North Carolina to recruit soldiers for the royal cause, it was the Highlanders who flocked to his standard. And it was the Highlanders who constituted the bulk of Ferguson's force when they were surrounded and captured at King's Mountain.

South Carolina was surpassed only by New Jersey in the diverse character of its population. The Charleston region was settled by a medley of Barbadians, English, Huguenots, Scotch and Dutch, while farther back at the head of tidewater were Scotch-Irish, Germans, Welsh and Swiss. At Williamsburg were a colony of Scotch-Irish who had sailed up Back River in 1732 to build their crude shelters around the "King's Tree" and hold their services in the little Presbyterian church. At Society Hill, in the old Welsh Neck on the Pee Dee River, a group of pious Baptists came from Delaware to make their home. Chester County, with its York and its Lancaster, was a region of "Pennsylvania Dutch"; at St. Matthews the cattle enclosures, the barns and the well sweeps marked it as a settlement of "Palatines"; Cheraw was peopled with Welsh from the Philadelphia region.

Thus the melting-pot has been active in the South from colonial days. Even among the purely English communities it has been an important factor, for in Maryland and Virginia families from Kent came into contact with families from Dorset, the Essex yeoman found that one of his neighbors hailed from Yorkshire, another from Somerset. The Virginia dialect, which became instantly recognizable, was the product of a number of English dialects. The charming cottages of the small planters had no direct prototype in the mother country, but borrowed one feature from one part of England, another from another part. New England was to a large degree East Anglia transplanted to America; Virginia east of the Blue Ridge was a cross section of all England shaken apart and reunited in a different pattern.

Over in the Shenandoah Valley the Scotch-Irish and Germans struggled to maintain their separate civilizations, yet both yielded slowly to the influence of the English and each borrowed from the other. The Ulster men derided the broad hats, the somber clothing, the long beards, the language of their German and Swiss neighbors, but they learned much from their system of agriculture and their craftsmanship. The Germans and Swiss, in turn, grudgingly gave up their "Pennsylvania Dutch" tongue, accepted English architecture and in some cases went over to the Methodist Church. Nor was it unusual for an English or a Scotch-Irish youth, tempted by a pretty face peeping out from a German sunbonnet, to marry a Dunkard or a Mennonite maiden.

The newcomers to the South, whether English, Scotch-Irish, Germans, French or Swiss, found it different indeed from their native lands. The Suffolk yeoman when settled upon his new plantation on the James was forced to discard the agricultural methods to which he and his father before him had been accustomed. In England he had been careful to use every foot of his tiny farm, to conserve the soil by a rotation of crops, to husband the manure of his cattle for fertilizer; on his 200-acre holding in Virginia or even upon the part of it which he put under cultivation, this was impossible. He found that English grain grew well enough in America, but since he had little sale for it he was forced to turn to the Virginia staple, tobacco. If he knew

3

nothing of the culture of this plant, he was not long in learning from his neighbors.

Life in the tobacco region he found very different from life in England. Whereas in the old country he was surrounded by neighbors, was within ten minutes' walk of the village and perhaps even closer to the church, in Virginia or Maryland he was almost alone upon his farm, which was little more than a clearing in the forest. His nearest neighbor might be a half mile, perhaps a mile away, there were no villages save the county courts and they were hamlets consisting of the court houses and a tavern or two, to attend church on Sunday might entail a journey of ten miles. It was inevitable that his habits, his amusements, his outlook on life, even his superstitions and his religion should be profoundly affected by his new surroundings.

In South Carolina, in the fourth decade of the eighteenth century, when the government set up a series of townships in the back country in an arc around Charleston and brought in groups of foreigners to settle them, conditions of soil and climate upset all their plans. These townships were modelled upon the New England towns, and Queenstown and Orangeburg were expected to become duplicates of Hingham or Harwich. But the Scotch-Irish and Germans were not New England Puritans, the South Carolina back country was not Massachusetts. It is true that little villages were founded after the New England manner, that each settler had his dividend of arable land, that the skilled Scotch-Irish weaver set up his loom, that the German shoemaker and cabinet maker for a while plied their trades. But in a few years the villages began to decline, the tradesmen closed shop, the "dividents" were enlarged into plantations, and the economic life of the townships became much like that of other Southern communities. Here and there German and Swiss farmers clung to the methods of their ancestors, but they too were eventually swept along by the impulse of local conditions and discarded the intensive agriculture of the Rhine Valley or of the hills of Switzerland for the more wasteful farming in vogue around them.

The Europeans who came to the South were almost overwhelmed by the riches nature bestowed upon them. From the

4

Pennsylvania border to Florida and from the Atlantic to the Appalachian ranges stretched a vast area of fertile soil, which if necessary could have fed all Europe and turned out in addition great quantities of timber, tar, pitch, turpentine, indigo and tobacco. The forests, which more than anything else had tempted the English to found colonies in America, and to which they had looked to supply them with naval stores, masts and other vitally needed products, the settlers found an annoyance rather than an asset. It is probable that enough timber was wantonly destroyed in the South during the colonial period in clearing the ground for crops to have built a dozen royal navies and reconstructed every house in England.

It was this very superabundance of riches which in the end proved the curse of the South. The policy of conserving labor at the expense of the soil eventually led to exhaustion and desolation. Today hundreds of thousands of acres, where once ripening tobacco leaves or yellowing wheat brought rich returns, have reverted to the forest. It was the soil, also, which brought on the South the curse of slavery. With land, rich land in almost unlimited quantities, to be had at very low prices, the constant demand was for cheap labor. There was almost no limit to what a planter could earn if he could secure workers for his tobacco or his rice fields. White wage earners proved unsatisfactory, not only because of the high pay demanded, but because as soon as they had laid aside a few pounds they purchased land of their own. The indentured worker did not serve the purpose since he was bound usually for but four or at most five years and then left to make his own bid for a farm and prosperity. But the slave served for life, he had intelligence enough for the tasks required of him, his labor was cheap, and ere long it was recognized that through him lay the road to wealth. Before the end of the third decade of the eighteenth century slavery had been fixed upon the tobacco and rice regions as the basis of their economic and social systems and even of their political systems. Slavery did not prosper in New England because the soil did not invite it; but in the South it was the very lavishness of nature's gifts which made it profitable.

5

It was the life upon the plantation, isolated as it was, which shaped the character of the Southern planter and differentiated him from the English yeoman or the English squire. It gave him a sense of security, of self-reliance, of dignity, of responsibility. He must be an agriculturalist, business man, perhaps doctor, builder, blacksmith, cooper. If he owned slaves, he must look after their welfare, see that they were properly housed, clothed and fed, insist upon work hard enough to insure a crop but not hard enough to injure their health. He must be the despot of a little community, a benevolent despot usually, but one upon whose shoulders fell the responsibility for the welfare of ten or twenty or perhaps a hundred human beings. The Englishman who gave up his manor or his leaseholds and migrated to the tobacco country to start life anew, could not escape the remoulding force of the plantation, became more and more a Virginian or Marylander, less an Englishman.

In the first stages of settlement the influence of the frontier was profound. The struggle with the vast forests, the battle with Indians, the handicap of great distances, the difficulty of educating children, all of which have proved so important as the frontier moved westward, influenced life on the banks of the James three centuries ago not less than in the old Northwest or on the prairies in later days. Hardships, suffering, danger made the settlers self-reliant, brave, resourceful, democratic. It is true that the deep-water frontiersman enjoyed a closer touch with Europe than did his successors after the frontier had moved on to shallow water and beyond. It was possible for John Rolfe to supply his family with clothes made in England; a century later for Peter Jefferson or Joshua Fry to bring boxes of English coats and gowns to their homes in the Piedmont was a costly and tedious matter; over the mountains in Kentucky or Tennessee it was almost impossible.

But the first pioneers deserve undying distinction as path-finders. John Sevier and Daniel Boone could avail themselves of lessons learned by their predecessors through decades of experience in woodcraft and in dealing with the Indians. But for the brave men and women who landed on the banks of the James under the guidance of Captain Newport or Sir Thomas Gates there

6

were no precedents, America for them was a land of mystery and unknown perils. They had to learn the ways of the Indian by bitter experience; they discovered the dangers of malaria only after it had taken a heavy toll of valuable lives; they had to experiment with building in the forests, for they did not have the art of log-cabin construction worked out for them in advance; it was only by trial and error that they knew what crops to grow, how to acclimate themselves to the excesses of heat and cold. The destiny of the South was shaped in no small degree by the many waterways—bays, sounds, rivers, with which nature had endowed her. The Chesapeake Bay, a great inland sea stretching from within a few miles of Pennsylvania to within a few miles of North Carolina, became an important highway of commerce. And up and down the broad rivers of the region—the Potomac, the Rappahannock, the York, the James, the Elizabeth, the Roanoke, the Cooper, the Ashley, the Savannah and many others, sailed the picturesque little vessels of the day with their cargoes of English manufactured goods or of tobacco or rice or staves or naval stores. It was their network of waterways which made possible for Virginia and Maryland thousands of private wharves but deprived them, for a century at least, of real ports, since it was easy for each planter to land imported goods and ship out his hogsheads of tobacco directly at his plantation. It was only in the eighteenth century, when the settlements had pushed back beyond deep water, that Norfolk and Annapolis became ports of some importance and that Alexandria, Fredericksburg, Richmond and other shipping towns came into being.

The rivers were of importance, also, in directing the course of settlement. The first plantations were on the river banks and decades passed before the ridges of the peninsulas in between were filled in. In selecting the site for a plantation the first consideration was fertility of soil, the second was facilities for transportation, for in both the tobacco and rice regions commerce was chiefly water-borne. Even when the colonists pressed on into the Piedmont, where the rivers were too shallow for large vessels, they still sought land bordering the streams so that they could float their produce down on rafts or in dug-out canoes. They were

7

influenced in their selections, also, by the discovery that in the upland river bottoms was some of the most fertile soil in all America. In the post-Revolution period it was the James River valley, from Lynchburg to Richmond, which was the garden spot of Virginia.

It would be difficult to exaggerate the influence of the rivers upon the life of the planter. Up the·rivers came the English vessels bringing the goods essential to his plantation and his family—farm implements, clothing, utensils, etc., and back they went with his rice or his tobacco. The rivers and creeks were to him what the hard-surfaced roads are to the farmers of today. Upon them he set out in his boat to visit neighbors, to attend church services, to join the throng at the county court on court days. If a planter, living in Surry on the south bank of the James, wished to visit a family in Gloucester twenty-five miles away on the York, he would probably make the trip by water, sailing perhaps seventy-five miles down to Hampton Roads, past Point Comfort and up the York River. In South Carolina every plantation had its pirogue, or huge canoe hollowed out of a cypress tree, with its crew of slaves, in which·to take the crop down to Charleston or to convey the family to church.

For the colonists the mountains which lifted their blue peaks majestically beyond the forests of the Piedmont and stretched northeast and southwest like a natural barrier to expansion, long were little more than a myth. A century after the founding of Jamestown not one in a thousand had ever seen the Blue Ridge, and their knowledge of it was garnered from hunters and the Indians. Yet the mountains affected their lives and their destiny far more than they suspected. It was the Appalachian ranges which determined the course of their rivers, shut them out of the vast Mississippi Valley, forced them to be agriculturalists rather than fur traders, influenced their rainfall and their climate.

And later, when new tides of immigrants poured into the South, it was the mountain valleys, stretching out like great natural highways, which invited into the back country thousands of Germans, Swiss and Scotch-Irish and so fixed for centuries the culture of that region. The tobacco civilization, when it

8

reached the Blue Ridge, had to leap-frog the extended line of foreigners before it could continue its westward advance. In Virginia, in the nineteenth century, the mountains proved an insuperable obstacle to unity, for they retarded the development of roads, canals and railways, cut off the western region from the east and foreshadowed, perhaps made inevitable, the creation of West Virginia as a separate State.

If local conditions in the South, more than in New England or the Middle Colonies, tended to break the bonds of tradition and mould a new and different civilization, the close and continuous contact with the mother country kept the section under her cultural dominance and reshaped the lives of the people in part in conformity with developments in England. The Virginian could not convert his plantation into an English manor, but he could pattern his residence after the English manor house, use the latest type of furniture in vogue in England, dress in English clothes, read English books. When he went to church he listened to a sermon by an English clergyman, his children might be under the instruction of an English tutor, his business correspondence was with an English factor. While his soil, climate, the rivers, the mountains, despite himself moulded him into a Virginian, his conscious efforts, seconded by his close intercourse with the mother country, kept him in part at least an Englishman.

The colonial South was far from being a unit with uniform economic conditions, life, culture and customs. It was, in fact, split up into at least five divisions with fairly well-defined boundaries—the tobacco country, the rice and indigo country, the mercantile belt, the naval stores and timber belt, and the back country. Although these divisions had close economic ties one with the other, their interests and their ways of life were often in marked contrast. The Maryland and Virginia planters had much in common with the rice planters of South Carolina, it is true, but from the thrifty farmers of the Shenandoah Valley, on the one hand, or the Norfolk merchants, on the other, they were far removed indeed. When William Byrd II visited Norfolk the place seemed as strange to him as though it had been a Dutch or a French town.

The tobacco country was the largest of the five divisions, extending as it did from the Mason and Dixon's line to Albemarle Sound, and from the eastern shore of the Chesapeake Bay to the Blue Ridge. It included most of eastern Maryland, almost all of tidewater and Piedmont Virginia and the northern tier of counties in North Carolina. With a population greater than that of New England, with the accumulated riches of its wide fields, with its fine mansions and its thousands of slaves, of vital importance in the English colonial system because of the great volume of its exports and imports, it played a rôle in the eighteenth century comparable to that of the Cotton Kingdom in the nineteenth. This was the region which gave to the country Washington, Jefferson, Madison and other great statesmen and took the lead in creating and launching the Constitution.

In the colonial period the bulk of the population·were engaged in growing tobacco, and the fields of yellow leaf surrounded every farmhouse, the humble frame cottage of the yeoman as well as the mansion of a Burwell or a Carter. There were other crops, of course—wheat, rye, barley, but it was for tobacco that the best soil was reserved, the planting and tending of the long rows of tobacco plants was the chief task of the slaves, it was with tobacco hogsheads that the English vessels were laden when they headed out to sea through the Virginia capes. The Indian weed became the backbone of the region because the soil was so admirably suited to its culture that no other part of the world could compete with it in supplying the growing European market.

✳ Society was aristocratic rather than democratic. Wealth, education, political power were concentrated in the hands of a comparatively small group who monopolized the seats in the Council of State and the General Court, and to a large extent in the Lower House of Assembly, filled the vestries, held all the important commands in the militia, built stately mansions, employed tutors for their children, owned each several plantations in addition perhaps to tens of thousands of unoccupied acres in the Piedmont or the Valley of Virginia. Next in order, and far more numerous, were the yeomanry—owners of little plantations of from fifty to two hundred acres. Prosperous, intelligent, self-reliant, jealous of their rights in the seventeenth century, they were the backbone of the region and their influence counted heavily in the General Assemblies. In the eighteenth century, when slavery fastened itself upon the country, their prosperity and power declined. Still numerous, they had to be reckoned with, but they looked to the aristocracy for leadership in both political and economic matters.

Lower still were the so-called poor white trash, or persons who owned no land or at best an old worn-out field or two on which to raise a few pounds of tobacco or a few bushels of wheat and corn. They had no slaves, no education, enjoyed no political influence, were despised even by the Negroes. Of greater moment, although few in numbers, were the professional men—doctors, lawyers, preachers; the merchants, whose little stores clung to the banks of the navigable streams or were scattered throughout the Piedmont, and the artisans—cabinetmakers, tailors, shoemakers, carpenters, wheelwrights. Last of all came the mass of Negro slaves upon whose shoulders fell the bulk of the manual labor and who had no education and no political rights.

The mercantile section stretched along the coast in a thin line from Savannah to Cape Henry, then up the Chesapeake Bay to Baltimore. It constituted, as it were, a fringe to three of the other districts—the tobacco district, the pine belt and the rice and indigo region. Yet it was sharply differentiated from any of them, for its life and economy linked it more with the mercantile centers of the North than with the tobacco and rice growers. Its activities were none the less vital to the agricultural districts, for the merchants of Baltimore, Norfolk, Wilmington and Charleston served as distributors of the crops and importers of goods needed on the plantations.

The mercantile system in the South was largely a growth of the eighteenth century, since the planters in the earlier days had their dealings directly with factors in England. It was only with the growth of trade and the expansion westward of settlement that the advantages of dealing with colonial merchants became obvious. The merchant himself was more than apt to be a Scotchman, a clerk in a Glasgow firm, perhaps, who had accumulated a little capital and set up for himself on the wharves of Norfolk or Charleston. Disliked by the tobacco planters both because of his mercantile pursuits and his Scottish accent, he won for himself a position of influence in colonial society. Some of the leading families of Virginia were founded by Scotch merchants who intermarried with the planter aristocracy and took their places at the bar and in political life.

Despite this affiliation with the planter class, the mercantile section was keenly conscious of its own separate interests and quick to defend them. Resentful of the passage of the Sugar Act, the Southern merchants joined with a whole heart in the protests against England's subversive policy in the decade from 1765 to 1775 and many were active on the committees of correspondence. But they drew back when war was threatened, for they visualized the complete ruin of their trade and even the destruction of their warehouses and the confiscation of their goods. Many became active Tories, supported the military and naval operations of the British, and when the royal forces withdrew from the South, loaded their vessels with personal effects, put their families on board and sailed away with them.

After the Revolution the mercantile section of the South continued its independent course in politics. The merchants were strongly in favor of the Federal Constitution and it was the weight of their votes which made ratification possible in some of the Southern States. When ratification became a fact they received the news with wild rejoicing and celebrated it with bonfires and processions. Throughout the early national period the mercantile South was not less strongly Federalist than the mercantile North. It opposed the embargo, derided Jefferson's gunboats, opposed the War of 1812, year after year sent Federalist representatives to Congress.

The pine belt extended along the eastern counties of South Carolina, North Carolina and Virginia, coinciding in part with the mercantile section. Here, hidden in the great forests poor whites and blacks lived in rude huts and occupied themselves with making tar and pitch, gathering turpentine and cutting timber. It was to this region that England looked for the naval stores to make her great merchant marine independent of imports from the Baltic, and her bounties were the chief incentive for keeping the kilns burning. It had been England's hope that New England would become a center for the production of tar, pitch and turpentine, but the northern pines were less suited for the purpose than the Carolina "lightwood." Travellers in the region noted with interest the tar kilns, the pine logs slanting in toward the center, the top covered over with sand and clay, and the tar oozing out through a funnel. In other parts of the woods they saw slaves collecting turpentine from the "boxes" set beneath gashes in the trees and pouring it into barrels for shipment. The barrels were made on the spot, the staves being split from pine logs, shaved, trimmed and hooped with oak saplings. These barrels when filled with their sticky contents were put on small boats for shipment to Norfolk or New Bern, or equipped with axles and shafts to which horses were hitched and rolled along like tobacco hogsheads.[1]

From the crudeness and poverty of the tar burners to the wealth and elegance of the rice planters was a long cry indeed. The rice region embraced parts of eastern Georgia and South Carolina and southeastern North Carolina. Here developed an aristocratic society of wealthy men who laid out their plantations in the low country, worked them with scores or even hundreds of slaves, built stately residences and lived the lives of cultured gentlemen. The rice aristocracy of the Cooper and Ashley Rivers was not so numerous as the tobacco aristocracy of the upper South, but it was in no way inferior in the development of "millionaires" and in the extravagance of its life. With the discovery that indigo could be grown profitably in this region and again with the spread of sea island cotton made possible by Eli Whitney's gin, the rice country took on new life, became even more wealthy.

The rice country of South Carolina revolved around Charleston. Here the planters brought their crops, here they made their purchases of European goods, here they built residences and

[1] R. H. Taylor, "Slaveholding in North Carolina," *James Sprunt's Historical Studies,* XVIII.

13

entertained lavishly, here they came to attend the theatre or to enter fine horses in the races, or to participate in dignified dances. In Virginia, Williamsburg was the center of the planter civilization, Norfolk the center of the mercantile interests, but Charleston was both, a place where planter families and merchant families lived side by side, attended the same church, perhaps became united by marriage. Here the agricultural section merged with the mercantile.

The rice-indigo section, although resembling the tobacco region in many respects differed from it in others, had its own culture, developed its own dialect from various English dialects, jealously guarded its peculiar economic interests. The Charlestonian would have been at home in Virginia society and would have conversed on even terms with Philip Ludwell on the Court gossip of London or on Shakespeare or the classic authors, would have held his own in the minuet at a ball in the Palace at Williamsburg, but he would have been recognized instantly as a South Carolinian. In the Constitutional Convention at Philadelphia the rice planters, so far from acting in concert with the Virginia and Maryland delegates, incurred their anger by allying themselves with the mercantile interests of New England.

Of the many contrasts in the old South none was more striking than that between the lowlands and the back country. When a Dulaney or a Carroll left eastern Maryland to visit Frederick or Hagerstown, he found himself in a strange country; when a Virginia planter from Gloucester or even Albemarle crossed the Blue Ridge into the Valley of Virginia many of the people were as foreign to him as though they had been Turks; a Pinckney or a Huger could go sixty miles from Charleston and be in the midst of people whose tongue he could not understand.

The back country farmers were a diverse group, a medley of Germans, Swiss and Scotch-Irish from Pennsylvania; Germans, Swiss, Scotch-Irish and Scotch Highlanders directly from Europe; and yeomen and poor whites from the tidewater and the Piedmont, with an occasional tobacco aristocrat thrown in for good measure. With them they brought their native tongues, their religious beliefs, their folk art, their customs, their crafts, their agriculture. Faced with difficulties of transportation and accustomed to intensive farming, they refused to yield to the westward advance of plantation economy with its staple products, its slave labor and its waste of good soil. In South Carolina much of what was at first thought of as back country, in the nineteenth century was annexed to the Cotton Kingdom and its farms converted into plantations, but in North Carolina, Virginia and Maryland the tobacco civilization, although it succeeded in gaining a foothold here and there, never conquered any considerable part of the upland region.

Had the Southern back country been organized into one colony or one State, instead of cutting across Maryland, Virginia, North Carolina and South Carolina, it could have defended its interests to better advantage. But in each State the back country people were in the minority, and found it difficult to make their weight felt in the government or to protect their interests. Leaders of thought or government in western Maryland, let us say, seldom came in contact with leaders in western North Carolina save perhaps at a church synod or more rarely on the floor of Congress. Yet the back country frequently acted as a unit, more because the people thought alike and had similar interests than because of a conscious program agreed upon in advance. It opposed the land grabbing of influential easterners, protested against discrimination in taxation, fought for its proper representation in the legislatures and demanded State aid for roads and canals. The back country on the whole was in favor of the Revolution despite the Tory leanings of the Highlanders and the pacifism of many of the Germans; it was suspicious of the new Federal Constitution and many of the people voted against ratification. In the War between the States the section was divided, the Maryland back country remaining firm for the Union while the Valley of Virginia and the small farmers of North Carolina generally cast in their lot with the Confederacy.

The failure to differentiate between the major subdivisions of the old South has led to much confusion. There has been a tendency, even among historians of note, to emphasize the planter classes of the tobacco and rice regions, while neglecting or even

15

ignoring the back country, the pine belt and the mercantile district. We hear much of the New England merchants, their enterprise, their widespread trade and their wealth, but few realize the volume of business done by the traders of Norfolk or Charleston. Yet a Niel Jamieson, or a John Goodrich, or a Henry Laurens, with their privately owned ships, their great warehouses, their trade to Europe and the West Indies were a match for the keenest merchant of Boston or Newport.

It is necessary for us to distinguish between the divisions of the colonial period if we are to understand the later South, not only of the time of the War between the States, but of the present. "How does it happen that the South, the land of the mint-julep, should vote so consistently for prohibition," many persons in the North have asked in perplexity. They fail to realize that the mint-julep drinkers are confined to a not very numerous class, in one or at best two of the great subdivisions of the section. The yeoman farmers, the poor white trash, the merchants and sailors, the tar burners, the pious Mennonites and Dunkards have never been fond of the julep. As for the Solid South, it is a complete misnomer, for the South is not now and never has been solid. In every great issue, in every national election, there have been differences and conflicts within the section. So when we write of the South we must be careful to state what part we have in mind, and what class in that part.

Emphasis upon the subdivisions of the South is necessary, also, for a proper understanding of the vast regions to the west to which the Southern population expanded, taking with them their psychology, customs, culture, religions, traditions. The younger son of a rich tobacco planter who settled on the Ohio, had a point of view on religion, politics and farming very different from that of the Rockbridge Scotch-Irishman who took up land near him. Their fellow settlers from New England or from Europe might consider them merely as Southerners, distinguishable by their broad hats and baggy trousers, but their contributions to the new civilization which was springing up west of the mountains were far from identical.

The cultures of the Ohio Valley, or the Great Lakes region,

16

or of Texas, or of any other part of the vast West, were shaped
by the same forces which created the civilization of New England
or of the tobacco country or the rice and indigo country—inheritance, local conditions, contact with the mother regions and the
melting-pot. What England was to the colonies, the East was
to the West. From the East came most of the settlers, bringing
with them the cultures which had grown up on the banks of
the Ashley, or the uplands of North Carolina, or the hills of
Massachusetts or Connecticut. The Scotch-Irish, when they moved
over the mountains from the southern back country into Kentucky
or Tennessee, brought their Presbyterian faith, their interest in
education, their way of speaking. The Yankee settler in western
New York or on the shores of Lake Michigan did not cease to be
a Yankee—he clung to his Calvinist faith, established his township
system, built New England meeting-houses, retained the New
England nasal twang.

But the Virginian and the Yankee could no more remain a
Virginian and a Yankee than their ancestors had remained Englishmen in Virginia or in Massachusetts. The West gripped them,
changed their economy, modified their political institutions, affected deeply the forms if not the substance of their religions,
influenced their architectures. They found themselves, also, in
contact with other groups of settlers from other parts of America
or from Europe, and so were subject to the operation of the
melting-pot. There was a merging of Congregationalism and
Presbyterianism, a mingling of dialects—eastern Virginian, Scotch-
Irish, New England, Pennsylvanian; Southern agricultural
methods were modified by the thrifty habits of the Connecticut
farmer or the English immigrant; the son of a North Carolinian
might marry the daughter of a New Yorker, and their daughter,
in turn, mate with an Ulsterman from western Pennsylvania.

In most of the civilizations which developed in the West—for
there were numerous clearly defined civilizations—the influence
of the South was profound. In central Kentucky the tobacco
civilization to a large extent duplicated itself, not only because
the region was suited to the plant, but because thousands of
planters moved there from tidewater and Piedmont Virginia.

The Kentuckian was proud of his Virginia ancestry, built his plantation "great house" in the Jeffersonian style and imitated the Virginia slave economy. But his ties with the Southern back country were also strong, for while one parent might have come from Henrico or Orange, the other was perhaps a Scotch-Irish Presbyterian from the Valley of Virginia.

Soil exhaustion in the old South was a deadly blight for the region itself, but it gave the West a host of sturdy settlers. It was habitual, as the tobacco farms of the Chesapeake Bay region became less and less productive, for the younger sons to pull up stakes and move out to the land of promise beyond the mountains. In Alabama, in Mississippi, in Texas, in southern Ohio, Indiana and Illinois, in Missouri, even on the Pacific coast adventurous Southerners settled and added their share to the life and culture of their new home States. It was some years after the close of the War between the States that a Princeton graduate lost his way in the wilds of eastern Oregon and sought hospitality in the rude hut of a settler. When his host bade him good-bye the next morning, he remarked: "Stranger, it has been a pleasure to have you here, but I will confess that had I known in advance that you are a Yankee, I wouldn't have let you in."

So in studying the old South, in analyzing the forces which created its various civilizations, we are laying the foundation of a better understanding of what we call American civilization and of the various civilizations of which it is composed. A good lady once remarked to a distinguished educator: "Nothing good ever came out of the East." "Not even the Westerners?" queried the professor in reply. After all the East was the mother country of the West, sending out her sons and daughters and endowing it with her traditions, languages, cultures, political institutions, religious faiths. Modify them the West certainly did, remould them, stamp them as western, create out of them new civilizations, but we cannot know the region, we cannot know the United States as a whole, until we study the cradles of colonial civilization, and of these some of first importance were in the South.

*Chapter II*

# INTELLECTUAL LIFE OF THE
# TOBACCO ARISTOCRAT

THE aristocracies of colonial Virginia and Maryland were not transplanted from England, but were the products of America, of the tobacco plantation, the accumulation of wealth, the command of indentured workers and slaves. "This generation knows too well whence" our Virginia aristocrats come, wrote Sir Francis Nicholson sourly, in 1705. "The ordinary sort of planters that have land of their own, tho' not much, look upon themselves to be as good as the best of them, for he knows, at least has heard, from whence these mighty dons derive their originals."[1] Some years later Henry Callister remarked in similar vein on the absurdity of the claims of wealthy Marylanders to distinguished lineage, declaring, no doubt with exaggeration, that "some of our proudest families here—vaunt themselves of a pedigree at the same time they know not their grandfather's name—I never knew a good honest Marylander that was not got by a merchant."[2]

Had Callister twitted one of these gentlemen to his face he probably would have had no trouble in producing the family tree and proving that he was the grandson of a Somerset squire or the great-great-grandson of a Yorkshire knight. But Callister would have been unconvinced. He knew that the English gentry did not constitute a caste similar to that of Spain or of France, and that many an humble parson of a rural parish, many a stockingmaker outside Ludgate, many a merchant's clerk, could boast of descent from a squire, or a knight, or perhaps an earl. "Yeomen and merchants were constantly finding entrance into this class (the gentry) by marriage and by purchase of lands, and the

[1] *British Public Record Office,* CO5–1314, Doc. 43.
[2] *Callister Papers,* Maryland Diocesan Library, Peabody Institute, p. 154.

younger sons of the manorhouse normally passed out of it into trade, manufacture, scholarship, the Church or military service abroad, in some cases carrying with them their pretension to gentility, in other cases tacitly abandoning it."[3]

Philip Alexander Bruce devotes two weary chapters in his *Social History of Virginia in the Seventeenth Century* to tracing the ancestry of one immigrant after another to distinguished families. "The Corbins were sprung from Nicholas Corbin," of Hall's End, Warwickshire, he tells us; John Page "is supposed on reliable evidence to have belonged to a branch of the Page family of Harrow-on-the-Hill, which had, during many generations, enjoyed a high position among the rural gentry"; Colonel Peter Ashton was sprung from the ancient family of Ashtons of Lincolnshire.[4] But it meant little in the life of a merchant tailor, or a weaver, or a banker-goldsmith, or a woolen draper, or a "mariner," or yeoman, that a grandfather had been a member of the landed gentry, perhaps a knight of the shire, perhaps a rough country justice, dividing his time between the bench, the chase and the tavern. He might cling fondly to the coat-of-arms, that visible evidence of his attenuated connection with the gentry, but the reflection that many families had assumed this badge of gentility without a shadow of claim and that others had procured it through the corruption of the Heralds' College, must have added a tinge of sourness to his cup of pride.

But when he came to Virginia or to Maryland, bought a thousand acres of tidewater land, began the culture of tobacco with three or four indentured servants and a half score of African slaves, built a farm-house, became a member of the local vestry, a justice of the peace and, perhaps, a Burgess in the colonial Assembly, his connection with the English squirearchy became a matter of real concern. He began to realize that he himself was a squire. The fact that his great-grandfather had been so unfortunate as to be a younger son had kept him from being a member of the gentry, but by his own efforts he had made himself a Virginia gentleman, with an income perhaps several

[3]G. M. Trevelyan, *History of England*, p. 371.
[4]P. A. Bruce, *Social History of Virginia*, pp. 71, 73.

times that of the ancestors whom he had so much envied. Forgotten was the fact that he had been a tradesman, that his father had been a sailor, that his maternal grandfather had been a candle manufacturer, that one maternal great-grandfather had been a yeoman, the other a parson, forgotten were a host of other plebeian or semi-plebeian relatives, and all attention was focussed upon the old squire whose name he bore and to whose coat-of-arms he had a right.

Among the settlers who sailed hopefully in between Cape Charles and Cape Henry, as between two gateposts to a land of plenty and opportunity, were no titled English gentlemen, not an earl, rarely a knight, or even the younger son of a knight. By far the larger part were humble people—ill-paid, ragged farm workers; villeins who had deserted the manor; day-laborers from London or Bristol—carpenters, masons, coopers, blacksmiths, tailors, brickmakers; with now and then a sturdy yeoman crowded off his land by the insatiable maw of the enclosures; or a youthful tradesman or merchant tempted by the fertility of the Chesapeake soil and the reports of the huge profits to be had from the culture of tobacco; occasionally an unwary youth who had fallen asleep over his grog in a London tavern and awakened to find himself aboard a tobacco ship with four years of servitude awaiting him in America. They came from various parts of England, from East-Anglia as well as Devon, from Somerset, Surrey, Sussex, Essex; one planter might speak the dialect of Yorkshire, his neighbor that of Norfolk; one might have fought for King Charles I at Naseby, the other might have been in the Parliamentary army; one was staunch for the episcopacy and the Prayer Book; the other had leanings toward Calvinism.

Out of this mass gradually emerged an aristocracy. One planter accumulated wealth by supplementing the culture of tobacco with plantation manufacture; another by trading for deer skins with the Southern Indians; another by importing English goods and selling them to his neighbors at a large profit; still another by speculating in land. But the surest way for the planter to build up a large estate was to purchase slaves and base his economy upon their labor. The chief reliance of Virginia and Maryland throughout the seventeenth century was the indentured worker, and decade after decade a stream of laborers poured across the Atlantic to serve their terms in the tobacco fields. But the supply was never adequate, transportation was costly, the mortality very high. The Negro slave was far preferable, even though the initial cost was greater, for he served for life, was more tractable, and withstood better the tidewater climate. So when the occasional slave ship made its appearance in the James or the Potomac, the planters who had the means to buy vied with each other in securing the largest number of black workers. It was the differential profits which came from slave labor which were the foundation of some of the largest fortunes in Virginia and Maryland.

In the seventeenth century the planter aristocracy embraced in both colonies small but powerful groups. Robert Carter, William Byrd I, Philip Ludwell, Lewis Burwell, Ralph Wormeley, Nathaniel Bacon, Senior, were constantly widening their land holdings, lorded over their neighbors as justices of the peace, naval officers, vestrymen and officers in the militia, gathered four times a year in the quaint old Statehouse at Jamestown to sit as the supreme court of the colony, and less frequently as the upper house of Assembly, paid lip service to the Governor as members of the Council of State, though often bitterly hostile to him and intriguing through influential friends in England for his removal. These men constituted more than a landed aristocracy, they were the untitled nobility of Virginia. The great mass of the planters, sturdy yeomen who owned from 100 to 500 acres which they cultivated with their own hands aided by their sons, with occasionally an indentured worker, regarded the "great men" with something akin to awe, and it was only through their representatives in the House of Burgesses that they dared oppose their wishes.

The immigrants who laid the foundations of the leading Virginia and Maryland families brought with them in varying degrees the education usual for an English squire or merchant or skilled artisan or yeoman. If the newcomer was connected with the gentry, he was apt to have had a thorough grounding in the classics, to be intimately acquainted with the Bible, to know something of philosophy, geography, literature and history. The day had passed when learning was despised as proper only for clerics, when a gentleman's son was out of place among the monks and friars in the courts and common rooms of Oxford and Cambridge. No doubt, as Macaulay tells us, many a young squire "dawdled away" his time at the university and made "little addition to his previous scanty store of knowledge," no doubt, the entire library in many a manor-house consisted of the Bible, Hudibras, Baker's *Chronicle* and a few other volumes lying in the "hall window among the fishing rods and fowling pieces," but for the average Jacobean country gentleman this picture is decidedly overdrawn. Usually the young squire had gone through the grammar school, perhaps completed a few years at the university, had travelled in France, Italy and Holland, had absorbed much of the new Renaissance learning, had built up a creditable library, enjoyed good music.

If the immigrant were a merchant, dominated by the mercantile spirit, his education, while by no means inferior, was apt to be more practical. The trader to foreign countries might speak Latin fluently, not to enjoy the beauties of Virgil or Ovid, but to communicate with business men in foreign lands. As Latin declined as the international tongue, he found it necessary to master French, Dutch, Spanish or Italian. He was also versed in geography, and had read and marvelled at Hakluyt's *Principal Navigations,* or *Purchas his Pilgrimes,* or Captain John Smith's *A True Relation.* But he might also be acquainted with Roman and Greek literature, he was not less well versed in the Bible than the country squire, he knew something of the principles of navigation, had read *The Merchant Mirror,* and had dipped into history. The middle-class English father, ambitious for his son, and knowing that through the doors of the schools he might pass to high preferment, gave him what education was in his means before putting him at the loom or setting him behind the counting table. Even the universities and the Inns of Court were crowded with middle-class youths, seeking to improve their minds and to train themselves for careers in business, church or state.

23

Nor was this ambition dulled merely because a father chanced to move to Virginia or Maryland and established himself as a successful planter. The statement of John Brinsley, in 1622, that "there is no man, having the nature of a wise father, who would not have his child to have some learning," was as true for the colonist as for the Englishman who remained at home. Unfortunately he found the situation far more difficult. Isolated upon his plantation with one or perhaps two miles of tobacco fields and woods intervening between him and his nearest neighbor, he was apt to be thrown entirely upon his own resources in training his children. Even though an "old field" school happened to be near enough for them to make the daily ride on horseback, he realized that they would learn little more than could be had from the hornbook, forced down by an ignorant and perhaps brutal teacher. The planter's mind reverted wistfully to Eton or Westminster, and he weighed carefully the advantages of English school life against the expense and perils of a voyage across the Atlantic. Augustine Warner, of Gloucester county, must have had many misgivings as he said good-bye to his son, a lad of sixteen, when he set sail to take up his studies at the Merchant Tailors school, London, in 1658.[5]

The problem was not less acute three decades later, when William Fitzhugh, of Stafford county, bewailed the difficulty of securing "good education of children" in Virginia. He, too, had decided to send his eldest son to school in England, but "accidentally meeting with a French minister, a sober, learned and discreet gentleman," he persuaded him to take the boy into his home to tutor him.[6] Other fathers, not so fortunate as Fitzhugh, were forced to send to England for a graduate of Oxford or Cambridge, a poor youth who perhaps had worked his way through the university by making beds and fetching water, to teach his children. In this way they could imbibe the standard allotments of Cicero and Virgil and Xenophon under his own roof, while the expense might be lessened by admitting as day scholars the sons of his nearest neighbors. In many cases the

[5] *William and Mary Quarterly*, Vol. VI, p. 173.
[6] *Virginia Magazine of Hist. and Biog.*, Vol. III, p. 9.

planter himself brushed up his Latin and assumed the rôle of instructor. We follow "the same course that is taken in England out of town," wrote Sir William Berkeley in 1672, "every man according to his ability instructing his children."

Thoughtful Virginians were so alive to the importance of this problem, agreeing that their sons were "better never born than ill-bred,"[7] that in the more populous and wealthy communities they began to "join and build schools for their children." Occasionally public-spirited citizens, men of the stamp of Benjamin Symes and Thomas Eaton, would leave their property, consisting usually of a plantation with residence, servants, cattle, etc.,

---

NOTICE is hereby given, That *Symes*'s Free School, in *Elizabeth-City* County, will be vacant on the 25th of *March* Inft. a Tutor of a good Charaƈter, and properly qualified, may meet with good Encouragement, by applying to the Truſtees of the ſaid Schcol.

*N. B.* The Land Rent of the ſaid School is 31 *l. per Ann.* beſides Perquiſites.

---

FIGURE I. ADVERTISEMENT OF SYMES' FREE SCHOOL

as the endowment of a free school. (Fig 1.) The historian Beverley tells us that such schools had been established in "many parts of the country," the income from the property, together with the tuition fee "which gentlemen gave with their sons," providing the master with a comfortable subsistence.[8] However, the fact that wealthy men continued to employ private tutors or to send their sons across the Atlantic leaves us to infer that the instruction and accommodations of the Virginia schools were not of the best.

When the planter's son had absorbed his allotted share of Lillie's *Latin Grammar,* Comenius's *Janua Linguarum Reserata, The English Rudiments, Euclid, Hodder's Arithmetic, Goldmine of the French Tongue* and the globes, he was ready to enter a university. But here his father's difficulties began anew. There was no university in Virginia. He had the choice of sending the

[7] *Virginia Magazine of Hist. and Biog.,* Vol. II, p. 25.
[8] Robert Beverley, *History of Virginia,* p. 224. Among these were the schools endowed by Capt. John Moon and Henry King, in Isle of Wight, William Whittington, Richard Russell and Samuel Sanford. *Wm. and Mary Quarterly,* Vol. VI, pp. 77–82.

lad to Oxford or Cambridge, or of finding a tutor capable of directing him in advanced work. The Roman Catholic planters of Maryland not infrequently sent their sons to Jesuit colleges in France, while the Virginians looked to Oxford and Cambridge. Ralph Wormeley II entered Oriel in 1665 as a boy of fifteen; John Lee was at the Queen's College, Oxford; Wilson Cary studied at Trinity College, Cambridge;[9] William Byrd II, after studying in Holland and later under a tutor in England, entered the Middle Temple. But the average Virginia youth was forced to stay at home, making the most of what knowledge he could pick up from his tutor or the parish rector or from his father's library.

All Virginia was thrilled, then, when it became known in 1693 that the Reverend James Blair had secured a charter from King William and Queen Mary for a college in the colony. Soon Blair was back in Virginia accompanied by an English builder, with an order for about £2000, with plans by Sir Christopher Wren, and with permission to name the college William and Mary in honor of their majesties.

A notable occasion it was when the college held its first commencement exercises in 1699. Proud fathers and mothers, together with many leading men of the colony—the Governor, Councillors, Burgesses, wealthy planters—gathered in the Wren building to listen to addresses by some of the graduates. One of these spoke upon the advantages which would accrue to the colony from the college, since it would release parents from the necessity of educating their sons in England. It was cruel, he thought, to introduce a child from the colonies, "a bashful stranger" into an English school, to be "cowed and overawed" by "a school full of boys that with their mother's milk learn to condemn all others that are not of their own nation." At last when the lad had accustomed himself to his new surroundings and had completed school and college, he came home "fraught more commonly with luxury than with the learning of England," and could not brook the "more simple and less costly way of living in Virginia."

[9] *William and Mary Quarterly*, VI, p. 174.

Moreover, the cost was excessive. "I doe safely appeal to those parents who ever sent" a son to "England to be educated," said the young speaker, whether it "did not cost them as dear as what would have been reckoned a good portion for him in Virginia." It is a badge of servitude that we can't have "a minister, nor a physician, nor a lawyer, nor a statesman, nor a justice of the peace, nor an ingenious gentleman without going" to England. "The old stock of English gentlemen being dead," it is now "a common complaint that there are not men enough to be found to fill the bench" and that "we insensibly decline to a state or ignorance and abjectness of spirit, . . . for it is not so much the fertility of the soil . . . that makes a brave country, as the improving the spirits of the inhabitants with useful knowledge."[10]

Despite the arguments and pleas of our youthful speaker more fathers sent their sons to English universities after the founding of William and Mary than before. This is explained not so much by the deficiencies of the college, as by the vast increase in wealth following the importation of slaves in large numbers, and the desire of the well-to-do to have their sons acquire the ease of manner, the polish and culture which they associated with the English aristocracy. It was not enough to acquire a knowledge of the classics, with a smattering of philosophy, theology, law and modern languages; one must know something of architecture, gardening and music; one must be able to handle oneself gracefully in the minuet.

The years from the close of the war of the Spanish Succession to the American Revolution were the golden era for the wealthy Virginia and Maryland tobacco planters. Then it was that they extended their holdings over one plantation after another, doubled and tripled their stock of slaves, acquired vast tracts of land in the Piedmont region, built their stately homes on the banks of the James, the Potomac and the Severn, filled them with costly furniture and silver, laid out their formal gardens, entertained with the lavish hospitality of English noblemen. This increase in wealth was accompanied by a corresponding growth in numbers. Many families, looked down upon by the aristocrats of the

[10]*William and Mary Quarterly*, Series Two, Vol. X, pp. 325–328.

seventeenth century, rose through slave labor to the first rank in the eighteenth. Well-to-do Englishmen or Scotchmen, migrating to the colonies, purchased large estates, and established themselves among the aristocrats.

Many of the more thoughtful were fully aware of the evils of the slave system. They could witness its effect upon the poor planters, many of whom left Virginia and Maryland when they found themselves in competition with slaves, while others sank to a condition of abject poverty and ignorance. And though many yeomen saved themselves by purchasing one or two slaves, the yeoman class was no longer the independent, industrious, intelligent group of the seventeenth century. But the aristocrat, wealthy, powerful, cultured, could not bring himself to condemn utterly a system which was the basis of his own high estate. It had produced an aristocracy of which any region might be proud, even England itself, he thought, and that atoned for a multitude of sins.

In the meanwhile the English aristocracy was also undergoing rapid changes. The eighteenth century for the country gentlemen was a period of expanding wealth and widening culture. It was their delight to erect beautiful mansions, surround them with formal gardens, fill them with graceful tables and chairs and formal secretaries in the style of Chippendale, to cover their walls with portraits by Van Dyke, or Gainsborough or Kneller, to stock their libraries not only with the ancient classics but with the works of Shakespeare, Swift, Milton and Addison. Even the Squire Westerns threw off their boorish manners and became in a mild way patrons of art, science and the polite manners of the day. It was habitual for young gentlemen to travel on the continent and so to become familiar with the art, architecture, music and literature of France and Italy, which found immediate reflection in their residences, gardens and reading as well as in their manners and bearing.[11]

This great change was not lost upon the Virginia and Maryland gentlemen. When William Byrd II came back from England to the large estate which his father had amassed for him,

[11]G. M. Trevelyan, *History of England*, pp. 515, 516.

his chief thought was to model his life upon that of the wealthy English landlord. He too would build a beautiful residence, he too would have his garden with its box-wood walks and its statuary, he too would accumulate a fine library, he too would decorate his walls with family portraits. This urge was just as strong with planters who had never set foot in England. They had seen pictures of Eaton Hall or Mount Morris in Kip's *English Houses and Gardens,* had descriptions of the splendor of English country life in the letters of friends, had talked with newcomers or with young Virginians or Marylanders just back from Oxford or the Inns of Court of the new ideas in architecture, art, music, and literature.

The tobacco aristocrat was moulded in part by influences of inheritance; in part by local conditions—his life upon the plantation, the command of servants and slaves, the important position in local and colonial affairs which fell to his lot, by the climate of the Chesapeake Bay region; in part by the intimate contact with England resulting from the tobacco trade. George Mason, Mann Page, Edmund Berkeley were Virginians, would no doubt have been "spotted" instantly as tobacco planters in a London coffee house or at the Globe Theatre, but they were also Englishmen, speaking the English language, reading English books, accepting English law, living under English forms of government. They were citizens of the great British Empire, and as such looked to England not only for political and economic direction, but for the patterns in which they should shape, so far as possible, their everyday life, their reading, manners, dress, dancing, music, architecture, furniture, gardening, coaches, silverware.

It was inevitable that in education, also, the wealthy planter should continue to imitate the English system, promptly following suit as changes were made in the method of teaching and in the emphasis placed on different studies in the mother country. The teacher who could advertise not only that he had graduated from Oxford or Edinburgh or Cambridge, but had taught in some of the academies of England or Scotland, was apt to attract a large number of students. In tidewater and Piedmont Virginia and Maryland the schools were modeled after Westminster or

Eton or Winchester, and many of the masters were Anglican ministers, who welcomed the opportunity to add to their slender incomes by teaching. Since the clergymen were in most cases Englishmen who had received their early training in the English schools, they invariably pursued with their young charges the methods in vogue in the mother country.

We are left in no doubt as to the subjects pursued in the Virginia and Maryland academies. William Kean, master of the Queen Anne County school, advertised in 1765 that he instructed young gentlemen "in Latin, Greek, Hebrew, the Grecian and Roman Histories and Antiquities . . . reading, writing, arithmetic—vulgar, decimal and duodecimal—geometry, planometry, trigonometry, surveying, gauging, Italian bookkeeping, navigation and the proportions of the horizontal dials."[12] In the Lower-Marlborough school, Calvert County, attention was concentrated on "English, French, Latin, Greek, Hebrew . . . the several approved writing-hands, short-hand, arithmetic, etc."[13] Thomas Jefferson, in advising young Peter Carr in the selection of his studies, prescribed Goldsmith's *History of Greece,* then in order "Herodotus, Thucydides, Xenophontis Anabasis, Arrian, Quintus Curtius, Diodorus Siculus, Justin," then "Virgil, Terence, Horace, Anacreon, Theocritus, Homer, Euripides, Sophocles," followed by "Milton's *Paradise Lost,* Shakespeare, Ossian, Pope's and Swift's works in order to form your style in your own language. In morality read Epictetus, Xenophontis *Memorabilia,* Plato's *Socratic dialogues,* Cicero's philosophies, Antoninus and Seneca . . . You are now, I expect, learning French. You must push this, because" your books in "mathematics, natural philosophy, natural history, etc., will be mostly French."[14] Although one may suspect that the youthful Peter staggered a bit under this load, the mere recital of the volumes from which he was expected to store his mind speaks eloquently for the standards of the day, especially in classical literature and philosophy.

The efficiency of the academies depended chiefly upon the

[12]*Maryland Gazette,* January 17, 1765.
[13]*Ibid.,* December 13, 1759.
[14]Jefferson's *Writings,* Vol. V, pp. 84–87.

headmaster. That he was often a man of thorough education, of experience in teaching and gifted in understanding and handling boys we know from the testimony of former pupils. But some must have been more proficient with the rod than with Greek grammar and the globes. No doubt the experience of Governor John Page, of Virginia, could be duplicated by many another boy of the tidewater region. "My grandmother excited in my mind an inquisitiveness," he tells us, so that I read many books "from my father's and grandfather's collection, which was no contemptible library. In 1752, when nine, my father put me into a grammar school where the Reverend Mr. William Yates had undertaken the tuition of twelve scholars." For twelve months I had "to get by heart an insipid and unintelligible book called Lilly's grammar, one sentence of which my teacher never explained. But happily my new tutor, Mr. William Price, at Mr. Willis', soon enabled me to see that it was . . . an excellent key to the Latin language," and three happy years of profitable study followed.[15]

Many well-to-do planters throughout the eighteenth century preferred to continue the old practice of employing tutors. Visitors to a Maryland or Virginia plantation were surprised to find in a minor building adjacent to the great house some recent graduate of Oxford or Edinburgh or Princeton with Latin grammar in hand surrounded by his youthful charges. For years it was usual to send to Scotland for tutors, since a Latin master from Glasgow could be had for £20 a year, but when parents found that their children acquired from them a Scotch "burr" which took years to wear off, their popularity waned.[16] Some turned to the northern colleges for their tutors, for Princeton and Harvard graduates were well prepared for the work, while their travelling expenses were not so great. The tutor was treated with respect, even

---

[15]*Virginia Historical Register*, Vol. III, pp. 142–151. For a criticism of the Virginia school system in 1822 see *The Family Visitor*, Huntington Library, January 1, June 8, June 22, July 6, 1822. Among the schools advertising in the Richmond papers were Samuel Coleman's School, 1786, William Patton's School, 1786, Fitzwhylson's School, 1787, Matthew Maury's School, 1787, York Grammar School, 1787, Williamsburg Grammar School, 1787, Fredericksburg Academy, 1787, George Wythe School, 1787, McGuire School, 1787, Harris and McRae School, 1789. *Virginia Magazine of Hist. and Biog.*, XXII, p. 290.

[16]*William and Mary Quarterly*, Vol. XIX, p. 145.

deference, by his employer; he was provided with a comfortable bedroom, ate at the table with the family, accompanied them to church and to receptions, aided them in entertaining their guests. Occasionally he married the daughter of a neighboring planter or perhaps one of his own pupils.[17] The influence of these men in shaping the characters, in arousing the intellectual curiosity and in directing the mental trends of some of the leading men of the South can hardly be exaggerated.

The planter of the eighteenth century, despite the founding of William and Mary, still had to ponder over the desirability of sending his sons to England for work at Oxford or Cambridge or for a legal training at the Inns of Court. Among those who considered the college at Williamsburg best suited for young Virginians was Governor John Page. "Instead of sending me to England, as he had promised my mother he would," my father placed me at William and Mary. "Fortunately for me several Virginians, about this time, had returned from that place [England] (where we were told learning alone existed) so inconceivably illiterate, and also corrupted and vicious, that he swore no son of his should ever go there."[18] Yet the prestige of the great English universities was still great in Virginia and Maryland. Daniel Dulaney went to Claire Hall, Cambridge; the scholarly Ralph Wormeley, of Rosegill, was at Trinity Hall, Cambridge; Arthur Holt, Garvin Corbin, Philip Thomas Lee, Thomas Nelson and George Fairfax Lee, all matriculated at Christ College, Cambridge; William Stith and John Span entered The Queen's College, Oxford; John Tayloe was at St. Johns, Cambridge. The employment of Scotch tutors by the planters no doubt accounts for the very large number of Virginia boys who were educated at Edinburgh or Aberdeen, among them Joseph Goodwin, John M. Galt, Walter Jones, Arthur Lee, James McClung, Samuel Nicolls, Valentine Peyton, John Ravencroft, Gustavus Scott and George Steptoe.[19]

On the other hand, many Virginia parents thought it better

---

[17]Philip Vickers Fithian, *Journal and Letters*, p. 47.
[18]*Virginia Historical Register*, Vol. III, pp. 142–151.
[19]*Virginia Magazine of Hist. and Biog.*, Vol. XXI, pp. 198–199.

to send their sons to William and Mary. Here they would be under the instruction of able masters and professors, learned and pious men, most of them, and graduates of Oxford or Cambridge, without undertaking the ocean voyage and growing up almost as strangers to their families. In 1727 the Visitors drew up a plan of study patterned upon the system in vogue in England. The youth entered the grammar school, where he ran the usual gauntlet of Latin and Greek. When he had completed this work, usually in his sixteenth year, he went through the awe-inspiring experience of an examination before the president, the masters and the "ministers of Virginia skilled in the ancient languages." If he survived this test he ceased to be a scholar and assumed the title of student, donned the cap and gown and took up his work in one of the two philosophical schools. If he elected the school of natural philosophy and mathematics, he devoted himself to physics, metaphysics and mathematics; if he entered the school of moral philosophy, he took up rhetoric, logic and ethics and went on to natural and civil law. The dull grind of reading and class work was enlivened by "disputations" or debates and "declamations and themes on various subjects." It required four years to win the Bachelor of Arts degree and seven the Master of Arts. In addition, there were two divinity schools, one for study in Hebrew and the Bible, the other concentrating on "the commonplaces of divinity and the controversies with heretics."[20]

For many years this system seems to have been satisfactory. Scores of promising young Virginians who wished to enter the ministry took the regular courses, received their degrees, went to England for ordination and accepted cures in various parts of the colony. At the outbreak of the Revolution a considerable percentage of the Virginia parsons were native Americans. These men not only performed a splendid work in upholding the standard of morality and intellectual attainment for the clergy, but by acting as tutors and school masters stimulated education, culture and refinement in the colony.[21] Perhaps the most distinguished was James Madison, second cousin of the fourth President

[20]*William and Mary Quarterly*, Series One, Vol. XIV, pp. 72, 73.
[21]Edward L. Goodwin, *The Colonial Church in Virginia*, pp. 245–319.

of the United States, who had no sooner laid aside the student's cap and gown than he had to assume the professor's garb, becoming president of the college at the age of twenty-eight and at forty-one the first Episcopal Bishop of Virginia.[22]

But William and Mary was much more than a theological seminary. Some of the ablest young men in the colony, members of families long prominent in social and political affairs—the Carters, Carys, Amblers, Ballards, Harrisons, Nelsons, Pages—went through the grammar school and college, imbibed the cultural spirit that hovered over the old Wren building, listened reverently to the instruction and counsel of the learned professors. These men took with them to their plantation homes and into the legislative halls of the colony and later of the nation, a culture, a breadth of vision, a power of reasoning, a clearness of expression that speaks eloquently for the type of training they received at William and Mary.

Thomas Jefferson gives full credit to the influence of the college upon his career, singling out for especial praise Dr. William Small, Professor of Natural Philosophy and Mathematics. "To me he was as a father," he says. "To his enlightened and affectionate guidance of my studies while in college I am indebted for everything . . . He introduced . . . rational and elevated courses of study, and, from an extraordinary conjunction of eloquence and logic, was enabled to communicate them to the students with great effect." But Jefferson valued his association with learned and distinguished citizens of the little capital almost as much as his instruction in the college courses. Dr. Small "procured for me the patronage of Mr. Wythe, and both of them the attentions of Governor Fauquier, the ablest man who ever filled the chair of government here," he says. "They were inseparable friends and at their frequent dinners I have heard more good sense, more rational and philosophical conversations, than in all my life besides."[23]

George Wythe himself joined the faculty to become the first professor of law in any American college. Far in advance of his

[22]*Ibid.*, pp. 290, 291.
[23]*Writings of Thomas Jefferson*, Vol. XIV, p. 231.

time, he not only established a moot court for his students, but a school of public affairs. The moot court sat monthly or oftener in the court room of the deserted Capitol at the end of the Duke of Gloucester Street where Dinwiddie, Fauquier, Botetourt, Dunmore and other governors had sat as Chief Justices of the colony in many a weighty case. Here Wythe, with the other professors, took the part of judge, before whom the students pleaded their causes, while the leading citizens of the Williamsburg vicinity crowded into the room to listen. He also organized his students into a legislative body, over which he presided, strictly enforcing parliamentary rules and encouraging the young men to suggest amendments to existing laws and to debate thoroughly each point as it arose.[24] Such was the training of the remarkable group of students who went out from William and Mary in the Revolutionary period as judges and legislators—Thomas Jefferson, John Marshall, Benjamin Harrison, Carter Braxton, Thomas Nelson, Peyton Randolph, John Tyler, Edmund Randolph, James Monroe.

"I have ever thought . . . that William and Mary is the best place on the continent for the education of young men," wrote one observer. "If they do not acquire more knowledge they at least acquire more liberality and more ambition. They appear at once to discover their own ignorance and . . . retire to pursue the base and laborious plans of study which they have chalked out for themselves." After five or six years they emerge to "shine forth with a splendor that dazzles the continent. . . . The spirit of skepticism, which every student acquired, is the first step towards knowledge."[25]

But it was this very skepticism, combined with a large degree of freedom for the students and a laxness in the conduct of some members of the faculty, which deterred many parents from sending their sons to William and Mary in the years just preceding the Revolution. Skepticism might lead to atheism, and the Virginians were still devout church members. Nor was it a good advertisement for the college for Councillors and Burgesses, when they came to Williamsburg to attend the sessions of the

[24]*William and Mary Quarterly*, Vol. IX, p. 80.
[25]*Ibid.*, Vol. VIII, pp. 158–159. I. A. Coles to Henry St. George Tucker, 1799.

Assembly, to find professors playing cards all night in the public houses, or staggering down the Duke of Gloucester Street in a state of intoxication.[26] It was these defects, perhaps, which brought about a drastic reorganization of the college in 1779 and the establishing of schools of medicine, physics, moral philosophy, law, economics, mathematics and modern languages, taught by such eminent men as Rev. James Madison, Dr. James McClurg, Robert Andrews, George Wythe and Charles Bellini.[27]

In the education of the Virginia and Maryland planter the classics took first place. No grammar school teacher, no tutor could hope for a position unless he knew his Cicero, his Ovid, his Xenophon. The classical authors gave the model of clearness and good taste in writing. They held the key not only to the vast store of ancient knowledge—to the drama, poetry, philosophy, history, oratory of Greece and Rome, but to medieval thought—theology, philosophy, art. The accomplished gentleman was supposed to know his Homer and his Horace, perhaps to quote from them in his letters and conversation if it could be done without show of ostentation. "Faber quisque fortunae suae' is a boastful saying," wrote Francis Walker Gilmer to his son. "You should commit to memory the most beautiful passages of Ovid, such as the description of the palace of the sun in the beginning of the 2d book and the 'Certamen' between Ajax and Ulysses in the 13th."[28] Hugh Blair Grigsby, while attending one of the William and Mary commencements, got into a discussion with a gentleman seated next to him at dinner over a line of the Iliad. Turning to Charles S. Stringfellow, who was near him, he asked: "Well, our young friend is fresh from the study of the classics, what does he say?" To Grigsby's delight Stringfellow was able to corroborate him by quoting the entire sentence.[29]

William Byrd, of Westover, was thoroughly versed in the ancient languages, reading Hebrew, Greek and Latin at sight. It was his custom to rise at five o'clock, and before saying his prayers, taking his exercise and eating breakfast, to go over an

[26]Philip Vickers Fithian, *Journal and Letters*, pp. 106, 107.
[27]*William and Mary Quarterly*, Series One, Vol. XIV, pp. 76–78.
[28]*Tyler's Magazine*, Vol. VI, pp. 18–20.
[29]*Ibid.*, p. 70.

astonishingly large number of pages in two of the three languages. One morning he would read "two chapters in Hebrew and some Greek in Cassius," another Hebrew mixed with Lucian or Homer or Thucydides. He must have been thoroughly acquainted, not only with these writers, but with Josephus, Anacreon, Pindar, Horace, Plutarch, Sallust, Terence and others. On one occasion Byrd's talent for languages got him into trouble, for when he entered into a conversation in Latin with Reverend Dunn, while visiting at Arlington on the eastern shore, his wife became offended because she could not join in and "called it bad manners."[30]

Thomas Jefferson's letter of August 24, 1819, to John Brazier, explaining the benefits derived from a knowledge of the classics, expressed the views of the average intelligent planter. "The utilities we derive from the remains of the Greek and Latin languages are, first, as models of pure taste in writing . . . second, . . . the luxury of reading the Greek and Roman authors in all the beauties of their originals. . . . I think myself more indebted to my father for this than for all the other luxuries his cares and affections have placed within my reach . . . third, . . . the stores of real science deposited and transmitted us in these languages, to-wit: in history, ethics, arithmetic, geometry, astronomy, natural history, etc. . . . To the moralist they are valuable because they furnish ethical writings highly and justly esteemed . . . The lawyer finds in the Latin language the system of civil law most conformable with the principles of justice . . . the physician as good a code of his art as has been given us to this day. . . . The statesman will find in these languages history, politics, mathematics, ethics, eloquence, love of country. . . . All the sciences must recur to the classical languages for the etymon and sound understanding of their fundamental terms."[31]

Not only did Jefferson read Latin and Greek fluently, but he went to great pains to pronounce both languages as correctly as possible. Early in life it occurred to him that modern Italians and

---

[30]L. B. Wright and M. Tinling, Eds. *The Secret Diary of William Byrd of Westover,* p. 105.

[31]*Jefferson's Writings,* Vol. XV, pp. 207–211.

Greeks could pronounce Latin and ancient Greek better than other peoples. "For this reason I learnt and have used the Italian pronunciation of the Latin," he tells us. "But that of the modern Greeks I had no opportunity of learning until I went to Paris. There I became acquainted with two learned Greeks, Count Carberri and Mr. Paradise" who taught me the modern Greek pronunciation of ancient Greek.[32] In his declining years the sage of Monticello turned eagerly from the cares of state, from his voluminous correspondence, from the flood of guests, even from farming and the erection of his beloved University, to the "luxury" of reading Cicero, Homer, Ovid, Euripides, Sophocles and other classic authors.

Having grounded himself in the classics the next concern of the wealthy planter was to acquire a knowledge of law. This he did, not merely to add breadth to his education, but to equip himself for his career in the economic and political life of the colony. It would prove useful to him in the innumerable suits over land titles and boundaries, he could draw upon it as a member of the parish vestry if a squabble arose over the levying of tithes or the appointment of the rector, it was a part of his equipment as justice of the peace, he needed it as the representative of his county in the House of Burgesses, it was indispensable if he acquired that greatest of honors, a seat on the Council of State, entailing as it did membership in the supreme court of his colony. In other words, he had to be prepared to take his place as lawyer, judge and legislator, and for this an extensive reading in Blackstone and Coke and the laws of Virginia or Maryland was essential.

In the years prior to the opening of the William and Mary law school the youth who desired a thorough legal training was forced to study in Great Britain. Thus it happened that many a promising young Marylander or Virginian took up his lodgings in the Inner Temple or Gray's Inn or the Middle Temple or Lincoln's Inn to pursue his studies within the shadow of the law courts. There some of the future leaders of both colonies and of the nation—Daniel Dulaney, Edmund Jennings, Samuel Chase,

[32]*Jefferson's Writings*, Vol. XV, p. 182.

Charles Carroll, William Peca, Richard Henry Lee, Sir John Randolph, Christopher Robinson, William Byrd II, John Blair, Philip Ludwell Lee, Arthur Lee—sat under the great teachers of law and rubbed elbows with future members of the English bar.

But the average planter, for whom study at the Inns of Court was impracticable, was self-taught in the law. In his leisure moments, after he had made his round of the plantation or on rainy days, one might find him poring over *A Perfect Guide for a Studious Young Lawyer,* or *A Guide to Constables,* or *The Country Justice,* or *Virginia Justice,* or Montesquieu's *Spirit of Laws,* or Blackstone's *Commentaries.* The library of John Mercer, noted as the preceptor of George Mason, contained no less than five hundred volumes on law.[33] When Robert Bell, in 1772, printed an American edition of Blackstone's *Commentaries* at his shop in Third Street, Philadelphia, eighty-two Virginians subscribed, among them not only men in public life such as John Page, John Tayloe and Edmund Pendleton, but planters, merchants, doctors, as well as lawyers and law students.

With the commencement exercises over and with his diploma safely packed away in his saddle-bags, the young graduate of William and Mary mounted his horse and set off for the home plantation. Whether he remained here to assist his father, or established himself in one of the "quarters," it was the plantation life which was to influence most profoundly the intellectual interests of his maturer years. As a planter he was concerned with husbandry, often in its scientific as well as its practical aspects, as a member of the Anglican church and a vestryman he must be well read in biblical literature and even in theology, as a country gentleman who found delight in intellectual interests he must know something of architecture, art, landscape gardening, English literature, perhaps of philosophy, science, drama, music. "We that are banished from the polite pleasures [of London] are forced to take up rural entertainments," wrote William Byrd II. "A library, a garden, a grove and a purling stream are the innocent scenes that divert our leisure."[34]

[33]Helen Hill, *George Mason—Constitutionalist* (1938), p. 12.
[34]*Correspondence of William Byrd II,* Vol. III, Huntington Library.

We are introduced into the daily life of a wealthy Virginia planter in the closing years of the colonial period by the pages of the *Journal* of Philip Vickers Fithian, the Princeton graduate employed as tutor by Colonel Robert Carter, of Nomini Hall, in Westmoreland County. We see the Colonel practicing on the flute or the piano, or studying thorough bass, or reading philosophy, or conversing learnedly of eclipses, telescopes and the solar system, or speculating on the possibility of life on the planets. We follow Fithian himself as he strolls in the formal garden, or browses in the very extensive library, or plays the violin in a family musicale, or looks over the latest London newspapers, or wonders at a case of mathematical instruments which has just arrived from England, or expresses his admiration for the beauty and dignity of Nomini Hall itself. It is a fascinating picture of a refined, leisurely, cultured life, in which neither the business of managing a great plantation nor an occasional ball or marriage festival interrupts for long the customary school work, music, interesting conversation, the reading of the classics, law, philosophy and English literature.

Beyond doubt there were other Virginia and Maryland households where intellectual interests were thrust aside for less elevated pleasures—costly entertainment, horse racing, hunting, cock-fighting, card-playing, perhaps a visit to Williamsburg to see Hallam and his company at the theatre. But nothing can be farther from the truth than the belief that the gay life absorbed all the leisure moments of the typical wealthy planter. There were many, like Jefferson, who enjoyed a quiet moment with Cicero or Horace, many who delighted in an evening devoted to music, many who preferred Shakespeare to the fox hunt, many who turned enthusiastically to architecture, landscape gardening, art and philosophy. But they devoted themselves to these things in the spirit of the cultured gentleman, not as professionals, not as productive artists or scholars. They kept abreast of the best literature of their time, but they were not themselves poets or essayists or novelists; they built beautiful residences, but they were not professional architects; they were acquainted with theology, but did not enter into theological disputes. In statecraft and political theory alone did they forsake the rôle of the amateur and become creators, and in these fields their accomplishment was truly amazing.

Why was it, some may ask, if the Virginia and Maryland aristocrat was scholarly and enlightened, that he proved so backward in the very science upon which his livelihood depended? Why was he such a slovenly agriculturalist, who wasted the soil, was too negligent to adopt the three-crop system, failed to utilize manures to the best advantage and was ignorant of the latest advances in husbandry? But if we step into the planter's library to thumb over his books, we are surprised to find many treatises on agriculture, presenting the latest advances in scientific farming—Hale's *Husbandry,* in four volumes, Full's *Husbandry, The Complete Farmer,* Young's *Experimental Agriculture,* Duhamel's *Husbandry, The Husbandman's Calling, Rural Economy* or *The Practical Parts of Husbandry, Essays on Husbandry* and others. To these books he turned in the hope that they might prove serviceable in the economy of his plantation.[35] It is more than probable that George Washington acquired his early impression of scientific agriculture from *The Farmer's Guide,* Maxwell's *Husbandry,* Duhamel's *Husbandry, The New System of Agriculture,* in the library of Daniel Parke Custis, which came into his possession when he married Mrs. Custis.

Unfortunately the planter found books on English agriculture of very little practical use in Virginia and Maryland. He was not deeply interested in the three-field system when land could be had for a song; he could not heed the advice to enrich his fields with manure, for this would have necessitated the keeping of a great herd of cattle for which he had no need since the market for beef was small and for dairy products almost non-existent; he looked in vain in these books for chapters on the culture of tobacco and Indian corn, the two crops upon which his economy was chiefly based. Thus, he was forced to fall back upon experience for his guide—his own experience, his father's and grandfather's experience and the experience of the Indians before them.

[35] *Tyler's Magazine,* Vol. III, p. 124; *Virginia Magazine of Hist. and Biog.,* Vol. IV, p. 290, Vol. VII, p. 302, Vol. XVII, p. 404; *William and Mary Quarterly,* Vol. IV, p. 15.

The agriculture of the region for nearly two centuries was based, not upon European methods, but upon Indian crops and to some extent Indian methods, improved by European farm implements and so far as possible by West Indian and European knowledge of cultivation.

That the planters were students of agriculture, often ardent students, is shown by their experiments with various foreign plants. They were keenly conscious that they possessed rich soil smiled upon by sunny skies and watered by frequent and well-distributed rains. Might they not hope to produce wheat, barley, oats, indigo, hemp, cotton, melons, apples, pears, oranges and other European, Asiatic or Latin American plants, not only for their own use, but in some cases for the British or even the foreign market? "I thank you for the yams, eddoes, etc.," wrote William Mayo to a friend in Barbados in 1731, but "such things will not come to . . perfection in this climate. . . . I shall take what care I can about propagating the fruit-stones. I have had plum stones from England and planted them here."[36] It was five years later that Peter Collinson sent John Custis, of Virginia, some melon-seed from Russia, while in 1737 we find him trying "to secure strawberry seed as desired." In 1743 Collinson wrote that he had shipped various plants and trees, among them the "love apple" called "tomiatos," much used in "soups and broths."[37]

Over and over the colonial experimenter had the satisfaction of seeing the imported plant prosper in American soil. He had reason to rejoice as his wheat seed sprouted, grew and ripened under the Southern sun, or when his apple or pear trees bowed under the weight of their delicious fruit. But he soon discovered that he could not compete with foreign countries or with England itself in the production of foreign or English products. He could not sell his wheat in England, save perhaps in time of war, because the costs of labor and transportation were too high; he could not compete with European hemp, oats, wines. It was vain to think of shipping his apples and pears across the Atlantic before the days of ocean refrigeration, so that his orchards served

[36]*Virginia Magazine of Hist. and Biog.*, Vol. XXXII, p. 56.
[37]*Colonial Williamsburg Inc. Transcripts of Curwen Manuscripts.*

only to feed his family, his servants and slaves. For indigo, cotton and the silk worm, Virginia and Maryland were not well suited, yet the attempts to produce them, especially silk, were persistent. The London Company required every planter in Virginia to set out six mulberry trees, treatises on silk were forwarded to the colony, seed were imported from Valcenia, bounties were placed upon production. Despite early failures we find Edward Digges experimenting with the silkworm in 1654, Major Thomas Walker in 1664, and Sir William Berkeley in 1668.[38] Yet the two colonies clung to tobacco as their staple crop for two centuries, because in the famed Orinoco and Sweetscented they had a natural monopoly, which yielded large profits despite the high costs of labor and transportation. But this does not justify the frequently repeated charge that they were slovenly, unintelligent and unprogressive agriculturalists, ignorant of the latest advances in the science of husbandry.

The planter delighted in reading. Isolated upon his plantation; cut off from the association of poets, historians, scientists; deprived of the pleasure of attending concerts or of knowing professional musicians; regarding a visit to the theatre at Annapolis or Williamsburg as a rare treat; too far from his neighbors to organize a literary or a philosophical club, he turned to his books as his best companions and his revered perceptors. In his residence he set aside one room for his library, where he kept under lock and key the volumes which had come down to him from his father and his grandfather, side by side with those of his own purchase. On certain shelves were the cumbrous folios, on another the quartos, on others the octavos and on still others the little duodecimos. Here he could seclude himself after his rounds of the plantation, or while the young members of the household were enjoying country dances or the stately minuet, or when rain or snow made it unpleasant to venture out-of-doors, to ponder over Blair's *Sermons,* or to thrill at Cicero's eloquence, or to lose himself in *Hamlet* or *The Merchant of Venice,* or *Gulliver's Travels,* or *Peregrine Pickle,* or Pope's *Essay on Man.*

Some of these libraries were very extensive, cosmopolitan and

[38] P. A. Bruce, *Economic History of Virginia,* Vol. I, pp. 241, 242, 365, 399.

well chosen. George Washington owned nine hundred and three volumes, Robert Carter had a thousand and sixty-six at Nomini Hall and five hundred at his residence in Williamsburg; John Mercer, the guardian of George Mason, owned fifteen hundred; William Byrd II gathered around him in beautiful Westover nearly four thousand. In the building up of these collections the planter exercised the greatest care to secure the volumes best suited to his needs. Often he gave specific orders for the purchase of this set of Homer or that of Shakespeare, but sometimes he depended upon his factor in England to select for him the latest work of fiction or the best treatise on mathematics or navigation. "You know some of the newest books if they be ingenious will be mighty acceptable," wrote William Fitzhugh, in 1690.[39] In 1698 we find him waiting impatiently for the arrival of the English *Statutes,* the second and third parts of Ruckworth's *Collections,* Thomas Burnet's *Theory of the Earth,* Bacon's *Remains,* a *Bible, The Secret History of Charles II and James II,* and other books.[40]

The plantation library was a reflection of the planter himself, his education, his tastes, his mentality, his dependence upon the mother country, his daily life. In the seventeenth century works on religion probably constituted the largest group of books in the average library, followed in turn by works by the classic authors, books on law, history and biography, medicine, belles-lettres, science, geography and travel, politics and government.[41] In time the planter's interest in religious writings waned, while his attention was increasingly fixed on law and belles-lettres. In Robert Carter's library at Nomini Hall the classics predominated, with scores of volumes devoted to Caesar, Horace, Cicero, Ovid, Xenophon, Seneca, Livy, Virgil, Tacitus, Aristotle, Pliny, Plutarch, Sallust, etc. Colonel Carter must have been very fond of Ovid, for there were no less than thirteen volumes of his works in his plantation library. Mixed in indiscriminately with the classics were many books on law, most of them octavos, a comparatively

[39]*Virginia Magazine of Hist. and Biog.,* Vol. III, p. 255.
[40]*Ibid.,* Vol. VI, p. 72.
[41]Louis B. Wright, *"Rich. Lee II,"* The Huntington Library Quarterly, Vol. II, pp. 1–35. *Ibid.,* Vol. I, pp. 3–61, *"The Gentleman's Library in Early Virginia."*

small number on religion; a well assorted selection on philosophy, music, history, biography, geography, art, science, archæology, French literature, medicine, English literature, commerce, architecture, husbandry. Fithian, who took the pains to go over the library to jot down in his journal the title of every volume, found, side by side, Shakespeare's *Works* in nine volumes, Plutarch's *Lives* in nine volumes, *Gil Blas* in four volumes, *Devil upon Crutches* in two volumes, *Æsop's Fables* in Greek and Latin, More's *Utopia*.[42] Fithian must have smiled as he compared this planter's library with those of the New Jersey clergymen which once he had regarded as so impressive. "To speak moderately," he wrote his friend, Reverend Enoch Green, "he has more than eight times your number."

One finds very little of contemporaneous English literature in the comparatively small libraries of the seventeenth century. But we know from the collections of Ralph Wormeley, Godfrey Pole, Arthur Spicer, Edmund Berkeley and others that the Virginians of the time of William and Mary and Queen Anne were awakening to the worth of Shakespeare,[43] Bunyan, Francis Bacon and Herbert and were even reading William Penn's *No Cross, No Crown,* Sir Walter Raleigh's *History of the West Indies,* and the poems of Cartwright, Quarles, Donne and others. Two decades later English literature had so gained in favor that Robert Beverley, on his estate in the frontier country of Spottsylvania County indulged himself in Milton's *Paradise Lost,* More's *Utopia,* Pope's *Iliad,* Locke's *Works,* Evelyn's *Sylvia,* and books by Tillotson, Temple, Burnet, Shaftesbury and others.[44] In the same period the famous "King" Carter was reading Addison's *Works* in four volumes, the *Works of the Duke of Buckingham,* Abraham Cowley's *Works,* Defoe's *Reformation of Manners: A Satire,* John Oldham's *Works,* Sir William Temple's *Miscellanea,* Clarendon's *The History of the Rebellion,* etc.[45]

By mid-century the appetite for English literature had grown still further. "Lent in town, but to whom forgot, the following

[42]*Fithian Journal, MSS.,* Princeton University Library.
[43]*Virginia Magazine of Hist. and Biog.,* Vol. XXXV, p. 37.
[44]*Ibid.,* Vol. III, pp. 388–391.
[45]L. B. Wright, in *Huntington Library Quarterly,* Vol. I, pp. 53, 61.

books," John Bennett advertised in the *Maryland Gazette,* on May 18, 1756, *"Gulliver's Travels,* Vol. II, Dean Swift's *Miscellanies . . . The Tale of a Tub,* Rollin's *Ancient History,* Vols. I, VII and IX, three volumes of *The Guardian,* two volumes of the *Spectator."* The development of Williamsburg and Annapolis as centers of culture greatly stimulated interest in literature. In 1762 the indefatigable William Rind, editor of the *Maryland Gazette,* organized a circulating library, with dues of a guinea a year, which placed the best books within the reach of a large group of readers. Rind opened a bookstore at Annapolis, where planters, lawyers, doctors, school teachers and ministers might resort in search of the works best suited to their needs. Since Rind must have known the tastes of his customers, his advertisements in *The Gazette,* giving the titles of his latest importations, are an excellent criterion of the reading in colonial Maryland. Among his books arriving on the *Charming Nancy* in 1762 were: Smollett's *History of England;* Pope's *Works* in ten volumes; Swift's *Works* in twelve volumes; four volumes of *The Rambler;* Samuel Johnson's *The Prince of Abyssinia; Adventures of Sir Lancelot Greaves;* Hume's *Essays; The Turkish Spy; Peregrine Pickle;* Milton's *Paradise Lost and Regained;* Fielding's *Tom Jones, Amelia* and *Joseph Andrews;* Richardson's *Clarissa* and *Pamela;* Shakespeare; Pope's *Posthumous Works;* Pope's *Iliad; The Spectator;* Dryden's *Plays; Robinson Crusoe,* and many others.[46]

It is remarkable that so many of these volumes found their way to the colonies soon after their publication. Colonel Carter, of Nomini Hall, had on his shelves in 1772 a copy of *Tristram Shandy,* published in 1760–1769; Dixon and Hunter's bookstore was advertising for sale in 1775 *Humphrey Clinker,* published in 1771; William Rind imported in 1762 Johnson's *Dictionary,* put out in 1755, *Peregrine Pickle,* published in 1751, and *Roderick Random,* published in 1748. One might almost conclude that the Virginians and Marylanders were using their own judgment as to what was best in English literature, did we not know their habitual dependence upon the mother country in all cultural matters. If it became fashionable in London to read *The Rambler,*

[46]*Maryland Gazette,* August 26, 1762.

or *The Vicar of Wakefield,* or *Tom Jones,* they would before long make their appearance on the shelves of a Dulaney, or a Carter, or a Wormeley.

But the planter was not diverted from his more solid reading by the romantic effusions of Fielding, Richardson and Smollett. He still poured over his Ovid and his Homer, he still gathered around him ponderous volumes of law, he read Shakespeare, Milton, Pope, Swift, Defoe and Dryden. Colonel Carter "has the works of almost all the late famous writers," said Fithian, "as Locke, Addison, Young, Pope, Swift, Dryden, etc." Young Robert Hunter, who visited Archibald McCall at Tappahannock in 1785 and 1786, gives in his *Journal* a delightful picture of the intellectual life of a Virginia family. When not attending a wedding at a neighboring plantation, or celebrating Washington's birthday with a ball, or playing on the harpsichord, he was reading aloud to sweet Kate McCall from Madame de Sévigné's *Letters,* or Lord Chesterfield's *Letters,* or *The Vicar of Wakefield,* or retiring to his chamber to lose himself in Vertot's *Revolution in Sweden* or Montesquieu's *Spirit of the Laws.*[47] The Virginian or Marylander, when he met his friends in the drawing room of Westover, or Mt. Airy, or the Hammond house, who could not discourse intelligently upon the great English writers was considered an ignoramus.

The wealthy planter who visited England in the eighteenth century could not fail to be impressed with the dignty and beauty of the residences of the landed aristocracy. In his mind the balanced façade, the doric door, the Palladian window, the panelled reception hall, the carved stairway, the marble mantel became associated with the life of the country gentleman. And as he gazed at stately Eaton Hall or went through the luxurious rooms of Shobdon Court he resolved that he too, in faraway Westmoreland or Anne Arundel, would erect a residence worthy of his position as an American squire, even though it put in pawn his tobacco crop for years to come. So there arose on the banks of the James or the Potomac or the Severn a series of mansions which in dignity, in correctness of proportion, in charm of detail, would

[47] *Hunter's Journal of Travels in America.* Huntington Library.

have done credit to England itself—Westover, Carter's Grove, Brandon, Tulip Hill, Gunston Hall, the Hammond House, Mount Airy and many others.

Had the planter merely called in an architect and left the planning and the details to his judgment, the residence would not have been in the truest sense his own. But when he drew his plans with his own hands, pored over books on architecture for interesting details, made his own bricks, gave detailed instruction to his agent in England for the purchase of mantels or latches or panes of glass, superintended the raising of the beams and the laying of floors, the house became a true reflection of his tastes and desires. We do not know the true Jefferson until we know Monticello; Mount Vernon was more than the residence of George Washington, it was his creation.

Despite the paucity of evidence we have every reason to believe that it was customary for the planter, especially in the seventeenth century, to design his own house and superintend the construction. Often no other course was open to him unless he sent across the Atlantic for architect and builder. When certain work was needed upon a small building owned by Charles City County in 1672, it was entrusted, not to a regular contractor, but to Colonel Edward Hill, one of the leading planters of the colony. His report to the county court is illuminating as to the methods in use at the time. "I employed the workmen, procured boards, made bricks, found lime, etc. and in fine finished the said house . . . paid bricklayers for building the chimney and for filling and white liming the house, Mr. Place for ceiling boards . . . Mrs. Ann Bland for nails and shells,[48] the carpenters and laborers" for their work.[49] It may be taken for granted that Colonel Hill, when he erected his own house, followed the same procedure.

It would be interesting to know just how much of his own personality William Byrd II put into Westover, or Mann Page into Rosewell or John Tayloe into Mount Airy, but in most cases the records are too meager for us to say. It is probable that even when a professional architect was employed, as at Carter's Grove or

[48]For lime.
[49]*Virginia Magazine of Hist. and Biog.*, Vol. III, p. 245.

PLATE I—Plan from John James's *The Theory and Practice of Gardening,*
showing forms popular with southern colonial gardeners

PLATE 2—Mount Vernon

Gunston Hall, the owner collaborated with him in both the main plan and many of the details. That frequently there was neither architect nor contractor we know from scattered diaries, letters and court records. When Colonel Francis Taylor, of Orange County, built a house for his father in 1786–1787, he supervised in person each step in the work. "Began to dig my father's cellar," he jotted down in diary. "Charles Dickinson is at work on the stone (foundation) . . . C. P. sent fifteen rafters . . . H. T. sent for some bricks and lime . . . H. T. promised to send his waggon tomorrow with shingles and to bring plank from sawmill . . . Workmen put cornice on . . . began to shingle . . . Peter with cart and oxen brought bricks . . . for the chimney . . . J. Taylor's cart brought 325 feet flooring plank—C. D. began plastering."[50]

Most interesting was the development of the mansion at Mount Vernon under the direction of George Washington. "Washington was his own architect and builder, laying off everything himself," his adopted son tells us.[51] "The buildings, gardens and grounds all rose to ornament and usefulness under his fostering hand." The residence which Washington inherited from his brother seems to have been a typical frame cottage of the late seventeenth-century type, one and a half stories high, with end chimneys, dormers and hallway running through the center. When he became engaged to Mrs. Custis he decided to enlarge the house, adding a story, rebuilding the chimneys, replacing the weather boarding with planks bevelled to resemble cut stone, reglazing the windows, putting in new floors. It was a real grief to Washington that his part in the French and Indian War took him away from Mount Vernon while the work was in progress, but he found time amid marches and battles to order materials and send directions to the workmen. Send me "a marble chimney piece, cost not to exceed fifteen guineas, paper mâché for the ceiling of the two rooms, 250 panes of window glass, a dozen fashionable locks for partition doors, fashionable hinges," etc., he wrote to a merchant in London.

[50]*Diary of Colonel Francis Taylor*, Virginia State Library, Richmond.
[51]*Memoirs of Washington*, G. W. P. Custis (N. Y., 1859), p. 371.

49

For fourteen years Mount Vernon remained practically unchanged. But now Washington was a wealthy man, and it was but proper that he should have a residence comparable in dignity and beauty with those of some of his friends and neighbors. In 1773 George W. Fairfax moved to England, leaving his estate, Belvoir, in Washington's care. This it was, no doubt, which influenced him to remodel Mount Vernon upon lines so strikingly similar to Belvoir. At all events he designed additions, one embracing a library on the first floor, with bedrooms on the second and third floors, the other devoted to a two-story banquet hall. It was with a sigh of regret that Washington rode away from Mount Vernon in 1775 to take his seat in Congress, leaving his estate in the care of Lund Washington and the alterations to the mansion to a builder named Going Lamphoir. "I wish you would quicken Lamphoir and Sears about the dining room chimney piece as I wish to have that end of the house completely finished before I return," he wrote from Cambridge in August. Little did he realize that it would be eight years before he could seek once more the peace and joy which the life at Mount Vernon brought him. But when the war was over we find him again busy with alterations, this time the building of the great east portico and the erection of the cupola, to complete the imposing structure which Americans so much admire and venerate[52] (Plate 2).

Even more than in his residence the planter delighted in his flower garden. Perhaps he had seen some of the formal gardens of England—at King's Weston, Gloucestershire; or Wilton House, Wiltshire; or Squerries Court, Kent; or Wimpole, Cambridgeshire; perhaps their fame had reached him by report; perhaps he was fired to emulate the beautiful palace garden at Williamsburg. He might leave some of the details of the layout of walks, steps, terraces, hedges, gates to a professional gardener, more often he drew his own plans and superintended the work in person. The transplanting of trees, the growth of a box bush labyrinth, the importation of flowers and shrubs from abroad offered him unending diversion from the cares of managing a plantation.

The palace garden at Williamsburg, laid out early in the eigh-

[52]T. H. Ormsbee, "Mansion from a Cottage," *House Beautiful*, Feb., 1934.

teenth century, seems to have set the pattern for the Virginia gardens and many of those in Maryland. It, in turn, was patterned closely upon the European formal gardens of the second half of the seventeenth century. As one views the fragrant maze of the box garden, or the ballroom garden gay with many-colored flowers, or wanders through the walks of the north garden, or descends the steps to the canal and vine garden, or rests in the shade of the holly trees, all now carefully restored, one could well imagine himself at Eaton Hall or Wimpole, or even Hampton Court or Westbury Court. We would be surprised at the French flavor, evident throughout, did we not remember that John Rose, Gardener-in-chief to Charles II, studied under the French master Le Nôtre, and that *The Compleat Gardener* and *The Retir'd Gardener,* two books which had a wide vogue in England, were translated from the French. The palace garden was one of the show places of colonial Virginia, and the Governor's guests, after a sumptuous dinner or a stately ball, delighted in wandering, perhaps by moonlight, through its walks, or under its arbors, or beside the canal. There were none, not even William Byrd, who could hope to rival it in costliness and extent, but there must have been many, as they rode out of the little capital, who resolved to lay out in the shadow of their plantation residences little "palace gardens" of their own.[53]

Yet Byrd did create a beautiful garden at Westover which remains today as a testimonial of his good taste and the breadth of his intellectual interests. One cannot listen to the buzz of the thousands of bees which hover over the giant wistaria, or smell the fragrance of the box or view the monument over Byrd's grave at the intersection of two paths, without realizing that something of the man himself still lingers on nearly two centuries after his death. Colonel Byrd may have got the inspiration for his garden either during his many years abroad or from his frequent visits to Williamsburg, or he may have drawn his ideas from the books on gardening which filled an entire shelf in his library at the time of its sale in 1778—*The Compleat Gardener, Solitary Gardener, Rapin on Gardening, Dutch Gardener,* and many

[53]H. Batsford and C. Fry, *Homes and Gardens of England.*

others[54] (Plate 1). At all events his garden was his own delight and the delight of his visitors, who spoke admiringly of his "new gates, gravel walks, hedges and cedars finely twined."[55] "I am told that Colonel Byrd has the best garden in Virginia and a pretty greenhouse well furnished with orange trees," wrote Peter Collinson.

Before the end of the colonial period eastern Virginia and Maryland were filled with charming gardens—at Ash Grove, Belvoir, Brandon, Nomini Hall, Mount Airy, the Chew House, Wye House, and scores of others. "Mr. Tayloe has a large, well formed, beautiful garden, as fine in every respect as I have seen in Virginia," wrote Fithian in 1772. "In it stand four large beautiful statues."[56] The planters apparently relied upon their slaves only for the simpler tasks in the garden under their personal supervision or the direction of a professional gardener. Colonel Carter had two Negroes constantly at work, but when spring came a Mr. Gregory arrived to take control. Occasionally professional gardeners advertised in the gazettes, emphasizing their experience in England or stating that they were well versed in the art of mathematics.[57]

Not less interesting than the restoration of the palace garden at Williamsburg is that of the garden at Stratford Hall, the ancestral home of the Lee family, by the Robert E. Lee Memorial Foundation. All that remained of the original garden were a few old trees, some fig bushes and a broad, flat area partly enclosed by a brick wall. Into this area landscape architects dug down to discover the remains of old walls, paths, terraces and parterres, until the plan stood revealed. Drawing upon old letters, upon the memory of old people and upon their knowledge of the art of gardening in colonial Virginia, they reconstructed the garden as it must have been in the days when Light-Horse Harry Lee was a little boy. Today it stretches away to the east of the mansion, its gentle

[54]J. S. Bassett, *The Writings of Colonel William Byrd of Westover* (N. Y., 1901), pp. 422, 425. It is possible that some of these volumes may have been added by William Byrd III.

[55]*Bartram Papers*, f. 21., Penna. Hist. Society.

[56]Philip Vickers Fithian, *Journal and Letters*, p. 149.

[57]*Maryland Gazette*, Dec. 6, 1749, Nov. 4, 1773.

terraces, its gravel walks, its boxwood pattern of the Lee coat-of-arms, its wooden gateways, its holly bushes, its snowballs, its lilacs, its wall of old brick, in all their former dignity and beauty.[58]

There was no more enthusiastic landscape gardener and horticulturist in America than George Washington. With meticulous care he plotted out the grounds around his mansion—the serpentine driveway, the oval grass-plot before the rear door, the lawn, the vegetable garden to the left, the flower garden to the right. The location of each tree was jotted down on his detailed plan, here a holly, here a chestnut, here a maple, here an elm, here a poplar, and the days when he could go to the woods to direct the work of transplanting were among the happiest of his life. "Enjoyed myself the greatest part of the day in pruning . . . my trees and shrubs," he wrote in his diary. "Finished laying out my serpentine roads. Dug most of the holes . . . and planted some of the maples . . . Took up the clump of lilacs which stood at the corner of the south garden plot and transplanted them."[59] The flower garden was surrounded by a wall with an octagonal seed-house at one corner, a Sago palm at the intersection of the two main paths, and a large conservatory on the north side. Here Washington kept his rare plants, some of them purchased of John Bartram, others the gifts of admiring friends, among them some lemon trees and a fine century plant.[60]

The planter would have considered the walls of his residence bare indeed had they been unadorned with family portraits and engravings of famous paintings. In the seventeenth century he might have been content with tapestry[61] or later with wood panelling and carving, or with damask hangings, or wall paper.[62] But when he visited some of the English country seats, where the walls were hung with portraits or with paintings by Benjamin West or Claude Lorrain or Gainsborough, he came away with a new interest in art and a determination to surround himself with

[58]Ethel Armes, *Stratford Hall*, pp. 495–512.
[59]John C. Fitzpatrick, *The Diaries of George Washington*, Vol. II, pp. 345, 346.
[60]Benson J. Lossing, *The Home of Washington* (N. Y., 1870), pp. 154–161.
[61]P. A. Bruce, *Economic History of Virginia*, Vol. I, pp. 277, 278; *Virginia Magazine of Hist. and Biog.*, Vol. VII, p. 317, Vol. XXX, p. 3.
[62]*Virginia Gazette*, Dec. 28, 1769.

pictures in his own home. If he could not afford originals by the greatest living artists, at least he could employ a painter of distinction to make his own and his wife's portrait, and purchase prints by William Byrne after Van Swanvelt or John Wooton.

The Byrd family especially were lavish in their expenditures for portraits, and Mrs. William Byrd III in her will mentions no less than forty which were hanging at Westover, among them likenesses of William Byrd II, William Byrd III, Evelyn Byrd and other members of the family; of the fourth Earl of Orrery; of Robert Harley, Earl of Oxford; Charles Montague, Earl of Halifax; John second Duke of Argyle; Sir Robert Southwell; and John Percival, Earl of Egmont. In addition there were a Titian, a Rubens and various other paintings.[63] At Mount Airy, the residence of the Tayloe family, Fithian was surprised to find "various paintings and rich pictures." "In the dining room besides other fine pieces are twenty-four of the most celebrated English racehorses, drawn masterly and set in elegant frames."[64] At Elsing Green, in King William County, in addition to a room hung with Gobelin tapestry, were many valuable paintings, among them a copy of Holbein's Viscount Montague.[65]

Among the family portraits which looked down from the panelled walls of the Maryland and Virginia mansions were many by Sir Godfrey Kneller, Sir Peter Lely and others who never visited the shores of America, for the planter who went to England frequently took advantage of the opportunity to sit to some distinguished painter. But most of them were done by wandering artists who came to America and went from one estate to another, easel in hand in search of work. "The person who has the honor to wait upon you with this letter . . . is obliged to seek his bread . . . in a strange land," wrote William Byrd II to Alexander Spotswood in 1735. "His name is Bridges and his profession painting. . . . He has drawn my children and several others in this neighborhood and though he has not the master hand of a Lilly [Lely] or Kneller, yet had he lived so long ago as when places were given to

[63]*Virginia Magazine of Hist. and Biog.*, Vol. VI, pp. 346–358.
[64]Philip Vickers Fithian, *Journal*, p. 148.
[65]P. N. Clarke, *Old King William* (Louisville, 1897), p. 12.

the most deserving, he might have pretended to be sergeant painter of Virginia." Charles Bridges remained in Virginia for years, and many of his portraits have come down to us—of Lucy Park, wife of William Byrd II, Colonel Edward Hill III, Mann Page II, Colonel Matthew Page, Alexander Spotswood, Mrs. Lewis Burwell and others, his women easily identified by a lock of hair resting on or in front of the shoulder.[66]

Another English painter who found patronage in the estates of the planters was John Wollaston, who came to America in about 1758. After a stay in Philadelphia he came to Maryland and Virginia, painting the portraits of many prominent persons, among them Mary Ball the mother of George Washington, Martha Washington and her children, John and Martha Custis, Betty Washington and her husband Colonel Fielding Lewis.[67] Wollaston's work is much in the style of Kneller, and was greatly admired by the critics of his day. There were other itinerant painters who followed, some of whom did not hesitate to advertise in the gazettes. "Mr. Pratt, portrait painter, lately from England and Ireland" put a notice in the *Virginia Gazette,* of March 4, 1773, stating that he had a collection of paintings for sale, including copies of Corregio's *St. Jerome,* West's *Holy Family* and Guido's *Jupiter and Europa.* In 1770 J. Durand advertised that he would be glad to "wait upon" ladies and gentlemen who wished to have their portraits painted.[68]

Of even greater interest is a notice which appeared in the *Maryland Gazette* on February 9, 1764, stating that Charles Willson Peale, at his shop in Church Street was ready to serve the public by making chairs and repairing clocks. Persons who read this notice could not have foreseen that this young man was to become one of the most distinguished portrait painters in America. Apprenticed as a lad to a saddler, a failure in business, he took up painting with such success that several Maryland gentlemen advanced funds to make it possible for him to study in England. There he became a pupil of another American, Benjamin West,

[66]*Virginia Magazine of Hist. and Biog.,* Vol. IX, pp. 236, 237.
[67]*Tyler's Magazine,* Vol. IX, pp. 224–230.
[68]*Virginia Gazette* (Hunter), June 21, 1770.

and soon achieved a reputation as a portrait painter. He will always be known as the painter of George Washington, of whom he made no less than sixty portraits, but he has left us as well paintings of Mrs. Washington, Lafayette, General John Cropper, Arthur Lee, Henry Tazewell, Benjamin Harrison "The Signer" and others. Peale, although of humble origin and so not a product of the planter aristocracy, is none the less an evidence of that aristocracy's interest in art, for without the assistance of the gentlemen who sent him to study in England, his latent talent would never have come to fruition.

The interest of the planters in art found expression often in engravings, for oil paintings, save for a portrait or two, were beyond the reach of all but the very wealthy. In 1750 we find one dealer in Annapolis advertising in the *Maryland Gazette* that he had just received "sundry curious and delightful prospects of most of the public buildings, palaces, hospitals, etc. of Europe, views of shipping, inside prospects of sundry churches, rivers, lakes and fountains."[69] In 1784 a notice was inserted of the arrival of "an elegant parcel" of nearly five thousand of "the most esteemed prints." It was with eagerness that the wealthy Marylander went through these importations and picked out a copy of a West, or a Lorrain, or a Trumbull, with which to adorn the walls of Tulip Hill, or Homewood, or the Brice House.

George Washington surrounded himself at Mount Vernon with engravings of famous paintings—some in the hall, others in the banquet hall, still others in the little parlor, others again in the front parlor where they rubbed elbows with the family portraits, some were in the dining room and some upstairs. There were landscapes after Claude Lorrain, battle scenes of the French and Indian War and the Revolution, including West's "Death of Wolfe" and Trumbull's "Battle of Bunker Hill"; several prints of storms at sea reminiscent of Washington's boyhood dreams of a mariner's life, while his prints of Lafayette, General Nathanael Greene, General Anthony Wayne, David Rittenhouse and others attest his loyalty to his friends. This extensive collection represents the wide range of Washington's taste, his appreciation of

[69]*Maryland Gazette*, Feb. 21, 1750.

current art and the liberal character of his mind. Had he lived today, with ample means at his disposal, he would no doubt have collected the paintings of the masters and built up a private gallery rivalling that of a Mellon or a Huntington.

In music, as in art, the Virginia and Maryland planters were appreciative rather than creative. Williamsburg and Annapolis produced no musical genius, no great composer, no brilliant performer. It is true that every community had its fiddlers, but they contented themselves chiefly with English tunes, which according to the fastidious Callister they murdered "ten times worse than the country fiddlers" of England.[70] Yet there was a wide appreciation of good music, many of the well-to-do planters themselves performed upon the violin or the organ or the guitar, every young lady was expected to sing or play upon the harpsichord or the pianoforte, there were not infrequent public concerts, excellent music was the accompaniment of every ball, psalmody was a part of church services. The planters, regarding music as an innocent and elevating diversion, were at a loss to understand the Quaker and Puritan contention that singing and playing upon instruments turned one from God by bewitching the heart with temporal delight.

The advertisements in the *Maryland Gazette* and the *Virginia Gazette* reveal both the extent of the interest in music and the musical taste of the planters. In 1772 there was a sale of music at the post office at Williamsburg, which included Stamitz's *Orchestra Trios,* Fisher's favorite *Minuet,* Brewster's *Vauxhall* and *Grotto Songs,* Abel's favorite *Overtures,* Pasquali's *Thorough Bass Made Easy,* Burgess Senior's *Lessons for the Harpsichord,* Corelli's *Solos,* and other works by Schwindl, Richter, Campioni, Bezozzi, Just and Pugnani, and many other selections.[71] Cuthbert Ogle, a well-known music teacher of Williamsburg, left a large collection of classical music among which may be noted Pasquati's *Overtures,* ten books of Händel's *Songs,* six *Sonatas* by Shickard, Händel's *Appolo's Faust,* six *Concertos* by Burgess, Lamp's *Thorough Bass,* Corelli's *Sonatas* and Grannom's *Ballads.*[72]

[70]*Callister Papers,* pp. 54–55, Maryland Diocesan Library.
[71]*Virginia Gazette,* Purdie & Dixon, Sept. 17, 1772.
[72]*William and Mary Quarterly,* III, p. 252.

Ogle must have presented a picturesque figure as he went from plantation to plantation, violin and folio of music in hand, in his French gray coat and breeches, black silk waistcoat and flowing wig, or peered through his "temple" spectacles at his notes and kept time for his pupil at the harpsichord.[73] And there was an Ogle for almost every community. In 1771 Francis Russworm, of Nansemond, announced in the *Virginia Gazette* that he had opened a school for the violin, and the German and common flutes.[74] Unfortunately, this good man, "who played such a sweet fiddle," was drowned while crossing a ferry.[75] The music masters were not content with teaching their young charges "to thump the keys of a harpsichord into the air of a tune mechanically," but often insisted upon a study of basic principles. A Mr. Vogel, in Richmond, declared that in addition to giving lessons on "the Piano Forte" and the harp, he would devote especial attention "to bringing up his pupils in the knowledge of composition, thorough bass, etc."[76]

The wealthy planter who invited a group of guests to a dance in his stately ball room was as careful in the selection of his orchestra as any committee for an undergraduate "prom." But the musicians, the instruments and the music itself presented a striking contrast to the "jazz" orchestra of today. True there were reels and country dances, but usually the young people bowed and turned to the stately strains of the minuet. Another opportunity to hear good music came with the opening of the theatres at Williamsburg and Annapolis, for no play was complete without the accompaniment of music between the acts, by performers upon the French horns, trumpets and other instruments. When the *Beggar's Opera* was given at Williamsburg in 1768, the music was conducted by Peter Pelham, organist of Bruton church.[77]

That Mr. Pelham's appreciation of music was of a very high order we know from a letter from a young lady of Williamsburg who complained that the doors of the church were left open so

[73]*Ibid.*
[74]*Virginia Gazette,* May 16, 1771.
[75]*Ibid.,* June 24, 1773.
[76]*William and Mary Quarterly,* Second Series, V, p. 63.
[77]*Virginia Gazette,* May 26, 1768.

that there was "scarce an evening but we are entertained with performances of Felton's, Händel's, Vi-Vally's, etc."[78] Music played a far more important rôle in the services of the Anglican churches of Virginia and Maryland than in the Quaker, Congregational and Presbyterian services in the northern colonies. Not only do we have evidence of excellent church music in advertisements and inventories, but we know that in many communities singing schools were conducted in connection with the parish. When Philip Williams, clerk of St. Anne's, announced that he proposed to teach "psalmody in all its parts, treble, contra tenor and bass," he gives an interesting insight into the character of the singing in the quaint old church at Annapolis.[79] Fithian tells us that Colonel Robert Carter, of Nomini Hall, had "a collection of psalm-tunes, hymns and anthems set in four parts for the voice," which he insisted upon his family's singing "in their several parts" and with instruments.[80]

Music was Colonel Carter's especial delight. He had a good ear, "a vastly delicate taste," owned a harpsichord, piano, harmonica, guitar, German flute and an organ, performed well upon several instruments and was a student of thorough bass. There were many delightful evenings at Nomini Hall when the Colonel played upon the guitar, or his daughters Betsy and Fanny sang to the accompaniment of the harpsichord. Even more interesting were the evenings in the Palace at Williamsburg when Governor Fauquier, with the youthful Thomas Jefferson and several others, indulged their love of music with amateur concerts.[81] Jefferson gathered together a fine musical library, including selections from Bach, Händel, Haydn and other masters, which survived intact until a few years ago. Unfortunately it was not entrusted to the Virginia State Library or the Library of Congress for safekeeping, but was kept upon a shelf in the parlor of one of Jefferson's descendants. Apparently old masterpieces make excellent kindling, for a Negro house boy used the music piece by piece in making fires, until all save a few volumes were consumed.[82] In Maryland

[78]William and Mary Quarterly, Vol. XVI, p. 179.
[79]Maryland Gazette, May 10, 1764.     [80]Philip Fithian, Journal, Vol. I, p. 187.
[81]The Writings of Thomas Jefferson, Vol. XIV, p. 232.
[82]Antiques, Vol. XII, p. 484.

a small group, including Henry Callister, Reverend Thomas Bacon and several others formed a musical society which met at various plantations for performances upon the violin, the harpsichord and other instruments.[83]

The Virginia planter who wished to witness a performance of *Richard III* or the *Merchant of Venice* had to make a visit to Williamsburg; the Marylander could indulge himself and his family in the drama only by journeying to Annapolis. This was not so great a hardship as at first sight it might seem, since when the General Assemblies were in session or when the courts were sitting, thousands of people crowded into the little capitals, filling the taverns and inns to overflowing and imposing upon the hospitality of the surrounding planters. Williamsburg and Annapolis were the social and cultural, as well as the political centers of Virginia and Maryland, so that debates in the House of Burgesses and decisions by the General Court had to share the limelight with balls, assemblies, dinners and theatrical performances.

To Williamsburg belongs the honor of having the first theatre in the colonies. It was in 1716 that William Levingston formed a partnership with Charles and Mary Stegg, dancing teachers, who had just arrived from London. Levingston agreed to erect a "good, substantial house, commodious for acting," and the Steggs were to produce "comedies, drolls or other kinds of stage plays" and to share the expenses for "clothes, music and other necessaries." The partners were to send to England for actors and musicians. That this pioneer venture in the field of dramatics met with hearty approval in Virginia is shown by the list of patrons, which reads like a roll-call of the aristocracy—the Harrisons, Burwells, Nelsons, Lees, Ludwells, Randolphs, Blairs.[84] Performances at the little theatre continued for two decades, coming to an end with the death of Stegg in 1736.

Sixteen years later the capital was alive with interest when it was announced that a company of well-known English actors

[83]*Callister Papers*, pp. 215.
[84]Helen Bulloch, *Williamsburg and Its Theatres*, MSS. Report of Colonial Williamsburg, Inc.

were on their way to Virginia aboard the *Charming Sally.* In the group were Lewis Hallam, the actor-manager; his wife, noted for her work in both tragedy and comedy; their little son Lewis, destined to become famous; Mr. Rigby, his wife, and several others. There was some difficulty in securing a license, but eventually the Governor gave his permission and the first performance was announced. The company will open "with a play, called *The Merchant of Venice* (written by Shakespeare) and a farce, called the *Anatomist, or Sham Doctor,*" it was announced (Plate 4). "The ladies are desired to give timely notice to Mr. Hallam, at Mr. Fisher's, for their places in the boxes, and on the day of performance to send their servants early to keep them, in order to prevent trouble and disappointment."

There followed in quick succession plays by Shakespeare, Congreve, Garrick and Gay, in which tragedies were mixed with popular plays such as *The Constant Couple, The Provoked Husband, Miss in Her Teens or a Medley of Lovers, The Lying Valet.* To the planters and their families the performances were a source of great delight, and during the season the theatre was crowded night after night. Among the most enthusiastic patrons was George Washington. "Dined at the Speaker's and went to the play," he jotted down in his *Diary,* on May 3, 1771. "Reached Williamsburg before dinner and went to the play in the afternoon," he wrote on October 29, 1771. On November 4, he "dined with the Council and went to the play afterwards."

Sarah Hallam, niece of Lewis Hallam, became the queen of the colonial stage and wherever she went received the plaudits of the audience and the homage of the gallants. Charles Willson Peale painted her portrait as Imogen in *Cymbeline.* The announcement that she was to play at Williamsburg was enough to fill the little theatre to overflowing. During the Revolution, when theatrical productions were forbidden, she opened a dancing school at Williamsburg, and continued to live in the little capital, revered and loved by the townspeople, until her death at a very advanced age.

The Marylanders were no less enthusiastic than the Virginians over the theatre and the playhouse at Annapolis was the scene of many distinguished gatherings. In 1752 there were performances of *The Beaux Stratagem, The Recruiting Officer, The London Merchant,* the ballad opera *Damon and Phillida, A Bold Stroke for a Wife, The Beggar's Opera, The Constant Couple, The Lying Valet* and other plays.[85] "Monday last the theatre in this city was opened," says the *Maryland Gazette,* of March 6, 1760, "when the *Tragedy of the Orphan* and *Lethe* (a dramatic satire) were performed in the presence of his Excellency the Governor, to a polite and numerous audience, who all expressed a general satisfaction. . . . The Prologue and Epilogue [were] both written by a gentleman in this province."

"When I left England I little expected that my passion for the drama could have been gratified—at a distance so remote from the great mart of genius," wrote William Eddis, Surveyor of Customs at Annapolis, just prior to and during the Revolution. But he was surprised to find performers "equal at least to" the best in our "most celebrated provincial theatres" of England. Though the playhouse was small, the Governor, who was a patron of the American Company, had headed a subscription to erect a new one on a larger scale.[86]

"Just imported and to be sold by William Parks, in Williamsburg," stated a notice in the *Virginia Gazette* of October 24, 1745, "a large quantity of church and family Bibles and Common Prayer Books, sermons, etc., too tedious to mention." Perhaps Parks's unconscious humor indicated quite well the attitude of many of the wealthy planters, not toward religion, but religious treatises and ecclesiastical disputations. The Virginians and Marylanders built charming and sometimes costly churches, secured the ablest minister within their means, made a point of attending services when weather and distances permitted, read the *Bible, The Whole Duty of Man, The Practice of Piety* and the *Common Prayer Book,* but they were not deeply interested in theological disputations or controversies on abstract religious theories.

The planter accepted his religion as he accepted the sun and the ocean and the King, as a thing to be taken without question,

[85]*Maryland Gazette,* July 9, 16, 23, 30, August 13, September 28, 1752.
[86]William Eddis, *Letters from America,* p. 93.

as a part of his life and his being. There were few indeed who emulated Jefferson in "fixing reason in her seat" even to questioning with boldness "the existence of God," and reading the Bible with the same detached spirit that one reads Livy or Tacitus.[87]

The Bible was a best seller and the people read it constantly, with the reverence due God's word. And we need no better evidence that they read other religious books than the fact that thousands were imported from England and others printed by the local presses. In 1729 William Parks found a ready sale for three books of devotions, turned out from his press and bound together: *The Week's Preparation Towards a Worthy Receiving of the Lord's Supper, The Church of England-Man's Private Devotions* and *An Explanation of the Feasts and Fasts.* The price was two shillings, sixpence, with "considerable allowance to those that buy a quantity." This was followed in 1734 by *A Short and Easy Method with the Deists,* and some years later by a proposal to print the Thanksgiving sermon of Reverend Mr. Gordon, preached before the Governor of Maryland. In 1750 Parks called for subscriptions for two volumes on *Christian Knowledge and Practice,* "being a brief system of divinity, or summary of what is to be done or known by Christians in their respective duties to God and man . . . a collection from the most eminent . . . English writers by a clergyman of Maryland."[88]

No doubt the planters read these books in the privacy of their homes and reflected seriously over the questions of religious duty which they raised. But they seldom discussed them with their friends, were not constantly quoting from them, did not become excited over the more controversial points. Fithian divided the time at the church into three parts, "before service, giving and receiving letters of business, reading advertisements, consulting the price of tobacco, grain, etc., and settling either the lineage, age or qualities of favorite horses; in the church at service, prayers read over in haste, a sermon seldom under and never over twenty minutes, but always made up of sound morality, or deep studied metaphysicks." After the service was over the congregation lin-

---

[87]*Jefferson's Writings,* Vol. VI, p. 257.
[88]*Maryland Gazette,* December 5, 1750.

gered on for three quarters of an hour, not to discuss the preacher's words or argue over predestination or transubstantiation, but to gossip with neighbors and extend invitations to Sunday dinner.

It has been said that every man must become a physician if he hopes to live beyond the age of forty. The Virginians and Marylanders had to be physicians from the moment they assumed the management of their plantations. With perhaps a hundred persons under their control and often too isolated to have a doctor within reach, they must know how to treat malaria, dysentery and other maladies common to the region, or face the loss of their children, indentured workers and slaves. So they purchased copies of Brooke's *Practice of Physic,* Quincy's *Dispensatory, The Surgeon's Mate* and Lynch's *Guide to Health,* and at the first report of illness among their charges turned to them for guidance. Even when a practicing physician was available, the planter often ignored him. "I would have no doctor unless in very violent cases, they generally do more harm than good," wrote Joseph Ball, the uncle of George Washington, in 1744. Yet his own remedies must have taxed the strength of his slaves to the utmost. "When they are taken with a pleurisy they should be immediately blooded pretty largely and if they continue bad the bleeding must be repeated but not in such large quantities. And they must take for three or four days running a spoonful of linseed oil every day and be kept warm and dieted." One shudders for the poor blacks when he reads Colonel Ball's inventory of medicines and directions for their use. There was dark salve for sores, green salve for boils or for "blisters after they are cut," red salve for "sore shins," three vials of Friars balsam for green wounds and cuts. "Wipe the wound as clean as you can of the blood, then pour a little of the balsam into a clean oyster shell and with a fine rag dop the wound," he directed. Side by side with the balsam and salves were "Tartar emitick" to be "taken in Carduii's tea."[89]

If Robert Carter, of Nomini Hall, read all the books on medical science in his library, he must have possessed a knowledge of the subject equal to that of the average colonial physician. Side by side with his volumes on history and philosophy were Quincy's

[89]*Joseph Ball Letter Book,* Library of Congress.

*Dispensatory,* Harrison's *Accomplished Practitioner,* Lynch's *Guide to Health, Friend on Fevers and Small Pox,* Turner's *Syphilis,* McLung on *Bile,* etc.[90] Daniel Parke Custis, who died in 1757, was even more interested in medical science and his book shelves were crowded with volumes on surgery, anatomy, fevers, "fluxes," the diseases of children and on general practice.[91]

Despite the many discouragements to research, colonial Virginia boasted of one medical scientist of distinction—John Tennent, author of many scholarly papers. Noting that the Seneca Indians used rattlesnake root as a remedy for snake-bite, carrying it powdered in their shot bags, he began to experiment with it in cases of pleurisy, pneumonia, gout and intermittent fever. In 1736 he published *An Essay on the Pleurisy,* probably the first medical treatise printed in Virginia.[92] Two years later he followed this with *An Epistle to Dr. Richard Mead Concerning the Epidemical Diseases of Virginia, Particularly a Pleurisy and Peripneumony, wherein is Shown the Surprising Efficacy of the Seneca Rattlesnake Root.* He also wrote a *Treatise on the Diseases of Virginia and the Neighboring Colonies,* but apparently this work was never printed. Tennent seems to have spent more time upon his researches than his medical practice, for he fell heavily into debt. When the General Assembly voted him £100 for "publishing his discovery of the use of the Seneca rattlesnake root," the money was turned over to two of his creditors.[93]

The interest of Governor Francis Fauquier in medical science is shown in a most interesting way by his will: "As for the uninformed mass of clay which will remain after life . . . is departed from it," my desire is if I should die of "any latent disease, with the cause of which the physicians or surgeons . . . may not be well acquainted, my body should be opened if they desire it, that the immediate cause of my disorder may be known and that by these means I may become more useful to my fellow creatures by my death than I have been in my life."[94]

90Philip Fithian, *Journal,* MSS. *Princeton University Library.*
91*Virginia Magazine of Hist. and Biog.,* XVII, pp. 404–412.
92Frederick E. Brasch, in *The Scientific Monthly,* XXXIII.
93*Virginia Magazine of Hist. and Biog.,* XIV, p. 238.
94York County Virginia, Wills, etc., Book No. 21.

Despite their isolation from centers of scientific investigation, many of the planters were interested in botany, electricity, zoology, chemistry, etc. It was in 1773 that a Philosophical Society was organized at Williamsburg under the patronage of the Governor with a hundred members, "for the advancement of useful knowledge in this colony." John Clayton, author of the *Flora Virginica* was made president, John Page, of Rosewell, vice-president, Reverend Samuel Henley, Professor of Moral Philosophy, secretary, St. George Tucker, assistant secretary, and David Jameson, treasurer.[95] "There is a society at Williamsburg for the advancement of arts, manufactures and sciences," wrote Francis Hargreaves, "in humble immitation of the Royal Society, but it is yet in its infancy. They were to have the Claytonian library, petrifactions and microscope."[96]

Eminent among Virginia scientists was John Clayton, clerk of Gloucester County for nearly fifty years and an enthusiastic botanist. One finds him going from county to county, or prowling through the forests at the foot of the Blue Ridge, inspecting trees and plants, or busy with his great manuscript on the flora of Virginia or corresponding with Gronovius or Linnæus. To the Royal Society he wrote his observations on the action of lightning: "One time when the thunder split the mast of a boat at Jamestown, I saw it break from the cloud, which it divided in two and seemed as if it had shot them immediately a mile asunder to the eye. It is dangerous when it thunders standing in a narrow passage . . . or in a room betwixt two windows, though several have been killed in the open fields."[97] Clayton was a member of several learned societies of Europe and was held in high esteem by the leading botanists of the age. His *Flora Virginica* was published under the direction of Gronovius, but his two-volume manuscript book which he left at his death with instructions to the printer was destroyed during the Revolution.[98]

William Byrd's interest in science was more typical of the average wealthy planter. A member of the Royal Society, he

[95]*Virginia Gazette,* May 13, 1773.
[96]*William and Mary Quarterly,* IV, pp. 200, 201.
[97]Peter Force, *Tracts,* III, No. 12, p. 7.
[98]J. W. Campbell, *History of Virginia,* pp. 182, 183.

encouraged the study of natural phenomena and the importation of scientific instruments, and was in constant correspondence with learned men in England. He made no experiments himself, but collected native plants, roots and seeds which he forwarded to Sir Hans Sloane, secretary of the Royal Society, for study and classification. Whereas botany was for Clayton an all-absorbing life avocation, for Byrd it was but one of the many interests of a very busy man.[99]

Perhaps the ablest scientist of colonial Virginia was John Mitchell, member of the Royal Society, and contributor to the study of botany, electricity, medicine, agriculture and cartography. Born in Scotland and educated as a physician, he resided in Virginia for nearly half a century. In 1791 he published a paper in which he describes thirty species of plants, nine of which have been confirmed as true genera by subsequent botanists. But his intellectual curiosity was by no means confined to botany. Now we find him making a study of yellow-fever epidemics in Virginia, now he is inquiring into the causes of "the different colors of people in different climates," now he is working on the "preparation and uses of potash," now he gives his attention to the "force of electrical cohesion," now he writes for a "specimen of the water which turns iron to copper," and for "earth salts" for analysis, now he is publishing a two-volume treatise on agriculture in the colonies, now he is preparing a map of British America. In 1746 he sailed for England with more than a thousand specimens of native plants, for study and classification by his friend Linnæus and others, only to have his hopes dashed when the ship was captured by Spanish privateers. To some extent the damage was repaired by his friend John Bartram, of Philadelphia, with whom he corresponded and who sent him many specimens.[100]

There seems to have been a strange fatality which hovered over early Virginia science, for in addition to the loss of Mitchell's collection and the destruction of Clayton's great manuscript, John Bannister, another remarkable naturalist, came to death by a fall

[99]Frederick E. Brasch, *The Scientific Monthly*, Vol. XXXIII.
[100]F. E. Brasch, *The Scientific Monthly*, Vol. XXXIII.

while looking for specimens. Bannister was rector of Appomattox parish, but in the midst of his clerical duties he found time to study the fauna and flora of the colony. He was a contributor to the *Philosophical Transactions* of the Royal Society, writing on insects, on curiosities of Virginia, on "several sorts of snails, on the snake-root," etc. It was Bannister who completed the catalogue of Virginia plants published in John Ray's *Historia Plantarum*.[101]

Among the Virginians and Marylanders who contributed their bit to science were John Page, of Rosewell, who invented an instrument to measure the fall of rain and snow, calculated an eclipse of the sun and suggested the identity of electricity and magnetism; Professor William Small, of William and Mary; Robert Beverley who included in his *History of Virginia* a chapter on natural history; Reverend F. Feilde, who made a collection of fossil shells, discovered that the dirt-dauber left spiders in its nest for the sustenance of its young and made other investigations into the habits of insects;[102] Henry Callister, who was an amateur ornithologist and was described as "botanist, florist, philosopher, musician"; Lloyd Dulaney, who entertained his friends at his residence in Annapolis with "electrical experiments."

The influence of England in shaping the intellectual interests of the planters was profound. The educating of young Virginians and Marylanders at Oxford and Cambridge, the constant influx of ministers, some of them men of wide cultural interests, the employment of British tutors and professors at William and Mary, the migration of architects, landscape gardeners, musicians, physicians, the importation of English books, the contact with English ship captains—all tended to bind the two colonies more closely with the culture of the mother country. "The habits, life, customs, computations, etc., of the Virginians are much the same as about London which they esteem their home," declared Hugh Jones. "The planters and even the native negroes generally talk good English without idiom or tone and can discourse handsomely upon most common subjects, and conversing with

[101]*Amer. Antiq. Society*, Vol. XXV, p. 358.
[102]F. Feilde to Doctor McKenzie, Feb. 16, 1771, Huntington Library.

persons belonging to trade . . . for the most part they are much civilized."[103]

When the planter ordered a suit of clothes for himself or a gown for his wife, he directed that they should be in the latest London fashions; when he sent for a box of books he asked his agent to pick out the volumes most read in England; when he built his house, or laid out his garden, or purchased his silverware or furniture, he was guided by the prevailing taste in England. To a Virginian or a Marylander what was going on in New York or Boston was of little interest, but he kept abreast of the latest court gossip, read the English gazettes, corresponded with leading merchants and government officials in London.

The influence of Williamsburg and Annapolis, also, was entirely out of proportion to their size. At certain times of year, when the Assembly and the General Court were in session, the sleepy little capitals woke to bustling activity. From all parts of the colonies came Councillors, Burgesses and other leading planters, often with their families, to vary the seriousness of legislative and judicial sessions with concerts, theatrical preformances, dances and dinners. It was the governor who set the fashions, and the planters, when they returned home, kept in mind not only the stately palace and its beautiful gardens, but his Excellency's library, his furniture, his plate, the hangings on his walls, the music performed at his balls, the gown worn by his wife. In radio parlance, as London was the central station for cultural broadcasting, so Williamsburg and Annapolis were important in relaying the programs to the remote corners of Virginia and Maryland.

At the same time the planters, however keen their desire to imitate things English, however closely they patterned themselves after the English squire, could not escape the moulding influence of Virginia and Maryland, with their distinctive plantation system. William Byrd II might attend college in England, might pattern beautiful Westover upon the English manor house and fill it with portraits by English painters, he might wear English-made clothes and correspond with friends in England; yet he remained a Virginian and a tobacco planter. The isolation of life upon the

[103]Hugh Jones, *The Present State of Virginia*, p. 43.

plantation retarded education, made it difficult for men of intellectual interests to come in contact with each other, made the attendance upon concerts or the theatre or even the ablest sermons a matter of some difficulty, a treat rarely to be indulged in. The wealthy planter might turn over the larger part of the responsibility for running his plantation to his overseer and retire to his library to delve in the classics or history or philosophy, but he seldom had the opportunity of discussing them with men of like interests. Unless he lived in the vicinity of Williamsburg or Annapolis he must miss the stimulus of the literary society or the musical club. It was this, perhaps, which made the culture of the region receptive rather than creative. The plantation was not the place to create a Shakespeare, or a Newton, or a Beethoven.

That it proved to be a breeding ground for statesmen is explained by the fact that the very nature of political life tended to break down isolation. The aspirant for political honors had to break away from the plantation to mingle with the voters, to learn their views and impress them with his own opinions. Once elected to the House of Burgesses, he must visit the capital frequently, join in the debates with fellow members, defend the interests of Virginia or Maryland against the king or the proprietor, of his section or county against the representatives of other sections and counties. The colonial legislatures were all training schools for practical politicians and political thinkers, and those who came from isolated rural districts benefitted equally with those from cities and towns.

Certain it is that the widely spread belief that the Virginia and Maryland planters, even of the wealthy group, spent all their leisure in racing, cock-fighting, gambling at cards, hunting or dancing is entirely erroneous. Thomas Jefferson, George Washington, James Madison were not freaks of nature, whose interest in the classics, science, architecture, gardening, history was in contrast to the intellectual vacuity of the class to which they belonged; they were but outstanding examples of the educated, cultured, widely read wealthy class, whose interests varied from statecraft to astronomy, from music to philosophy, from medicine to gardening.

## Chapter III

# MANOR HOUSE AND COTTAGE

THE architecture of the English cottage in Tudor and Stuart times was marked by diversity. The picturesque stone houses of Somerset or Devon are in marked contrast to the ornate plastered houses of Suffolk, or the weatherboarded houses of Essex, or the half timbered houses of Middlesex. The East Anglian cottage, shaped in part by Flemish influence, would never be mistaken for a Cotswold cottage; Lavenham, in Suffolk, has no more in common with Castle Coombe, in Somerset, than with a French or a Dutch village. The prevailing types were determined by building materials, tradition and foreign influence. In the old days when there were no railways or canals, when the roads were often impassable and river transportation difficult, one built with the materials at hand. In the wooded districts, if lime and clay were available, half timber houses are common; in the limestone shires the stone cottage is almost universal; in the sand and clay region we find whole villages of brick.

Had the settlers in Virginia, like those of New England come chiefly from one part of England, their architectural inheritance would have been simple. They would have built insofar as conditions there permitted, little houses duplicating those of their native shires—Devon houses, or East Anglian houses, or Kent houses, or Cotswold houses. But since the Virginians came from various parts of England, their architectural traditions were as diverse as those of England itself. Among the men who accompanied Captain Newport, or Sir Thomas Gates, or Sir George Yeardley there must have been some who were acquainted with brick construction, others with half-timbering, still others with the laying of stone; some who were tile makers, some who were sawyers, some skilled in the thatching of roofs, some who understood the art of cutting clapboards.

On the other hand, there was probably not one who had

ever attempted to construct a log house. In Saxon days, when the forests still covered most of the English countryside and timber was cheap, houses were sometimes made of logs, smoothed on one side and left in the round on the other. But these logs or beams were laid vertically, not horizontally, with one end resting on a heavy squared ground sill, the other attached to the wall plate, the smoothed side facing in. The old church at Greensted, Essex, which is constructed in this manner, carries us back in fancy to the days of Edward the Confessor.[1] "Palisaded" houses, built in this way, were common in early New Jersey,[2] and may possibly have existed at Plymouth and elsewhere in New England, but there is no evidence that they ever appeared on the banks of the James.

There is also no evidence that log houses, similar to those of Sweden or of Germany, with the logs laid horizontally and notched at the ends, which became so common throughout the South in the nineteenth century, were constructed by the early settlers at Jamestown or Henrico. One may read the works of Captain John Smith, the letters of Percy, Newport, Hamor, Dale, Gates and Argoll and the records of the London Company from beginning to end without finding any mention of log cabins. Moreover, we search in vain through the thousands of pages of official documents, private letters, the acts of Assembly, and county records for many decades after the founding of the colony. Nor would one expect the first settlers, faced as they were with the tremendous difficulties of planting a colony in the wilderness, to lay aside all their former ideas of building for new and unfamiliar methods. Even though Captain John Smith was acquainted with the log houses of Transylvania and some of Captain Newport's sailors may have seen others in the Baltic region when on trading voyages for ship-stores or potash, they would have found it difficult to persuade the carpenters to imitate them. The people of New Sweden built log cabins, because they were accustomed to them in old Sweden; the settlers in the German parts of Penn-

[1] Martin S. Briggs, *The Homes of the Pilgrim Fathers, etc.,* pp. 56, 57.
[2] T. J. Wertenbaker, *The Founding of American Civilization, The Middle Colonies,* p. 149.

sylvania and Virginia built log houses, because they were common in Germany; the English did not bring log construction to America because they knew nothing about it.[3] The log house seems to have been introduced into Virginia by the German settlers of the Shenandoah Valley, and it was not until they had been in use there for a decade or two that the planters of the Piedmont region began to imitate them in the construction of slave cabins, tobacco houses and barns. As late as 1749 we find the Reverend Robert Rose, in the Piedmont frontier, erecting framed houses on his plantations.[4]

When Captain Newport's little band disembarked from the *Sarah Constant,* the *Discovery* and the *Goodspeed* at Jamestown in the spring of 1607, they had no opportunity to build any save the crudest shelters. To cut down trees, erect their fort, plant their crops, nurse their sick, explore the country and prepare a return cargo of clapboard took most of their energies. So they contented themselves with dugouts, or with what Smith called "cabins worse than naught,"[5] until they could construct crude houses "set upon crackets" and covered with turf and sedge laid over rafters. It was considered a great improvement when the bark of trees was used for roofing, possibly in the manner of half cylinder tiles, and large framed chimneys of wattles and clay.[6] In time these gave way to "rows of houses all of framed timber," two stories high with garrets or corn lofts,[7] while at Henrico, higher up the river, Sir Thomas Dale built "three streets of well-framed houses,"[8] the "first story all of bricks."

The old chronicles fail to tell us whether these frame houses of the first decade of Virginia history, like the frame houses of England, were half timbered with filling of wattle, clay and lime, or whether they were covered with clapboards. When builders migrate to a new country they almost invariably try to

[3]See Harold R. Shurtleff, *The Log Cabin Myth,* Samuel E. Morison, editor. The article in the *Virginia Magazine of Hist. and Biog.,* Vol. 44, pp. 287–295, by George C. Gregory, which tries to prove that log houses were built by the early settlers in Virginia, seems quite unconvincing.

[4]Robert Rose, *Diary,* December 5, 1749.

[5]Arber, *Works of Captain John Smith,* pp. 957, 502, 503.

[6]Purchas His Pilgrimes, Lib IX, p. 1752.     [7]Ralph Hamor, *A True Discourse,* p. 33.

[8]L. G. Tyler, *Narratives of Early Virginia,* p. 305; Peter Force, *Tracts,* I, No. 7, p. 14.

duplicate the houses of the homeland. It would be unusual, indeed, if the Jamestown carpenters had ignored the half-timber construction to which many must have been accustomed, for all the needed materials were at hand—trees for timbers, and wattle, clay and lime for fillings. Since we know that chimneys occasionally were made of "wattles plastered with clay,"[9] it hardly admits of a doubt that in some of the houses the spaces between timbers were filled in with the same materials. Perhaps this explains the rapidity with which these early houses fell into decay, for the heat of the Virginia summer and the cold of winter may well have caused the clay to crack or crumble, or the shrinkage of the green timbers with which the frames were constructed may have loosened the wattle. It is remarkable that the houses which were described in one year as goodly or strong, the next had become so ruinous that the settlers were kept busy repairing them, or tearing them down to make room for new structures.[10] Not until a decade or more of experimentation did they learn how to build houses that would endure, and were "convenient for both seasons."[11]

The Council of Virginia stated in 1624 that the houses which had just been erected were forty times as good as those of former years. It is possible that the improvement came not only from using seasoned timbers, but from the substitution of weatherboarding for wattle and clay. The settlers had no sooner set foot in Virginia than they began to cut clapboard for return cargoes for Captain Newport's little fleet,[12] and they probably were not long in recognizing the wisdom of using them in their own houses. Their chief hesitancy must have arisen from the strenuous labor involved in splitting logs into clapboards by hand, a far more tedious matter than the settling of wattle between the timbers of a house and daubing it with clay and lime.

[9]In 1623 a church in Accomac was described as "constructed of roughly riled logs, cemented loosely with wattle." *Virginia Magazine of Hist. and Biog.*, Vol. V, p. 128.

[10]P. A. Bruce, *Economic History of Virginia*, Vol. II, p. 527.

[11]*William and Mary Quarterly*, Second Series, Vol. VI, p. 119. This affords additional evidence that the early houses were not log cabins. It is a poor log house, indeed, which will last only a year or two. Some of the log houses of the German settlers in Pennsylvania, built two centuries ago, are still standing.

[12]Alexander Brown, *Genesis of the U. S.*, Vol. I, p. 109.

Thus, despite the abundance of trees, weather boarding was by no means cheap prior to the period of saw mills. And even when the whirr of the horse-driven saw had become comparatively common in the Virginia forests, the custom of splitting clapboards continued. It was the considerations of durability and comfort, then, rather than of cheapness which made the planters construct their houses of wood.

But tidewater Virginia, even in the first half of the seventeenth century, was not exclusively a land of frame houses, for here and there throughout the region one might have found a tiny church or a quaint farmhouse built of brick. Among the early settlers at Jamestown and Henrico were trained brickmakers, who had no difficulty in finding clay out of which bricks could be made as good as any in England. Since lime for mortar was procured by burning oyster shells, the only drawback to building substantial brick houses was the heavy expense of making and laying the bricks in a new country where labor costs were excessive. The house of Secretary Richard Kemp, erected in 1639, thirty-two years after the founding of Jamestown, and described as "the fairest that ever was known in this country for substance and uniformity," was perhaps the first house in Virginia to be built entirely of brick.[13] That others followed we know from the statement in *The New Description of Virginia,* published in 1649, that the colonists had "lime in abundance for their houses, store of bricks made, and house and chimneys built of brick."[14]

The discovery of fragments of slate and tile at Jamestown leads to the conclusion that some of the houses of the little village were covered with these materials.[15] If we may credit the statement of Secretary Thomas Ludwell, that the terrific hailstorm of 1667 "beat holes through the tiles of our houses,"[16] tiling must have been fairly common. Yet twenty-two years later, when William Byrd I wanted a supply of pantiles, he found it necessary to import them from England.[17] There is every reason to think that most

---

[13]*Virginia Magazine of Hist. and Biog.,* Vol. III, pp. 29, 30.
[14]Peter Force, *Tracts,* Vol. II, *The New Description of Virginia,* p. 7.
[15]*Virginia Magazine of Hist. and Biog.,* Vol. XII, p. 123.
[16]*British Public Record Office,* C61–21, November, 1667, Ludwell to Lord Berkeley.
[17]*Virginia Magazine of Hist. and Biog.,* Vol. XXVI, p. 31.

of the buildings in Virginia from a very early period were covered with shingles, and it was the silver gray of cypress or pine mellowing in the southern sun rather than the glaring red of the tile, which characterized the roofs of the planter's residence, tobacco house and barn.[18]

In outward form the early houses must have differed greatly, one bearing the stamp of Surrey, another of Middlesex, another, perhaps, of Kent or Devon. But gradually there emerged a type of cottage, differing from anything in England, which became so common that we are justified in calling it the mid-seventeenth century Virginia house. The voyager up the James or the York in the days of Sir William Berkeley would have seen here and there, half hidden in a grove of trees and surrounded by fields of tobacco, the charming little residences of the middle-class planters. If he had picked out one at random and drawn near to inspect it, he would have seen a structure reminiscent of England, yet bearing the unmistakable stamp of the New World. It would have been constructed, perhaps, of hewn timbers covered with clapboards, perhaps of brick laid in English bond, some forty-five feet by twenty, one story and a half high, with casement windows, brick chimneys, one within and the other without the end walls, sharply rising roof covered with shingles and pierced perhaps with a dormer or two.

Most distinctive of all was the porch, a projection from the center of the front wall, about ten feet by eight, and rising two stories to a pediment which was joined to the roof like an overgrown dormer. Below was an enclosed entry with open arches or at times a door in front and windows on the side, and a small bedroom above. A few of these old seventeenth-century porches still stand—on Bacon's Castle, Christ's Cross, the Jones Cottage at Fort Eustis, Foster's Castle—while we know that there were porches to Malvern Hill, the Neale house, Westmoreland; the Edward Lockey house, York; the Robert Beverley house, and many others. (Plate 6.)

Passing through the porch one found himself in a room of

[18]Peter Force, *Tracts,* Vol. II, "New Description of Virginia," p. 7; Hugh Jones, *Present State of Virginia,* p. 32.

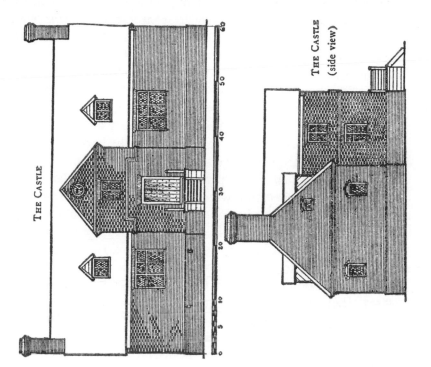

THE CASTLE

THE CASTLE
(side view)

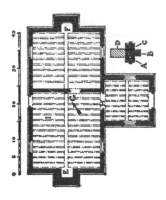

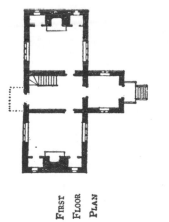

FIRST
FLOOR
PLAN

FIGURE 2.  THE CASTLE

perhaps twenty-five feet by eighteen, with a large fireplace at one end flanked by closets, a staircase at the other, the walls plastered and whitewashed, the partition of plain boards, the whole mellowed by the light which filtered in through the tiny panes of the casement windows. In the middle of the room was the dining table, flanked by benches, while the trammel, the bellows, the skillets, the pot-hook, the pans, the forks gathered in or around the fireplace announced that this was the kitchen as well as dining room and parlor. A door in the partition opened into a chamber, about eighteen feet square, while the staircase led to the corn loft, converted perhaps into one or more bedrooms. The floors of the lower story were often of brick, but more usually of wide, smoothed boards. In the houses of the well-to-do the entire end wall of the main hall around the fireplace was covered with simple, but graceful pine paneling. (Fig. 2.)

Typical of the early Virginia houses, and one of the most interesting in the country, is Christ's Cross, New Kent. Upon entering the main hall one's eyes fall immediately upon the huge summer beam running lengthwise in the center of the ceiling from one end of the house to the other, supported by the walls and by a post in the partition. The summer and wall plates are elaborately moulded on the lower edges, while at the top of the supporting beam is a remarkable shield enclosing two scrolls, and depending from a curious impost moulding. The double front door, hung in a heavy frame, on wrought-iron strap hinges, is panelled on the outside and battened within.[19] The atmosphere of the old house is redolent of the seventeenth century, and one sees in fancy the housewife bending over the huge fireplace, or the planter, weary from his arduous labor in the tobacco fields, waiting for his evening meal at the table board.

Especially interesting are the exterior chimneys of the Virginia colonial cottage, which rise in successive stages to a single stack, like an elongated pyramid (Plate 7). Often the lower section, which has to be large enough to enclose the great hall fireplace, is twelve feet by three. The chimney in some cases, instead of hugging the end wall, above the main floor stands apart cul-

[19]*Virginia Magazine of Hist. and Biog.*, Vol. XLIII, pp. 1–7.

minating in two stacks. Brick seems to have been the customary material for more than a century after the founding of Jamestown, so that when a contract was signed for the construction of a house it was taken for granted that the chimneys should be of this material. But in the eighteenth century it became common for poor planters to construct wooden chimneys and daub them on the inside with clay.[20] This caused so many fires that the Assembly, beginning with the Act of 1732, passed a series of laws requiring those in existence to be pulled down and prohibiting their construction for the future.[21]

Many of the planters had "glazed windows" according to John Hammond, and the others contented themselves with "shutters which are made very pretty and convenient."[22] In 1644 the Assembly passed an act to confiscate all the lead of the colony to make bullets for use in the war against Opechancanough, the "lead upon glass windows only excepted."[23] The panes must have been very small and the glass rough and not entirely transparent. When Lady Berkeley vented her spleen against the Commissioners sent by Charles II to investigate Bacon's Rebellion by having the common hangman act as their postillion, she had to avail herself of "a broken quarrel of the glass" in her window "to observe how the show looked."[24] Possibly the first sash windows in Virginia were those of the capitol built at Williamsburg,[25] and these, no doubt, were imported from England. But when sashes appeared in the governor's "palace" and in the newly erected residences of rich planters, the old casements with their little diamond or square panes gradually disappeared.

In 1647 the Assembly passed an act for building prisons, which were to be "such houses as we frequently inhabit" and "built according to the form of Virginia houses,"[26] Thus was it recognized before mid-century that the colony had developed a domestic

[20]J. F. D. Smyth, *A Tour in the U. S.*, Vol. I, p. 49. This gives further evidence that log construction was unknown to the early settlers at Jamestown.
[21]Hening, *Statutes*, Vol. IV, p. 376; Vol. V, p. 209.
[22]Peter Force, *Tracts*, Vol. III, "Leah and Rachel," p. 18.
[23]*Virginia Magazine of Hist. and Biog.*, Vol. XXXIII, p. 237.
[24]*British Public Record Office*, CO5–1371–220, 231.
[25]Hening, *Statutes*, Vol. III, p. 420.
[26]*Ibid.*, Vol. I, p. 340.

architecture of its own, with houses so different from those of the mother country as to be termed Virginia houses. In its antecedents, of course, the early Virginia cottage was English, but local conditions—the summer's heat and the winter's cold, the costliness of labor, the abundance of timber, clay and lime, the scarcity of stone, the high freight rates to England—had so transformed it as to give it an individuality which was instantly noted by visitors to the colony. "Pleasant in their building," says John Hammond, "which although for most part are but one story besides the loft, and built of wood, yet contrived so delightfully that your ordinary houses in England are not so handsome."[27]

One may search in vain for the English cottage from which the early Virginia house was derived—in the quaint villages of Surrey, along the narrow roads and lanes of Sussex, in the hills of Somerset, in Berks, Oxford, Cambridge, Norfolk, Suffolk. One has no difficulty in finding the ancient porch. It occurs in various parts of England, but is especially common in Sussex. There is a particularly charming old stone porch near Wisborough, and a brick porch on a house near Chiddingfold (Plate 5), either of which would have fitted perfectly into the front wall of Bacon's Castle or Christ's Cross. The Virginia chimney occurs frequently in Surrey. But the form of the Virginia cottage, the one and a half story house, long and narrow, with steeply rising roof and end chimneys is to be found in Cambridge, Norfolk and Suffolk. So many perfect examples occur in Cottenham, a few miles north of Cambridge, that one would almost infer that that quaint little village sent more than its share of builders to the Chesapeake Bay region. That this type of house came to England from Flanders is clearly indicated by lingering features typical of that region—mouse-tooth brick work or more rarely the stepped gable-end. At Ely there is a fourteenth-century stone house which is as Dutch as though it had been built in Amsterdam itself. Perhaps it is not by chance that the Flemish cottages of the lower valley of the Hudson are similar in form to the houses of the early planters on the James and the York.

Gradually the early type of Virginia farm house began to take

[27]Peter Force, *Tracts*, Vol. III, "Leah and Rachel," p. 18.

PLATE 3—Early Virginia Hunting Scene
From a contemporary frieze found in an old Virginia mansion

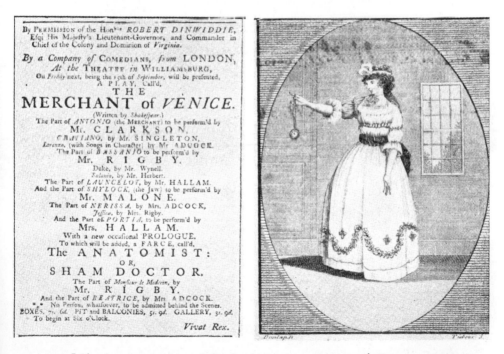

PLATE 4—*Left:* Announcement of the first appearance of the Hallams in America.
*Right:* Mrs. Hallam as "Marianne" in "The Dramatist"

PLATE 5—*Top:* Surrey House near Chiddingfold, showing porch. *Center:* Cottage at Cottenham, near Cambridge. *Bottom:* So-called Adam Thoroughgood House, Princess Anne County, Virginia

on a new aspect, to become more distinctly American, better suited to the needs of the planters. Many essential features remained unchanged—the proportions, the sharply rising roof-lines, the wooden shingles, the walls of timber or brick, the end chimneys, the casement windows. But the ancient porch disappeared, the bond changed from English to Flemish, the use of dormers became more common, and a hallway was introduced through the center of the house.

These changes were made partly to keep step with architectural developments in England, and were introduced by the carpenters and bricklayers who came over in response to the ever urgent demand for men in the building trades. The new bond, which consists of alternating the heads and sides of the brick throughout, greatly changed the aspect of the Virginia cottages, since the habit of burning the heads until they assumed a bluish glaze set them out in contrast to the sides and produced a pleasing checker-board effect. It was the glazed header, also, which gave the bricklayer the opportunity to weave designs into the walls. Although very few such designs by the Virginia artisans have come down to us, the diamond patterns of Malvern Hill and the diaper work of the Keeling house, Princess Anne County, rival even the remarkable work in the early Quaker houses of southern New Jersey. It is said that the Flemish bond became popular in England after the great London fire of 1666, when workmen were brought in from the Netherlands to aid in rebuilding the ruined city.

It is probable that the ancient porch became unpopular because it was unsuited to the long, hot summers of Tidewater Virginia. The porch opened directly into the main living room, protecting the front door from rain and cold and obviating the need of a lobby, but also interfering with the refreshing breezes of summer. So they discarded it in favor of a hallway running through the house with doors at each end, as Hugh Jones tells us, "for an air draught in summer."[28] In like manner the increased use of dormers came with the conversion of the corn loft into bedrooms, and the consequent increased need for light and air.

Many examples of the second type of Virginia cottage remain

[28]Hugh Jones, *The Present State of Virginia*, p. 32.

today, mute witnesses of the good taste, sense of proportion, sincerity and skill of their builders—the so-called Adam Thoroughgood house (Plate 5), the Keeling house and the Wishart house, in Princess Anne County; the Blair house, Williamsburg; the Warren house, Surry; the Rising Sun tavern, Fredericksburg, and many others. In some cases old seventeenth-century cottages have survived as wings to later structures, the owners, when the influx of slaves brought them wealth, having added a larger building as the main residence. The difference between the life of many families in the early days and in the mid-eighteenth century is strikingly illustrated by the contrast between the unpretentious rear wing of Little England, Gloucester County, once the main residence, and the huge expanse of the Georgian house to which it is attached.

In the third decade of the eighteenth century, there came still another innovation in the Virginia cottage, the so-called Virginia and Maryland gambrel (Plate 7). Originated by the French architect François Mansard, the gambrel roof spread far and wide, assuming different aspects in different countries. Common in England, especially in the neighborhood of Bath, it was carried across the ocean to the Chesapeake Bay colonies, where it received a hearty welcome from builders who saw an opportunity to give more space and air in the upper bedrooms of the cottages of the small planters. So popular did the new style become that owners at times actually rebuilt the roof of standing houses to conform to it. Unfortunately what was gained in comfort was lost in beauty, for the almost perpendicular lower slope and the very gentle upper slope combine to give an awkward boxlike effect. The Virginia gambrel is not to be compared with the graceful Flemish gambrel of the lower Hudson region.[29] It occurs chiefly on small cottages, and even here it never entirely superseded the old seventeenth-century type of roof.

In the meanwhile, across the Potomac, there was developing a cottage architecture akin to that of Virginia, yet having its own peculiar characteristics. Maryland and Virginia were sister colo-

[29]In the Weblen house, Princess Anne County, this transition is clearly indicated by the joint where the old roof lines were built out to make the gambrel.

nies, with the same type of society based on the culture of tobacco, the same large group of small planters, the same small clique of aristocrats. Maryland, like Virginia, was dotted with little plantations, each bearing a name of its own—Parrott's Cage, Spout Farm, Bachelor's Hope, Mills' Point, Industry, Dear Bought, Want Water, Philip's Purchase, Watermelon Point, etc.

The East Anglian cottage, the long, narrow house, with one story and loft, steep roof and end chimneys, was less common in Maryland than in Virginia. Yet many charming examples survive—Resurrection Manor, St. Mary's County; Graeme house, Calvert County; Fassit house and Fairfield, Worcester County; Make Peace and Lankford house, Somerset County; Woolford house, Dorchester County.[30]

In the mid-seventeenth century many of these little houses had the ancient porch, some of one story for the entry only, and some having a "porch chamber" above. Of great interest is the porch of Bond Castle, with its overhanging second story and the turned spindles in the entry. In Maryland the gambrel became very popular, and many houses still standing testify to the fact that in some cases it can be graceful as well as useful. The old Paul Jones house and quaint Otwell show the Maryland gambrel at its best.

It is characteristic of the complexity of cultural currents that St. Mary's County should have developed a cottage architecture of its own. Its depth in comparison with the breadth was much greater than in the East Anglian house, the roof lines were gentler and in some cases there were four chimneys in place of two. One entered a hallway, leading usually through to a back door, with the winding stairway tucked away in an alcove at the rear. On one side of the hallway was a living room with a small room or den behind, on the other the dining room with a kitchen behind.[31] Most interesting of all was the pent-roof connecting the two exterior chimneys at each gable-end, enclosing one or more closets, shown in Bard's Field, The Folly, Cross Manor and many other cottages. In time the pent was raised to give closet space on the second as

[30]Henry C. Forman, *Early Manor and Plantation Houses of Maryland* (Easton, Md., 1934).
[31]*Ibid.,* pp. 46, 47.

well as the first floor, as at Woodlawn and the Davis house.[32] The chimney pent spread north and west to Calvert, Charles, Prince George, Anne Arundel, and other counties, but it was rare on the Maryland Eastern Shore and in Virginia, and in no other county did it become so common as in St. Mary's.

The Maryland bricklayers were fond of the Flemish bond, and we recognize on all sides the distinctive checker-board effect so common in Virginia. Peculiar to Maryland, and rare even there, is the all-header bond, where the glazed brick, unrelieved by the dull red of the stretchers, glares in the sun like a giant window pane. Here and there the builders indulged in diaper work, perhaps the continuous diamond, as at John's Point and Genezir, perhaps the single diamond of Clover Fields and Bowlingly, perhaps the interlocking diamonds of the Paul Jones house, perhaps the figure eights of Sweet Air, perhaps the zig-zags of Fassit house, perhaps the inverted V's of Make Peace.[33] The patterns of the Maryland bricklayers, while less interesting and intricate than those of southern New Jersey, were more common and elaborate than those of their fellow artisans across the Potomac in Virginia.

Although the old belief that Virginia in the seventeenth century was the land of rich planters owning thousands of acres and scores of slaves has proved fallacious, it is true that there was a small group of influential men in the colony, some of them possessed of considerable wealth. Robert Carter, Lewis Burwell, Nathaniel Bacon, Sr., Robert Beverley, Ralph Wormeley and others, despite the excessive cost of building, owned residences more pretentious than those of the poorer planters. Although time has dealt heavily with these houses, old wills and inventories sometimes give us a hint of their size and form. The house of Nathaniel Bacon, Sr., contained the old and the new hall, an inner room over the hall, an outer room, an upper chamber, Mrs. Bacon's chamber and the chamber above it—seven rooms in all besides the kitchen, dairy and storeroom which seem to have been in separate buildings. Rosegill, in Middlesex, the home of Ralph Wormeley, which for a brief time was used as the capitol of the colony, had a parlor

32*Ibid.*, p. 27.  33*Ibid.*, p. 24.

with a chamber above it, a chamber with a second chamber above it, an old and a new nursery, the lady's chamber with a chamber over it, an entry, two closets and a storeroom.

The Arthur Allen house, the so-called Bacon's Castle, has come down to us in a fair state of preservation (Plate 6). As one stands before this ancient residence he forgets that he is in America, and is carried in fancy to the beautiful Suffolk countryside into which it would fit perfectly. The ancient porch in front matched by a like projection behind to inclose the stairways, the English bond, the graceful curves of the Flemish gable-ends, the S-shaped beam-anchors, the massive chimneys terminating in three stacks set diagonally, combine to make this one of the most interesting houses in the United States. From the porch we enter a hallway with parlor on one side and dining room on the other, and then descend the winding staircase in the rear to the basement which contains kitchen, storeroom and milk room. On the second floor are two large bedrooms and above, in the attic, three bedrooms. By replacing the modern sash windows with casements, the tin roof with shingles, and removing the ugly addition to the right, patching the brick work, and repairing the interior, we would have a perfect example of the residence of the well-to-do Virginia planter of the years from 1650 to 1670. As we wander through its ancient chambers or stand beneath the great beams of the attic, we seem to see Bacon's men standing guard at the doors, or pacing back and forth on the lawn below, or anxiously peering out over the James to see whether Sir William Berkeley's fleet was coming to land men to attack them.[34]

That there were other residences in Virginia similar to Bacon's Castle in general form we know from a study of old inventories. The Southey Littleton house, Accomac, with its entry, parlor and dining room on the first floor, two large bedrooms and porch chamber on the second floor, and two rooms in the attic would have been almost identical had the kitchen been in the basement instead of in a separate building.[35] But we know nothing of the

[34]*Virginia Magazine of Hist. and Biog.*, Vol. IV, p. 153. It is sincerely to be hoped that steps may be taken to preserve this priceless monument of a departed age. It is as valuable in throwing light upon the culture and life of Virginia in the seventeenth century as are the beautiful houses at Williamsburg of the eighteenth century.

[35]P. A. Bruce, *Economic History of Virginia*, Vol. II, p. 157.

architectural details of this house, or of the scores of others which have fallen victims to fire or decay or the destructive hand of man. Certain it is that not all of the residences of the well-to-do conformed to the Bacon's Castle type. William Fitzhugh states that it was customary for gentlemen, when planning to build, to send to England for the necessary artisans.[36] In such cases the master mechanic or carpenter no doubt shaped the structure to accord with the prevailing type in the part of the mother country from which he came. Carter's Creek, Gloucester County, the home of Major Lewis Burwell, was built in imitation of the E-shaped English manor house. The thick walls, the tiny panes of the narrow windows, the towering Tudor chimney stacks, the massive cellar arches, the linen-fold panelling of the hall carved to represent drapery, link this old house with the England of the sixteenth rather than the seventeenth century. Its destruction by fire in comparatively recent times was an irreparable loss to the history of American architecture.[37]

In Maryland perhaps the most interesting of the larger plantation houses which came down to recent times was Bond Castle, Calvert County, destroyed in recent years to make room for an ugly farm structure. This old building seems to have been originally about fifty feet by twenty-one, with two-story porches in front and rear, steep roof, free-standing chimneys decorated with inset arches, battened doors, beamed ceilings, small stairs, wall paintings over the mantels and a kitchen fireplace large enough to receive a six-foot log. Later wings were added to right and left retaining the original balance of the structure, and giving a new sense of spaciousness, but spoiling the charm of the free-standing chimneys. Bond Castle speaks eloquently of the forces which created American civilization, for it was a bit of English medievalism expressed in the American medium of timber and plank.[38]

The church architecture of seventeenth-century Virginia was in the main quite simple. So thinly settled were most parishes that there was no need for large buildings, and so moderate the means

[36]*Virginia Magazine of Hist. and Biog.*, Vol. II, p. 23.
[37]*Ibid.*, Vol. X, pp. 1, 106, 107; Mary N. Stanard, *Colonial Virginia* (Phila., 1917), pp. 63, 64.
[38]H. C. Forman, *Early Manor and Plantation Houses of Maryland*, pp. 62, 63.

of the parishioners that costly materials and ornate decorations were usually impossible. "In every county there are one, two or three churches," Francis Louis Michel tells us, "according to the population. . . . Most of them are of timber, without towers or bells."[39] These little temples of God were scattered over the tidewater region, hidden away in the forests, occupying some "old field," or perched upon the bank of navigable rivers and creeks. From the contract between the churchwardens of Hungers Parish, Accomac County, and the architect and builder, Simon Thomas, we gain some idea of their main features. Thomas agreed to construct a church forty feet by twenty-five, the framework to be of seasoned oak resting on locust blocks and covered with weatherboarding. The ceiling of the former church was to be transferred to the new, where it was to be supported by wooden arches. There was no mention of tower, bell or porch.[40]

At Jamestown, after the first rude structure "covered with rafts, sedge and earth" had fallen in ruins, Captain Samuel Argall erected a substantial church building. An ancient foundation of brick laid on a footing of cobblestones, unearthed in recent years, seems to locate this church and to fix the dimensions. The slightness of this substructure and the absence of buttresses clearly indicate that the building was made of timber.[41] Here it was that the first representative assembly in the New World came into being. "The most convenient place we could find to sit in was the choir of the church," say the minutes, "where Sir George Yeardley, the governor, being set down in his accustomed place, those of the Council of State sat next him." The Burgesses, in "the body of the church," were called by name and took the oath of supremacy.[42]

Twenty years later we find Governor John Harvey bustling about to collect money from "the ablest planters" and "masters of ships" for a brick church. The new structure was built around the old, and it is probable that during week-day services the noise of the trowel or the saw mingled with the sound of singing from within. The walls were of brick, built on a heavy foundation, and

[39]*Virginia Magazine of Hist. and Biog.* Vol. XXIV, p. 22.
[40]P. A. Bruce, *Institutional History of Virginia* (N. Y., 1910), Vol. I, pp. 104–105.
[41]S. H. Yonge, *The Site of Old Jamestown* (Rich., 1907), pp. 65–68.
[42]L. G. Tyler, *Narratives of Early Virginia*, p. 251.

strengthened with buttresses. The proportions and details of the old square tower, which still stands, the dimensions of the foundation and the existence of buttresses lead us to the conclusion that this church resembled charming old St. Luke's, near Smithfield. It is even possible that the two churches were designed by the same builder, so that the pointed window arches and the stepped gable-ends of the restored Jamestown church are based on something better than mere conjecture. The church, like other buildings in Jamestown, went up in flames when Bacon's enraged followers applied the torch in 1676, but it was restored later, probably within the old walls.[43]

As for St. Luke's, there can be no controversy as to what it looked like, for it still stands beside the highway, an interesting relic of colonial times (Plates 8 and 9). If we may trust tradition and the finding of a brick in the wall dated 1632, this little church was a century old the year George Washington was born. The architect was probably an Essex man, and well acquainted with the little church at Woodham Walter, for the two buildings resemble each other closely.[44] St. Luke's, with its buttresses and its pointed arches, is the only survival of the Gothic in colonial ecclesiastical architecture, while the stepped gable-ends and the bond show Flemish influence. The heavy square tower, which is out of proportion with the rest of the building, seems to have been added at a later date. As we view the little building, tucked away in a grove of ancient trees, visions come to us of exciting scenes of long past days—visions of ministers in flowing robes holding forth from the quaint pulpit, of reverent men and women listening from the stiff pews or the panelled gallery, of prying Indians looking in at the arched windows, of Bacon's patriot rebels marching by, or of red coats encamped in adjacent fields.

Quite different was Bruton church, at Middle Plantation, built in 1683.[45] We are grateful to Francis Louis Michel for leaving us a drawing of this building, but we can only regret that he was so poor an artist. His crude sketch shows an oblong, brick build-

---

[43]*British Public Record Office*, CO5–1371–401; Bacon's Proceedings, p. 26.
[44]Martin S. Briggs, *The Homes of the Pilgrim Fathers*, pp. 195–198.
[45]*William and Mary Quarterly*, Vol. XVI, p. 9.

PLATE 6—*Left:* English gambrel, Cambridge.
*Right:* Bacon's Castle, Surry County, Virginia

PLATE 7—Moore House, Yorktown, showing Virginia gambrel. The terms for the
surrender of Cornwallis's army were drawn up here

PLATE 8—St. Luke's—Rear

PLATE 9—St. Luke's, Smithfield, Virginia

ing, with rounded window arches, double door and Flemish gable-end.[46] As the century drew to an end, the erection of brick churches became more frequent. In 1691 the Lynnhaven congregation built a "good, substantial brick church," forty-five feet by twenty-two within the walls, with a brick porch, and "good and sufficient lights of brick, well glazed with good glass." The roof was covered with "oaken boards," and the interior was "well sealed with good oaken boards, archwise, and painted with good lime."[47] To this early period belongs Yeocomico church, Westmoreland County, built in 1706. This quaint little building, which at one time was abandoned and served as a shelter for cattle,[48] has been restored to its original condition. The flaring eaves of the roof supported by end brick brackets which receive the block cornice, the circular window in the gable-end, the porch with diaper work over the door, the tiny panes of the windows mark this as one of the most interesting churches in Virginia. Here it was that Philip Fithian, the Princeton graduate who served as tutor in the family of Councillor Robert Carter, listened reverently to the sermons of Parson Thomas Smith, and looked on in disapproval as the congregation lingered in the churchyard to discuss politics, or the next horse race, or the price of tobacco or wheat.

Seventeenth-century Virginia could make no boast of pretentious public buildings. There were few hidden taxes, and the planters objected to increasing the tithable, or poll tax, to adorn Jamestown with a stately capitol, or to erect costly court houses in the various counties. For many years after the founding of the colony it was customary for the justices to meet in private houses or in taverns, and when the first court houses were erected they were usually little frame buildings, fitted with plain benches, the floor earthen.[49] The only public building which had any architectural interest was the State House at Jamestown, built in 1666. The discovery and excavating of the basement,[50] together with an occasional reference in the records to a window or a partition or to

46*Virginia Magazine of Hist. and Biog.*, Vol. XXIV, p. 275.
47Mary N. Stanard, *Colonial Virginia*, p. 322.     48*Tyler's Quarterly*, Vol. IV, p. 172.
49*William and Mary Quarterly*, Vol. XXIII, p. 55.
50Samuel H. Yonge, *The Site of Old "James Towne,"* p. 87.

this room or that make it possible for us to reconstruct the old building with some degree of certainty. When Bacon, the patriot, drew up his fusileers on the green and defied the enraged old governor, he saw a two-story brick structure, seventy-seven feet by twenty-four, with sharply rising roof, old-style porch about thirteen feet square, casement windows and two rear chimneys. It looked more like a comfortable English farm house than the capitol of a growing colony. The first floor was divided into two apartments, the Council chamber or court room and the secretary's office, probably separated by a hallway containing the stairway, while above was the long Assembly Hall and the tiny clerk's office in the porch. It was from the windows of the Assembly Hall that the Burgesses looked down upon the exciting scenes below in 1676, when Bacon demanded a commission as general of the forces to fight the Indians and Governor Berkeley bared his breast and dared him to shoot. A few weeks later Bacon returned with his little army and laid the State House, with the rest of the village, in ashes.

To the Englishman who visited Virginia and Maryland in the closing decade of the seventeenth century, the architecture must have seemed strange and at the same time familiar. The little farm houses looking out from groves of trees over the surrounding tobacco fields were distinctive of the Chesapeake Bay region, were obviously not English cottages, were different from the Cotswold cottage, or the Sussex cottage, or even the East Anglian cottage. Our visitor would have recognized the English influence in this architectural feature or that, in the ancient porch, the pitch of the roof, the pyramidal chimney, the bond of the brick work, but he would have noted that these features were cast in a new and characteristic pattern, a pattern distinctive of Virginia and Maryland. This new architecture, the architecture of the tobacco planter, would undoubtedly have become more and more distinctive, would have grown further and further apart from English domestic architecture, had the colonies been cut off from the cultural dominance of the mother country. But the Virginians and Marylanders were as much subject to the cultural dictates of London as to the political and economic control of the King and Parliament. "The habits, life, customs, computations, etc. of the Virginians are much the same as about London, which they esteem their home," wrote Hugh Jones.[51] So as architecture in England changed, the colonists somewhat belatedly followed suit.

Even in the first half of the seventeenth century the Renaissance influence was transforming English architecture, for it was in 1619 that Whitehall was begun after the plans of Inigo Jones, while in later decades the genius of Sir Christopher Wren brought it to new heights of beauty and dignity. Under the influence of the new school functional considerations such as high chimney stacks, mullioned casements, exposed beams, and irregular spacing of windows, gave way to those of pure form, space, mass and surface. Following in the footsteps of Jones and Wren came a group of able men—Sir James Gibbs, Sir Roger Pratt, John Webb, Captain Wynne and others—who diffused the new style throughout England until during the Hanoverian period it became so universal that the name Georgian was applied to it.

A strange mingling of influence the Georgian was. Based on Palladio, the classical tone was always obvious—the balancing of window spaces, the Doric or Ionian or Corinthian doors, the ornate cornice, the front pediment, the interior decorations. With the classical there was a strong touch of French and Dutch expressed in the steeply rising hipped roof, the towering chimneys, the roof balustrade and the cupola. In the last decade of the seventeenth century not only were some of the most distinguished architects in England Dutchmen by birth and training, but the tastes of the Dutch King William III influenced architecture profoundly. Yet, despite all, the Georgian was English, fitted to English life, utilizing English materials and English artistry and English mechanical skill.

The conquest of the American colonies by the new architectural ideas constitutes an instructive chapter in the history of American civilization. The prevailing forms in the various colonies, based on European inheritance and shaped by local conditions, the quaint timbered houses of New England, the Dutch houses of New Amsterdam, the Flemish cottage of the Lower Hudson Valley, the

[51]Hugh Jones, *Present State of Virginia*, p. 32.

half-timbered and log houses of the Pennsylvania German, the picturesque little cottages of the tobacco planters, gradually gave way before the all-conquering Georgian. It brought a uniformity to colonial architecture unknown in the seventeenth century. In Portsmouth, New Hampshire, in Salem, in Providence, in western New Jersey and eastern Pennsylvania, in Annapolis, in Alexandria, in Charleston there are many stately old residences strikingly similar to each other and to innumerable houses in England built during late Stuart or early Hanoverian times.

The new style was brought to the colonies in part by English architects who came over to practice their profession in America, in part by Americans who went to England to study architecture, and in part by the importation of English books showing plans and elevations and exterior and interior details. "If any gentleman should want plans . . . for any fabric or public edifice, he may have them by applying to" John Ariss, lately from Great Britain, "at Major John Bushrod's, at Westmoreland County, Virginia, where may be seen a great variety and sundry draughts of buildings in miniature, and also some buildings near finished after the modern taste," says an advertisement in the *Maryland Gazette* of June 5, 1751. Beautiful Carter's Grove, near Williamsburg, was designed by David Minitree, who came over from England for the purpose. William Buckland, the architect of some of the superb Annapolis mansions, learned his profession as an apprentice to his uncle, James Buckland, "carpenter" of Paternoster Row, London.[52]

The native Virginia or Maryland architects, even those who found it impracticable to serve their apprenticeship in England, had no difficulty in adapting themselves to the new school, since its principles were set forth in one book after another. In 1715 appeared a complete edition of Palladio, the great apostle of the classical revival, while the designs of Inigo Jones were published in 1727. The next year came James Gibbs's book of designs intended to aid those "concerned in building, especially in remote parts of the country, where little assistance in design is to be secured."[53]

[52]Lecture by R. T. H. Halsey.
[53]Fiske Kimball, *Domestic Architecture of the American Colonies*, p. 58.

This was the signal for a long series of volumes giving suggestive details for residences, with drawings of mantels, doors, capitals, pediments, stairs, windows, by Robert Morris, Abraham Swan, William Halfpenny, William Pain and others. Copies of these works found their way into the hands of American builders, who conned eagerly over the plates and explanations to acquaint themselves with the "modern taste" in design.

No doubt the planters themselves had a large hand in the designing of their residences and churches, for Hugh Jones tells us that they were good "mechanics in building, wherein most are capable of directing their servants and slaves."[54] We may imagine William Byrd II, or Carter Burwell, or George Mason poring over the plans for their stately houses, suggesting changes here, the insertion of a classic mantel here or of carved panelling there. The architect might be an intimate friend, a member of an influential family who united building with tobacco planting. Henry Cary, son of Councillor Miles Cary, built some of the finest structures in Virginia—the Capitol and the Palace, at Williamsburg, the York Courthouse. His son, Henry Cary, Jr., gave the colony the William and Mary Chapel and president's house; St. Paul's Church, Hanover; lovely St. John's, Hampton; his own home, Ampthill, in Chesterfield, and other churches and courthouses.[55]

It was no minor figure who drove the entering wedge for Renaissance architecture in Virginia, but the great Sir Christopher Wren himself. When King William and Queen Mary consented to the erection of a college in Virginia and donated the money from royal funds, they seem to have asked Wren, then the royal architect, to draw the plans. "The building is beautiful and commodious, being first modelled by Sir Christopher Wren, [and] adapted to the nature of the country by the gentlemen there,"[56] wrote Hugh Jones in his *Present State of Virginia*. Although this testimony has been questioned, there would seem to be no valid reason to doubt it. Hugh Jones was a minister who was called to William and Mary as professor of mathematics twenty-two years

[54]Hugh Jones, *Present State of Virginia*, p. 38.
[55]Fairfax Harrison, *The Virginia Carys*, p. 88.
[56]Hugh Jones, *Present State of Virginia*, p. 26.

after the erection of the building and must have been correctly informed as to its architect. That the drawings are not found in the Wren papers is what one would anticipate, since Blair and the builder, Thomas Hadley, would obviously take them along when they sailed for Virginia. Nor is it true, as has been stated, that the college was unlike Wren's other work, as any one who examines the design of Trinity College, Oxford, will see at a glance.[57]

The college was by far the largest building in the colony, and to those of the planters who had never seen the great edifices of England, it must have seemed very imposing. Today, restored to its original form, it impresses the visitor by its quiet dignity and the beauty of its proportions (Plate 10). As one catches the soft tones of the brick showing red through the great trees of the campus, or views the quaint windows, the rows of dormers, the spreading stairs leading up to the front door, the balcony above, the hipped roof, the graceful cupola, he peoples the building once more with dignified, bewigged professors and students in cap and gown.

The carpenters and plasterers were still at work on the Wren building, when the burning of the old State House at Jamestown brought about the removal of the capitol to Middle Plantation. Here the ground was higher, there were fewer mosquitoes and less malaria, the place was more accessible to the people of the York River and all northern Virginia. So Sir Francis Nicholson busied himself with the planning and surveying of streets, which at first he designed to lay out in the form of the letters W and M in honor of King William and Queen Mary. When this proved to be a bit too complicated, he contented himself with a long central avenue running east from the college past Bruton church, named Duke of Gloucester Street, with parallel streets to the north and south named for himself. At the end of the avenue, facing the Wren building was to be the capitol, while north of the church the governor's residence was to look out on a long, narrow green. Williamsburg he called the place, in honor of King William.

[57]The building, which was burned several times and greatly changed with each reconstruction, has been beautifully restored by the Williamsburg Restoration.

The two public buildings were to follow, not the old style of the "Virginia house," but the new Renaissance architecture already established by the Wren building. We do not know who designed the Capitol (Plate 11). It may have been Henry Cary, who was the builder, it may have been one of the distinguished English architects, possibly Sir Christopher Wren himself. It would seem more likely that it was the work of one of King William's Dutch architects, possibly William Wynne or Sir John Vanbrugh, as the building in certain features shows a strong Dutch influence. The half-round projections with conical roofs look as though they might have been lifted bodily from the city walls of Alkmaar or Leiden. The suggestion of Dutch influence is strengthened, also, by a comparison of the building with the New York City Hall built in 1696 when Dutch influence was still strong on Wall Street, for the similarity is obvious.

It was in April, 1699, that the specifications for the Capitol were laid before the Assembly. The building was to be in the form of an H, each wing to be seventy-five by twenty five feet, with a connecting gallery thirty feet long "raised upon piazzas" or an arcaded porch. There was to be a hip roof, with dormer windows, covered with cypress shingles and surmounted by a cupola which was to have a clock placed in it and over which "on occasion" should wave the British flag. One wing was set aside for the use of the Council of State and General Court, the other for the House of Burgesses.[58]

This interesting building, now so beautifully restored, was the scene of many of the most exciting events in Virginia history. It was in the Hall of Burgesses (Plate 12), with its dignified Speaker's Chair, its rows of benches, its arched side windows, its charming panelling that the people's representatives bearded Governor Dinwiddie and penned a decade before the passage of the Stamp Act their protest against taxation without representation; that the youthful George Washington received a vote of thanks for his remarkable mission to the French in the Ohio Valley; that Patrick Henry delivered his famous address in which he compared George III to Cæsar, Tarquin and Charles I; that Richard Henry Lee was

[58]W. W. Hening, *Statutes at Large*, III, pp. 420, 421.

instructed to introduce into Congress resolutions for American independence. Across the porch in the other wing is the courtroom (Plate 13), where the Governor's seat, the chairs of the justices on either hand, the clerk's desk, the railings, the gallery, the benches for witnesses and spectators, bring back scenes of bewigged justices, eloquent appeals by George Wythe and Peyton Randolph and of decisions momentous in the political and social life of the colony. The Council Chamber, in the same wing, is also rich in history, for here it was that Alexander Spotswood thundered out his defiance of the Virginia aristocracy and vowed to break their power; here the decision was made to send across the mountains the expedition which precipitated the French and Indian War; here Governor Francis Fauquier conferred with the Council on what steps should be taken to quell the Stamp Act riots.

With the Capitol completed the Assembly proceeded to the erection of the Governor's residence, or Palace, as it was called (Plate 15). The building was to be of "brick, fifty-four foot in length and forty-eight foot in breadth, from inside to inside, two story high, with convenient cellars underneath and one valt, sash windows . . . and a covering of stone slate."[59] Once more we are left in the dark as to the architect. Of the school to which the Palace belongs, however, there can be no doubt. If one thumbs over the fascinating pages of Johannes Kip's *English Houses and Gardens,* he will see many country mansions of the late seventeenth century in form, detail and setting akin to this building. The rectangular mass, the Georgian door with pyramidal steps, the hip roof rising sharply to a balustrade, the towering chimneys, the rows of dormer windows, the slender cupola, make it probable that this is the work of Sir Roger Pratt, or William Wynne, or John Webb. One cannot fail to note the similarity to Pratt's Eagle House, Surrey; to Webb's Ashdown House, Berkshire; to the wings of Buckingham Palace.[60] With Eaton Hall, near Chester, the resemblance is so striking that we are tempted to

[59]W. W. Hening, *Statutes at Large,* III, p. 285.
[60]Nath. Lloyd, *History of the English House,* p. 232; Reginald Blume, *A History of Renaissance Architecture in England,* pp. 130, 190, 192.

PLATE 10—Wren Building, College of William and Mary

PLATE 11—The Capitol, Williamsburg, Virginia

PLATE 12—House of Burgesses, Capitol, Williamsburg, Virginia

PLATE 13—The General Court, Capitol, Williamsburg, Virginia

believe that the architect of the Palace had the plans before him when he took his rule and pen in hand (Plate 14). Not only are the two buildings themselves similar, but the front courts flanked by outbuildings, the formal side gardens, the summer houses, the lakes as well.

As one wanders through the restored Palace with its beautiful hall, its great ball room, its three dining rooms, the somewhat massive staircase, its many bedrooms, or gazes out of the windows over the court or the box garden, one peoples it again with colonial governors and their families, with dignified visitors and with humble Negro servants (Plate 15). Now Alexander Spotswood and his Council drown their enmity in deep drafts of punch; now the kindly Gooch gathers around him the cream of the colonial aristocracy; now the doughty Dinwiddie confers with the youthful Washington on the conduct of the French and Indian War; now we see a gay party strolling over to the little theatre nearby on the green for a presentation of "Othello" or "Hamlet"; now Fauquier entertains his friends with discourses on Palladio, or on music, or medicine, or the classics; now Lord Dunmore and his charming lady lead the minuet in the stately ballroom.

The restoration of colonial Williamsburg, which was begun in 1927 and is still in progress, is a major contribution to American history. It is more than the rebuilding of old houses, it is the re-vivifying in a charming and visible way of the life of the people who lived in them. Architecture, decoration, the arts and crafts, horticulture, costume, music, drama, education, social customs—all are involved in this great undertaking. And since Williamsburg was the center and chief expression of the civilization of tidewater Virginia, what we have is in fact a "restoration" of that civilization. Nor is this all. Since from this region went out many thousands of settlers—to Piedmont Virginia, to the Shenandoah Valley, to Kentucky, to southern Ohio, to Alabama, to Missouri, to Texas, even to the Pacific slope—we are dealing with a society which has affected profoundly the life of the United States. One may stumble upon a Williamsburg cottage in far-off California, or find a family in Oregon who point with pride to their descent from the Spotswoods or the Cloptons, or visit in a Missouri home

97

where the table silver goes back to Carter's Grove or Westover.

In an architectural way Williamsburg is interesting in showing the old and the new styles side by side. The very outhouses of that typically Renaissance building, the Palace—the kitchen, guard

FIGURE 3. THE RALEIGH TAVERN

house, "quarters," office—are merely old Virginia cottages. When we leave the Capitol to stroll down the Duke of Gloucester Street we pass one little house after another which would have fitted perfectly into the seventeenth-century plantation or into the Jamestown of Nathaniel Bacon's day—the James Galt house, the

Travis house, the Blair house, the Prentis house. But the court-house, the Wythe house, the Norton house, the Ludwell-Paradise house, all speak of a later and more pretentious age.

The Raleigh Tavern, the Faneuil Hall of Virginia, is as interesting architecturally as historically (Fig. 3). Originally a small cottage of the second Virginia type, it was gradually enlarged until its proportions were entirely changed. But the L form which it now assumes, the entrance with steps and door hood, the hipped

WHEREAS some ill-difpos'd Perfons have reported, that the Subfcriber hath not fufficient Entertainment : This is to give Notice, That all Gentlemen who will favour me with their Company, may depend on good Entertainment, at the *Crown* Tavern, oppofite to the *Printing-Office*, in *Williamfburg*, by
Their humble Servant,
*William Dunn.*

FIGURE 4. ADVERTISEMENT OF CROWN TAVERN

roof, the central chimneys cannot disguise the kinship of the building with other old houses to right and left. To the day, in December, 1859, when flames devoured the old structure, it had little in common with the architectural periods which came and went, and remained in fact a seventeenth-century cottage. Many were the famous guests who lodged here or stepped into the bar for a drink of rum, or dined in the famous Apollo room. Here Thomas Jefferson danced with his fair Belinda,[61] here George Washington often joined his friends at dinner, here patriots assembled in 1773 to organize a committee of correspondence. In 1769, when the protests of the House of Burgesses against the duties laid on tea, paper, glass, etc., by Parliament forced Lord Botetourt to dissolve them, the members poured out of the Capitol, walked the short distance to the Raleigh Tavern, and reassembled there in unofficial session. After declaring an association or boycott against British goods, they made it clear that their defense of American rights and liberties in no way weakened their loyalty for the mother country by drinking toasts to the King, the Queen and Royal Family, Lord Botetourt, a Speedy and Lasting Union between Great Britain and her Colonies, the Duke of

[61]Rebecca Burwell.

99

Richmond, Colonel Barri, etc. We are not informed whether the exhaustion of the punch or of the list of toasts brought the meeting to an end[62] (Fig. 4).

Though the cottages of the Georgian period continued in the old quaint style of the late seventeenth century, it was the Palace which set the fashion for the pretentious houses of the wealthy planters. Westover, Carter's Grove, Eltham, Belair, the Wythe house, the Carlisle house, Elsing Green and many others, while differing in details and often in proportions, show so unmistakably the influence of the Palace that one wonders whether the architects deliberately took it as their model. Carter's Grove, as we have seen, was designed by an English architect, David Minitree, whom Carter Burwell brought to Virginia for the purpose, but he drew his plans, not in the latest Georgian style, then becoming popular in the mother country, but of the late seventeenth-century Renaissance style, typified by the Palace. This stately mansion, like the Williamsburg houses, has recently been restored to all its former beauty. Some years ago it had fallen into a sad state of dilapidation, with red, white, and blue paint covering the richly carved wainscoting, and a stovepipe thrust through the cornice of the hall. Today these disfigurements have been removed and the native wood of pilasters, frieze, cornice, the hallway arch, the superb balustrades of the staircase stand revealed.[63]

The house stands on a terraced elevation overlooking the James River, its stately beauty typifying the golden era of the Virginia plantation. The pedimented doorway with pyramidal front steps, the evenly spaced windows, the towering chimneys, the hipped roof, all proclaim its kinship with the Palace. But unlike the Palace there is no front court, the flanking minor buildings being in line with the front façade. This disposition of the office, or kitchen, or schoolhouse, which became very common in Virginia and Maryland, balances the main residence and adds greatly to its dignity. Carter's Grove was famous for the hospitality of its owner and for the polish and charm of the society which graced its beau-

[62]Governor Botetourt's letter of May 19, 1769, British Public Record Office.
[63]William O. Stevens, *Old Williamsburg,* pp. 209–217; Edith T. Sale, *Manors of Virginia,* etc., pp. 172–182.

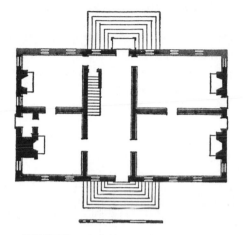

WESTOVER, CHARLES CITY COUNTY, VA.

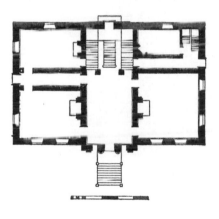

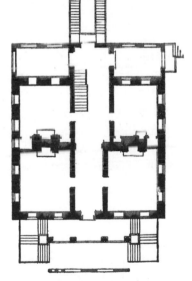

CHASE HOUSE,
ANNAPOLIS, MD.

MILES BREWTON HOUSE,
CHARLESTON, S. C.

FIGURE 5. PLANS OF SOUTHERN MANSIONS

tiful rooms. Here it was, in the famous "refusal room," that Thomas Jefferson stammered out his confession of love to Rebecca Burwell and received the reply which sent him away, for the moment at least, completely wretched.

In the same style as Carter's Grove was Eltham, the mansion of

FIGURE 6. STAIRWAY AT WESTOVER

Burwell Bassett, in New Kent County. The pedimented front door with Doric pilasters, the evenly spaced windows, the hip roof, the high chimneys, the balancing wings, marked this fine residence as a typical Virginia modification of the English Renaissance manor house. And like Carter's Grove, Eltham was the scene of lavish entertainment and hospitality. George Washington, who was the brother-in-law of Mrs. Bassett, was a frequent visitor. Eltham went up in flames in 1870.

Even more stately than Carter's Grove, but resembling it closely, is Westover, built by William Byrd II. Strip this beautiful house of its wings, add a roof balustrade and cupola and you have a close approximation of the Palace. But the superb front door with its broken pediment resting on Corinthian pilasters, and the marble

FIGURE 7. IRON GATE, WESTOVER

bands between stories give a touch of elegance lacking in the Palace façade. The wings of Westover, like those of Carter's Grove, were originally detached from the main residence, but in recent times have been joined to it by connecting units (Fig. 5). The beauty of the interior matches that of the exterior, the drawing room with its famous black marble mantel, its elaborate cornice, and its fluted pilasters, and the hallway eighteen feet wide with its graceful stairway set off by twisted balustrades of mahogany, being especially impressive (Fig. 6). Around this old building

103

have surged the storms of two wars, with the British invaders making themselves at home in its halls during the Revolution and McClellan's troops encamped under the great tulip poplars in the Civil War; here Evelyn Byrd pined away after her father forbade her marriage to an attractive young fortune-hunting baronet; here was entertained the young Marquis de Chastellux, who declared that Westover surpassed "them all in magnificence" (Fig. 7).

Before the middle of the century the Palace type of residence began to give way to the Georgian, under the pressure of English influence. The colonial architects, as they turned over the pages of Swan's *The British Architect* or James Gibbs' *A Book of Architecture*, could not resist the temptation to utilize some of the "modern" plans presented there. So the gable roof replaced the hipped roof, the main façade was lengthened, the depth shortened, the interior arrangement took on a more stereotyped pattern with room balancing room on either side of a central hallway. Kenmore, in Fredericksburg, the residence of Colonel Fielding Lewis; Chatham, near Falmouth, built by William Fitzhugh; stately York Hall, used by Lord Cornwallis as headquarters during the siege of Yorktown; Little England, Gloucester County; Poplar Hall, Princess Anne County, Chelsea, famous for the carved panelling of the reception hall, and many others are in the Georgian style.

Of the various types which evolved in the colonies out of the English Georgian, none was more beautiful than the Annapolis school. The group of stately mansions which graced the streets of the little capital or looked out over box gardens or groves of trees to the Chesapeake Bay, akin though they were to the old houses of Berkeley Square, bore the indelible stamp of Maryland itself (Plate 16). Could we have looked on as William Buckland laid his drawing paper before him and began work on the plans for the Hammond house, the evolution of this school would have manifested itself before our eyes. We see him taking a design from Gibbs, adding height to the central structure, reshaping the wings, simplifying the connecting links, modelling his front door after a detail in Kent's *The Designs of Inigo Jones,* his windows after another in Pain's *The Builder's Companion,* his mantels from

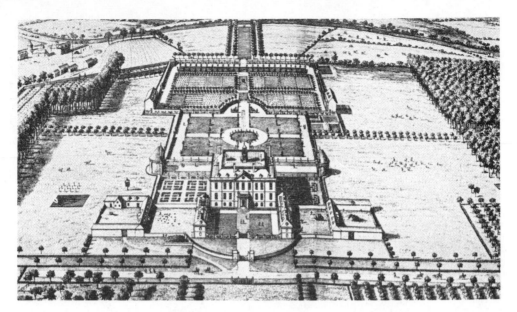

PLATE 14—Eaton Hall and Garden

PLATE 15—Palace from Garden

PLATE 16—Tulip Hill, Anne Arundel County, Maryland

still another in Halfpenny's *The Modern Builder's Assistant.*
When the drawings have been completed we discover that there
is a harmony in proportion and a beauty of detail which make
the work distinctively Buckland's own.[64]

The Annapolis Georgian is characterized by the central structure, which in some cases towers a hundred feet above the ground,
by balancing wings connected with it by unobtrusive links, by the
perfection of proportions, by the absence of exterior shutters, the
bold height of the chimneys, the unique brickwork, the flush trim
and heavy muntins of the windows, the very high ceilings, the
beauty and delicacy of both exterior and interior carvings[65] (Fig.
5). A perfect example is the Hammond house, considered by
many the most beautiful residence in America (Plate 18). The
perfect balance of central pavilion and wings, the brick façade relieved by elaborately carved wood doorway, windows and cornice,
the brick band between stories, the brick pilasters of the garden
front combine to give an impression of great simplicity and dignity. The brick is of a rich, dull salmon color, laid in the Flemish
bond, with white mortar joints finely pencilled. It seems almost
certain that Buckland had James Gibbs' *A Book of Architecture*
at his right hand when he designed this building, for the large
decorative cartouche obviously came from Plate 110, the banded
laurel theme of the woodwork occurs frequently in Gibbs and the
front doorway is strikingly similar to the one shown in Plate 108.
Associated with the old house is a story of blighted love, for it is
said that when the bride-to-be, for whom it was built broke her
engagement, Hammond was so broken-hearted that he remained
always a bachelor. The Hammond house has been purchased by
St. John's College, beautifully restored and fitted up with appropriate furniture.

In church architecture Maryland and Virginia showed a surprising reluctance to submit to the Renaissance influence. If the
planters who visited London were impressed by the beauty of St.
Mary-le-Bow or St. Clement Danes or St. Brides, they gave no
evidence of it in their own church structures. Whereas South

[64]*Monograph Series,* XV, No. 5.

[65]*Ibid.,* Lewis A. Coffin, Jr. and S. C. Holden, *Brick Architecture of the Colonial Period
in Maryland and Virginia,* pp. 3–6, plates 1–34.

Carolina, on the one hand, and the northern colonies on the other were imitating Wren and Gibbs, the tobacco colonies, despite their close contact with the mother country, especially with London, in church architecture turned their backs on them. It seems probable that Commissary James Blair and other leading Anglican clergy-men, like Dean William Sancroft, who so bitterly opposed Wren's plans for St. Paul's cathedral, considered the Renaissance style with its pagan traditions unsuited for a house of worship.

So the Virginia and Maryland churches of the first third of the eighteenth century were in the main merely elaborations of the early simple structures. The rectangular nave was enlarged, transepts were added, the wooden walls gave way to brick laid in Flemish bond, in some cases a massive square tower was built at one end. The result was most pleasing, in some respects quite as pleasing as the beautiful Wren churches themselves. As we stand before Bruton, in Williamsburg; or St. Paul's, Norfolk; or St. John's, Hampton; or Blanford, Petersburg, we are charmed by the harmony of lines and excellence of detail. Although they are basically Gothic in origin, these buildings are at the same time distinctly Virginian.

The thousands of visitors who pour into Williamsburg each year stand in admiration before old Bruton, or enter its doors with a mingled sense of reverence and deep interest, or wander through the churchyard to read the inscriptions on the old tombstones (Plate 17). It was in 1711 that Governor Alexander Spotswood submitted to the vestry "a platt or draught" for a new church to replace the old structure. Whether he himself drew these plans or whether he employed an architect, we do not know, but whoever the designer he had a fine sense of propriety and proportion. The builder was James Morris, "carpenter and chief workman in the city of Williamsburg." The church was completed in 1715, and enlarged to its present dimensions in 1751. The nave, the aisles, the choir, the roof lines remind us that the Gothic influence was not yet dead, but the absence of buttresses, the tall windows with rounded arches, the simple cornice, are in the simple Virginia style. The massive but plain square tower surmounted by a wooden belfry in two stages, although built half a century after the completion of the church, harmonizes perfectly with the rest of the structure.[66]

Bruton was to the religious life of the colony what the Capitol was to its political life. From its pulpit held forth James Blair, founder of William and Mary and Commissary for the Bishop of London; here each Sunday came the student body of the college to occupy part of the gallery; here in a pew elevated above the main floor and richly canopied, sat a long list of governors— Spotswood, Gooch, Fauquier, Botetourt and others; here worshiped Sir John Randolph, Peyton Randolph, Robert Carter Nicholas and other leaders of the Virginia aristocracy; here sat George Wythe, Thomas Jefferson, James Monroe, John Tyler and other leaders of the Revolutionary movement; here came the members of the Council of State and the House of Burgesses when the Assembly was in session; here gathered the wives and daughters of the nearby planters to listen to the sermons and display their gowns and hats. During services a long line of vehicles waited outside, while the liveried coachmen and postilions conversed with each other or perhaps sat reverently and humbly in the part of the gallery reserved for slaves.

In the same style as Bruton, but each having its own individuality, were St. Paul's, Norfolk, which was burned during the Revolution but later restored; Blanford, with its steep roof and flaring eaves, its plain door, its rounded window arches; Vawter's church, Essex County (Plate 19); St. John's, Hampton, its checkerboard brick walls peeping out from behind a group of willows.

The resistance of Virginia to the spell of Wren was perhaps fortunate, for it made possible the eventual rise of a unique type of Georgian churches which stand out as a real American contribution to architecture. These buildings constitute an abrupt break with tradition, for they contrast so radically not only with the older Virginia churches, but with the Gothic and the Wren churches of England, that to the older generation they were hardly recognizable as houses of worship. Some architect, or group of architects, taking the Georgian residence as the basis of their designs, created a type of structure which vies with the best in sim-

[66]*Virginia Gazette*, Dec. 15, 1768.

plicity, dignity, individuality and charm. In some cases built in the form of a Greek cross, in others of a rectangle, the brick walls laid in Flemish bond and rising usually high enough for two rows of windows, the roof sloping back gently on the four sides to a short ridge; the lower windows usually rectangular, those above with rounded arches; the cornices heavy and often elaborate; the doors adorned with pediment and pilasters, we marvel at the beauty of these churches when we stumble upon them beside the road or search them out in some secluded grove of ancient oaks.

Christ Church, Lancaster County, built with money left by Robert Carter, of Corotoman, with the stipulation that a pew be set aside for his family and the chancel reserved as their place of burial, led the way for this new group of buildings. The structure is in the form of a Greek cross, with high walls three feet thick, narrow windows set with small panes and topped with round arches, with gently sloping roof flaring above the elaborate cornice. It is only upon entering that we are conscious that this is, indeed, a church, but the ceiling which rises in graceful arches thirty-three feet above the floor, the great square pews panelled in black walnut, the pulpit with its quaint sounding board and winding stairs, the carved chancel rail and the massive communion table, are more nearly in the conventional style. Christ Church remains today practically as it was when the proud Carter family first took their seats in their high-backed pew and listened to the sermons of the rector.[67]

The new style is exemplified by Abingdon Church, Gloucester County; St. Paul's, King George County; Aquia, Stafford County, and four churches in Fairfax County—Pohick, Christ Church, Falls Church and Upper Church. These last four, all of them within the original limits of Truro parish, of which George Washington and George Mason were vestrymen, were so similar in design that one cannot escape the conclusion that they were designed by the same man. Since we know that it was one James Wren, and not George Washington, as Lossing states, who drew the plans for Pohick, it is possible that it was he who was responsible for the church Georgian of all northern Virginia. Unfor-

[67]Robert A. Lancaster, Jr., *Historic Virginia Houses and Churches*, pp. 316–319.

PLATE 17—Bruton Church, Williamsburg, Virginia

PLATE 18— Hammond House, Annapolis, Maryland

PLATE 19—Vawter's Church, Essex County, Virginia

PLATE 20—*Left:* Christ Church, Alexandria, Virginia. *Upper right:* Pohick Church, Fairfax County, Virginia. *Lower right:* Acquia Church, near Fredericksburg, Virginia

tunately, we know almost nothing about him save that his work reveals him as a man of great talent, if not of genius, one who was not afraid to discard old ideas and to modify new architectural conceptions to his own ends. These little church structures approach more closely an original American style than any other type of architecture in the first two centuries of our history, unless it be the four-square meeting houses of New England. We can trace the octagonal churches of New Jersey and New York to Holland, the Virginia cottage to East Anglia, beautiful Christ Church, Philadelphia, was modelled on St. Andrew by the Wardrobe, while even the so-called Dutch colonial turns out to be merely the Flemish farmhouse transplanted in America. But one may search all England from the Scottish border to the channel without finding the prototype of the Virginia Georgian church, and to the English traveller as to other visitors, they seem unfamiliar, a unique and interesting type of church architecture.

It was on April 7, 1769, that Washington and the other members of the vestry signed the contract with one Daniel French for the building of the Pohick church (Plate 20). An interesting document it was. The church was to be "sixty-six feet in length and forty-five and a half in breadth, from out to out, the walls twenty-eight feet high from the foundation to be built of good bricks well burnt. . . . The corners of the house, the pedistals and doors with the pediment heads to be of good white freestone and the returns of the arches of the windows to be of rubbed brick. The doors to be made of pine plank, two inches thick, moulded and raised pannells on both sides . . . the lights to be of the best crown glass, eighteen in each window, eleven inches by nine, the window and door cases to be made with double archatraves . . . a modillion cornice on the outside and a cove cornice on the inside. . . . The isles to be laid with flaggstone, well squared and jointed. . . . The pews to be wainscoted with pine plank. . . . The altar-piece to be twenty feet high and fifteen feet wide, done with wainscot after the Ionic order. . . . The Apostles creed, the Lord's Prayer and the Ten Commandments to be neatly painted on the altarpiece."[68]

[68]Philip Slaughter, *The History of Truro Parish* (Phila., 1908), pp. 73-75.

The pulpit with its curved steps and sounding board faced the side entrance, while George Washington's pews, numbers 28 and 29, were to the right in the main body of the church. George Mason's family sat in numbers 3 and 4, "magistrates and strangers" in number 1, their wives on the opposite side in No. 11, "vestrymen and merchants" were in No. 2, their wives in No. 12; ten pews were reserved for the "most respectable inhabitants and housekeepers," the men sitting on one side, the women facing them from the other. An exciting scene it was as the congregation drove up for services. "The church-yard on Sunday resembles rather a race course than a sepulchral ground," observed a visitor, "the ladies come to it in carriages, and the men after dismounting from their horses make them fast to the trees. . . . I was stunned with the rattling of carriage-wheels, the cracking of whips, and the vociferations of the gentlemen to the negroes who accompanied them."[69]

The Upper Church, or Payne's Church, built in 1768 on the old Braddock's Road, differed from Pohick in having only one tier of windows, but in other respects it was similar, and the rectangular form, the low-hipped roof, the classic doors, the rounded arches, the cornice mark it as the work of James Wren or the architectural school he represented. This old church was abandoned after the Revolution and eventually fell into the hands of the Baptists. During the War Between the States it was torn down by Federal troops, who used the brick to build chimneys and hearths for their winter quarters.[70]

Christ Church, Alexandria (Plate 20), also designed by James Wren, is even more than the Upper Church, an approximation of Pohick. The interior is especially beautiful, the Tuscan arches and pediments, the Ionic altar-piece, pulpit and canopy, the boxlike pews and the quaint windows giving an impression of great harmony and charm. The tower, which was added after the days of Washington and Wren, no doubt to make the building conform to the popular conception of a house of worship, is entirely out of place, overshadows the original building and obscures its lines.

[69]Howe, *Historical Collections*, p. 255.
[70]Philip Slaughter, *History of Truro Parish*, pp. 50, 51, 68.

Bad as this is, the tower is a thing of beauty compared to the little boxlike structure which has been placed atop the Aquia church and gives to that lovely structure the appearance of a fire-house (Plate 20).

· The Virginia Georgian churches in one respect illustrate most interestingly the dependence of architecture upon local materials and available means of transportation. The only freestone quarry in northern Virginia was on Aquia Creek, where the stone was within a few feet of the wharf and could be loaded directly upon the boats. This made it available for any buildings on deep water. So the Aquia freestone was used for coins, pediments, pilasters and capitals on Christ Church, which was within a few hundred yards of the Alexandria wharves; Pohick, where the stone was probably brought up Pohick Creek; and Aquia church which was but a short distance from the quarry itself. But for the Upper Church it proved too costly to cart stone ten or fifteen miles over the dirt roads of the day, so we find that "the corners of the house, the windows and doors," as well as "the arches and pediment heads of the doors and windows" were of "bricks, rubbed, gauged and set in putty."[71] For the same reason at Falls Church and St. Paul's the ornamental work had to be done either in brick or wood, even though the latter building was within a score of miles of the quarry itself.[72]

The Revolution swept over the colonies, the United States sprang into being, a new epoch opened for the people, yet Geor gian architecture, both domestic and ecclesiastical, continued to hold sway in Virginia and Maryland. There was one young man, however, who made a personal "declaration of independence" in architecture even in the colonial period, when he was a student at William and Mary. Why it was that Thomas Jefferson, despite his keen appreciation of beauty and proportion, could see nothing save ugliness in the lovely Georgian buildings of tidewater Virginia, it is difficult to understand. Carter's Grove, where he spent so many happy days, the Palace, Westover, the Capitol held no charm for him, while he spoke of the college buildings as "rude, misshapen piles, which, but they have roofs, would be taken for

[71]*Ibid.*, p. 52.    [72]*Aquia Freestone* (Pamphlet—Alexandria, Virginia).

brick kilns." As for the frame cottages of the region, he thought it "impossible to devise things more ugly."

One of the many delights which Jefferson found in his frequent visits to Governor Fauquier, was the thumbing over of the volumes of his very extensive library. Here, one day he ran upon a copy of Palladio. As he viewed the various plates, studied the classic orders and worked over the formulæ, his imagination was deeply stirred. From that moment he became an ardent devotee of classical architecture, whose beauties he longed to transplant to his native Virginia. No doubt, as he left the Palace after an hour or two of music or of conversation with the Governor and his circle of friends, he often stopped on the green to look back at the building and consider how it might be converted into a Roman temple by lowering the roof and adding classical porticoes in front and behind.

When Jefferson was in France, he received a request from the Virginia government to engage an architect for a new state capitol at Richmond. Instantly he was all enthusiasm. First he decided upon the beautiful Roman temple at Nîmes, known as the Maison Carrée, as his model, and then took the matter up with Clérisseau, architect and classical enthusiast. Together they worked out the adaptation of the temple to modern needs and to available building materials, drew the plans and supervised the making of a model. As a result the first state capitol in the United States is also, perhaps, the most beautiful. The portico, approached by a wide flight of steps, with its eight Ionic columns and well-proportioned pediment, the beautiful cornice, the pilasters, the two tiers of windows combine to give a sense of beauty, dignity and elegance.

As this building rose on Capitol Hill to look down serenely upon the turbid James and across to the woods and fields of Chesterfield, it became apparent that a challenge had been issued to the established architecture of Virginia, perhaps of America. Here was no meek submission to the cultural dictates of England, for Jefferson had gone not to the London architects for his inspiration, but to Rome through Palladio. Fiske Kimball says of the Capitol: "It has been little realized that the design long preceded

PLATE 21—The Lawn, University of Virginia

PLATE 22—Monticello, near Charlottesville, Virginia

PLATE 23—West Lawn, University of Virginia

anything similar abroad. The classic revival was indeed a movement which already had its beginnings there . . . but the Virginia Capitol preceded the Madeleine, in Paris, first of the great European temple reproductions, by more than a score of years." Jefferson's fertile mind had furnished the impetus for one of the few early cultural movements in which America led the way.

Although the Capitol showed the way for the classical movement, it is improbable that it would have been so widespread and universal had not Jefferson himself followed it with many other beautiful designs, and had not fresh classical currents set in from Europe in the early nineteenth century. One can hardly contend that the Massachusetts State House, the United States Bank and Girard College, in Philadelphia, were inspired entirely by the building on Capitol Hill, nor that Latrobe, Hoban and other foreign architects were mere imitators of the great Virginian. None the less, within the half-century following the erection of the Capitol the entire countryside from New England to the far South was dotted with Greek and Roman temples, and the classic portico graced the house of the Nantucket fisherman and the Georgia planter, of the wheat grower of the Valley of Virginia and the Boston merchant.

Jefferson, himself, was never happier than when he could steal a few hours from his duties as governor, or president, or political organizer to work on his own beautiful residence or draw the plans for the houses of friends and neighbors. If he had to deal with a house already standing, he used great ingenuity in concealing every Georgian feature behind an imposing array of classical columns; if a new house was contemplated he turned joyfully to his numerous copies of Palladio for fresh inspiration. It was Jefferson who gave us his own Poplar Forest, the octagonal house near Lynchburg built as a retreat to which he could flee from the hordes of friends and curious visitors, and drawn, apparently, from William Kent's *Designs of Inigo Jones;* Edgehill, designed and built for his daughter Martha, who married Thomas Mann Randolph; Farmington, the residence of George Divers, which he transformed from the original Georgian by adding a rectangular front with octagonal ends and front portico. The Jeffersonian flavor is very strong, also, in Redlands, built by Robert Carter; Estouteville, the residence of John Cole III; Montpelier, which Jefferson seems to have remodelled for his friend President Madison; Oak Hill, to which James Monroe retired from the presidency, where the style of the original house is carefully hidden by an imposing elevated portico; beautiful Bremo, the mansion of General John Hartwell Cocke.

But the gem of Jefferson's domestic buildings is his own Monticello, perched on the little mountain which overlooks the Piedmont to the east and Albemarle County on the west stretching out in rolling woods and farmlands to the Blue Ridge (Plate 22). An architectural feast it was for Jefferson as he seized upon one Palladian feature after another to create a whole of extraordinary harmony and charm, and to his dying day he revelled in the two porticoes, the beautiful cornices, interior and exterior, the well-proportioned dome, the roof balustrade, the classical mantels, the pedimented doors, the carved balcony brackets.

The greatest of Jefferson's architectural creations was the University of Virginia. It was his desire that there should be "an academical village rather than one large building," with separate "lodges" for the professors, joined by dormitories "opening into a covered way." This idea eventually found expression in the Lawn, a rectangular space dominated by a rotunda at one end and flanked by two-story pavilions and student rooms united by colonnades (Plate 21). Behind East Lawn and West Lawn charming gardens were enclosed by the famous serpentine brick walls, and further on were the rows of dormitories fronting on low arcades known as East Range and West Range. The fact that the Lawn ascends to the north in successive terraces lends added dignity to the rotunda, so that the great dome and stately south portico dominate the entire group. Jefferson modelled this building upon the Pantheon, reducing the scale one half, and rearranging the interior "to the purposes of a library for the university, with rooms for drawing, music, examinations," etc. A later generation disfigured this noble structure by placing a pepperbox skylight atop the dome and joining a shapeless structure for classrooms, auditorium and laboratories to the north front. A not-too-unfortunate fire in 1895 offered the opportunity for a restoration in keeping with the original plans.

The pavilions on the lawn were either taken from the pages of Palladio, or modelled after existing Roman structures. Pavilions I and VIII were based on Diocletian's baths, Nos. III, V and VII came from Palladio, Nos. II and IX were based on the Temple of Fortuna Virilis, Nos. VI and X on the Theatre of Marcellas, No. IV on Albano. Each pavilion not only fits perfectly into the general scheme, but is a thing of beauty in itself (Plate 23). Jefferson was loath to spoil the classical effect by adding such modern accessories as chimneys, and when necessity forced him to yield, conducted all flues in each pavilion to one centrally placed stack. The University of Virginia has made it a policy in all recent expansions to adhere to the original style, but though able architects have been employed, nothing they have done compares in beauty, dignity, balance and charm with Jefferson's Lawn.

Others took up Jefferson's work to spread classical architecture through Virginia and Maryland, especially through those regions where wheat and tobacco growing was creating new fortunes— Montibello, the seat of the Cave family, put into line by the addition of a Doric portico; Horse Shoe, built by the Moncure family in a wide bend of the Rapidan River; Tuleyries, built by Colonel Tuley, and spared by Sheridan's men because of the eagle over the doorway; Long Branch, in Clarke County, built by Robert Carter Burwell; Carter Hall, imposing with its fluted columns and carved Ionic capitals; the Confederate White House, at Richmond, designed by the famous architect, Robert Mills; McKim School, Baltimore, built in 1821. Surpassing all others in stateliness, perfection of proportions and richness of detail is Berry Hill, Halifax County, Virginia, the seat of the Bruce family. This Doric temple, for such it is, stands forth like a vision of ancient Rome from a grove of mighty oaks. The stone steps and the eight massive columns of the portico stretch the entire width of the house. The great hall, with its circular stairways rising on either side to a common landing, the mantels of carved Italian marble, the colonnade in the rear are noteworthy features of this noble mansion.

The forces which turned the English colonies into laboratories of American civilization are admirably illustrated by the history of Virginia and Maryland architecture. The power of tradition, which was the first element thrown into the crucible, was as strong on the banks of the James and the Potomac as it afterwards proved at Plymouth, New Amsterdam and Philadelphia. The settlers at Jamestown and St. Mary's brought with them English building methods, English tools, English ideas of house design; they wished to build their cottages and churches as nearly as possible like those they had been accustomed to in their native villages or shires.

But they were forced to modify their plans by other great factors, the first of which was the melting pot. Early Virginia and Maryland architecture, it is true, was not a mixture of two or more European architectures, since the settlers were overwhelmingly English in blood, but the early Virginia cottage was in part a conglomerate of certain types of English cottages, the early Maryland a fusion of others. And both alike were profoundly influenced by local conditions—the high cost of labor, the absence of stone, the cheapness of wood, the climate, difficulties of transportation, etc. Thus in each colony distinct architectures developed, both born partly of England, partly of America, like each other in some respects, different in others, each having a charm and an individuality of its own.

But the continued contact with England prevented the uninterrupted development of these two architectures. Virginia and Maryland were even more subject culturally to the mother country than politically, so that when Renaissance architecture became the vogue, it was not long before it swept over the Atlantic to the colonies of the Chesapeake Bay region. This was the more inevitable since the new style was especially fitted to the golden age of the tobacco civilization, when the accumulation of large fortunes led to the erection of so many stately mansions. But that Americans were capable of asserting at least a degree of cultural independence is shown by their refusal to follow Sir Christopher Wren and other Renaissance architects in designing their churches during the early years of the eighteenth century, and later developing a charming and unique ecclesiastical architecture of their own. And even in domestic and public buildings the influence of America was not to be denied, so that eventually they assumed distinct regional characteristics. Westover, English Renaissance though it is, would be out of place beyond the limits of eastern Virginia; the Hammond house, although Georgian in every line and detail, is typical of Maryland and Annapolis.

The significance of Jefferson's classical revival lies in the fact that it was perhaps the first important instance in which America led the way in a great cultural movement. It was not a reversal of the transit of civilization, since England did not borrow Jefferson's ideas, but merely hit upon the path he had followed several decades earlier. But it presaged the time when the United States would no longer look to London for leadership in literature, art, music, science, as well as in architecture, perhaps even the day when the current would set the other way and Europe be forced to make acknowledgment for the profound influence of American civilization upon her life and thought.

*Chapter IV*

## ADVANCE INTO PIEDMONT

WE MAY imagine William Byrd II standing in the front door of stately Westover, looking out over the broad expanse of the James. To him the river was a great pathway leading to the Chesapeake and the Atlantic, and so to England—the England whence came his ancestors, the England where he was educated, where lived many relatives and friends, which sent him the clothes on his back, the silver on his table, the books in his spacious library, the tools with which his slaves cultivated the fields, the coach in which his wife drove to church. He knew that goods which his English agent placed on shipboard for him at Gravesend would remain untouched until he unloaded them at his plantation wharf. So, despite the three thousand miles of water which separated him from London, the James, gliding past his door, gave him a comforting sense of nearness.

It was their dependence on the mother country which made the colonists for a century after the founding of Jamestown continue to hug deep water. Their plantations, with their quaint brick or timber residences surrounded by outhouses, their orchards, gardens and wide fields of tobacco, lined the bank of the Potomac, the Rappahannock, the York and the James as far as the ocean-going vessels of the day could go. But the rich region beyond was a vast forest, given over to the Indian, to bears and wolves, or to an occasional hunter or fur-trader. Despite the remarkable explorations of Abraham Wood in 1671, Sir William Berkeley died knowing little more of the Shenandoah Valley than of the Congo or the Arctic.

During the seventeenth century the planters looked upon themselves as occupying an outpost of Europe rather than the threshold of America. Their faces were turned east toward the world whence they came, not west to the great, mysterious world of America. Had any one predicted that in the second century after the first permanent English settlement the frontier would be pushed beyond the mountains into the Ohio Valley, and in the third extended to the Pacific Ocean, he would have been ridiculed. "If it has taken us one century to advance a hundred miles into the interior with the aid of deep water transportation," the most thoughtful would have asked, "how will it be possible in two more centuries to sweep on over mountains and plains, for a distance thirty times as great? How will the settlers get their crops to market? How will it be possible for them to import English goods? How can the mother country defend them from the attacks of French, or Spaniards, or the Indians?"

Yet, with the dawn of the eighteenth century it became more and more evident that the time had come for the colonists to throw off their swaddling cloth, to let go the hand of mother England and attempt to walk alone. Tobacco is very exhausting to the soil, and the planters had found land so abundant and cheap that little or no effort had been made to preserve its fertility. It was their practice to secure holdings far in excess of their immediate needs, to clear only a small part and to sow the same crop year after year until the diminishing yields warned them that it was time to make use of their land reserves. A plantation of five hundred acres might consist of fifty acres of cultivated land, two or three abandoned fields and a goodly expanse of virgin forest. In time, as the proportion of "old fields" increased and the area of "fresh land" dwindled, the planter faced the alternative of moving on to some other part of the colony, or of adjusting his life to diminishing returns from his exhausted fields.[1] A hard alternative it was—to abandon the old homestead, to say farewell to neighbors and friends, to write down as a loss the labor of decades, to move into a wilderness, to clear away the great trees, to build a new residence, new barns, new fences, to brave the

[1]"Plantations are every day left by tobacco-planters, who quit and sell them at low prices in order to retire backwards for fresh land." *American Husbandry* (London, 1775), Vol. I, p. 247.

hardships and dangers of the wilderness, or to struggle to maintain the old standard of living in the face of mounting debts, diminishing crops and run-down barns and tobacco houses. Their excuses to the English merchants for their failure to meet their debts give us the story. "I am sorry that the freshet this year destroyed a part of my crop," writes one. "I now have a new overseer and so hope to send you more hogsheads by the next fleet," says another.

In the middle of the eighteenth century, the golden era of the tobacco aristocracy, when the number of rich planters had multiplied, extravagance and a desire to surpass one's neighbors in courtly living and sumptuous entertainment vied with soil exhaustion in bringing many families to ruin and so forcing them to start life over again in the Piedmont. "Williamsburg was the center of taste and fashion and refinement," William Henry Foote tells us. "The entertainments of the Governor and Council in the capital were answered by entertainments in the country. . . . Wealth, dress, and address were everything, and the two latter were often obtained at the expense of the former. A season unfavorable for tobacco brought dismay to those who were in the habit of anticipating their income. Sometimes, unhappily the father left his son his expensive habits, a worn-out plantation and a heavy debt; then degradation and poverty, premature death, or emigration to the western borders were the alternatives. Too spirited to be degraded and too proud to be mean, many families carried to new settlements in the wilderness easy manners, dear bought experience and social refinement."[2]

The movement to the West was accelerated by the introduction of slaves in large numbers. In the seventeenth century the deep-water region was covered with small plantations on which the labor of cultivation was performed usually by the owner and his sons with an occasional indentured servant or two. Only the rich, and there were few rich men in Virginia during this period, worked their plantations with slave labor. But in the closing years of the seventeenth century, when the English first secured their full share of the slave trade, the blacks began to arrive in an ever-

[2]William Henry Foote, *Sketches of Virginia* (Phila., 1850), p. 149.

increasing stream. Men of means stocked their plantations with the black workers, while the smaller planter stretched his credit to the limit to make purchases. In 1670 Governor Berkeley estimated the number of slaves at 2000 in a total population of 40,000; sixty years later, when the population was 114,000, no less than 30,000 were Negroes.

This great increase in the number of slaves added a strong impulse to the opening of new tobacco lands. The blacks so cheapened the cost of production that the Virginia and Maryland leaf could undersell all rivals in the European market and still leave a large margin of profit for the planters.[3] When Robert Carter, or William Fitzhugh, or Lewis Burwell found that every African they set to work was bringing in handsome returns, they began to think of extending their operations by opening new plantations of untouched soil. Since fresh soil was scarce in the deep-water region and abundant in the Piedmont above the Fall Line, they began to cast their eyes westward to Spotsylvania, Goochland and Chesterfield.

If these wealthy men, after acquiring their Piedmont tracts, set out on horseback to supervise the laying out of plantations and the transportation of farm implements and slaves, they might have passed on the way many a poor farmer—trudging beside the wagon which carried his wife and children, a hoe or two, an axe, and perhaps a few household goods. He, too, was impelled by slavery to seek his fortunes in the Piedmont, for with tobacco bringing lower and lower returns, the worn-out soil of his farm in Gloucester or Surry no longer yielded him an adequate living. The newly opened country, like the tidewater, was to be the home of both rich and poor, was to be dotted with humble farms as well as with large plantations.

The poor man had to face all the hardships of the frontier with none to help him save his wife and his children. They had to make a clearing in the forest, build an humble cabin, lay out the crop of corn and tobacco, plant an orchard and a vegetable garden. But the rich often left the pioneer work to an overseer with a gang of slaves. No doubt the procedure of the Reverend Robert

[3]Francis Fane to the Lords of Trade, British Public Record Office, CO5–1322.

Rose was typical. This remarkable man, who was a successful planter, as well as a minister of the gospel, decided to give up his plantation and his cure in Essex County in tidewater Virginia, and move to the upper James River region.

His first step was to secure title to several tracts of land in what is now Amherst and Nelson Counties, in the shadow of the Blue Ridge. Then, in February, 1740, he employed a certain John Ray to conduct a group of slaves to his new property and establish several plantations;[4] or quarters, as the Virginians called farms conducted by overseers. Now and then Mr. Rose, mounting his horse and leaving his home and his flock, would ride a hundred miles or more over rough roads and forest paths to see how things were progressing and what supplies were needed, and to give directions for the building of houses and the laying out of crops. But it was only in September, 1747, seven and a half years after the plantations were laid out, that eleven hogsheads of tobacco reached Atcheson's warehouse, near the head of deep water on the James, ready for exportation to England, "The first fruits" of Mr. Rose's investment.[5]

This so encouraged him that he got the rather grudging consent of the Governor to give up his parish in Essex, and made preparations to remove his residence to his quarter on Tye River. Riding to the site, he selected "a place for to build a house on a hill," and then returned to Essex to prepare for the removal. Busy days followed. On November 16th his "people," as Mr. Rose invariably called his slaves, set out for Tye River, driving before them herds of cattle and sheep,[6] while the family servants, under indenture for six years, and supplies of all kinds followed. But it was a full year later, when all was in readiness to receive them, that Mrs. Rose and the children left the old home in Essex and, after breaking the journey at Colonel Fry's and other hospitable plantations along the way, eleven days later reached Tye River.

Rose found that most of his neighbors were men of very moderate means, who had few if any slaves and so might be classed as

---

[4]*Diary of Robert Rose*, copy, Virginia State Library.

[5]*Diary of Robert Rose*, September 10, 1747.

[6]*Ibid.*, November 16, 1747. *Landmark's of Old Prince William* (Rich., 1924), Vol. I, p. 250.

farmers rather than planters. The region was still the frontier, and rich men were slow to leave their beautiful estates on the lower James or Potomac until it assumed more the character of a civilized community. If they wished to put a part of their Piedmont holdings under cultivation, they established "quarters" under the supervision of overseers. Thus it was the poor man who led the van as the line of settlement moved westward. In the years from 1722 to 1729, when Spotsylvania was still a frontier country, the deed books show that of 197 land transfers, 44 were for 100 acres or less, 110 for 300 acres or less, while the average was 487 acres.[7]

The records of one frontier county after another tell the same story, the story of the wilderness, given over to bears, wolves and panthers, with a few pioneers living in huts, with no schools, no churches, no organized government. Gradually the little clearings in the forest expand, new settlers come in, lumber mills and blacksmith shops appear, roads take the place of bridle paths; but society is still primitive, still democratic, the average farmer does his own work without the aid of slaves. In time, however, slaves make their appearance, usually in groups of twenty or more and under the supervision of an overseer to open tobacco quarters. When Mr. Rose took up his residence on the Tye River in what is now Amherst, Nelson and Albemarle were dotted with this type of plantation. We find Mr. Rose stopping overnight at Webb's quarter, christening a child at Blackely's quarter, travelling past Gray's Point quarter, dining at Lomax's quarter.

In time, as rivers and roads were improved, the more fortunate or the abler farmers began to acquire wealth, to increase their land holdings, buy slaves and build fine residences. Sons of wealthy planters in the tidewater region took possession of quarters in the Piedmont and made them their permanent homes, or, deserting the wasted fields of their ancestors, purchased tracts of virgin land there and made a fresh start in life under the shadows of the Blue Ridge. As a consequence a region which was still in the pioneer stage during one decade might boast of a large degree of wealth and culture the next. Cumberland was cut off from

[7] W. A. Crozier, *Virginia County Records,* Vol. I, pp. 88–110.

Goochland and constituted a separate county in 1748, yet ten years later some of its leading families could afford to employ tutors for their children and to entertain with lavish hospitality. "Mr. Swann's house was a place of great resort," says Devereux Jarratt. "Scarce a week in the year passed without a company for cards, dancing, etc. The same was the case, more or less, with all the wealthy families in the neighborhood."[8]

Settlers from England, or Wales, or Ireland, or France, men of considerable capital some of them, cast in their lot with the new region. In Halifax we find the Raglands and Craddochs, of Welsh origin; Fontaines and Flournoys, of French origin; the Bruces, the Adams, the Faulkners, the Carringtons, the Bookers,[9] in Albemarle, the Carters, the Dabneys, the Southalls, the Randolphs, the Peytons, the Pages and similar families creating a society which vied in culture and wealth with that of the tidewater region. Oak Hill, North Wales, Monticello, Ash Lawn, Farmington, Estouteville, Montpelier, Bremo, Berry Hill, Prestwould and other Piedmont mansions bear testimony to wealth and refinement of taste and sumptuous living. One needs only to see them to people them in imagination with courtly gentlemen and handsomely gowned women and liveried slaves. Even the stately dignity of life at Westover or Carter's Grove in the eighteenth century did not surpass that of Berry Hill in the nineteenth. This costly mansion, built in the classical style typical of the early national period, was furnished in sumptuous style, even the basins and bowls of the bedrooms being of silver. Here lived James C. Bruce, surrounded by hundreds of slaves, "a sort of feudal chief on his great landed estate."[10]

We have seen that Spotsylvania prior to 1730 was still a pioneer county peopled chiefly by small farmers; yet before the end of the century it had its full quota of rich planters. Of the 505 slaveholders listed in 1783 no less than 76 owned 15 or more slaves, of whom 19 owned 35 or more and 1 owned 159. It is interesting to note that 49 per cent of the owners had 5 slaves or less and 70 per

[8]*Life of Devereux Jarratt* (Balt., 1806), p. 54.
[9]*William and Mary Quarterly*, Ser. II, Vol. V, pp. 67, 68.
[10]*Virginia Magazine of Hist. and Biog.*, Vol. XI, p. 332.

cent 10 slaves or less in both Spotsylvania and the tidewater county of Gloucester.[11]

Society in the Piedmont tended to reproduce that of the tidewater region because of the profitable use of slaves in agriculture. So long as the poor farmer who tilled his fields with his own hands had to compete with the slave labor of his neighbor, he could hope for the barest living. When the owner of forty slaves could make profit fifteen times as great as the owner of four, the creation of large estates would be inevitable. "To make a due profit on tobacco a man should be able to begin with twenty slaves at least," said a shrewd observer in 1775, "because so many will pay for an overseer. None, or at least very few, can be kept without an overseer, and if fewer than twenty be the number, the expense of the overseer will be too high."[12]

He goes on to show that a planter who owned twenty or more slaves should, even with ordinary care and economy, save enough each year to purchase additional slaves and so build up a handsome fortune. The reason why more did not acquire wealth was the common fault of extravagant living, for the planters lived like country gentlemen of fortune, and so luxurious were their buildings, furniture, dress and diversions that it was surprising that they could keep out of bankruptcy. But "to live within compass, and to lay out their savings in an annual addition to their culture, requires in the conduct a fixed and settled economy, and a firm determination not to depart from it at least until a handsome fortune is made."[13]

"But it does not follow," he continues, "that settlers are precluded from these colonies who cannot buy twenty negroes; every day's experience tells us the contrary." He who owns one or two slaves only, often makes a profit by being a "farmer for corn and provisions," and yet own a few slaves to produce tobacco. This makes a small business profitable, "and at the same time easy to be attained, nor is anything more common throughout both Maryland and Virginia."[14]

[11]*Virignia Magazine of Hist. and Biog.*, Vol. IV, p. 298, Vol. V, pp. 414-416.
[12]*American Husbandry*, Vol. I, p. 246.
[13]*American Husbandry*, Vol. I, p. 238.      [14]*Ibid.*, p. 248.

Despite the basic similarity of society in the Piedmont and the Tidewater region, differences existed, some of them very important, indeed. It would have been remarkable had a vast movement of this kind, involving the migration of tens of thousands of families to a new region, resulted in an exact duplication of the old life.

The key to the situation was transportation. The frontier could not pass the Fall Line until the settlers were assured of getting their tobacco hogsheads to deep water. Tobacco is a bulky commodity. It might cost so much to transport it to the nearest warehouse and wharf available for ocean-going vessels that all profit from its culture would be eaten up. The freight charges on a hogshead from Louisa to Richmond, a distance of but forty-six miles, might be greater than the freight to London. What would it avail to have the richest soil in the world, if he were cut off from the world markets? The settler wanted to know, also, how he was going to bring back needed English goods—boxes of clothing, farm implements, furniture, salt, fire-arms.

In the days when William Byrd I sent out his traders with their packhorses hundreds of miles from his store at the falls of the James, they travelled over Indian trails which had existed long before the days of Powhatan and Captain Newport.[15] But an Indian trail was a poor highway, indeed, over which to transport tobacco, so the pioneers of the Piedmont found it necessary to widen them by cutting trees and underbrush on either side. In some cases they made entirely new roads through the forests leading directly to a tobacco wharf, or connecting with some through highway. Rolling-roads the settlers called them, since the tobacco hogsheads were rolled over them to points of shipment.

In the deep-water region it had long been the custom for the planter or his slaves to get behind a hogshead to roll it from the tobacco house to the wharf.[16] Sometimes the crews of the merchant vessels were required to perform this service, which they did with many a lusty oath and curses upon Virginia and the Virginians. When the plantations crept westward into the Piedmont, it was no longer feasible to propel an eight hundred or thousand

[15] *American Husbandry*, Vol. 2, p. 441.    [16] *Ibid.*, p. 466.

pound hogshead twenty-five or fifty or a hundred miles by hand, so the planters substituted horses or more frequently oxen.

Hogsheads intended for rolling were especially constructed, being "closer in their joints than other hogsheads" and strongly tied with hickory hoops (Fig. 8d). Driving two large pins of wood into the butts of either end to serve as axles, the cooper attached shafts to them, so that the hogsheads could be drawn along like giant rolling-pins.[17] On the shafts, behind the horses a box was affixed for provisions, provender, an axe and other tools. Unfortunately, the jolting over rough roads often injured the tobacco and so battered the hogshead that long stops for repairs were necessary. This led to the invention of fellies, or wooden tires affixed to the body of the hogshead by means of wooden pins driven into the staves. This device elevated the hoops and staves above the road and saved them from much battering.[18] One would suppose that when the hogsheads splashed through the water of the numerous fords the tobacco would be ruined, but such was not the case. "Tobacco, if well packed and prized duly, will resist the water for a surprising time," says William Tatham. In proof of this fact he cites the case of some hogsheads which had been washed away in the James River flood of 1771, and were still in good condition when found twenty years later lodged in a mass of driftwood.[19]

In the spring and autumn overseers and slaves might be seen driving the plodding oxen with their clumsy load through the forest, over half-finished roads. Often the drivers from one plantation joined company with those from others, so that cavalcades of considerable size were formed. The habit of sleeping in the woods, the red mud which splashed over their clothes, the exposure to rain and dew made these journeys arduous, but camp-fire stories and rustic amusements helped pass the time.[20] Despite the slowness and costliness of the trip thousands of hogsheads were brought down in this way from Albemarle or Cumberland Coun-

[17]Isaac Weld, *Travels in North America*, I, p. 155.
[18]William Tatham, *Essay on Tobacco*, pp. 58–61.
[19]*Ibid.*, pp. 48, 49.
[20]*William and Mary Quarterly*, XVI, p. 127. See also Hening, *Statutes at Large*, IV, p. 206; Francis Taylor, *Dairy*.

ties on the upper James to Rocky Ridge or Richmond, or from Orange and Culpeper to Fredericksburg and Falmouth.[21]

Dissatisfied with this clumsy and costly method of transportation, the settlers began to cast longing eyes at the upper reaches of their great rivers. True the James, the Rappahannock, the Mattapony, the Pamunkey and the Potomac were shallow, interspersed here and there with rapids or falls, and subject to freshets or floods. None the less, they began to build "rafts and flats to course down the current for many miles with their commodities to market and the warehouses." In returning with English manufactured goods "they put their crafts along shore back again with poles." "Were it not for this piece of industry, they would labour under great difficulties and hardships in bringing down the crops by land carriages over mountains and stony ways."

But the settlers found it no easy task to steer these clumsy craft down stream without wetting the cargoes, while to pole them back was arduous in the extreme. Realizing that the prosperity of the region was involved in a proper solution of this problem, many began to give it serious consideration. If the Indians could navigate these waters in their dug-out canoes, why could not the white man devise a vessel for transporting his merchandise equally suited to shallow water navigation? Such a vessel would make it possible to get a hogshead to market at a fraction of the cost of "rolling," and despite the difficulty of going upstream against the current, would also facilitate the transportation of European goods from the Fall Line ports.

Among those who pondered over this problem was our friend, Reverend Robert Rose. As he sat on the banks of the James watching its waters glide by, or perhaps as he urged his horse through the fords on his clerical duties, he must have wondered whether the canoe itself could not be so modified as to answer the purpose.[22] Unfortunately, although the canoe was swift, drew but a few inches of water, and could easily be steered through rapids and around rocks, it was so frail that it could never support the weight of a hogshead of tobacco. Even an outrigger would not insure stability with a thousand pounds wabbling on the gunwales.

[21]*Tyler's Quarterly Magazine*, IV, p. 247.   [22]*Diary of Robert Rose*, May 19, 1749.

But then it occurred to him that by fastening two canoes together he could secure a steady support for his bulky freight, without sacrificing speed and ease of navigation[23] (Fig. 8a).

Early in 1749 we find him busy directing the making of canoes, and on March 16 he took a short trip down Tye River "to see the nature of the navigation."[24] Undeterred by a drenching when he tumbled out into the river, he went ahead hopefully with his plans. Late in March he put his idea to the test, accompanying his "people" in the canoes as they started off with their cargo. Although the eight or nine hogsheads which were rolled on to the gunwales of the two canoes and fastened firmly in place made "an almost incredible burden" for such frail craft, the experiment was entirely successful. We may only guess at Rose's elation as his little fleet glided swiftly down stream, under the skillful guidance of his boatmen. A few weeks later he jotted down in his diary: "This evening my watermen got home, having safely carried down fifty-two hogsheads of tobacco, twenty-nine of which are mine."[25] A new era had opened for the Piedmont region.

Soon every well-to-do planter on the upper James had his watermen and his canoes to send down his tobacco to Richmond or Rocky Ridge and bring back imported goods. "Nothing is more common than to see two of these tottering vehicles, when lashed together, . . . carrying down our upland streams eight or nine heavy hogsheads of tobacco," wrote Reverend James Fontaine in 1756.[26] In making these vessels the planters did not go through the long and expensive process of laying a keel, attaching ribs and adding the planking. Harking back to Indian tradition they selected a log fifty or sixty feet long, and four and a half feet to five feet in diameter, and fashioned their craft out of it. Two canoes were clamped together with cross beams and pins, so that there could be no danger of their parting company.[27]

The canoes were manned usually by Negro watermen, who learned to know every rock and every bend in the river and ac-

[23]James Fontaine, *Memoirs of a Huguenot Family* (N. Y., 1853), pp. 388, 389.
[24]*Diary of Robert Rose,* March 16, 1749.
[25]*Diary of Robert Rose,* June 27, 1749.
[26]James Fontaine, *Memoirs of a Huguenot Family* (N. Y., 1853), pp. 388, 389.
[27]William Tatham, *Essay on Tobacco,* pp. 62, 63.

quired great skill in handling their frail craft.[27a] On one occasion, when the river was unusually high, a boatman, who was paying more attention to his bottle than his steering, was swept by the torrent into the rapids at Westham. But sobered by his peril, he avoided every threatening rock, so that those who followed to search for his body found him safely moored seven miles below at the Shokoes warehouse.[28] During the Revolution the Virginia government made good use of tobacco canoes for conveying supplies up and down the James, paying the planters £500, Virginia money, for a ten hogshead canoe.[29] The double canoe seems to have remained the most practical method of navigation until a new type of boat was brought into use designed especially to meet conditions on the upper James.

It is said that Thomas Jefferson was present at the launching of the first James River bateau, designed by one Anthony Rucker.[30] This boat was not unlike a canoe, long and narrow, elevated at the bow and stern and drawing only a few inches of water[31] (Fig. 8b). It could carry a larger cargo than the double canoe, however, was easily steered by a Negro helmsman with a giant oar, and made the journey from Lynchburg to Richmond in seven days. But the bateau required a crew of three men, it was difficult to steer it past certain places at low water, and being lightly constructed to lessen the laborious task of propelling upstream, its life was only two or three years.[32] Even after the James River Company had improved the river channel, the bateau-men often had to wait for a rise in the water before setting out on their journey. In these strange craft the commerce of the upper James and its tributaries as far west as Rockbridge and Botetourt flowed back and forth until the fourth decade of the nineteenth century. Doctor George W. Bagby recalled seeing them moored in fleets on the river bank at Lynchburg,[33] taking on their cargoes of tobacco and

[27a]*Calendar of Virginia State Papers*, Vol. II, p. 362.
[28]J. F. D. Smyth, *A Tour in the United States* (Lon., 1784), Vol. I, p. 33.
[29]*Calendar of Virginia State Papers*, Vol. I, p. 451.
[30]*William and Mary Quarterly*, Ser. 2, Vol. II, p. 153.
[31]Isaac Weld, *Travels in North America*, Vol. I, p. 210; *Virginia Board of Public Works, Report*, Part III, 1819, p. 28.
[32]*Ibid.*, p. 94.
[33]George W. Bagby, *Selections, etc.* (Rich., 1884), Vol. I, p. 123.

A.

B.

C.

D.

FIGURE 8. FOUR WAYS OF TAKING TOBACCO TO MARKET

flour, and discharging bags of salt and fertilizer or boxes of imported goods. Similar boats, about forty feet in length, were used on the upper Roanoke to bring the tobacco and wheat of Mecklenburg, Halifax and Pittsylvania down to deep water at Weldon.[34]

The Negro bateau-man was selected with the greatest care, for he must possess courage, strength, skill and resourcefulness. "I can see him now," writes Doctor Bagby, "striding the plank that ran along the gunwale . . . his long iron-shod pole trailing in the water behind him. Now he turns and after one or two ineffectual efforts to get his pole fixed in the rocky bottom of the river, secures his purchase, adjusts the upper part of the pole to the pad at his shoulder, bends to his task and the long, but not ungraceful, bark mounts the rapids like a sea-bird bresting the storm. His companion on the other side plies the pole with equal ardor and between the two the boat bravely surmounts every obstacle, be it rocks, rapids, quicksands, hammocks, what not. A third Negro at the stern held the mighty oar that served as a rudder. A stalwart, jolly, courageous set they were, plying the pole all day, hauling in to shore at night under the friendly shade of a mighty sycamore to rest, to eat, to play the banjo and to snatch a few hours of profound, blissful sleep."[35] The voyage down stream was swifter, less strenuous, and as the current of the stream bore the bateau along, the crew would often sing in unison:

> "I'm gwine down ter town,
> I'm gwine down ter town,
> I'm gwine down t' Richmond town,
> Ter cyar my baccer down."[36]

As the canoe gave way to the bateau, so the bateau gave way to the canal boat (Fig. 9). With the construction of the James River and Kanawha Canal, and the introduction of enclosed boats carrying a far heavier burden of freight, there was no need for the lighter craft. Soon they became obsolete, and the passengers of the slow-moving canal boats, when they saw groups of the old

[34]*Virginia Board of Public Works, Report*, 1825, p. 72.
[35]George W. Bagby, *Selections, etc.* (Rich., 1884), Vol. I, p. 123.
[36]*Virginia Magazine of Hist. and Biog.*, Vol. VII, p. 415 n.

vessels moored at the mouths of creeks or at old wharves, regarded them curiously as relics of a by-gone age.

In the meanwhile progress was being made also in overland transportation, for many of the Piedmont plantations were so remote from the rivers that water passage was impractical. Gradually the most important rolling roads were widened, straightened,

FIGURE 9. CANAL BOATS, RICHMOND, VA.

cleared of rocks and stumps and placed under the care of surveyors. Ferries were provided over the larger streams,[37] while for creeks and small rivers bridges began to take the place of fords.

Waiting for an opportune moment, when the roads were not muddy and the horses not needed at home, the planter loaded his wagons, two hogsheads of tobacco to each wagon, together with provisions, liquor and provender, joined company with his neighbors and set out for the nearest inland port (Fig. 8c). Along the way they encamped in the woods, knowing there would be no

[37]*Francis Taylor, Diary,* Virginia State Library, I., July 27, 1786; Thomas Jefferson, *Works,* II, p. 34.

objection from the owners, and by the side of a "good rousing fire" spread their meals and exchanged anecdotes. After the hogsheads had been safely deposited at the warehouses, they took on goods for their plantations—cloth, farm implements, household utensils, salt, etc.—and turned their horses' heads homeward.[38]

Merchants also used the roads regularly in shipping goods from their warehouses at Falmouth, or Dumfries, or Petersburg to their stores scattered over the Piedmont.[39] The wheat and tobacco of Frederick poured over the Williams Gap and the Vestals Gap roads down to Alexandria, or over the Ashby Gap road to Falmouth at the head of navigation on the Rappahannock.[40] The Swift Run Gap road was the only highway of commerce for parts of Spotsylvania and Fauquier, all of Culpeper, Madison and Orange, and parts of Albemarle, Louisa and the Shenandoah Valley[41] (Fig. 10).

Over these roads rolled the heavy merchant wagons, the Negro driver directing the six or eight mules without reins, but with many a gee and haw. When Benson J. Lossing visited Virginia he found the highways leading into Richmond dotted with these picturesque vehicles.[42] He also found the roads exceptionally bad. "Worst roads I never expect to travel," he complained as he drove through Sussex. "Oftentimes Charlie would sink to his knees in the soft earth, which was almost as adhesive as tar."[43] Nor were native Virginians less harsh in their criticisms. Jefferson wrote Madison in April, 1801, that the road through Fairfax Court House was practicable till you came to Little's Lane. "I passed it yesterday, a wagon being there stuck fast in it, nor do I suppose any four-wheeled carriage could have got through the spot."[44] "You can scarcely conceive the difficulty in finding the proper roads," wrote Major Anburey, "as they can hardly be guessed at by those who have often used to travel in America; when one is bad they make another in a different direction."[45]

[38]William Tatham, *Essay on Tobacco*, pp. 55–57.

[39]*Allison Papers*, Virginia State Library, *John Hook Letter Book*, Virginia State Library; *Andrew Shepherd Account Book*, Virginia Hist. Society.

[40]See *Jefferson and Fry Map, Allison Papers*, Virginia State Library.

[41]*Virginia Board of Public Works*, Vol. I, Part 3, p. 57.

[42]Benson J. Lossing, *Field Book of the Revolution*, Vol. II, p. 325.

[43]*Ibid.*, p. 348.      [44]Thomas Jefferson, *Writings*, Vol. XIX, p. 124.

[45]Thos. Anburey, *Travels* (Lon., 1791), Vol. II, pp. 300, 301.

Thus for more than a century after the opening of the Piedmont, transportation, whether by rolling hogsheads, by rafts, canoe,
by bateau, or by wagon, was a costly matter. It must have been
discouraging, indeed, to the Albemarle farmer to find that the

FIGURE 10. VIRGINIA TOBACCO WHARF

expense of thirty-eight cents for moving a barrel of flour from
Columbia, at the mouth of the Rivanna, to Richmond, had eaten
deep into his profits,[46] or the tobacco planter on the upper Roanoke to pay $17.00 a hogshead wagonage to Petersburg.[47] It must
have been still more discouraging to pay the charges on transporting European goods up country, especially if they had to be polled

[46]*Virginia Board of Public Works, Report,* 1819, Part III, pp. 100, 101.
[47]*Ibid., Report,* 1825, p. 7). "Tobacco of no bad quality is produced toward the west,"
said Schöpf, "but the profit from it is greatly diminished, because it must be hauled over
long and difficult roads to the places where it can be received by the European ships."
T. D. Schöpf, *Travels in the Confederation,* Morison, Ed. (Phila., 1911), pp. 34, 35.

up stream in canoes or bateaux. The cost to the Albemarle or Buckingham planter of an imported table or plow, a bag of salt or fertilizer, or of a cask of distilled liquor was far greater than to the planter of Gloucester or Westmoreland, who could unload the goods at his private wharf.

It was this matter of transportation which differentiated the Virginia planter of the Piedmont from the planter on deep water. When a Carter or a Randolph moved into the "mountains," as they called the upland region, they expected so far as possible to duplicate the life to which they had been accustomed. Taking with them their overseers, their slaves, their live-stock, their farm implements, their experience with tobacco culture, their plantation economy, their architectural tastes, their social customs, they hoped to begin life in Buckingham or Albemarle where they had left off in James City or Surry. The westward movement was to be merely the expansion of Eastern Virginia, not the creation of a distinct section.

To some extent this is what it was. The plantation economy of Tuckahoe or Bremo on the upper James was not fundamentally different from that of Westover or Carter's Grove on the lower James. Both in the colonial and national periods prior to the Civil War the Tidewater and the Piedmont usually thought alike and voted alike on matters of local and national interest, both took the patriot side during the Revolution, both supported Jefferson and his Democratic-Republican party, both opposed the demands of the far western counties for greater representation in the Legislature, both voted for secession. None-the-less there was a very real difference between the Piedmont and the deep water region, a difference based on isolation.

The up-country planter was more self-reliant, more aggressive, more independent than his fellow of the Tidewater region. To him England seemed very far away indeed, the authority of Crown and Parliament somewhat shadowy. He seldom came in contact with a native Englishman, he read the *Virginia Gazette,* not the London papers, he knew little of what was going on in court circles, the coffee house gossip seldom reached his ears, the London merchant had a weaker hold upon his pocketbook, the Anglican bishop upon his spiritual life. For tables and chairs and highboys, his clothes, his hardware, his shoes, which the Tide-water planter imported from England, he usually turned to the local cabinet-maker, tailor or blacksmith.

Although the average planter who moved to the Piedmont was no Daniel Boone or a Sevier, he found life more independent, rougher, more primitive than in the Tidewater region. He might have to jump out of bed in the night to defend his sheep against the attack of wolves; if his wife became ill he must play the doctor and himself bleed her or administer the dose of Jesuits' bark or Bateman's drops; when he visited his nearest neighbor, he might have to ride through the woods and ford some swollen creek; to attend services at the nearest church might entail a ten-mile journey. Reverend Robert Rose, when he set out to attend to his pastoral duties, usually prepared for a hundred-mile journey. We find him preaching in lonely chapels or in private homes, stopping at a farm-house to marry a young couple or to christen a baby, now he is plunging his horse through the waters of the James, now he is lost in the forest, now sleeping on a hillside, with the earth his bed and the heavens his canopy.[48]

Isolation necessitated a degree of self-sufficiency in the plantation economy unknown in the deep water region. It is true that the advantages of utilizing products which would otherwise go to waste—cowhides, apples, peaches, persimmons, wool, tallow, etc.—had induced far-sighted men like Robert Carter, Ralph Wormeley and Lewis Burwell to include shoemakers, coopers, tanners, spinners, distillers among their indentured workers and slaves, and so to free themselves in part from dependence on the English merchants. But the Piedmont settlers, well-to-do planters and small farmers alike, supplied many of their own needs because they could not afford to pay the charge of transportation. The freight on a box of nails from London to Williamsburg might be no great matter, but to bring it from Richmond to Charlottesville by wagon or to pole it up the James and Rivanna in a bateau was costly indeed. So costly in fact that Jefferson, when he built his beautiful home at Monticello, preferred to have his blacksmith hammer out the nails on the spot.

We can follow a Piedmont planter as he directs some of the

[48]*Robert Rose Diary,* December 8, 1748.

varied activities of his household through the vivid pages of the diary of Colonel Francis Taylor, of Orange. We see him setting up a kiln to burn oyster shells for white-wash, planting hemp, flax and cotton for rope, linen and cotton cloth, shearing his sheep so that he might have wool for his spinners, running his own still, bottling persimmon beer, dipping candles, making hogsheads for his tobacco, and clothes and shoes for his slaves.[49] It was by no means uncommon for the thrifty planter to have his own blacksmith shop, his brick kiln, his distillery, his tan yard, his shoemaker's shop, his own loom, his cooperage, his grist mill. Thomas Jefferson wrote in 1788 that in almost every family cloth was manufactured for private use which was always good in quality and often tolerably fine. "They make excellent stockings of cotton," he added, "weaving it in like manner chiefly by the family. Among the poor the wife weaves generally and the rich either have a weaver among their servants or employ their poor neighbors."[50]

Major Anburey gives us an interesting picture of home industries among the poorer planters of the Piedmont. "The inhabitants of the lower sort, through the scarceness and difficulty of procuring clothing for themselves and their Negroes, pay greater attention to it (cotton) at present than tobacco. . . . The seeds . . . are cleaned by means of a machine called a gen, which is made of two smooth rollers placed close and parallel to each other in a frame and move in contrary directions. . . . The carding and spinning of cotton is the chief employment of the female Negroes. . . . Both male and female are clothed with their own manufacture, the superior class as an example to their inferiors, who are compelled by necessity. . . . The cotton of which (my own clothes are) made I obtained from my landlord, and saw the whole process of its growth and manufacture from the seed being sown till it came out of the loom."[51]

[49]*Francis Taylor Diary*, Virginia State Library.

[50]Thomas Jefferson, *Writings*, Vol. VII, p. 48.

[51]Thos. Anburey, *Travels*, Vol. II, pp. 376–378. "I now wear a good suit of cloth of my son's wool, manufactured, as well as my shirts, in Albemarle and Augusta counties," wrote W. Nelson to John Norton, in 1770. Frances N. Mason, *John Norton & Sons* (Rich., 1937), p. 122.

Anburey described conditions as they were during the Revolution when imports from England were cut off, but Johann David Schöpf, who travelled through the Piedmont some years later, found that the resumption of trade had had little effect on home industry. One of the families with whom he stopped "had flax, cotton and wool, which were woven into articles of clothing; hides, for shoes and other purposes. There was no lack of all kinds of meat, and in drinks the orchard furnished a sour cider and whiskey, and a sweetish, not unpleasant beer is made from the persimmon. . . . Tobacco pays for what they need besides . . . pays the taxes, gives the women their indispensable silks and laces, procures their foreign wares, coffee, tea, sugar, drugs and everything which is not produced at home."[52]

Home and plantation industry was often accompanied by an interchange of services. Robert Rose's joiners might be called upon to make a coffin when one of the neighbors died unexpectedly;[53] Francis Taylor might have some of his smith's work done at James Madison's blacksmith shop,[54] or send his corn to his grist mill; he might draw on Robert Taylor's kiln for bricks; he might have seventeen dozen candles made at C. Taylor's. Frequently a planter would call in a specialist to do a limited amount of work, perhaps a wheelwright to make a pair of cart wheels, or a tailor to make clothes for the family, or a shoemaker to fashion their shoes, or a cooper to set up his hogsheads.

It was isolation which gave encouragement to the hawker and peddler, that picturesque petty merchant of the American backwoods. Leading his pack horse over lonely bridlepaths and forests, fording rivers and creeks, often facing danger from robbers or even wild animals, he went from farm to farm, never scorning even the humblest home. The women of the family accorded him a hearty welcome, and it took but one glimpse at the laces and other finery which he brought forth from his pack to send them to the hiding place of their hard-earned shillings and pennies. The storekeepers of Albemarle County in 1806, feeling the com-

[52]J. D. Schöpf, *Travels in the Confederation* (1911), pp. 36, 37.
[53]*Diary of Robert Rose*, January 4, 1749.
[54]Francis Taylor, *Diary*, March 3, 1787; W. W. Scott, *History of Orange County* (1907), p. 73.

petition of the peddlers, seem to have insisted that they be prohibited from selling goods unless they could produce a license granted by a regular court, for five peddlers had their licenses duly recorded that year, and another, one Michael Duffy, had a license issued to him.[55]

Gradually, as the country became more thickly settled, professional artisans set up shop at cross roads, or at the county courthouse, or on a river at the head of navigation.[56] Every community had its blacksmith shop, where the planters brought their horses to be shod, their wagons, their farm implements, their hardware to be repaired. The blacksmith might be a former indentured worker who had completed his term of service, he might be a free Negro trained at some nearby plantation smithy. Important, also, were the shoemaker and the tailor, while here and there were tanners, coopers, wagonmakers, gunsmiths, saddlers, wheelwrights, cabinet-makers.

In Albemarle County when the planter wished his horse shod, he could take him to Durrett's smithy or John Cole's smithy; when he needed a new rim on his wagon wheels to Moore's Iron Works or Old's Forge; he could have a new pair of shoes made at Lazerous Cameron's or John Meillious'; he might dispose of his cowhides to Cornelius Schenk, John Watson or Frederick Gauder, the tanners; he could find a harness for his team at William Watson's, Daniel Maupin's, James King's or some other saddler; he might have his yarn or cotton woven into cloth by John Daniels; if he needed a carriage or a cart, Giles Rogers could make it for him. Indispensable in the up-country economy was the grist mill, which not only ground grain for the farmer's table, but for exportation of flour to Europe (Plate 32). In Albemarle County one stumbled upon these mills at every turn, on Mechum's River, Ivy Creek, the Hardware, here and there on the Rivanna, in fact on almost every stream where it was feasible to build a dam and start the wheel going.[57]

In time hamlets appeared here and there among the plantations

[55]*Order Book, Albemarle County, Virginia*, 1806, pp. 276, 374, 385, 427.

[56]Joseph Martin, *Gazetteer of Virginia* (Charlottesville, 1836), pp. 113, 114, 153, 158, etc.

[57]*Order Book*, Albemarle County, Virginia.

which in some cases developed into villages. Around the court-house, the church, the school, the tavern clustered the workshops of the artisans, their doors open for business, their picturesque signs swinging in the breeze. At Charlottesville, in the years just preceding the advent of the railway, were four tailor shops, three tan-yards, three saddlers, one tinner, two cabinet-makers, three wheelwrights, one chair-maker, two coach and gig makers, two jewelers, two shoe factories, a hatter, four smithies, a brick-yard and two book-binders. Beside this imposing array, Everettsville, with a tavern, a store, a blacksmith and a wheelwright; or Variety Mills with two mills, a store, a tan-yard and a cooperage sank into insignificance.[58] In the vicinity of Orange were W. Gibson and W. Ingram, cabinet-makers; John Smith, shoemaker; a wheel-wright, a spinning-wheel maker, besides several carpenters, tail-ors, etc.

The cabinet-makers of the Piedmont developed great skill and a degree of artistry. There were among them no Duncan Phyfes, no Benjamin Randolphs, no Thomas Afflecks, but their mastery of their chief medium, Virginia walnut[59] was complete. Their tables, chairs and secretaries were well constructed, with simple and pleasing lines and delicate and artistic inlaying. Although we know the names of some of these up-country cabinet-makers, and although an appreciable part of their work has been preserved, they have escaped even passing mention by the historian of early American culture[60] (Plate 43).

The development of an intelligent, reasonably prosperous ar-tisan class was a matter of prime importance for the Piedmont. It added an element of democracy in a society based in large measure on slavery. The local cooper or cabinet-maker was not regarded as an equal by a rich planter, was not invited to a dance at his home, but if he were called in to set up his hogsheads or repair his secretary, he took his meals at his table. The skilled artisan ranked about on a par with the small slave-holder, perhaps above the overseer, and distinctly above the poor planter who

[58]Joseph Martin, *Gazetteer of Virginia* (Charlottesville, 1836), pp. 113, 114.
[59]*Francis Taylor, Diary,* April 28, May 1, 1787.
[60]Among the cabinet-makers of Orange County were W. Gibson and W. Ingram.

owned no slaves. It was unfortunate, then, that with the advent of the railway he was thrown into competition with the northern factories and in company with his fellow craftsman in other parts of the country was slowly driven out of business. But his elimination was a matter of a half century or more. I have a vivid recollection of standing as a small boy open-eyed before the bearded gunsmith at Charlottesville as he plied his trade, or of wondering at the skill displayed by the local locksmith, or the saddler, or the founder.

Though the advance into the Piedmont thus brought about important economic changes, in certain other aspects it had little effect on the life of the people. We find that in their new homes they continued almost unchanged the sports and other amusements of the old. It is true that in the early years of settlement the sparseness of the population and the comparative crudeness of life made it impossible to imitate the sumptuousness and elegance of entertainment so noticeable in the tidewater region. Joshua Fry and Peter Jefferson could not hope to rival in their modest Albemarle homes the brilliant ball given by Richard Lee, of Lee Hall, in Westmoreland County, described by Philip Fithian.[61] But as soon as the country began to fill up, when tobacco growing had brought a degree of wealth to some of the planters, when pretentious residences began to appear atop some of the rolling hills of Orange, Culpeper or Albemarle, social life took on a great dignity and elegance. Thomas Jefferson rather prided himself upon the plainness of Piedmont society, but there is abundant evidence of gaiety and elaborate entertainment at Bremo, Farmington, Blenheim, Montpelier and even his own Monticello.

It was in 1786 that Francis Taylor noted in his diary the interesting news that Mrs. Lewis was going to open a dancing school at Colonel Alcock's, having engaged fifteen pupils.[62] The Colonel seems to have been himself a devotee of the art of dancing, for two years later we find his residence the scene of a gay and numerous company assembled to indulge in the stately minuet or the more familiar reel.[63] Perhaps the winter of 1788 was especially

[61]Philip Vickers Fithian, *Journal and Letters*, pp. 94–97.
[62]Francis Taylor, *Diary*, March 13, 1786.    [63]*Ibid.*, February 8, 1788.

festive in Orange because of the successful framing of the Constitution the previous summer, for Colonel Alcock's ball was followed two weeks later by a dance at the residence of James Madison.[64] Often, when a group of young ladies had a quilting party, they followed it with a dance which lasted far into the night.[65]

Hardly less popular than dancing was the barbecue, which was brought from the deep-water region apparently unchanged. These open-air feasts were awaited with eager anticipation by old and young alike, for they afforded an opportunity for widely separated friends to see each other. The three hundred persons gathered at Orange Court House for a barbecue in July, 1788, enjoyed a feast of beef, mutton, lamb, shoat, bacon and vegetables, served with punch, wine and grog. Colonel Taylor tells us of a barbecue at Waugh's Fort, where there was a numerous company of every rank and age, but where the fun was spoiled by a shower, which "made it disagreeable returning."[66]

The Piedmont was a paradise for the hunter, for not only were there partridges, wild pigeons and other birds in abundance, but raccoons, opossums, foxes, and even wolves and bears. Horse-racing, while perhaps not so frequent as in the tidewater counties, was very popular. The traveller Smyth tells us that "there are races established annually almost at every town and considerable place in Virginia, and frequent matches, on which large sums of money depend, the inhabitants, almost to a man, being quite devoted to the diversion of horse-racing." The Virginia horses, he thought, would make a good showing in England itself, for Virginia gentlemen spared "no pains, trouble or expense in importing the best stock and improving the excellence of the breed by proper and judicious crossing."[67] If the planter in the Piedmont tired of hunting or horse-racing, he might divert himself with cock-fights, or fishing, or play at whist or at fives. The muster, where the militia went through its invariably ragged maneuvers, the men in homespun and the officers in gorgeous uniforms, always assumed the character of a social gathering.

[64]*Ibid.*, February 25, 1788.  [65]*Ibid.*, November 11, 1786.
[66]Francis Taylor, *Diary*, August 11, 1798.
[67]J. F. D. Smyth, *A Tour in the U. S.*, Vol. I, p. 21.

St. Andrew's Day, 1737, witnessed at Old Field near Captain John Bickerton's, in Hanover, a merry scene, indeed, for there were horse races, spiced with many "whimsical and comical diversions." At one moment the crowd was entertained by a cudgelling contest after the manner of Robin Hood and Friar Tuck, the next by a wrestling match by a "number of brisk young men with a pair of silver buckles as the prize, the next by a fiddling contest, the next by the efforts of songsters who had all of them liquor enough to clear their wind pipes." Although there were feasting and drinking of healths to his Majesty, to the Governor and others, the mirth was "purely innocent" and all immorality was "discountenanced with the utmost rigor."[68]

When the Tidewater planter moved up beyond the Fall Line he often found that he had severed the old personal tie with the English merchant to whom he, and perhaps his father before him, had for decades consigned their tobacco. Micajah Perry, or John Cooper, or Peter Paggin were much more to a William Byrd, or a William Fitzhugh than mere importers and exporters; they were their representatives in England to whom they turned for every kind of service. The merchant might be called upon to place the planter's son in school, buy his clothes and remit the money for his tuition; he might have to select the planter's silver, his furniture, even the wig on his head; he might have to browse in the bookshops and pick out a book or two for the planter's library. But the Piedmont tobacco grower, instead of consigning his crop to a firm in England, usually sold it outright to a dealer in Virginia.

This dealer might be a junior partner or an agent for a British firm, or he might be an independent merchant, but in either case he no longer served to keep the planter in intimate touch with life in England. He might be a Scotchman acting as agent for a Glasgow firm, and so himself a stranger to London, or he might possibly be a native Virginian. The merchant established himself at some convenient point on deep water, at Norfolk, or Yorktown, or Dumfries, or Alexandria, or Falmouth, where he built a warehouse to receive the tobacco and flour of Virginia and Maryland

[68]*Virginia Hist. Register,* Vol. VI, pp. 99–101.

on the one hand, and British and West Indian goods on the other. In some cases he dealt chiefly with commission merchants at Richmond, Petersburg and other Fall Line towns, in others he bought directly from the planter himself. Some firms built up a series of stores on the more important rivers and highways, which served as distributing centers for their imports and as agencies for collecting tobacco and other local products.[69] Niel Jamieson, of Norfolk, sent his sloops out to Port Tobacco, Falmouth, Petersburg, Baltimore, Suffolk and elsewhere within the great network of Virginia and Maryland inland waterways, to deliver rum, sugar, molasses and other West Indian goods and bring back to his storehouses the tobacco, flour, corn, shingles and barrel staves of the back country.[70]

It was either with the local store, whether one of these chains or independent, or with the merchant at the head of deep water, that the planter had his dealings. William Allason, of Falmouth at the rapids of the Rappahannock, did a thriving business, not only in nearby Stafford County, but in Fairfax, Prince William and Frederick. We find him selling John Chinn, of Stafford, an ivory comb, a gallon of rum, some Irish linen, 2000 nails, a bushel of salt and some pepper, which Chinn paid for with two hogsheads of tobacco at Caves' warehouse. Mr. Henry Threlkeld, in Culpeper, bought handkerchiefs, powder, paper, sugar, knives, pins, rum, cloth, a trunk, a thimble, a coffeepot, a looking glass, etc., to the value of £38.13.10½.[71]

The correspondence of John Hook, a Scotch merchant, who managed two stores in Bedford County just prior to the Revolution, in connection with a firm of importers and exporters, throws much light upon the business methods of the time. His partner, David Ross, had failed to send up any sugar for nearly six months, he complained, the stills had come in very bad order, the pewter was the most brittle stuff he had ever seen, he was almost bare of linen and shoes. The success of their trade depended upon the dispatch, exactness and judgment with which the orders are filled, yet he was having difficulty in getting tobacco, for it was like

[69]*American Husbandry*, Vol. I, p. 227; Thos. Anburey, *Travels*, Vol. II, p. 318.
[70]*Niel Jamieson Papers*, Library of Congress, Vols. X, XI, XII, XIII.
[71]*Allason Ledger*, Virginia State Library, December, 1762, to October, 1763.

dragging an ox to the slaughter to get the planters to sell at the present price. In the meanwhile Ross was active with his part of the business. From Richmond he wrote that the *Melham* would land part of her cargo at Norfolk and would then proceed up the James River to Warwick in time to land the European goods and to take on the tobacco Hook was sending down. Their West Indian goods had arrived and they would need wagons for four hogsheads of rum, two hogsheads of molasses, three barrels of sugar, four cases of Jamaica rum, two boxes of candles and one bag of coffee.[72]

Despite the difficulties in transportation, the emphasis put upon home industry and the development of a group of artisans, the agricultural economy of the Piedmont at first was closely patterned upon that of the deep-water region. In both sections tobacco was the staple crop upon which the planter relied for the main part of his income, in both all save the poorest depended upon slave labor, in both wheat, Indian corn, vegetables and fruits were raised only for consumption on the plantation itself, in both soil and forests were ruthlessly sacrificed in order to save labor costs.

It had been the forests, with their wealth of wood for houses and ships and fuel which had first drawn the attention of the English to Virginia. But the planter regarded the great trees merely as an impediment to tobacco planting which must be destroyed by the easiest and quickest method. "The manner of clearing land is, by cutting a circle round the tree before the sap arises, which kills it," Anburey informs us. "They then clear the small brush-wood and cultivate the ground, leaving the tree to rot standing. . . . A large field in this state has a very singular, striking and dreadful appearance."[73] Thus enough wood to supply the royal navy for a decade was ruthlessly destroyed. Why should we expend costly labor in cutting down trees, the planters asked, when the cost of getting the logs to market is greater than the price we can get for them? Trees in this region are worth nothing; while transportation and labor are dear.

As it was with the forests, so it was with the soil. Whereas soil,

[72]*Letter Book of John Hook*, Virginia State Library.
[73]Thos. Anburey, *Travels*, Vol. II, p. 188.

rich soil, could be had for a few shillings an acre, a young Negro cost £50.[74] "The planters are not interested in the product of tobacco per acre," we are told, "all their ideas run in the proportion per working hand." To secure the highest return they must plant in the richest soil, and this, of course, was "fresh woodland where ages have formed a stratum of rich black mould. . . . This makes the planters more solicitous for new land than any other people in America." It did not pay to import fertilizers, the number of cattle was insufficient to provide manure, there was no rotation of crops since there was little demand for wheat or rye or barley. "The culture was tobacco and maize as long as they would bring enough to pay the labor," Jefferson tells us. "Then they were turned out. After four or five years' rest they would bring good corn again and in double that time perhaps good tobacco. Then they would be exhausted by a second series of tobacco and corn."[75]

N. F. Cabell, writing in 1855, gives us a vivid and perhaps a somewhat prejudiced picture of this wasteful system. Upon approaching a plantation one would "see a garden and a lot for vegetables about the homestead receiving as much of the little manure . . . as could be spared. . . . The two or three outer fields in the meantime were cropped, or grazed without mercy, until the poorer parts . . . were turned out to reclothe themselves in pine or broom sedge." The corn field "was scratched to the depth of two or three inches by a 'trowel hoe' " drawn by a single horse. "The wheat was severed from the 'field,' more frequently 'the patch,' by a reaphook, was trodden out by the feet of animals, or was beaten from the straw by flails. It was separated from the chaff by being thrown against a barn door in windy weather, or further cleansed by a handscreen. . . . The corn was rubbed from the cob by the hard hands of the laborers. . . . The axe and the hoe were still the favorite implements."[76]

Thus was begun in the Piedmont the agricultural system which had brought ruin to so much of eastern Virginia. Soil exhaustion followed hard on the heels of the frontier, and what had been virgin forests one decade might be dotted with "old fields" the

[74]*American Husbandry*, Vol. I, p. 229.
[75]Thos. Jefferson, *Writings*, Vol. IX, p. 142; Vol. V, p. 18.
[76]*William and Mary Quarterly*, Ser. I, Vol. XXVI, p. 147.

next. In one lifetime a district might rise from the pioneer stage into blooming prosperity, and then decline into comparative desolation. "The perfect cultivation, the abundance, the ducal splendor, one might almost say, of the great estates that lay along the [James River] canal in the old days have passed away in a great measure," said George W. Bagby. Here were "greatly successful farmers. . . . The land teemed with all manner of products, cereals, fruits, what not! negroes by the hundreds and the thousands. . . . A mighty change has been wrought."[77]

The work of ruin was hastened in the uplands by soil erosion. "Our country is hilly and we have been in the habit of ploughing in strait rows whether up and down hill, in oblique lines, or however they lead and our soil was all rapidly running into the rivers," wrote Jefferson.[78] As a small boy, when visiting my grandparents in Richmond, I complained of the muddy drinking water. But an uncle silenced me with the remark that I was drinking the sacred soil of my native Albemarle, and so should be the last to complain. Even as early as the Revolution the river, always tinged with red, after every freshet took on the appearance of "a torrent of blood."[79]

As soil exhaustion in eastern Virginia was an important factor in the advance into the Piedmont, so soil exhaustion and erosion in the Piedmont added its quota to the settlement of Kentucky. "A new country called Kaintuckey . . . is reckon'd the finest country in the world," wrote one observer, "affording almost all the necessities of life spontaneously."[80] Anburey was amazed at the extent of the migration over the mountains, as he looked on while one family after another went by, travelling "like the patriarchs of old," with their "horses, oxen, sheep and other cattle, as likewise all kinds of poultry. . . . I saw a family setting off . . . leaving behind them a neat habitation" that seemed all that one could wish as "the mansion of content and happiness."[81]

[77]Geo. W. Bagby, *Selections from Works*, pp. 130, 131.

[78]Thos. Jefferson, *Writings*, Vol. XVIII, p. 278.

[79]Thos. Anburey, *Travels*, Vol. II, p. 360.

[80]*Virginia Magazine of Hist. and Biog.*, Vol. XXIII, p. 413, *Letters of John Joyce*.

[81]Thos. Anburey, *Travels*, Vol. II, p. 361; see also Francis Taylor, *Diary*, August 9, 1786, October 9, 1787; and *William and Mary Quarterly*, Vol. XXVI, p. 149. "All our most independent and married men seem to be running to the west, the greater proportion to the Kentucky and Tennessee States," wrote J. Watkins in 1796. *William and Mary Quarterly*, Vol. XIV, p. 94.

This movement was an important factor in bringing about revolutionary changes in the agriculture of Virginia. The Kentucky soil was so rich that the settlers could pay the heavy cost of transporting their tobacco to market and still undersell the planters of either the tidewater region or the Piedmont. As the stream of flat boats made their way from the Kentucky creeks and rivers into the Ohio, from the Ohio into the Mississippi down to New Orleans, there to transfer their hogsheads to ships bound to Great Britain, the Virginians and Marylanders were forced to turn their attention to some other crop.

To find a new staple when the old becomes unprofitable is usually a difficult task and sometimes proves hopeless, so the Virginia and Maryland planters were fortunate in shifting from tobacco to wheat. Jefferson tells us that the culture of tobacco was fast declining at the commencement of the Revolution and the transition to wheat continued intermittently until far into the nineteenth century. Many planters first lessened their tobacco acreage and finally abandoned the leaf entirely. With the boost in prices in 1815 and 1816 from $16.00 to $35.00 a hundred pounds, many farmers were tempted to resume tobacco culture, but they repented bitterly when prices collapsed in 1817.[82] In the end tobacco retreated from all the eastern and northern counties and took refuge south of the James.

The transition to wheat was caused not only by soil exhaustion, erosion and the competition of Kentucky, but by the increased demand for breadstuffs in Europe occasioned by the French Revolution and the Napoleonic wars and by the introduction into Maryland and Virginia of gypsum.[83] The planter discovered that it was better to raise wheat at a dollar a bushel than tobacco at $8.00 a hundred pounds. It was observed that those who put their fields out in grain soon became comfortable, with well-kept barns and fences, and increased stocks of slaves and cattle, while the tobacco planter exhausted his soil, his slaves "became sickly and his stock unproductive."[84]

With the shift to wheat there came a realization that the salva-

[82]*William and Mary Quarterly*, Vol. XXVI, p. 155.    [83]*Ibid.*, p. 164.
[84]D. B. Warden, *Account of the United States* (Edin., 1819), Vol. II, p. 211 n.

tion of the planter lay in a study of scientific farming, rotation of crops to preserve the fertility of the soil, vigorous measures to halt erosion, and the general use of fertilizers. There was much conning over Jethro Tull's *The Horse-hoing Husbandry,* while at social gatherings, in the churchyard before services and at the county seat on court days, new farming methods was the ever recurring theme. Agricultural societies were organized, treatises were published, letters on fertilizer or plows or rotation of crops appeared in the gazettes. Washington, Jefferson and others distinguished in public life took the lead and prided themselves upon their ability as scientific farmers.

Jefferson's son-in-law introduced a method of plowing, which, had it been universally adopted, would have put an almost complete stop to erosion and saved thousands of tons of fertile soil from running off into the rivers. "We now plough horizontally," Jefferson wrote in 1813, "following the curvatures of the hills and hollows, on the dead level, however crooked the lines may be. Every furrow thus acts as a reservoir to receive and retain the waters, all of which go to the benefit of the growing plant, instead of running off into the streams. In a farm horizontally and deeply ploughed, scarcely an ounce of soil is now carried off. . . . The improvement of our soil from this cause the last half dozen years strikes every one with wonder."[85] It is a sad commentary upon the intelligence of the average man that the United States Government today, a century and a quarter after Jefferson wrote this letter, is spending millions of dollars in an effort to convince the farmers of the nation of the advantages of contour plowing.

But even the checking of erosion was of secondary importance in the Piedmont to the restoration of fertility to the exhausted soil by the use of fertilizers. In 1784 a Loudoun County farmer named John A. Binns while at Alexandria, then the chief port of northern Virginia, purchased "two small stones, weighing about fifteen pounds," which he took home, "pounded fine in a mortar," and sifted "through a hair sifter." A long series of experiments followed which so convinced Binns that he had found the secret of successful farming that he published a pamphlet to speed abroad

[85]Thomas Jefferson, *Writings,* Vol. XVIII, p. 278.

the gospel of gypsum,[86] "which has made my farm, from . . . being tired down, or the natural soil worn out, a rich and fruitful one." Like all innovators Binns was derided by many of his neighbors, but his own blooming fields of clover, wheat and Indian corn converted many a doubting Thomas. In the end he had the satisfaction of making his native Loudoun, "exhausted and wasted by bad husbandry" as it was, not only the richest county in Virginia, but the leader in the movement for agricultural regeneration.[87] Before the end of the second decade of the century gypsum in great quantities was pouring up the Potomac, the Rappahannock and the James for use upon the farms of the Piedmont.[88]

The larger planters, men of education and scientific interests many of them, were the first to adopt new methods and new aids, but it was difficult to persuade the poorer farmer to follow suit. "You have capital and are well able to buy such things," he said, "the benefit of which I do not deny, for I see it. But with my limited income, which with economy is barely sufficient to meet the present demands upon it, I cannot afford to purchase them." None the less, the entire region began to thrill with new hope, with the realization that the future held in store something better than poverty and ruin.

Many farmers began an intelligent system of crop rotation. "We reckon it a good distribution to divide a farm into three fields," wrote Jefferson, "putting one into wheat, half a one into maize, the other half into pease and oats and the third into clover, and to tend the fields successively in this rotation."[89] In 1811 he wrote to Charles W. Peale: "Our rotations are corn, wheat and clover; or corn, wheat, clover and clover; or wheat, corn, wheat, clover and clover; preceding the clover by plastering."[90] There was an awakening also to other phases of intelligent farming. The plowing was deeper than before, more attention was paid to stock breeding, threshing machines appeared on some of the larger

[86]Plaster of Paris.

[87]William and Mary Quarterly, Ser. II, Vol. XXVI, pp. 20–39.

[88]Virginia Board of Public Works, 1819, Part III, pp. 102, 103. "Upwards of 3000 tons of plaster, lime, etc." entered the port of Richmond in 1833. Martin's Gazetteer, p. 192.

[89]Thomas Jefferson, Writings, Vol. XIV, p. 263.

[90]Ibid., Vol. XIII, p. 79.

farms, timothy, red-top and other grasses came into use. The farmers began to husband their supplies of manure, meadows were fenced off, the best methods of combating insect pests were eagerly studied.[91]

The wheat and flour era of Piedmont history was far sounder than the tobacco era, for it did not mortgage the future for a fleeting period of prosperity. The farmer not only gained a fair living for his own family, but could take satisfaction in the thought that his fields would still yield abundantly for the families of his sons and his grandsons. As tens of thousands of barrels of flour poured down the rivers, or canals, or highways, or railways to Richmond, Petersburg, Fredericksburg and Alexandria for shipment to Europe or the West Indies, there came a sense of security, of lasting well-being, which had been lacking in former days. Richmond became one of the great flouring centers of the country. The Gallego mills, Haxall's mills and Rutherford mill, with Mayo's mill at Manchester, their brick walls and steep gabled roofs rising five or six stories above the ground, their windows white with flour dust, dominated both sides of the river.[92]

But prosperity is often a fleeting thing, especially prosperity based upon one staple commodity. Ere long the wheat growers of the Piedmont, like their tobacco-growing fathers, began to feel the competition of the vast agricultural acres of the West. The stream of wheat and flour which poured into New York with the completion of the Erie Canal became a torrent as one railway after another spanned the Appalachians and reached out to the Mississippi and the Missouri. This was followed by the disaster of the Civil War, and the Civil War in turn by Reconstruction. Much of the old wheat land reverted to woods, the Georgian residences of large planters and the humble houses of the poor farmers alike fell into disrepair, the wheels of the local mills ceased to turn, the great Richmond mills stood empty, ghostly reminders of a departed age. Virginia still raises wheat, some of her old mills

---

[91]*William and Mary Quarterly,* Vol. XXVI, p. 165.

[92]Martin's *Gazetteer,* p. 193. In 1833 Richmond exported 152,000 barrels of flour and 133,000 bushels of wheat. *Ibid.,* p. 192. The United States Commissioner of Agriculture stated in 1864 that the Gallego mills turned out 190,000 barrels of flour in one year.

built in the eighteenth century still grind, but in total output she ranks only nineteenth among the states.[93]

The weakening of the economic ties with England resulting from the advance into the Piedmont was accompanied by an equally significant weakening of religious ties. Colonial Virginia had been traditionally staunch for the Church of England. In the days when the Puritan Parliament had conquered and beheaded Charles I, Sir William Berkeley held the colony firm for Crown and Church until a Parliamentary expedition forced him to yield. The clergy, headed by the Governor himself and by the Commissary of the Bishop of London, paid from public levies, backed by the full force of law, had the field quite to themselves. Had they met fully the spiritual needs of the planters their complete ascendency would probably have continued throughout the colonial period.

But they were far from meeting all the needs of the planters. Even in the seventeenth century the Bishop of London became aware that not all was well with the Virginia Church. The parishes were too large for the ministers to serve properly, the salaries were inadequate, some of the clergy were unsuited to their calling. Commissary James Blair, backed by the full force of the Crown and the Anglican Church in England, had attempted to bring about a reform by founding a college for training ministers, by raising salaries and by enforcing ecclesiastical discipline, but his efforts in the main had been unsuccessful.

It was universally conceded that there were pious and learned ministers in Virginia, but to visitors of intense religious conviction they seemed as a whole ill-suited to their calling. "Some of them are companions of drunkards and partakers in their sottish extravagancies," it was said; they "are stupidly serene and unconcerned" for their parishioners' souls, and do not alarm them with solemn, pathetic and affectionate warnings, . . . their common conversation has little or no savour of living religion . . . instead of intense application to study or teaching their parishioners from house to house, they waste their time in idle visits, trifling conversation, slothful ease." With what Gilbert Tennent would have

[93]*Virginia Magazine of Hist. and Biog.*, Vol. XLIII, p. 106.

called "unconverted ministers" to guide them, the people took their religion less seriously than some of their northern neighbors. The devout young Philip Fithian was shocked to find that "all the lower classes of people and the servants and the slaves consider it (Sunday) as a day of pleasure and amusement. . . . The gentlemen go to church to be sure, but they make that itself a matter of convenience, and account the church a useful weekly resort to do business."[94]

With the westward movement the difficulties of the clergy multiplied. If in the deep-water region parishes sometimes extended twenty miles or more along the river banks, in the Piedmont they stretched out over the semi-wilderness for hundreds of square miles. If the minister of Gloucester or James City, with his many wealthy parishioners found his income inadequate and his duties exacting, the frontier parson could be thankful for the barest living. And it required the burning ardor of the religious zealot to carry the Gospel to the scattered plantations and farms of the uplands, and there were few among the Anglican clergy in Virginia either qualified for the task or willing to undertake it.

That there were notable exceptions the careers of such men as Robert Rose and Anthony Gavin amply testify. "Hearing that a frontier parish was vacant and that the people of the mountains had never seen a clergyman since they settled there," Gavin wrote the Bishop of London in 1738, "I desired the governor's consent to leave an easy parish for this I do now serve. I have three churches, twenty-three and twenty-four miles from the glebe, in which I officiate every third Sunday, and besides these three I have seven places of service up in the mountains, where the clerks read prayers, four clerks in seven places. I go twice a year to preach in twelve places, which I reckon better than 400 miles backward and forward and ford nineteen times the North and South Rivers."[95]

Mr. Gavin's duties were no more exhausting than those of Robert Rose. We may follow this good man on one of his periodic tours to minister to his widely scattered parishioners in the pages

[94]Philip Vickers Fithian, *Journal and Letters*, p. 202.
[95]W. S. Perry, *Historical Collections*, etc., Vol. I, p. 360.

of his *Diary*. Starting off on a crisp March day from his Tye River plantation, we find him crossing the James, losing his way in the forest and arriving at night at the home of one Glover on Slate River, preaching on two successive days at private residences, coming up the James River to Albemarle Court House to deliver another sermon, going at night to christen Captain Caball's grandchildren and, after five days of constant riding, returning to Tye River.[96] Again we find him jotting down: "Very cold. Rode to Captain William Allen's on Hunt Creek. Preached on John. Then crossed Slate River and lodged with Mr. Gideon Marr.—Mr. Marr conveyed us along a ridge marked for a road to John Goodman's whose son I christened,—lost ourselves and went to one Blackely's quarter . . . where I christened another child—got to Captain Caball's at night. Got home before 3 P.M. after a journey of about 130 miles in discharge of my duty as minister of St. Anne's parish in Albemarle."[97]

Unfortunately there were few among the clergy of the stamp of Gavin and Rose, and thousands were left without the services of any minister at all, while others were forced to content themselves with but one or two sermons a year. Even when a regular clergyman became available with the gradual filling up of the region, he was apt to perform his duties in a way so perfunctory as to have little appeal to his parishioners, especially persons of the poorer class. Altogether the Anglican Church was ill prepared to hold the Piedmont against the impending attacks of the militant zealots of the Great Awakening.

Governor Gooch and Commissary Blair would not have been so cordial in their welcome to George Whitefield, when he visited Williamsburg in 1739,[98] had they realized that he was the forerunner of a movement which was to deliver large parts of Virginia into the hands of the dissenters. His sermon preached from the text, "What think ye of Christ," attracted a "numerous congregation," and won "the admiration and applause of most of his hearers." The interest aroused by this visit may account for the fact that soon afterward a small group of men in Hanover County

[96]*Diary of Robert Rose*, March 23 to 28, 1749.
[97]*Ibid.*, December 26 to 28, 1748.　　[98]*Virginia Gazette*, December 21, 1739.

began to hold private meetings for the reading of some of White-field's sermons, together with Luther's *Commentary on Galatians* and *Boston's Fourfold State*.[99]

When this movement gained such headway as to cause pew after pew in the parish church to remain vacant at Sunday services, several of the leaders were hauled before the justices and fined. Against this treatment they appealed to the English Act of Toleration, and so in due time were summoned to Williamsburg to appear before the Council of State and declare their creed. This caused them no little perplexity, as they "knew but little of any denomination of dissenters, except Quakers," with whom they were not in full harmony. Standing hesitant before the Governor and his Councillors in the stately Council chamber, they recollected that "Luther was a noted reformer" and so declared themselves Lutherans. This shielded them from prosecution as disturbers of the peace,[100] and they returned to Hanover to continue their meetings, to establish Reading Houses and to spread their doctrines.

Such was the situation when word came that the Reverend William Robinson, a New Light Presbyterian, a former student at the Neshaminy Log College and a man of piety, zeal and devotion, was travelling through Amelia and Lunenburg counties and preaching there with great success. So they sent messengers to overtake him with an urgent invitation to come to Hanover. Robinson stayed only four days, but his forceful preaching produced a profound effect. Some "who had been hungering for the word before were lost in agreeable surprise" and publicly declared their "transports," others who had come out of curiosity were convinced of their ignorance of religion and anxiously inquired what they should do to be saved.[101] Robinson's visit to Hanover brought the dissenting group into the Presbyterian fold, for when they found that the eloquent preacher was of that denomination they attached themselves to the Presbytery of New Castle.

After Robinson's departure Hanover was visited by a succession of Log College missionaries—John Blair, John Roan, Gilbert Ten-

---

[99]W. H. Foote, *Sketches of Virginia* (Phila., 1850), pp. 121, 122.
[100]*Ibid.*, p. 124.          [101]*Ibid.*, p. 128.

nent, Samuel Finley, William Tennent and Samuel Blair—followed in 1745 by George Whitefield.[102] After listening to this array of brilliant men, the good people of the region must have found the sermons of the Reverend Patrick Henry, their Anglican minister, dull and uninspiring. At all events Mr. Henry, tired of speaking to empty pews, complained bitterly to Commissary Dawson of the itinerants and their methods. "They thunder out mawful words and new coined phrases," he wrote, ". . . calling the old people gray-headed Devils, and all promiscuously damned, whose (souls) are in hell though they are alive on earth and imps of hellfire. . . . All the while the preacher exalts his voice, puts himself into a violent agitation, stamping and beating his desk unmercifully, till the weaker part of his hearers being scared cry out, fall down and work like people in convulsive fits to the amazement of the spectators . . . and these things are extoll'd by the preachers as the mighty power of God's grace in their hearts, and they . . . are carress'd and commended as the only penitent souls who come to Christ, whilst they who don't are often condemn'd by the lump as hardened wretches."[103]

On one occasion Dawson visited Hanover and spent an entire evening talking with Parson Henry about "the new religion which hath of late got footing in this county." We may imagine that they reiterated their indignation at the unjust reflections cast by the New Lights upon the Anglican clergy, ridiculed the excesses of the itinerant preachers and considered the question of appealing to the Governor and Council to enforce the laws against them.[104] But one wonders whether they had a clear understanding of the forces which were undermining the established church in the Piedmont—the vast distances, the poor roads, the comparative poverty of the people, the unwillingness of the clergy to make sacrifices for religion's sake.

When William Robinson had completed his four days' visit to Hanover and was taking affectionate leave of his new friends, he discovered that they had collected a considerable sum of money which they had hidden in his saddle bags. The good man agreed

[102]W. M. Gewehr, *The Great Awakening in Virginia*, pp. 52–58.
[103]*Dawson Papers*, Library of Congress, Henry to Dawson, February, 1745.
[104]*Ibid.*, Rev. Patrick Henry to Dawson, 1747.

to take it on condition that it should be used, not for his personal needs, but to aid in the education of a pious youth who was studying for the ministry. "It may be that by your liberality you are preparing a minister for yourselves," he told them.[105] Five years later on a Sunday a group of Presbyterians stood before their Hanover meeting-house in troubled silence, reading a proclamation posted there requiring the magistrates to suppress all preaching by itinerant ministers. But before a week had passed their grief had turned to joy with the unexpected news that young Samuel Davies had come to Virginia as their resident minister and had already qualified himself according to law.[106] The youth whom their money had helped to educate was to be the great Presbyterian apostle of the Piedmont.

It seemed suicidal for Davies to assume this exacting post, for he was very ill with tuberculosis, but he preferred "to expire under the fatigues of duty rather than in voluntary negligence." As it turned out, these very fatigues undoubtedly prolonged his life, for he was forced to spend a large part of his time in the saddle, breathing the pure air of the Virginia forests. From his residence about ten miles north of Richmond he had to ride, not only to his three meeting-houses in Hanover, but to Henrico on the south, New Kent to the east, northward to minister to ten or twelve families in Caroline, west into Goochland and Louisa, and across the James River into far-off Cumberland.[107] In the summer of 1757 he rode nearly five hundred miles and preached forty sermons in the space of two months.[108] "My heart at times is set upon nothing more than to snatch the brands out of the burning . . . and hence it is I consume my strength and life in such great fatigues."[109]

Nor was his zeal wasted, for he succeeded in bringing hundreds into the fold of the Presbyterian Church. It is said that during his ministry "a mother might often be seen rocking her infant in a cradle, sewing some garment for her husband and learning her catechism at the same time. A girl employed in spinning would

[105]W. H. Foote, *Sketches of Virginia*, p. 129.
[106]*Ibid.*, pp. 157, 162.          [107]*Ibid.*, p. 183.
[108]W. M. Gewehr, *The Great Awakening in Virginia*, p. 93.
[109]W. F. Foote, *Sketches of Virginia*, p. 205.

place her book of questions at the head of the wheel, and catching a glance at it as she ran up her yarn on the spindle, would thus practice for public catechising." Plow-boys, reclining under an old oak, while their horses were feeding at mid-day, took out their book to learn the weekly lesson.[110]

In 1759 the Synod of New York and Philadelphia made the mistake of directing Davies to lay down his pastoral work in order to assume the Presidency of the College of New Jersey. The change from the outdoor life in Virginia to the confining work at Princeton proved fatal to his health, and he died in less than two years after leaving Hanover.[111] Had he been permitted to continue in central Virginia, he might have converted that region into a Presbyterian stronghold. As it was, he did not succeed in building up a group strong enough to challenge the dominance of the established church. The significance of his career lies in the fact that he drove an entering wedge into the old ecclesiastical order, and thus created a breach into which other denominations were quick to rush. The Presbyterian invasion of the Piedmont was to be followed by the more formidable invasions of the Baptists and the Methodists.

If the Anglican ministers were critical of the preaching of Whitefield and Robinson and Davies, they were infinitely more disgusted with the Baptists. The Presbyterian New Lights, despite their insistence upon religious experience and their objection to formalism in worship, were men of classical education and seemly deportment, but the Baptist missionaries were often ignorant, uneducated persons who had formerly been tinkers, shoemakers, or carpenters.[112] "The Baptist preachers were without learning, without patronage, generally very poor, very plain in their dress, unrefined in their manners and awkward in their address," testifies R. B. Semple, the Baptist historian.[113]

Their emotional harangues, in which the imminence of eternal

---

[110]Ibid., p. 294.          [111]Ibid., p. 303.

[112]William Murphy, one of the most prominent Baptist preachers in Virginia, was declared "so ignorant that he cannot read plain or write his name." Dawson MSS., September 8, 1759.

[113]R. B. Semple, A History of the Rise and Progress of the Baptists in Virginia (1810), p. 26.

damnation was held vividly before the imaginations of the listeners, often aroused frenzies of despair or of exaltation. Compared with a Baptist meeting the Presbyterian revivals in Hanover, to which the Reverend Patrick Henry objected so strongly, were models of decorum. Daniel Fristoe tells us that at one gathering he saw "multitudes, some roaring on the ground, some wringing their hands, some in extacies, some praying, some weeping, and others so outrageous cursing and swearing that it was thought that they were really possessed of the devil."[114] "The manner of conducting the general revival was somewhat extraordinary," admits Semple. "It was not unusual to have a large proportion of a congregation prostrate on the floor, and in some instances they have lost the use of their limbs, . . . screams, cries, groans, songs, shouts and hozannas, notes of grief and notes of joy all heard at the same time." If several ministers were present they all would "exercise their gifts at the same time in different parts of the congregation, some in exhortation, some in praying for the distressed, some in argument with opposers."[115]

The Presbyterian preachers had escaped persecution under the English Act of Toleration, but the Baptists refused to recognize the right of civil authorities to regulate their preaching or their places of worship. Since, then, they would not comply with the act, they were subjected to serious persecution and their preachers were repeatedly imprisoned. When William Webber was preaching in Goochland and "a magistrate pushed up and drew back his club with design to knock Webber down, some person behind caught the club." But being "backed by two sheriffs, the parson and a posse," he seized not only Webber, but three other preachers who were with him and lodged them in jail. Ignoring the swarms of fleas, they borrowed a candle of the jailor and had a brief service of song and prayer. For many days they preached regularly to crowds who flocked to the prison to hear them; "their words seeming to have double weight when coming from the jail," until the authorities were in the end glad to get rid of them.[116]

The emotional preaching of the Baptists, the plainness of their

[114]W. M. Gewehr, *The Great Awakening in Virginia*, p. 110 n.
[115]R. B. Semple, *A History of the Rise and Progress of the Baptists in Virginia*, p. 37.
[116]*Ibid.*, pp. 17–19. See *The Life of the Reverend Jas. Ireland* (Winchester, Virginia, 1819), pp. 158–181.

ministers, the persecutions to which they were subjected by magistrates and the Anglican clergy all gave them a strong appeal to the lower classes, persons of little property and less education. William Frisloe says that most of them were "of the mediocrity or poorer sort among the people," reputed to be "an ignorant, illiterate set."[117] Within this class the Baptist doctrines, in the decade preceding the Revolution, spread with great rapidity. The Regular Baptists, entering Berkeley county in 1743, gradually spread over northern Virginia, until in 1770 they had ten churches scattered over seven counties. The Separate Baptists, invading the colony from North Carolina, swept over county after county like a conquering host. In 1770 they had only ten churches in Virginia, but in 1771 the number had mounted to fourteen, and in 1774 to no less than fifty-four.[118]

Whereas the Baptists stormed over the battlements of the Anglican Church, the Methodists entered the citadel in a Trojan horse. One of the most interesting men in the history of colonial Virginia was the Reverend Devereux Jarratt. The son of a New Kent artisan, trained as a plow-boy and carpenter, self-educated, he received ordination from the Bishop of London and became a power in the Virginia Church. Although throughout his life a staunch Anglican, he adopted many of the principles and methods of preaching and teaching of the New Lights. Warning his congregations of their condition of sin, explaining the curse under which mankind labored and their inability to evade the strokes of divine justice, he inaugurated a religious revival which affected all southern Virginia and parts of North Carolina. The rotund figure and smiling face of this evangelical Anglican minister were a common sight from Franklin to Caroline and from Bedford to Surry. When he was denied the pulpit of some fellow clergyman, or when the church building was too small to hold the crowds who flocked to hear him, he preached in the open air "under trees, arbors or booths."[119]

The good man was elated at his success. To see my congrega-

---

[117]Quoted by Gewehr from Wm. Frisloe's *History of the Ketocton Baptist Association*, pp. 64, 148.

[118]R. B. Semple, *A History of the Rise and Progress of the Baptists in Virginia*, pp. 90, 91, 141, 174, 208, 219, 232, 233, 260, etc.

[119]*Life of Devereux Jarratt*, p. 96.

tions "listening to the word preached with attention, still as night, eagerly drinking in the balmy blessings of the gospel, dispensed by . . . their pastor, their teacher, their guide, their father . . . was a little heaven upon earth," he wrote. When this "little heaven" was threatened by the Baptists in 1769 and 1770, he defended it vigorously and on the whole successfully.[120] But the Methodists caught him off guard. When they told him that they were "true members of the Church of England, that their design was to build up not divide the Church," he gave them his support and co-operated with them in organizing religious societies. In this way Methodist principles were instilled throughout the entire region over which Jarratt had labored so hard to revive and revitalize the established church, and when, in 1784, the Methodists broke off to form their own organization, they took with them the mass of his followers. "Instead of crowded churches" I have now only a handful, and my former friends "look so strange at me that I can take no satisfaction in the company of any," he wrote sadly.[121]

Thus the advance into the Piedmont tended to weaken one more important tie with England. So long as the people revered the Anglican Church and looked across the Atlantic for their supply of ministers and for guidance in religious matters, the mother country still retained a strong hold upon the life and thoughts and the affection of the colonists. But when Presbyterians, Baptists and Methodists rushed in, attacking the Anglican ministers and drawing off thousands from the Church, a new spirit of independence and hostility developed. The rôle of the persecutor is always unlovely, and in Virginia as in New England, the clergy who assumed it weakened themselves and the church they represented. The Baptist enthusiast, as he preached through the bars of his prison to the crowds gathered under his window, since he was an earnest advocate of religious independence, found himself allied with the prophets of political independence.

When Jefferson espoused their cause by including the separation of Church and State and complete religious freedom in his great reform program during the Revolution, they rallied behind

120*Ibid.*, p. 105.          121*Ibid.*, pp. 123, 124.

him with enthusiasm. The Scotch-Irish and the German dissenters of the Shenandoah Valley would perhaps have been content with toleration and freedom from taxation for the support of the Episcopal clergy, but the Baptists would have no half-way measures. In the end, however, Baptists, Presbyterians, and Methodists alike united to vote for Jefferson's bill for religious freedom in 1785, which decreed that "no man shall be compelled to frequent or support any religious worship, place or ministry whatsoever . . . but all men shall be free to profess, and by argument to maintain, their opinions in matters of religion."[122]

It would be unsafe to assume that without the advance into the Piedmont there would have been no Great Awakening in Virginia. The dissenters, especially the Baptists, invaded the older counties as well as the new, establishing their congregations almost in the shadow of the time-honored churches of Gloucester, Middlesex, Northumberland or Essex. But it was the newer regions, beyond the Fall Line, where tradition was less respected, where the spirit of independence was more pronounced, where the Anglican system was less effective and the Anglican ministers too few in number to meet the needs of the people, that they made their greatest inroads. The same isolation which weakened the English merchants' control over the economic life of the Piedmont planter weakened the Bishop of London's control over his religious life.

It weakened also the control of King and Parliament. "The farther removed from Williamsburg the less the dependence upon the King," says Foote, "the more embosomed in the mountains, the more resolutely did the pioneers contend against authority that was not warranted by necessity and the plainest dictates of law. Above Tidewater the people, simple in their habits, plain in manners and accustomed to a roving and independent life, questioned every demand made upon their property, their persons or their enjoyments. Their children were republicans; in England they would have been styled rebels."[123]

122W. W. Hening, *Statutes at Large*, Vol. XII, p. 84.
123William H. Foote, *Sketches of Virginia*, p. 149.

## Chapter V

## TUCKAHOE AND COHEE

IT WAS in 1716 that Governor Alexander Spotswood, with a gay company of gentlemen, accompanied by a dozen rangers and four Indians, scaled the Blue Ridge mountains at Swift Run Gap, between High Top and Saddle Back, and looked out over the smiling Valley of Virginia. Descending the western slope he pressed on to the South Fork of the Shenandoah River, where he "took possession for King George the First of England." Then the company "drank the King's health in champagne and fired a volley, the Princess' health in Burgundy and fired a volley and all the rest of the royal family in claret and a volley." Such was the expedition of discovery by the famous Knights of the Golden Horseshoe.

Although it was not immediately followed by the settlement of the Valley, it presaged the coming of a mighty host, the westward sweep of the Tuckahoes, or people of eastern Virginia. Spotswood was a scout, as it were, for the civilization which had grown up on the banks of the James, the York, the Rappahannock and the Potomac, with its wealthy planters, owning scores of slaves, wide tobacco fields, stately residences, extensive libraries and beautiful gardens; its multitude of small farmers, some with a few slaves, some with none; its established church, to which the vast majority of the people were still loyal; its wasteful agriculture which economized in labor costs at the expense of the soil. Who could tell how far westward this civilization would move? Already it was invading the Piedmont, creeping up the fertile river valleys above the Fall Line, and the day was not distant when it would reach to the foothills of the Blue Ridge. Would it sweep over the mountain passes and fix itself on the banks of the Shenandoah? Would it go still farther, out to the Ohio region and beyond to the vast plains of the Mississippi Valley? Would

there be a new race of Byrds and Carters and Burwells and Beverleys in what is now Missouri or Minnesota or Colorado; was the
civilization which then centered around Williamsburg to inherit
the lion's share of the American continent?

Before many decades had passed it became apparent that there
were various impediments in the path of the Tuckahoes which
would certainly slow up their westward march and threatened
to bring it to a complete halt. Slavery, which was the foundation
of their system, required fertile soil, suitable for the production of
staple crops. It could not be used to the best advantage for intensive farming with diversified crops; it could not get a foothold
in mountainous territory. Moreover, it was at a great disadvantage
wherever transportation was difficult and freight rates high, since
it was essential for the slaveholder to get his money crop to
market and his imported manufactured goods back to his plantation. The Blue Ridge offered no serious barrier to the Piedmont
planter in moving his family and slaves to the Valley of Virginia,
but it proved a very real obstacle to his prosperity when once he
had settled there, for it was a costly matter to send tobacco hogsheads over the passes in wagons, while to roll them was almost
impossible.

Piedmont Virginia was linked to the tidewater by the upper
reaches of the great rivers, all of them flowing in a southwesterly
direction. But the Valley, shut in on the one side by the Blue
Ridge and on the other by the Alleghanies, shed its waters to the
north and the south. A farmer in Rockingham or Page who
wished to avail himself of water transportation, would have to
ship his produce down the shallow North or South Forks into
the Shenandoah to Harper's Ferry, thence by the upper Potomac
past a series of formidable falls. By the time he had got his barrels
of flour or his hogsheads of tobacco on board a merchant vessel
at Georgetown, his profit had been whittled down to nothing.
The case of a planter in Botetourt or Rockbridge in the upper
Valley was almost as bad, for he had to trust his goods to the
turbulent waters of the James as they burst through the Blue
Ridge and hastened on to Lynchburg and Richmond.

On the other hand, the richness of the Valley soil was a standing invitation to the planters to bring their slaves, lay off their plantations and begin the cultivation of tobacco or wheat. George Washington, who had devoted so many of his early days to defending this region from the Indians and knew every foot of it from Natural Bridge to the Potomac, spoke of it as the "Garden of America."[1] The prevailing soil, a stiff clay loam, durable and fertile, is admirably suited to all kinds of grain. The settlers were not long in recognizing four distinct types of land—the natural bluegrass land, suited for stock raising and dairying; the heavy clay lands which could with proper care yield rich harvests of corn and wheat; the lighter slaty soil, famous for its heavy yields of wheat; the poorer ridge lands, suitable for sheep raising.[2]

The temptation to settle in the Valley was all the greater in that eastern Virginia planters owned large parts of it. William Beverley had an enormous tract, known as Beverley Manor, on the headwaters of the South Fork of the Shenandoah; Carter Burwell, Robert Burwell, Carter Page, Robert C. Nicholas and others held thousands of acres in the lower Valley through grants to Robert Carter. Moreover, the wearing out of the soil in eastern Virginia and even in the Piedmont was a constant impetus for movement further westward. The march of the Tuckahoes, by the end of the third decade of the eighteenth century, was approaching the foot of the Blue Ridge; it was inevitable that it would flow into the fertile woods and prairies of the Shenandoah.

The small farmers led the way. Many a poor man, when he had used up his last acre of "fresh" soil, when his family was growing and the returns from his old fields diminishing, began to have dreams of better things farther west. So when the agent of William Beverley or Lord Fairfax or Joist Hite, or John and Isaac Van Meter came to him with an offer of six hundred acres as a freehold or perhaps as a tenancy on very favorable terms, he pulled up stakes and began his trek over the mountains. Piling his possessions in the farm wagon—his hoes, axes, and

[1]Letter to Sir John Sinclair, 1796, *The Writings of Washington*, Jared Sparks, Vol. XII, p. 325.

[2]Ted. Hotchkiss, *Virginia—A Geographical and Political Summary* (Rich., 1876), pp. 32, 33.

other farm implements, his clothing, a few pieces of furniture, his pewter plates and mugs, his pots, pestle, grinding stone—he started off, with his wife holding the reins while he strode beside the creaking vehicle. Slow work it was as they drove through the mud or the deep ruts of the Piedmont road, or made the laborious ascent of Ashby Gap, or Swift Run Gap, or Snicker's Gap. It was with elation that they halted on the summit of the Ridge and looked down upon the promised land with its great forests, its smiling open spaces, its winding streams glittering in the sunlight and far away to the west the hazy ranges of the Alleghanies.

Across the Potomac in Maryland the right flank of the advancing planters—wealthy slaveholders and poor farmers alike—was pushing northwest from Montgomery and west from Baltimore County into Frederick. Some of the large proprietors, reserving a portion of their manors for their own use, sent overseers to establish quarters or perhaps themselves migrated to the west. Benjamin Tasker, at Tasker's Chance; Daniel Carroll at Carroll's Delight; Governor Thomas Johnson, on his Monocacy plantation three miles from Frederick; Governor Thomas Sim Lee, at his splendid estate, Forest of Needwood, and others laid out large fields of tobacco, or wheat, built stately residences, and duplicated the life and culture of the Maryland tidewater. Accompanying them, or in many cases preceding them, were the thousands of small planters, many owning no slaves, to buy or lease a few hundred acres from a Carroll or a Dulaney and begin life anew in the fertile plains of Frederick or Washington.[3]

Far to the south, also, the planters, rich and poor alike, were advancing their settlements into the upper Roanoke Valley, in Charlotte, Mecklenburg and Halifax Counties in Virginia, and in Person, Caswell and Rockingham Counties across the border in North Carolina. Here the soil was well suited for staple crops and here the Dan, the Staunton and other tributaries of the Roanoke made it possible to get heavy products to market. There were few very large slaveholders in this region in the eighteenth century, but already Governor Alexander Martin, Valentine

[3]J. T. Scharf, *History of Western Maryland*, Vol. II, p. 981.

Allen, Joshua Coffen and others had extensive plantations cultivated in the manner of the eastern planters. By 1790 there were several thousand slaveowners in western North Carolina, most of them possessing from one to five slaves, a fair proportion from five to twenty, and a mere handful over twenty.[4]

Thus the hosts of tidewater civilization, the civilization which had developed on the shores of Chesapeake Bay and Albemarle Sound and on the banks of the rivers which flowed into them, the civilization of tobacco and wheat planters, of slaveholders, big and small, of poor whites owning no slaves, the civilization of Englishmen who had been changed into plantation Americans by the region in which they lived, were pushing on in a line three hundred miles long from the borders of Pennsylvania to Greensboro or Winston-Salem. The flanks of this line in Maryland and North Carolina were still in the Piedmont region, east of the mountain barrier, but in Virginia it had spread to the foot of the Blue Ridge and now was beginning to pass over into the Valley of Virginia.

At this point the easterners came into contact with another stream of settlers, coming chiefly from Pennsylvania, but partly directly from Europe through Pennsylvania and Maryland. Some of these people, crossing the Mason and Dixon's Line into Frederick County, Maryland, stopped there to make their homes; others went on into the Shenandoah, swarming over Berkeley, Frederick, Rockingham, Augusta, Rockbridge, Botetourt and other counties; still others continued southward, driving their wagons or their pack horses over the Blue Ridge and settling in southwest Virginia or western North Carolina. It was the march of the Cohees—of Germans, Scotch-Irish, Irish, Swiss, Quakers— who thrust themselves directly athwart the line of advance of the easterners and threatened to bring them to a dead halt.

There is no more instructive chapter in the history of American civilization than the clash of civilizations in the backwoods of Maryland and North Carolina and in the beautiful Valley of Virginia. Would slavery win over the thrifty German, the pious Scotch Presbyterian and the gentle Quaker and convert them

[4] U. S. Bureau of the Census, North Carolina, 1790.

into plantation owners who imitated the farming methods, the culture, the mode of life of a Dulaney or a Burwell or a Berkeley? Or would the newcomers adhere to their own economy, preferring the intensive agriculture of the Palatinate or of Ulster to the wasteful methods of the Tuckahoes? Would the Germans continue to speak their native tongue, would they build their houses and their barns in the manner of their ancestors, would they cling to their Volkskunst, would they prefer their own labor and the labor of their sons to that of Negro slaves? Would the Scotch-Irish convert the upper Valley into a new Ulster with their Presbyterian churches, their Latin schools, their bagpipes and their distinctive accent? The answers to these questions were of vital importance to the region itself, and to all America. Had the Cohees halted slave civilization in the upper South, had they confined it permanently to the region east of the Blue Ridge, the history of the United States would have been very different, there might have been no war between the States.

The Germans and Swiss who settled in Maryland, Virginia and North Carolina were, for the most part, merely the continuation of the great migration from the Palatinate and Switzerland to Pennsylvania. They were hard working, peaceable, pious peasants and artisans, fleeing from religious persecution, the ravages of war and political oppression. Arriving in Philadelphia, they found that the best lands of southeastern Pennsylvania had already been appropriated, while settlement in the northwest beyond the Blue Mountains was blocked by the Indians. Many laid out little farms on the least fertile soil, others worked for wages until they had accumulated enough capital for a new start. Then they pulled up stakes and set off for the southwest, where fertile land was cheap, and where the large proprietors were offering every inducement to settlers.

We gain a vivid impression of the difficulties encountered by these pioneers in travelling scores, perhaps hundreds, of miles through the wilderness to take possession of their lands, from an account of the journey of a group of Moravian brethren from Pennsylvania to North Carolina. A picturesque sight they made with their straight, dark coats without lapels, their broad-brimmed, low-crowned hats, their knee-buckled trousers and round-toed shoes, their lumbering Conestoga wagon with its canvas cover and its load of tools, farm implements and other supplies.[5] The roads, where there were roads, were execrable, provisions for the men and oats and hay for the horses had to be taken along with them, rivers had to be forded. One night it rained so hard that the water ran through their tent and they were all soaked. The next morning the sun came out, but it shone down on roads so muddy that in ascending hills the horses slipped and fell to their knees, and half the load had to be taken off before any progress could be made. On approaching the James River the decline became so steep that the brothers locked the wheels and held back with all their might to avoid smashing into "stump and stone."[6]

In Maryland the Germans settled on both sides of the South Mountains, a continuation of the Blue Ridge, in central and western Frederick County and in Washington County. With their keen scent for good soil they picked out fertile spots in the woods, made their clearings, built their cabins and barns and planted fields of wheat and corn. Some were Lutherans, others Reformed, still others Mennonites, while here and there were groups of Dunkards, conspicuous for their plain costume and deep piety. The Moravians established themselves at Grace-ham, about twelve miles north of the town of Frederick, where they created a "woodland sanctuary" with its *Gemeinhaus,* its communal life, its quaint costumes, its emphasis upon peace and brotherhood.[7]

If one examines the names of the settlers in western Maryland, it becomes apparent that the region was by no means entirely German, for many, perhaps a majority, are clearly English. But the presence of Dietrich, Diffendorfer, Fechtig, Geiger, Ott, Leider, Schroder and similar names indicates that German culture had a very strong hold on the region. If we had stepped inside

[5]Jacob J. Sessler, *Communal Pietism Among Early American Moravians,* pp. 97–99.
[6]Adelaide L. Fries, *Records of the Moravians of North Carolina,* I, pp. 77–81.
[7]*Transactions of the Moravian Hist. Soc.,* IX, 1913.

one of the little log churches, we would have heard sermons delivered in German; if we visited a school we would have listened to the teacher expound the lessons in German; if we entered one of the stores of Hagerstown or Frederick the merchant would have quoted his prices in German; if we had stopped a passer-by on the street to make an inquiry, the reply would probably have been made, if not in German, in broken English; if we had called for a newspaper we might have got the *Deutsche Washington Correspondent*. When J. F. D. Smyth, the English traveller, was arrested and brought before the Frederick Committee of Safety during the Revolution, he could hardly restrain his disgust when one of them asked: "Howsh can you shtand sho shtyff for King Shorsh akainsht dish koontery?"[8]

In the Valley of Virginia large landholders were offering great inducements to settlers. In 1732 Jorst Hite brought sixteen families from Pennsylvania to the Opequon, and other groups followed—Lutherans, Mennonites, Reformed, Dunkards. They laid out their farms and built their cabins and barns on both sides of the Massanutten Mountains in Page, Shenandoah, Rockingham and Warren, gained a strong foothold in Frederick and Augusta, and spread out into parts of Clarke, Berkeley and Jefferson. With them came so many skilled artisans, who set up their tanneries, potteries, wagon factories, gunsmith shops, blacksmith shops, shoe shops, that Winchester, Strasburg, Woodstock, and Stephensburg were·practically German towns. Even Charlestown and Staunton had their quota of Germans.

It was this predominance of the Germans in the towns which gave the impression to travellers that all the Valley, from Augusta to the Potomac, was overwhelmingly German. "Our next stopping place was Woodstock," wrote Charles Hodge in 1816, when he and Doctor Archibald Alexander visited the Valley. "This being their court-day the whole place was filled with the oddest-looking, old-fashioned men and women I ever saw. The Doctor enjoyed the scene very much and was constantly telling me not to laugh, while his own mouth was wide open."[9] La Rochefoucauld

[8] J. F. D. Smyth, *A Tour in the United States,* II, p. 274.
[9] A. A. Hodge, *Life of Charles Hodge,* p. 45.

Liancourt gained a similar impression and wrote that both Strasburg and Woodstock were entirely peopled with Germans or the sons of Germans.[10] Yet, if we may judge from the non-German congregations in the Valley, other nationalities were in the majority in every county save Shenandoah and perhaps Rockingham.

Visitors to the Valley half a century before Hodge's day saw hundreds of the people who seemed so "odd-looking" to him, travelling through on their way to take up lands in North Carolina. In the Conestoga wagon was their bedding, the decorated dower chest, the farm implements, perhaps the plates for a stove; the able-bodied men on foot driving before them a few cattle, sheep and hogs. Picking out fertile spots in the Carolina Piedmont, along the banks of the Cape Fear River in Alamance and Guilford, or of the Yadkin in Davidson, Rowan and Stanley, or of the Catawba in the shadow of the Blue Ridge, they purchased small tracts from Lord Granville or secured patents from the government and settled down to build their cabins and barns and to plant wheat and corn.

In Forsyth and Davidson the Moravians got title to 100,000 acres which they called *der Wachen* or Wachovia. Here they made several settlements—Bethabara, or House of Passage, Bethania, Salem—erected churches, brothers' houses, sisters' houses, mills, waterworks; established their- communal economy, developed the various German crafts, indulged in their distinctive religious exercises enlivened by singing and the music of trumpets and organs. It was not only a bit of Germany which these brethren established in the woods of western North Carolina, but a distinctive type of German civilization, the civilization of the Unitas Fratrum. But the Germans of North Carolina, unlike those of western Maryland and the Valley of Virginia, seem to have been greatly outnumbered by the English, and even the Scotch and Irish. The census of 1790 lists 4960 Germans in the Salisbury District, out of a total population of 58,425, and but 1884 Germans in the Morgan District in a population of 30,687.

Had we stopped at the farm of a Maryland, Virginia or North

[10]*Voyages*, V, pp. 65, 66.

Carolina German he would probably have told us that his ancestors and the ancestors of his neighbors came from Pennsylvania. In the fireplace we would see an iron plate with the stamp of the Reading Furnace across its face; on the table the old German Bible, the names of Pennsylvania ancestors written in the blank pages; our host might address us in the distinctive "Pennsylvania Dutch" dialect; in the corner might be a dower chest ornamented with tulips made in Dauphin County by Johann Rank or John Selzer.[11] But there were some, tempted by the agents of William Byrd II and other large landowners, who came directly from Germany or Switzerland, using Philadelphia as no more than a landing-place, or coming in through one of the Southern ports. In the years from 1752 to 1755 over a thousand arrived at Annapolis alone.[12]

The Germans brought with them, not the civilization of Germany, but the civilization of German Pennsylvania. The society which had developed in the region west and northwest of Philadelphia in the fertile valleys of the Lehigh, the Schuylkill and the lower Susquehanna, was a composite of South German, the Rhine Palatinate and Swiss cultures. Herr Schröder, of York, or Herr Geiger, of Reading, had they visited Berlin, might have had difficulty in making themselves understood, for they spoke a medley of German dialects which came to be known as Pennsylvania Dutch. Before a Beltzhoover or a Boreoff or a Dietrich crossed the Maryland line to make his home at Frederick or Hagerstown he had probably discarded the clothing of his German ancestors for the English styles prevailing in Philadelphia or for the rough garb of the frontier. He had turned his back upon the Palatinate courtyard or the Black Forest peasant house to erect residences more in keeping with life in America, residences in most cases made of logs. The German agricultural village had given way under the force of cheap land to privately owned farms, while the Swiss peasant house, shorn of its residential section, became the universal model for the Pennsylvania German barn.

[11]G. D. Bernheim, *German Settlements in North and South Carolina*, p. 150.
[12]T. J. C. Williams, *History of Frederick County, Maryland*, p. 7.

Yet the German American, despite these changes, retained much of the culture of the fatherland, had by no means yielded entirely to the melting pot. He clung to his religion, whether he was a Lutheran, a German Reformed, a Mennonite, a Moravian, a Dunker; he brought with him his mechanical skill as cabinet-maker, or cooper, or tanner, or iron worker, or potter, or wagonmaker, or turner; his spirit still found expression in his Volkskunst, whether in his slipware or sgraffito pottery, or in his dower chests, or in his stoves, or his barn decorations, or his fractur work, or his sacred music. In short, the emigrant to western Maryland, Virginia or North Carolina had grown up in an American Germany, based on the old Germany of Europe, but profoundly modified and changed by America itself.

So far as he could he re-established this American Germany in the southern backwoods. Great was his satisfaction when he tested the soil of his new farm and found it similar to the best of southeastern Pennsylvania and quite as fertile, while the climate, though somewhat warmer, was much the same. But he was more isolated than in his old home, it was more costly to get his produce to market, the need for economic self-sufficiency greater, and in no part of the South was he surrounded by his fellow Germans in sufficient numbers to present a united front against the cultural encroachments of his English and Scotch-Irish neighbors. He must anticipate that his sons or his grandsons would some day have to give up Pennsylvania Dutch for English, relinquish the fascinating peasant art, perhaps even purchase a slave or two; in short, cease to be a German or a Pennsylvanian and become a Marylander, a Virginian or a Carolinian.

The Germans of the South introduced very little of real German architecture. We look in vain, save in the Winston-Salem region, for the steeply rising roof-lines, the successive tiers of dormers, the quaint half-timbering of the Rhine Valley. The Miller house, near Harrisonburg, which was a crude replica in logs of the Black Forest peasant house, seems to have been exceptional.[18] One suspects that the builder of this house came

[18]T. J. Wertenbaker, *The Founding of American Civilization—The Middle Colonies,* p. 306.

174

to the Valley directly from Germany, whereas most of his neighbors were Pennsylvanians who had never seen a German village. They were the second generation of pioneers, and were acquainted only with frontier architecture, the architecture of the log house or the crude stone house.

Whereas the tobacco-raising region of the South for more than a century after the founding of Jamestown was the land of frame and brick residences, the Cohee region was from the first the land of the log house. When Philip Fithian visited Hagerstown he found some of the houses of stone or brick, "but the greater part" of "logs neatly squared."[14] La Rochefoucauld Liancourt described New Market, Winchester and Frederick as log-house towns,[15] while we know from the records of the North Carolina Moravians that their first buildings were put together with hewn logs. Not only residences, but stores, the quaint little churches, the great Swiss barns, in the early days were almost universally of log construction.

Most of these old houses have disappeared, some through decay, some because their owners replaced them with better buildings, many because Sheridan's troops in the Shenandoah sent them up in flames. But enough have survived to make it clear that they were German log houses, not Swedish. The Germans, in Pennsylvania, as well as Germany itself, usually squared the logs and then notched them with a hatchet with great neatness and exactness. Often the upper end of the log was cut in an obtuse angle like the roof of a house and fitted into a notch made in the log above, the spaces between being filled in with clay mixed with straw. More complex but making a stronger house was the *Schwalbenschwanz* notching, in which each surface drained outward. Of these two types the former seems to have been the more usual in the South. An old house near Winchester which I found several years ago falling into ruins, several of the log houses at Catoctin Village (Plate 24), Maryland, Level Green, Jefferson County, West Virginia, the old house on Lawrence Street, Charlestown, and others all have the simpler roof-like type of notching.

[14]P. V. Fithian, *Journal*, Albion and Dodson, eds., pp. 9, 10.
[15]*Voyages dans les États-Unis*, V, pp. 55, 65.

When with the accumulation of wealth and the passing of the frontier the German built a more pretentious house, he took as his model the simple Georgian architecture of Pennsylvania or of Piedmont Virginia. The John Kline house, the Beery house, the Coffman house, the John Zigler house, all in Rockingham County, Virginia; the old houses of West Patrick Street, Frederick, and of Locust Street, Hagerstown, the farmhouses of Stokes County, North Carolina, the so-called Old Stone Fort, Frederick County, Virginia, have far more in common with the architecture of the tobacco regions than with that of the Rhine Valley. The Barbara Frietchie house, made famous by Whittier's poem, is typical of the early colonial cottage architecture of tidewater Virginia.

Yet the motorist, when he stops to examine some of the old buildings of western Maryland and the lower Shenandoah, is not long in discovering certain German features which have escaped the hand of time and the encroachments of English influence. He may be surprised to see a stone spring house or cow shed covered with shingles laid in the German style, with each shingle not only partly under the row above, but under its neighbor to right or left. Examples of this German shingling survive in the office at Greenway Court, the Lord Fairfax estate in Clarke County, Virginia; in one of the outhouses of the Burr house, near Charlestown, and elsewhere (Plate 24). Our motorist will be interested, also, in the old mill near Martinsburg, Virginia, with its massive stone walls and its perfect example of the German gambrel roof.

The huge Swiss barns which are the invariable accompaniment of every farm in themselves link the region with German Pennsylvania (Plate 24). In the pioneer days these structures were built of logs, but later generations turned to stone and timber as more convenient and enduring. The smaller barns are 40 feet long, the largest 120 feet. The lower floor, which stables the horses, cattle and sheep, is usually dug out of the side of a slope, so that in the back it is underground and in front looks out on the barnyard. Above, and extending over the barnyard for several feet, is the main story, with threshing floor in the center

PLATE 24—*Upper left:* Wachovia Historical Society Museum, Winston-Salem. *Lower left:* Mabry Mill, Floyd County, Virginia. *Upper right:* Barn, Jefferson County, West Virginia. *Lower right:* Log House, Cacoctin, Frederick County, Maryland

PLATE 25—Bethabara Moravian Church

PLATE 26—*Left:* Michael Brown House, Rowan County, North Carolina.
*Right:* Moravian Clay Products, Winston-Salem

and at either end, rising twenty or thirty feet to the peak of the roof, the storage rooms for hay or grain. "Woe to the poor swain whose lot it is to pack the hay or wheat up against the rafters and scorching roof on some sultry day in July or August."[16] So wide and strong is the threshing floor that heavily loaded wagons may enter through the wide door in the rear. The Switzer barn is the lineal descendant of the picturesque peasant houses of Switzerland and Upper Bavaria.[17]

To see German architecture in the South in its purest form we must visit Winston-Salem and some of the nearby villages. Wandering through South Main Street and Church Street and in the old Moravian cemetery we imagine that we are actually in far-off Saxony. Here is the quaint Winkler Bakery, here the Brothers' House, here the Home Moravian Church, here the noted Chimney House built in 1789 of hand-hewn logs, all clearly German in their antecedents. The Moravian brothers were more successful in resisting the influence of English architecture than their fellow Germans because they retained a closer contact with the fatherland. They were in constant communication with the American church headquarters at Bethlehem, and the Bethlehem brothers took their orders from the Moravian center Herrnhut, in Germany. It is even possible that some of the drawings for the Salem houses were made by architects at Bethlehem.

The brethren, when they reached their forest retreat in the Carolina Piedmont, built of logs in the crudest form. The first house in Salem, put up in 1766, lacked even the characteristic German notching, the round logs being laid one on the other and the interstices stuffed with clay. At Bethabara, in 1755, when the house of the shoemaker became infested with rats he took the logs down one by one, so that he could get rid of the pests, and by evening they had been nearly all laid up again.[18] Later, when not so pressed for time by the necessities of pioneer life, the Moravians began to improve the quality of their houses by

[16]J. W. Wayland, *The German Element in the Valley of Virginia*, p. 191.

[17]T. J. Wertenbaker, *The Founding of American Civilization—The Middle Colonies*, pp. 320–324.

[18]A. L. Fries, *Records of the Moravians in North Carolina*, I, p. 148.

squaring the logs and resorting to their characteristic notching.

At Salem half-timbering followed close upon the heels of the crude log cabins. "I find three family houses ready for use, all made of framework covered with clay, or framework filled with brick and clay," wrote Frederick William Marshall in 1768. He then explains why it was that thousands of European settlers who in their own homes had been accustomed to half-timber construction, in America would have none of it, a fact which has long puzzled the historians of architecture. "I imagine we shall have to cover the walls with weather-boards, which in this country is the most expensive method and not a good one on account of the sharp lightning and other danger of fire, but without lime it seems to be the only thing we can do." Clearly the brothers had hoped that their half-timbering would be sufficient, for they had followed the European method used in the Ephrata Sisters' House and other Pennsylvania German buildings. Wattle was fixed between the posts and "wrapped around with a straw clay," after which a thin coat of mortar was added to fill all interstices.[19] Without lime, however, this mixture cracked and crumbled before the sun and the driving rains, so that an outer sheathing of boards became indispensable.

The surviving Moravian houses of Salem, constituting a unique architectural group, were built, some of logs, some of timber, some of stone, some of handmade brick. Their steep roofs covered with red tiles, the arched hoods over the doors, the vaulted cellars, the octagonal cupola of the church with its onion-shaped dome, not only link these buildings with Germany but give them an individuality of their own. Most interesting of all, perhaps, is the Brothers' House built in two units, one in wood in 1768 and the other in brick in 1786. The two hooded doorways, the tiers of shuttered windows, the hand-wrought guard rail, the two tiers of dormers add to the charm of this old building where formerly the unmarried men had their residence. Similar is the Sisters' House, now occupied by the faculty of the Salem College, which was completed in 1786, with its handmade brick laid in Flemish bond, its dormer windows, its steep roof covered with

[19] Ibid., II, p. 604.

German tiles, its floors of stone and wide plank. Here the Sisters, in their light-blue or white gowns, and "snipe bill" caps with lace around the forehead, had their bedrooms and worked busily at their spinning and weaving.

The Museum of the Wachovia Historical Society, built in 1796, is marked by a simple brick façade relieved by arched window headings and a wrought-iron door lamp (Plate 24). The tiled roof, the vaulted cellar, the old oven, emphasize the German touch. The charm of the little village comes back to us also when we visit in turn the Vierling house, where lived the community physician; the house of Henry Lineback, the photographer; the bakery operated for a century by the Winkler family; the Moravian church, notable for its beautiful brick masonry; the office building of the Moravian college; the house of John Vogler, the silversmith and cabinetmaker; the house of Christian Reich, the tinner; the Salem tavern; the Chimney house.

When one views the red tiles of the Museum, the Sisters' House, and other Salem buildings, one has visions of the red roofs of the quaint villages of the Rhine Valley. Brother August Joseph Miller, in his brickyard, made tiles which duplicate those of German Pennsylvania exactly,[20] there being the same grooving designed to conduct rainwater away from the joints between tiles, the same lug underneath which was hooked over a horizontal lath to hold the tile in place, the same color, the same rounded corners. They were laid, also, in the same pattern, with each tile resting on its fellow below and the joints carried through both vertically and horizontally.[21]

In the nearby Moravian villages of Bethabara and Bethania, time has dealt heavily with the buildings so that little remains in either place save the two churches. Of these the Bethabara church is the more interesting, the more clearly German (Plate 25). The carefully cut blocks of stone, the recessed window headings, the octagonal cupola with dunce-cap steeple, the ancient mellow-toned bell, the worn steps leading down to the vaulted

[20]*Moravian Records,* I, p. 328.

[21]T. J. Wertenbaker, *The Founding of American Civilization—The Middle Colonies,* pp. 300, 310.

cellar, all bring back visions of pious brothers in dark coats without lapels, knickerbockers and broad-brimmed hats, of lengthy sermons and inspiring singing. The Bethania church, built in 1807, with its brick façade, hooded entrance and open cupola, is more in the style of the church at Salem. Here the organ made by Joseph Bullitschek in 1773 still retains its original sweetness of tone.

The Germans brought with them to the South their love of music, instrumental as well as vocal. William Penn's opinion that "to bewitch the heart with temporal delight by playing upon instruments and singing, was to forget God,"[22] had no meaning for them. Music, they thought, was a noble expression of God's love for man, a joyous manifestation of the triumph of life over death, a symbol of paternal affection. The Moravians, both at Graceham and Wachovia, even in the pioneer stage of their settlements, made singing a part of their worship and their festivals. They had a large collection of hymns and lay music brought over from Germany, to which they added by composing verses with a local or personal significance.[23] In fact, music entered into almost every phase of the Moravian life. When Governor Tryon visited Bethabara in 1771, the trombonists greeted him a short distance out of town and escorted him to his lodgings;[24] when a brother or sister departed life the "home-going" was announced by the musicians;[25] when the corner-stone of the Bethabara church was laid, the congregation formed in a circle around the spot while the "trombone choir" led the singing; a betrothed pair received good wishes by the singing of verses of blessing by the unmarried brothers and sisters.[26]

The first settlers at Bethabara were forced to carve out a wooden trumpet from a hollow limb of a tree, but later they procured the finest musical instruments—French horns, trombones, violin, organs. It was in 1800 that the Graceham congregation sent to Europe for a set of trombones and only in 1802

---

[22]William Penn, *No Cross, No Crown*, p. 306.
[23]A. L. Fries, *Records of the Moravians*, II, p. 831.     [24]*Ibid.*, p. 620.
[25]*Ibid.*, p. 901.
[26]*Transactions of Moravian Historical Society*, p. 141.

that they were thrilled by the news of its arrival. So beautiful was their sacred music on Easter Sundays that Graceham was crowded with visitors from Emmitsburg, Frederick and even Hagerstown.[27] The Wachovia brothers were fortunate in having an organ builder in Joseph Bullitschek comparable to the celebrated David Tanneberg of Lititz. In May, 1772, he was at work on the Salem organ and five months later with Brother Graff's help he tuned it, and immediately tried it in the *Singstunden*.[28] It is said that Bullitschek's keen ear was so offended at the playing of Doctor Schumann, the local physician, that he reversed the pipes and so cured him of the habit, a trick not quite in keeping with the brotherly love so emphasized by the Moravians.

It must not be imagined that the Moravians alone among the Germans of the South were musical, for other congregations also had their organs and their hymns, and the *Gemainschaftliches Gesangbuch* was in use among Lutherans and German Reformed throughout the back country.[29] In the Valley of Virginia, Joseph Funk, a Mennonite, settled in Mountain Valley, under the towering peaks of the Alleghanies, built a log house and opened a music school. For nearly half a century this obscure place became a center for the practice and study of vocal music and a source of inspiration not only for the people of the Valley, but of the entire western region. Establishing a press, Funk sent forth one musical volume after another from his retreat at what became known as Singer's Glen, most of them written by himself and his sons, among them the famous *Harmonia Sacra* which went through seventeen editions. In the meanwhile the Funks began to travel from one end of the Shenandoah Valley to the other, singing, teaching, bringing a better appreciation of music. After the War between the States, Aldine S. Kieffer, a grandson of Joseph Funk, kept up the family tradition by publishing the *Christian Harp* and the *Temple Star,* which carried the message of Singer's Glen to hundreds of thousands of music lovers.[30]

[27]*Ibid.*, p. 183.          [28]*Records of the Moravians*, II, p. 723.

[29]G. D. Bernheim, *History of German Settlements and the Lutheran Church in North and South Carolina*, p. 149.

[30]J. W. Wayland, *The German Element in the Valley of Virginia*, pp. 172, 173.

In art, as in architecture, the Germanism of the settlers in the South was weakened by the prolonged pioneer period through which they had to pass. The Palatine, when he took up his residence in Pennsylvania, usually lost something of the old creative spirit of Volkskunst; to his son who moved on to the Valley of Virginia to start life again on the frontier, it became still weaker. The symbolic meaning of the tulip or the drooping fuchsia or the unicorn was fainter in his mind than it had been for his grandfather and his great-grandfather, and these figures appeared less frequently in his pottery, or his furniture, or in fractur work.

None the less, German peasant art did find its way into the South, in some cases in a most interesting form. In pottery especially the Germans of Wachovia and the Valley of Virginia won fame for their artistry as well as the excellence of their wares. So early as 1755, Brother Gottfried Aust was at work at Bethabara digging clay to "make pottery for which the people were eager."[31] A year later it was triumphantly announced that "the great need is at last relieved, every living room now has the ware it needs and the kitchen is furnished. There is also a set of mugs of uniform size for Lovefeast."[32] The reports that the Moravian brothers were making pottery spread joy throughout the Carolina back country. On May 21, 1770, after Aust had had a burning, an unusual concourse of visitors poured into the quaint little village in their crude farm wagons, some coming sixty or eighty miles, to purchase "milk crocks and pans." They bought the entire stock, many securing only half what they wanted, and others who arrived late going away empty-handed.[33] In 1768 Aust moved to Salem where again he was forced to run the pottery at full capacity to meet the demands of the people. When word arrived that the little settlement was to have a visit from the North Carolina Assembly, he was urged to make "a quantity of chocolate cups, bowls and plates," for the reception of the distinguished guests[34] (Plate 26).

One suspects that good Brother Aust had his training as a

[31] *Records of the Moravians*, I, p. 149.
[32] *Ibid.*, p. 172.
[33] *Ibid.*, p. 412.
[34] *Ibid.*, IV, p. 1724.

potter in Germany, for the Carolina plates and dishes smack more of the fatherland than of Reading or Lancaster. Although sgraffito was common in Pennsylvania, it was rare, if not unknown, in Wachovia, Aust and other Carolina potters working, apparently, always with the slip cup. The floral motifs were inferior to those of Pennsylvania, the conventional border design superior; inscriptions were rare. But the clay was similar, the tulip was in evidence and occasionally the figure of a bird or a terrapin appeared on the bottom of the plate. The range of colors was wide, with backgrounds of light red, or creamy white, or dark reddish brown, or a very dark chocolate. The Wachovia brothers made plates, dishes, sugar jars, pitchers, jugs, flasks, etc., decorated usually with conventional ornaments.[35] That the Moravians were not the only potters among the Germans of western North Carolina is shown by the existence of a village near Hickory called Jugtown. Here the Weaver family, who came originally from Reybach, Germany, to Pennsylvania, and thence to North Carolina, for many years turned out interesting slip ware.

The potters of western Maryland and the Valley of Virginia, even more than those of Wachovia, drew their inspiration from Germany, and Peter Bell, Sr., whose sons and grandsons dotted the region with their little shops and turned out plates, jugs and dishes by the thousands, is said to have learned his trade in Wiesbaden. His pottery at Hagerstown was the training school for the Virginia and Maryland potters, and here they were instructed in the art of constructing kilns, mixing the clay, moulding it to the desired form, making the slip designs, doing the glazing. We follow the activities of Peter Bell, Jr., through the musty pages of his account book. Now he is engaging an apprentice, now he sends to Chambersburg for a load of clay, now he purchases wood to fire his kilns, now he sells two dozen quart bottles to the apothecary, now he sends out a wagon load of mugs, pitchers, milk pots, dishes, jugs for distribution to his customers.

In 1824 Bell moved to Winchester, where he continued his work. His sons, Samuel and Solomon, later set up shop at Stras-

[35] *Antiques*, Jan., 1935, "A Note on North Carolina Pottery."

burg, the beginning of eighty years of pottery which made that place the "Pot Town" of the Valley. Solomon was chiefly responsible for the production of the wares, while Samuel "wagoned" them up and down the Shenandoah. They were not without competition, however, for Anthony W. Baecher, a Bavarian potter who settled near Winchester, proved an artist, and many a Valley house was furnished with his crocks, jars, pitchers, jugs, vases and urns. Baecher used no mould for his creations, but sat on an elevated saddle and turned the potter's wheel with his foot by means of a treadle while he shaped the clay with wooden and leather forms. His designs of flowers and birds, his umbrella stand representing the trunk of an oak, his figures of animals, or of men with pipes or canes, were famous.[36]

The Valley pottery was noteworthy for brilliant colors, often a medley of greens, yellows, etc. Many were set off by raised figures of birds, leaves or flowers, while the potter might indulge his fancy by moulding a bottle in the form of a man, or making a hanging flower basket, or a reclining fawn, or a jardinière with tulips on each side, or even a Negro cabin. When we view a collection of these interesting pieces we fancy ourselves in the Hessisches Landesmuseum, at Kassel, or the Oldenburg Museum, for they all bear the stamp of Germany.[37] In their slip ware the Maryland and Virginia potters have more in common with their fellows of North Carolina than of Pennsylvania. Often one finds a brown glaze, with white, yellow and black slip decorations, usually of floral or conventional designs.

The vitality of German pottery in the South is explained by the fact that there was no interruption in the transit of methods and designs by the pioneer period. Unlike the builder, the potter did not have to discard old traditions when he came to Pennsylvania, and so he handed them on to the son, who moved on to Maryland or Virginia. And when the passage of time began to weaken the old ties, the arrival of potters direct from the fatherland gave them new strength. The German potters of the South continued to ply their trade throughout most of the nineteenth

[36] A. H. Rice and J. B. Stoudt, *The Shenandoah Pottery* (1929), p. 90.
[37] Konrad Hahn, *Deutsche Volkskunst*, Plates 165, 166.

century and were forced out of business only by the modern factory.

That the German settlers in western Maryland and the Valley of Virginia brought with them their distinctive five-plate stoves, decorated with Biblical scenes and set patterns, we know from inventories and wills. The historian Kercheval, who spent his life in the Valley, states that the early houses usually had a central chimney with a room on either side, one containing a fireplace, the other the so-called stove room.[38] The stove consisted of five plates fastened together to form top, bottom, front and two sides, while the rear, left open, was placed against an opening through the partition into the fireplace in the adjoining room.[39] In this way one fire heated both rooms. But the stoves are heavy, and the cost of transportation in wagons from the Pennsylvania iron works must have been almost prohibitive. So when they began to burn out, their manufacture was taken up by the local foundries—the Marlboro Iron Works, the Mossy Creek Iron Works, Vestal's Iron Works, etc. One of these stoves made in 1768 in Frederick County, has a wedding scene depicted on the front plate done in the style of the Pennsylvania Germans.[40] But the failure of collectors and local historians to preserve the old plates leaves us in considerable doubt as to how far and how long German peasant art found expression through this medium.

In their customs the Germans stubbornly resisted change. A small outpost of the Teutonic world, cut off from the fatherland by thousands of miles of water, isolated in the backwoods of America, surrounded by peoples of other nationality, they kept doggedly to the ways of their ancestors as long as conditions made it possible. Herr Koiner continued to sleep under his *plumeau,* that thick bed comfort stuffed with feathers; he smacked his lips over his sauerkraut, he took his place every Sunday in the little Lutheran or Reformed or Dunker church; he clung to his native tongue; on his table was the huge Bible his grandfather or great-grandfather brought from Germany;

[38]Samuel Kercheval, *History of Valley of Virginia,* p. 153.
[39]T. J. Wertenbaker, *The Founding of American Civilization—The Middle Colonies,* p. 337.
[40]Rice and Stoudt, *The Shenandoah Pottery,* p. 99.

his sons and daughters worked in the field or at the spinning wheel as did their ancestors before them. "It matters not to him," said James K. Paulding, "whether the form of sideboards or bureaus changes or whether other people wear tight breeches or Cossac pantaloons in the shape of meal-bags. Let fashion change as it may, his low, round-crowned, broad-brimmed hat keeps its ground. . . . His old oaken chest and clothes press of curled maple, with the Anno Domini of their construction upon them, together with dresser glistening with pewter plates, still stand their ground."[41]

Paulding was struck by the solidity of the German farmers. "The houses are of stone and built for duration, not for show. If a German builds a house its walls are twice as thick as others, if he puts down a gate-post, it is sure to be nearly as thick as it is long. Everything about him, animate and inanimate, partakes of this character of solidarity. His wife is even a jolly, portly dame, his children chubby rogues, with legs shaped like old-fashioned mahogany bannisters, his barns as big as fortresses, his horses like mammoths, his cattle enormous."[42]

In the pioneer days the German settlers, like every one else, wore the frontier garb, with hunting shirt, fringed cape, a belt tied behind, moccasins of dressed deerskin. But the old costume which he or his father had brought across the Atlantic was usually tucked away in the family chest ready for use on Sundays or festive occasions. Before the Revolution the married men shaved their heads, protecting them from the sun or from cold with wigs or white linen caps. The common male costume consisted of a coat with broad back, straight short skirts and outside pockets, a waistcoat whose skirts came down halfway to the knees; short breeches fastened around the knee with a band and buckle; a wool or fur hat with low crown and broad brim. The women wore short gowns and petticoats of plain materials, tight calico caps, with feet and arms bare.[43] In time, however, traditional costumes gave way before English influence, so that one could no

[41]Jas. K. Paulding, *Letters from the South*, p. 142.     [42]*Ibid.*

[43]*Virginia Magazine of Hist. and Biog.*, Vol. XI, p. 115; Samuel Kercheval, *History of Valley of Virginia*, p. 256.

longer distinguish the German by his clothes, unless his religious faith dictated what he should or should not wear. The Dunkers to this day retain their simple costume, the men in severe black clothes destitute of ornamental buttons and the women with sunbonnets.

The thrift of the Germans was proverbial. Starting life with little or nothing, by incessant labor and close economy they usually became prosperous or even well-to-do in the second and third generation. Paulding declared them "as four square, solid and deliberate smokers as e'er put pipe in mouth. They are of the genuine useful class of people who make two dozen ruddy blades of clover grow where never a one grew before, who save all they make, work harder and harder the richer they grow. . . . Mynheer Van Schimmelpenninck or Van der Schlegel, he is the man of saving grace, that is, he saves something every day and considers he has lost a day when he has not saved a penny."[44]

The German wedding was marked by quaint customs handed down from generation to generation. Katrina and Hans were honored with the fattest calf or lamb, the best chickens and turkeys, the finest bread, butter, milk, honey, home-made sugar and wine in overwhelming abundance. They were attended by eight "waiters," four pretty girls and four young men, who served the wedding dinner and guarded the bride's slipper. If the slipper were stolen the poor bride could not dance until it had been restored. The groomsmen were conspicuous for fine white aprons, beautifully embroidered.[45] The Moravians had wedding customs of their own. The young pair were solemnly betrothed at a meeting of the entire congregation and about a week later they took leave of the unmarried brothers and sisters in a special gathering featured by the singing of benedictory verses. The wedding itself, which took place in the presence of the married men and women in the Saal, was followed by the feast at the house of the bride or groom.[46]

The Germans took very little interest in politics, since in Germany they had never been permitted to have a voice in the

[44]J. K. Paulding, *Letters from the South*, p. 137.
[45]Samuel Kercheval, *History of the Valley of Virginia*, pp. 56, 57.
[46]*Transactions of Moravian Historical Society*, IX, p. 141.

conduct of government. When they came to America it seems not to have occurred to them that they would be expected to do their part in safeguarding and expanding the liberties they enjoyed and which protected them from the misfortunes from which they had fled. "In neither war nor politics have any great number of the Valley of Virginia Germans been eminent leaders," says the historian John Walter Wayland. "The quiet virtues of home and the common duties of the simple citizen have seemed to charm their ambitions most."[47]

From the day when the first German set foot in the southern back country there began a struggle for the survival of the German tongue—the so-called Pennsylvania Dutch. Had the newcomers been in a large majority in any county or group of counties, they might have preserved their language, as have the Pennsylvania Germans. But they were stretched out along a three-hundred-mile front, surrounded by English-speaking peoples, forced to conduct all legal proceedings in English and to do business with English or Scotch merchants. Bitterly did they strive against the inevitable. "We have no need of English," they argued, "if we hold fast to our language and religion, establish churches and schools of our own means and support ministers and schoolmasters out of our scanty earnings."[48]

It was with deep satisfaction that they greeted the appearance of newspapers in their native tongue, and they pored eagerly over the pages of *Der General Staatsbode,* printed at Frederick, or the *Hagerstown Westliche Correspondenz,* or *Der Virginische Volksberichter und Neumarketer Wochenschrift,* or the *Teutscher Virginischer Adler* of Staunton. It was a signal victory in the battle of languages, they thought, a guarantee that German would always survive. The German papers followed the ordinary four-page form, with reprints of foreign news, and with editorials, notices and advertisements. But in time, as the younger Germans learned to speak English and the number of those who could read these papers became smaller and smaller, one by one they discontinued publication.

[47]J. W. Wayland, *German Element in the Shenandoah Valley,* p. 134.
[48]S. R. Wentz, *Lutheran Church of Frederick, Md.,* p. 101.

For decades, however, even the English newspapers were often forced to print legal and other notices in German. In Bartgis' *Maryland Gazette,* printed at Frederick, we read in 1792: "Es wird verlangt, Ein Knob zu der Walkmül-Handierung (or der Fulling Business) der 16 or 17 Jahr alt ist."[49] Often the papers gave notice that they printed hand-bills in either German or English or advertised for a journeyman type-setter who understood both languages.[50] Almanacs in German were turned off regularly by the presses, while occasionally there appeared some more pretentious volume. The publication in German by Matthias Bartgis in 1810 of *The Life of George Washington* with the Declaration of Independence, showed that the German-American had no intention of permitting his patriotism to weaken his love of his native tongue.[51]

The first signs of weakening came in the churches when Moravian, or Lutheran, or Reformed ministers began to preach in English to neighboring congregations or when visitors came to their own churches. "As there were many English friends present, Brother Schlegel was obliged to yield to their request and preach English as well as German sermons," state the Graceham records of 1805.[52] This seemed harmless enough until some of the younger people, who had learned to speak English fluently and perhaps knew little German, began to demand that at least some of the regular sermons be in English. A storm of protest resulted and when finally English preaching actually began many of the older people resigned.[53] In Bethabara English preaching once a month was instituted so early as 1790;[54] the first regular sermons in St. John's Lutheran Church, Hagerstown, were after 1815.[55]

In the end English conquered. Gradually more and more English words crept into the local German, especially in matters relating to business. Ochse became Stier, Scheffel became

---

[49]Bartgis' *Maryland Gazette,* August 7, 1792.
[50]Frederick *Republican Gazette,* May 9, 1812.   [51]*Ibid.,* March 24, 1810.
[52]*Transactions of Moravian Historical Society,* IX, p. 183.
[53]G. D. Bernheim, *History of German Settlements and the Lutheran Church in North and South Carolina,* p. 188.
[54]J. H. Clewell, *History of Wachovia,* p. 182.
[55]J. T. Scharf, *History of Western Maryland,* pp. 508, 1089, 1093.

Buschell, Gestell became Frem, Bretter became Borts.[56] The older people looked on with sadness and alarm as their sons and grandsons gradually dropped the use of German, for to them it was not only a break with their traditional culture, but also with their religion. "Most of our theological books are written in German," Reverend David Henkel pointed out. "If knowledge of German is lost, the peculiar doctrines of our church will be forgotten." It was feared that with the change of language the German church music would be abandoned for "syncopations" and the hymnal for "odes and airs," that German sincerity would give way to compliments, and the shaking of hands to "deep bows," that for simplicity would be substituted finery and the "curling of the hair."[57]

At Wachovia German put up a sturdy resistance, but elsewhere in North Carolina the Lutherans and other denominations began to yield before the end of the eighteenth century. "About twenty years ago there was a rather strong congregation in the city of Salisbury," wrote Paul Henkel in 1806, "but since the Germans degenerated into English, the German services have disappeared." Eighteen miles away there was another Lutheran church where Henkel held services every fall from 1785 to 1789 and gave religious instruction to some of the older people, but there too the Germans were mingling with the English and the mother tongue was rapidly disappearing.

Even at Salem the surrender to English was merely a matter of time. As German gradually became unintelligible to the younger people it was pushed into the background, until in 1855 English won official recognition by the keeping of church records in that language.[58] In the Maryland churches German was dropped in the early years of the third decade of the nineteenth century, but in the Mennonite churches of Rockingham County, Virginia, not until the fifth decade. "But the old order has changed," says Doctor Wayland with a note of sadness. "As one generation has succeeded another, the circles in which the German language and customs are preserved have steadily nar-

---

[56]*North Carolina Historical Review*, XIV, p. 308.
[57]*Ibid.*, XII, p. 9.     [58]J. H. Clewell, *History of Wachovia*, p. 218.

rowed, until at the present time [1907] it is not probable that over five per cent of the German families of the Valley still use the German language."[59]

Though the German was forced to change his language and many of the old customs, he clung tenaciously to his system of agriculture. His father or grandfather, when he left the old country to settle in Pennsylvania, had abandoned the German manorial system with its central village and surrounding fields, for the privately owned farm.[60] His holdings in Berks or Lancaster, although not extensive when compared with a Southern plantation, were to him of princely size, perhaps larger than the entire agricultural community in the Palatinate from which he came. So it was the farm which from the first formed the basis of his economy in Maryland, Virginia and North Carolina.

Even as he made the first clearing in the forest and built his log cabin, the German visualized his farm establishment of the future. There must be low ground with running water for meadows; there were to be fields of wheat, corn, rye, barley, potatoes, with smaller divisions for hemp and flax; this space near the house was to be an orchard, this one a vegetable garden; there on the hillside he would erect his Swiss barn; here he might put up a tan-house; here on the banks of a brook was the right place for a grist-mill. If his arduous labors were not enough to realize this dream in his lifetime, it was sure to be completed by his son or his grandson.

Notices in the local newspapers, wills and inventories give us a clear picture of the usual German farm. Typical was an estate in Frederick County, Maryland, advertised for sale in 1792, comprising 304 acres, of which about 100 acres had been cleared and fenced in. The meadow of 20 acres was well watered, there was a good apple orchard of about one hundred "choice trees," a number of cherry and peach trees, a dwelling, a large barn, outhouses and several large springs of water.[61] Similar notices in the Virginia papers show that the German farm economy underwent no

---

[59]J. W. Wayland, *German Element in Valley of Virginia*, p. 102.
[60]T. J. Wertenbaker, *The Founding of American Civilization—The Middle Colonies* p. 271.
[61]Bartgis' *Maryland Gazette*, August 28, 1792.

change in passing over the Potomac. "Land for sale," we read in the *Virginia Sentinel and Gazette,* about 100 acres cleared of farming land, 18 acres of which is meadow, a considerable part . . . watered, a good orchard with 25 bearing trees, 60 more coming on planted out last spring, a dwelling house 32 feet by 20 feet, . . . a good barn 47 feet by 18½, with other necessary buildings, a never failing spring next to the house."[62]

The German farmer sought to make his farm so far as possible a self-sufficient unit, requiring little of the outside world and sending out little in return. From the stores at Hagerstown or Frederick or Winchester or Staunton he had to buy some indispensable articles—salt, medicines, bottles, scythes, plows, nails, etc., giving in return not cash but wheat, rye, hemp, etc.[63] But he produced his own food, raised his wool and hemp, spun his own yarn, perhaps weaved his own cloth, often did his own carpentry, raised his own cattle and tanned their hides. "In nearly every family the father or one of his sons was blacksmith enough to forge a nail and shoe a horse," Doctor Wayland tells us. "The men raised sheep, clipped the wool, carded it or had it carded . . . the women spun it into yarn, dyed it, knitted it into gloves, suspenders and stockings and wove it into cloth. . . . They grew flax and turned it into linen. They raised geese and plucked their feathers for beds and pillows. The housewives, by some magic touch, transformed old wornout clothes into new carpets, and stores of old meat rinds and grease . . . into blocks of excellent soap."[64]

The German differed from the Tuckahoe in abhorring waste, especially the waste of fertile soil. He was not content to buy a farm, clear a part of it and then plant year after year until his fields refused to yield. His land, like his barn, he wished to hand on to his sons in the very best condition. So he avoided a succession of exhausting crops in one field, was careful to allow part of his land to lie fallow each year, husbanded manure to use as fertilizer.[65] However cheap land was he would never

[62]February 18, 1793.
[63]*Virginia Sentinel* or *Winchester Mercury,* March 25, 1789.
[64]J. W. Wayland, *German Element in the Valley of Virginia,* p. **195.**
[65]La Rochefoucauld Liancourt, *Voyages,* V, p. 78.

sacrifice it to save labor, even the labor of himself and his sons, so that today, when vast areas in the Tidewater and Piedmont regions have reverted to forest, western Maryland and the Valley of Virginia still retain their fertility.

Thus the Germans, after they had planted themselves athwart the line of advance of Tuckahoe civilization, resisted it stubbornly and successfully. They might accept English architectural ideas, adopt the English language, obey English common law, wear English clothes, in some cases take English names and join English churches, but they never gave up their agricultural economy for the plantation system. In fact, not only did they bring to a dead halt in many locations the westward expansion of this system, but converted thousands of eastern settlers to their own.

They were the more successful in that their thrift and in many cases their religion kept them from the temptation of purchasing slaves. "I want father to buy a black woman," one little Valley girl told Paulding, "but he says they are more trouble than they are worth."[66] This opinion seems to have been widespread, and the traveller Vaux encountered it in Hagerstown when he asked an old farmer, "How do you do without Negroes?" He replied, "Better than with them. I occupy of my father eighty acres in this valley and hire all my hands and sell five loads of flour, while some of the Marylanders and Virginians cannot raise enough to maintain their Negroes, who do but little work."[67]

Many of the Germans, especially the Mennonites, Dunkers and Quakers, would not hold slaves because they considered it a sin and displeasing to God. The Mennonites, in their general conference, put themselves on record as opposed to the slave trade and the owning or even hiring of a slave. The Moravians, for their part, expressly forbade slaveholding, and Bishop Glossbrenner is said to have expelled his own father-in-law for a breach of this regulation. In fact, almost every German denomination in the South at one time or another made official protests against slavery as contrary to Christian ideals.[68]

[66]J. K. Paulding, *Letters from the South*, p. 146.
[67]R. G. Thwaites, *Early Western Travels*, XII, p. 22.
[68]J. W. Wayland, *German Element in the Valley of Virginia*, pp. 181, 182.

Even when the dislike of Negro inertia or religious scruples were disregarded, the German seldom purchased more than one or two slaves, for in his agricultural economy there was no place for the overseer and his gang. He could make use of no more Negroes than could work under his eye in the wheat field, or under his wife's eye in the household. "He has few or no slaves," says Paulding, "and those he has work with him, side by side, in the fields. This creates a sort of good fellowship between them, that the people of the other side of the mountain would consider degrading."[69] In many cases the Negroes of the German farmers spoke only German and were looked upon more as members of the family than slaves.[70]

In the counties and parts of counties where the Germans were numerous the census shows that the percentage of slaves was small. In Shenandoah, the great stronghold of the Germans in the Valley of Virginia, in 1840 it was 9 per cent, in Rockingham 11 per cent, in Page 13 per cent. Thus the slave population was far smaller than east of the mountains and considerably smaller than in Rockbridge, Botetourt and other non-German counties in the Valley itself. In North Carolina conditions were similar, the slave population of Stokes, Rowan, Guilford and other counties where the Germans were numerous being small in comparison with those of the tobacco-raising sections in the east and north.[71] In Maryland in 1850 there were only 3913 slaves in Frederick County in a population of 41,000; in Washington County 2090 slaves in a total population of 34,767.[72]

When the tide of German settlers poured into the South, there came, side by side with the farmers, hundreds of mechanics with an inheritance of skill and careful training in their trades. Picking out the main villages as their permanent abode, they hung out their signs, unpacked their tools and got to work. When the Reverend Harry Toulmin visited Winchester, he noted with interest that it was filled with artisans—"saddlers, hatters, shoemakers, weavers, braziers, smiths, clockmakers, rifle-smiths, cab-

[69]J. K. Paulding, *Letters from the South*, p. 139.

[70]G. D. Bernheim, *History of German Settlements and the Lutheran Church in North and South Carolina*, p. 148.

[71]U. S. Census, 1790.   [72]Gazeteer of Maryland, pp. 71, 100.

inetmakers, a painted chair-maker, an earthenware maker, a coachmaker, a buckskin breeches maker."[73] Stephensburg became the center for the manufacture of wagons, and its nine shops sent out to all parts of Virginia vehicles which were inferior to none.[74] As we have seen, the pottery industry centered at Strasburg, while Middletown boasted of many clockmakers whose reputation grew as the old wooden-wheels gave way to brass and the simple mantel clocks to elaborate eight-day grandfather clocks. In Hagerstown one saw swinging before the quaint old shops on the public square or one of the side streets the signs of Bendor, the wheelwright; Boreoff, the smith; Dietrich, the book-binder; Greiner, the brass-founder; Geiger, the tanner; Grubb, the cooper; Heyser, the coppersmith; Woltz, the cabinet-maker; Fechtig, the potter.[75]

In the community life of the Moravians, both in Wachovia and at Graceham, the artisan played an important rôle. Among the brothers at Salem were masons, carpenters, sawyers, cabinet-makers, wagonmakers, weavers, dyers, tailors, blacksmiths, gunsmiths, locksmiths, sickleomiths, nailsmiths, saddlers, shoe-makers, leather-breeches makers.[76] At Graceham, grouped near the old Gemeinhaus, were the shops of Philip Willar and George Hahn, the weavers; of Jacob Christ, the gunsmith; of John Herback, the smith; and of other artisans—tanners, shoemakers, nailsmiths, carpenters, millwrights, tin-smiths, linen weavers, stocking-makers, etc.[77] These skilled workers, with their German tools and methods, constituted as much a part of the German civilization of the South as the German tongue, or the German religious denominations, or German peasant art. Nor did contact with the English and Scotch-Irish weaken the Teutonic craft tradition until the factory and large-scale production undermined the artisan class throughout the nation.

Today, after the lapse of two centuries, the Germans of western

[73]Harry Toulmin, *Journal*, p. 94. Huntington Library; *Virginia Sentinel* or *Winchester Mercury*, January 21, 1789.

[74]*Martin's Gazeteer*, p. 539.

[75]J. T. Scharf, *History of Western Maryland*, p. 1061.

[76]A. L. Fries, *Records of the Moravians in North Carolina*, II, p. 830.

[77]*Transactions of the Moravian Historical Society*, IX, p. 191.

Maryland, Virginia and North Carolina have retained much of their native culture. They cling to their agriculture, their huge barns, their religious faiths, their thrifty habits, in some cases to their superstitions. But their language, their architecture, their peasant art, the crafts have fallen before the assaults of other nationalities, new surroundings, the industrial revolution and vastly bettered transportation facilities. Yet the German, even at the time when he was lamenting the gradual disuse of his native tongue, or the passing of old customs, could boast that he had resisted to the very end the advance of Tuckahoe civilization, that he had never discarded his traditional economy to become a large slaveholder and staple-crop planter.

In this his neighbors, the Scotch-Irish, were not quite so successful. The origin of the sturdy immigrants who poured into this country from Ulster in the eighteenth century is still a matter of controversy. Charles A. Hanna insists that they were Scots who in Ireland had mingled freely with English Puritans and with refugee Huguenots, but not with the pure Irish. Whenever he questioned an Ulsterman as to his origin he got the same answer. "We're no Irish but Scoatch."[78] On the other hand, J. C. Lineman points out that the number of Irish names among the settlers from Ulster proves that intermarriages were not uncommon, and that the province sent out a "mingled race, Irish, English and Scotch," who always "considered themselves Irish."[79]

A visitor to the north of Ireland in 1810 noted that the population was sharply divided into three classes, "the gentry, who are the English Irish; the merchants, shop-keepers and manufacturers, who are the Scotch-Irish; and the servants and laborers, who are mostly composed of the native Irish."[80] The migration to America of some members of the third class under terms of indenture no doubt accounts in part for many of the purely Irish names in the Scotch-Irish regions of America. The problem has been complicated, also, by the migration of many Roman Catholics from South Ireland and Presbyterians directly from Scotland who often

[78]C. A. Hanna, *The Scotch-Irish or the Scot in North Britain, North Ireland, and North America*, I, p. 163.
[79]J. C. Lineman, *The Irish Scots and the Scotch-Irish*, pp. 62, 63.
[80]John Gamble, *Sketches of History*, p. 285.

settled in close proximity to the Scotch-Irish. The United States census of 1790 distinguished between the two races by listing Scotch and Irish separately, and making no mention of Scotch-Irish.

That the Scotch strain predominated in the group as a whole is obvious from the almost universal attachment to Presbyterianism, and even in the eighteenth century the log or limestone Presbyterian meetinghouses at crossroads or hidden in the woods could be counted by the score. The people spoke with the Scottish "burr," read Scottish books, their first ministers were educated at Glasgow,[81] they were steeped in Scottish traditions. Yet there were enough Irish among them, or enough Irish in their veins, for them to venerate the patron saint of Ireland. "It was customary for the Dutch on St. Patrick's Day to exhibit the effigy of the saint with a string of Irish potatoes around his neck and his wife, Sheeley, with her apron loaded also with potatoes," Kercheval tells us of the Valley of Virginia Germans. "This was always followed by a riot. . . . On St. Michael's Day the Irish would retort and exhibit the saint with a rope of sauerkraut about the neck."[82]

Whatever the racial origins of the Scotch-Irish, we know that in Ulster itself the people were occupied chiefly with agriculture and the manufacture of woolens and linen. When Arthur Young visited the province it seemed to him that it was entirely peopled with weavers. Yet no weaver thought of supporting himself by his loom alone, for he always devoted part of his time to his patch of potatoes, his field of oats, his flax and his cow. His farm was small, ten acres at the most, because he had neither the time nor the inclination to cultivate more.[83] Despite the fact that many of these little holdings were leased from English proprietors, Ulster at the end of the seventeenth century was prosperous and contented.

Then a series of blows brought ruin to the province, impoverished and embittered the people and drove tens of thousands into

[81]J. G. Craighead, *Scotch and Irish Seeds in American Soil*, p. 286.
[82]Samuel Kercheval, *History of the Valley of Virginia*, p. 179.
[83]*Arthur Young's Tour in Ireland*, Ed., A. W. Hutton, II, p. 215.

voluntary exile. In 1699 an act was passed by Parliament, in response to the demands of the English weavers, prohibiting the exportation of Irish woolens. When the people then concentrated their attention on making linens, discouraging restrictions were placed upon that also. At this moment, when the Ulstermen were regarding their idle looms in sullen anger, the English landlords added to their burdens by doubling or tripling rents.[84] And when, from his dwindling income he had to pay tithes to support in idleness the Anglican minister whose sermons he never listened to, or to repair the Anglican church while his own Presbyterian meetinghouse fell into decay, his cup of bitterness was full.

And so the tide of emigration set in. Disposing of his belongings, all save clothing, the family Bible and perhaps his loom, the Ulsterman turned his back on the place which had been his home and the home of his father and grandfather before him and set out for Belfast, there to take passage for America. Landing in Philadelphia, he made inquiries as to vacant lands, and then started on his trek for western Pennsylvania, or southwest into Maryland, the Shenandoah or North Carolina. A few months later we find him in his wilderness home. Many settled in the shadow of the South Mountains, or on the banks of the Monocacy, and though greatly outnumbered by the Germans, made a lasting imprint upon the region. Western Maryland would have been less progressive, less prosperous had it not been for the McCoys, the McCardells, the McIntoshes, the McDonalds.

In the Valley of Virginia the Scotch-Irish were even more numerous, and whole counties were so impregnated with the culture of Ulster that one could not go to market or to church without hearing on all sides what Philip Fithian called the Scottish "roll and whine."[85] At Kernstown Fithian found the "large and genteel society" mostly Scotch-Irish, while at Stephens City, at Vance's Meeting House, Berkeley County and throughout Augusta, all were "Irish, all Presbyterians." In Botetourt they were so numerous that the huge Beverley Manor was often spoken of

---

[84] S. S. Green, *The Scotch-Irish in America*, II, p. 260; Wm. Douglass, *British Settlers in North America*, I, pp. 367, 368.

[85] P. V. Fithian, *Journal*, Albion and Dodson, p. 140.

as Irish Tract. When he preached at Hall's Meeting House, near Lexington, or the Stone Meeting House, in Augusta, or at the log church in the beautiful Cow-Pasture, he found his congregations made up of Kirkpatricks, Alexanders, Campbells, McClanehans, McCullochs and others with names similarly Caledonian.[86]

Had his clerical wanderings taken him farther south into western North Carolina, he would have found just as many Presbyterian meetinghouses, would have heard on all sides the Scottish accent, for the tide of Scotch-Irish immigrants had flowed also into the rolling hill country of the Carolina Piedmont, to Guilford, Alamance, Caswell and Orange, and along the upper reaches of the Catawba under the shadow of the Blue Ridge. "In the year 1746 I was up in the country that is now Anson, Orange and Rowan counties," wrote Acting-Governor Matthew Rowan in 1753. "There were not then above one hundred fighting men; there is now at least three thousand, for the most part Irish Protestants and Germans."[87] Some of the settlers came directly from Ireland, for Governor Gabriel Johnson, a Scotchman, and Governors Matthew Rowan and Arthur Dobbs, both Ulstermen, did all in their power to encourage migration.[88]

The pure Irish among the settlers in the South were in most communities too few in numbers to establish a congregation, and gradually relinquished their faith to join some one of the Protestant churches. Here and there, however, they joined hands with English and German Catholics to build a church and secure the services of a priest. At Hagerstown the congregation included Condins, McGonigles, Roachs, Bradleys, Murphys, Barrys, Drinens, all born in Ireland. The little Catholic congregation at Winchester were too weak to have a priest of their own, and were forced to content themselves with the occasional ministrations of a clergyman from Maryland. In western Maryland the census of 1790 lists 728 Irish heads of families, or about 2 per cent of the population; in the Salisbury district, North Carolina, 1277 heads of families or 2.2 per cent.

[86]*Ibid.*, pp. 17, 132.
[87]R. D. W. Connor, "Race Elements in the White Populations of North Carolina," *Pamphlets on the Southern States*, IV, p. 85.
[88]*Colonial Records of North Carolina*, V, xi.

The Scotch-Irish farmer, though perhaps not so good an economist as the German, was far in advance of his Tuckahoe neighbor. "As you approach his residence you will be struck with the neatness and cleanness of his system of farming, so different from the more slovenly course pursued on a large eastern plantation," said one observer. "His gates, his fences, his outhouses are all substantial and neat. His barn is always three times as large and handsome as his house. . . . His table is loaded with abundance and almost everything is the product of his own farm, even the liquor which, though temperate as he is, he presses upon you."[89]

Like the German the Scotch-Irishman had his fields of wheat, corn, and rye; his well-watered meadow; his flourishing orchard; his horses, cows, sheep and hogs; his great barn. But he was apt to have more ground laid out in flax, his wife and his daughters spent more time at the loom, he boasted of a larger distillery. "To be sold, plantation in Rockbridge, estate of the late Archibald Alexander, 350 acres, 80 acres cleared and farmed, 30 acres low ground, 6 to 7 acres watered meadow," states a notice in 1792 in a local newspaper. "Good dwelling house, kitchen, etc., large double barn, almost new apple orchard."[90] William McKee owned 538 acres near Lexington, Virginia, where he raised wheat, rye, corn and hemp, and had a dwelling, kitchen, spring house, barn, stables and orchards. In the eyes of Mr. McKee the property was the more valuable in that it was convenient both to several Presbyterian meetinghouses and merchant mills.[91]

Unfortunately for the Scotch-Irish their skill in weaving, although of great value to the individual families and to the regions where they settled, could not lead to the development of a major industry. They were too isolated, transportation costs were too great, the competition with English weavers too strenuous. Yet there were spinning wheels in almost every farmhouse—big for wool and little for flax—and a loom-room or perhaps a loom house. The farmer, after shearing his sheep, sent the wool to the nearest shop for carding. When it returned it was spun and

[89]*Knickerbocker Magazine*, Vol. 52, p. 279.
[90]*Winchester Sentinel and Gazette*, August 27, 1792, Library of Congress.
[91]*Ibid.*, October 1, 1792.

woven by the women of the family, after which it went to the
fulling mill. Out of the finished cloth were made jeans for men,
linsey for the women, blankets and flannels. The good housewife
took pride in displaying her towels, sheets and blankets made by
herself or her mother or grandmother.[92]

Every Scotch-Irish maid was taught to pull flax, to sew, to spin
and to weave. One good mother who could not resist the temptation of showing off to Paulding the accomplishments of her
daughter, ushered him into the best room, which was festooned
with short gowns and petticoats. "They certainly constituted a
very respectable dower in chintz and striped linsey woolsey," he
remarked.[93] Fithian, when on his preaching tours, often found
the women "at their wheels." So late as 1858 we are told that the
farmer clothed himself in domestic cloth save on court days,
election days or at muster. Then he put on his "blue coat, glittering with brass buttons and surmounted by one of those immense, stiff collars which belong to the style of the Court of
George III."[94]

The Scotch-Irish, though they never adopted the plantation
economy of the east, made much greater use of slave labor than
the Germans. When La Rochefoucauld Liancourt was in Augusta
he noted that there were no rich planters and few slaves.[95] In time,
however, as the farmers grew richer, the temptation to purchase
became irresistible, so that it was not uncommon to see Negroes
in gangs of five or six working in the fields. In both Botetourt
and Rockbridge, where the Scotch-Irish were very numerous, in
1840 the slaves amounted to 25 per cent of the population. In
Augusta, where many Germans had taken up land side by side
with the Ulstermen, the percentage was twenty.[96]

We witness the transformation which America wrought in the
Irish immigrant by following the career of John Robinson. This
remarkable man lost his parents when a lad in County Armagh
and was forced to earn his bread as a weaver's apprentice. Hard
work this was, but it stood him in good stead when, upon his

[92]*Jas. Sprunt Hist. Studies*, XVI, p. 54.
[93]J. K. Paulding, *Letters from the South*, pp. 146, 147.
[94]*Knickerbocker Magazine*, Vol. 52, p. 279.
[95]La Rochefoucauld Liancourt, *Voyages*, V, p. 47.      [96]U. S. Census.

arrival in Virginia, he carried on his trade beneath a swinging sign in one of the streets of Lexington. Possessing the typical Scotch shrewdness, he was not long in adding to his earnings by horse-trading and by speculating in Revolutionary soldiers' certificates. With riches in his hands his thoughts now turned to the gentleman's life, and in Virginia, even west of the Blue Ridge, the proper vocation for the gentleman was agriculture. So the former apprentice boy purchased a plantation of about 400 acres on the North River, became the owner of numerous slaves and laid out large crops of wheat, corn and rye. And, like other good Scotch-Irish Presbyterians, seeing nothing antagonistic between religion and whiskey, he established a large distillery which, he boasted, turned out the best liquor a gentleman could buy.[97]

Distilling, in fact, vied with weaving as an accustomed part of the farm routine in all "Scotch-Irish Virginia," and copper stills imported from England found their way in large numbers up the James and the North rivers to Botetourt and Rockbridge.[98] It is said that while the builders were at work on the Bethel church, the congregation held services in the Bumgardner Distillery near-by.[99] The presence of a distillery on a farm always enhanced its value, and the owner or agents if they had to offer it for sale emphasized the number of stills and tubs. Even if there were no distillery, they might point out that the presence of good running water made the situation advantageous for erecting one.[100]

The Ulstermen as mechanics lacked the diversified and careful training of the Germans, save in weaving, in which they excelled. So in Hagerstown, Winchester, and other towns, whereas the potters, coopers and shoemakers were apt to be of German origin, the weaving was done by men named Douglass, or Arnold or Campbell.[101] The merchandise business also fell in large part into the hands of the Scotch-Irish or Scotch. Had some of the visitors to Winchester who spoke of the place as chiefly German cast their eyes around, they would have been the Sign of the Spinning

---

[97]Henry Boley, *Lexington in Old Virginia*, p. 68.
[98]*John Hook Letter Book*, Virginia State Library.
[99]Henry Boley, *Lexington in Old Virginia*, p. 69.
[100]*The Washington Spy*, November 26, 1796.
[101]J. T. Scharf, *History of Western Maryland*, p. 1026.

Wheel swinging before the store of O'Neal and O'Loughlin; Joseph Tidball's Sign of the Umbrella; John Murphy's liquor and grocery store; John and James McAlister's Sign of the Tobacco Hogshead,[102] etc.

When a neighboring farmer entered one of these stores, he left outside his wagon laden with flour, or wheat, or corn, which he sought to barter off to the merchant for medicines, salt, coffee, farm implements, hardware, or cloth. The storekeeper, once he had accumulated a sufficient quantity of country produce, shipped it off to the most convenient port for sale to some exporting firm. If he had his business in Hagerstown or Frederick, he traded with Philadelphia, or Baltimore or Georgetown; if in Winchester with Alexandria, Falmouth, Baltimore and Philadelphia; if in Lexington with Richmond; if in western North Carolina with Charleston, Edenton and Richmond. Whatever the direction of trade the journey was long, costly and often dangerous. "They must go from here to Charleston, S. C., about 300 miles," stated one of the Wachovia brethren, "and the length of the way is not the worst part, for there is little but bad water to be had and there is danger of robbers; or else they must go to Boling's Point, Virginia, on a branch of the James River, but it takes several weeks for the trip and the road is bad, with hills and streams."[103]

It must have been an exciting moment when Daniel Hollenbach, the Winchester wagoner, backed up to the McAlister store and lifted on the barrels of flour and bags of wheat, and started off on his monthly trip to Philadelphia. A long hard journey it was, which taxed the strength of his four or six sturdy horses, with dangerous crossings of great rivers on fragile ferries, jolting over rough roads, stops at many wayside taverns. The trip to Alexandria, while much shorter, was even more arduous, for the wagons had to cross the Blue Ridge at Snicker's Gap or Ashby's Gap, contend with the mud of Piedmont Virginia and perhaps splash through swollen creeks.[104] The wagoners charged a fee for every barrel of flour or bushel of grain, which varied with the

[102]Frederic Morton, *The Story of Winchester in Virginia*, p. 118.
[103]*Records of Moravians in North Carolina*, I, p. 44.
[104]*Winchester Sentinel*, April 2, 1792.

distance, the condition of the roads and the season of the year. In the early spring when rains and the melting snow of the mountains made the roads impassable, business was at times almost entirely suspended for weeks at a time, while the merchants anxiously scanned the skies in hopes of seeing a rift in the clouds or wondered whether the wagons with goods from Alexandria or Philadelphia were stuck in the mud.[105]

When feasible the merchant availed himself of water transportation, and every improvement in the Potomac or James or Roanoke was watched with eager interest. "There is a fair prospect of the Potomac's being a common channel of commerce," said the *Virginia Gazette and Weekly Advertiser,* on May 14, 1789. "Colonel Darek's boat last week brought down a load of 262 barrels of flour from Shepherdstown and passed Shenandoah and Seneca Falls with safety and ease." On the Shenandoah River during the winter months navigation was very uncertain, while even in the summer a succession of rainless days might bring the waterlevel down to a point too low for the boats. Goods were carried in part by professional boatmen, in part by boats owned by the merchants themselves. But large parts of the "back country" were shut off from river transportation, so that they were almost entirely dependent upon the covered wagon.

The Scots, Irish and Scotch-Irish brought with them to the American frontier their customs, superstitions, costumes, dialects, music, religion, educational methods. At one place Fithian noted with interest the "shrill, acute accent" of the people and their "many odd phrases." When a good lady told him that her son "lately lost his foot in the smallpox," she meant he could not stand. "Will you take a check?" she asked, meaning will you have a late dinner? "Our neighbor, McOlahlan, since you left us has flitted," meant he had moved away.[106] At Kernstown a Mr. Glass at church services raised the tune "in a primitive, genuine Presbyterian whine and roll."[107] In time, however, the Scotch "burr" was toned down under the influence of the soft Southern accent, the pronunciation of words became more and more Eng-

---

[105]*North Carolina Historical Review,* IV, p. 407.
[106]*P. V. Fithian Journal,* p. 6.     [107]*Ibid.,* p. 17.

lish, interesting old expressions went out of use. Today, the Southern Scotch-Irish, although by no means duplicating the broad A, or other distinctly English features of the Tuckahoe dialect, no longer speak the language of Scotland or of Ulster.

In church music the Scotch-Irish in America sang the "Scotch or David's Psalms," ignoring Doctor Watts' paraphrastic version of the Book of Psalms. And the Ulstermen, though not so devoted to music as their German neighbors, brought with them their own Scottish songs to enliven festive occasions or beguile the tedium of work. Fithian, in one home, was charmed by "two young misses" who were "singing at their wheels." "There is something harmonious in a well-tuned face," noted the young minister, "but when it is improved by real sound, surely there is then intrinsic harmony."[108] "I always loved the 'Scotch tunes,'" he added, "and Scotch tunes are good." But he was not charmed by the "incessant scraping on the Caledonian Fiddle," nor by the beating of drums, the sound of fifes and the whine of bagpipes which accompanied the drilling of the backwoods militia just before the outbreak of the Revolution.[109]

In food, as in many other things, the Ulsterman had to adapt himself to new conditions in his American home. It was hard for his wife to do without her cup of "tay," so she made a kind of tea from sassafras roots. In Ireland the potato had been the stand-by of the family larder, the foundation of most of the dishes; in the backwoods Indian corn took its place. For porridge was substituted mush and milk; as an especial delicacy at breakfast were served fried mush and honey from a nearby bee tree; for dinner roasting ears and succotash.[110] And with the growth of prosperity came a variety and abundance almost unknown in Ulster. Fithian in his wanderings found no coffee nor chocolate, nor other "superfluous nick-nacks," but in their place "plenty of rich milk in large basons and noggins, large platters covered with meat of many sorts, beef, venison, pork, and with these potatoes, turnips, cabbage and apples beyond your asking. A low bench for a table you will have covered with such provisions three times

[108]*Ibid.*, p. 123.  [109]*Ibid.*, p. 24.
[110]Robert Garland, *The Scotch-Irish in Western Pennsylvania*, p. 31.

every day."[111] In Augusta the people enjoyed not only fruit, cheese, butter, and other rich food, but "cyder, whiskey and peach-brandy" which they saw no harm in setting before the young minister.[112]

When the Scotch-Irish family came to America they brought with them, not only the clothes on their backs, but their best dresses and suits neatly packed in the chest or carried in bundles. There they remained, while their owners donned the frontier garb, until a wedding, a frolic or a sermon brought them forth again. In far-off Buffalo Valley Fithian preached in the open to a gathering in which richly clothed women were so numerous that he called it his "silk gowned congregation."[113] Yet on week days he might find many of these same women in coarse clothes, barefooted, working at the churn or the distaff. Fithian, who always viewed the ladies with either an approving or a critical eye, noted that girls who were exposed to "the curse of the Irish" wore "rolls and their hair high." A Mr. Wilson, "lately from Ireland," was conspicuous because of his "short, trite, yellow wig." Yet at one place he found the women "drest in plain good taste" and some of the men "made as an important figure" as one would wish to see in town.[114]

With the Scotch-Irish the wedding was an occasion of hilarity, mirth and feasting. It was customary for some of the young men after the ceremony to race to the bride's residence for a bottle of spirits decorated by a white ribbon. Away they went over rock and stumps and through mud, until the leader dashed up and took it from the hands of the bride's father. The winner then wheeled and returned with it to greet the bride and groom, who tasted it and then passed it around to the guests.[115] Scotching flax often offered occasion for frolics which were attended by scores of young people and enlivened by dancing, for unlike some of the German sects the "Irish" saw no harm in the country reel.

The Scotch-Irish brought with them from Ulster little that was distinctive in architecture. They had been accustomed to simple

[111]P. V. Fithian Journal, p. 151.  
[112]Ibid., 140.  
[113]Ibid., p. 52.  
[114]Ibid., p. 100.  
[115]Samuel Kercheval, History of the Valley of Virginia, p. 58.

stone houses, two stories high, rectangular in form, without ornaments, the walls of great thickness as though the masons had built for future generations. John Gamble, who visited the north of Ireland in 1810, thought the Ulster farmhouse an accurate reflection of the character of the people. It was no more than an unhewn mass of stone, without pretense to beauty—"a picture without a frame, a bed without a curtain, a drawing-room without a carpet." "It is astonishing how little idea the Presbyterian has of pastoral beauty," he adds. "If he builds a cottage, it is a prison in miniature. . . . The fence of his grounds is a stone wall, seldom a hedge, his garden is kale, but never has flowers."[116]

Upon his arrival on the American frontier, the Ulsterman found it impossible to reproduce the stone house of his ancestors and had to content himself with a log cabin, patterned after those of the neighboring Germans. When Paulding became a paying guest in a Valley of Virginia farmhouse, he described it as "built of square pine logs, lapping over at the four corners, the interstices filled up with little blocks of wood plastered over and whitewashed very neatly. Before the establishment of sawmills it was cheaper and less laborious to build in this manner than to bring boards from a great distance."[117] The first meetinghouses were also of logs, and Fithian often had to preach in these little buildings with the wind whistling through the cracks. The Old Derry Church, which was still standing in western Pennsylvania in 1876, was typical. "The building is constructed of oak logs, about two feet thick, which are covered over with hemlock boards on the outside," A. Boyd Hamilton tells us. The pews and floors were of yellow pine, cherry and oak, the nails were hand-wrought, the hinges and locks of the most primitive character.[118]

With the passing of the frontier, the Scotch-Irish began to avail themselves of stone in their building. Even before the Revolution, here and there, a prosperous farmer converted the log house where he had been born into a kitchen or a stable, and erected a more pretentious residence of uncut limestone. Plain, rectangular, two-

[116]John Gamble, *Sketches of History, Politics and Manners, taken in Dublin, and the North of Ireland, in the Autumn of 1810* (London, 1811), pp. 235, 236, 287.
[117]J. K. Paulding, *Letters from the South*, p. 145.
[118]W. H. Egle, *An Illustrated Hist. of the Commonwealth of Pennsylvania*, p. 367.

story houses, they were not dissimilar to those of Ulster. In some cases the log house was left as a wing of the new structure. The Smith Thompson house, at Staunton, is half log, half brick, with an outer covering of clapboarding. The Michael Brown house, near Salisbury, was typical of the early stone houses, its rough, sturdy masonry, its end chimneys, its arched windows, its lack of adornment—no porch, no classic doors, no quoins, no pilasters— differentiating it from the Georgian residences of the tobacco planters (Plate 26).

In keeping with their deeply religious nature, the Scotch-Irish also substituted for their log churches larger buildings of stone as soon as their circumstances permitted. A charming example was the Fort Defiance Church, near Staunton. The sturdy walls, the large expanse of roof broken by a hip at each end, the simple rectangular windows, the absence of tower or cupola, all seemed in keeping with the early Presbyterian spirit. It is said that "men, women and children labored at the erection, transporting sand from Middle River on horseback and timber and stone in like manner,"[119] and that "all the iron work, the glass, the sashes were carried across the Blue Ridge from Williamsburg on pack-saddles."[120] Similar in spirit and architectural design were some of the Scotch-Irish Presbyterian churches of Pennsylvania—the Hanover Church, Dauphin County, Old Paxtang Church, Donegal Church and others.

In these little rustic churches was to be found the spirit of Presbyterianism, and in Presbyterianism was the spirit of the Scotch-Irish. The seriousness, self-discipline, sturdiness, hardihood, the neglect of the æsthetic were all in keeping with Calvin and his doctrine. The Scotch-Irish had no folk-art comparable to that of the German peasant, he lacked the gentleness of the Dunker and the Mennonite, he was more interested in politics, he was a better Indian fighter, his religion was more militant.

He was determined that the frontier life should not weaken the tie with his church. Where there was no church he joined

---

[119]J. A. Waddell, *Annals of Augusta County*, p. 50. The old church has been disfigured in recent times by the addition of a wing and a portico.

[120]*Knickerbocker Magazine*, Vol. 52, p. 279.

PLATE 27—Rose Hill, Frederick County, Maryland

PLATE 28—Wheatland, Jefferson County, West Virginia

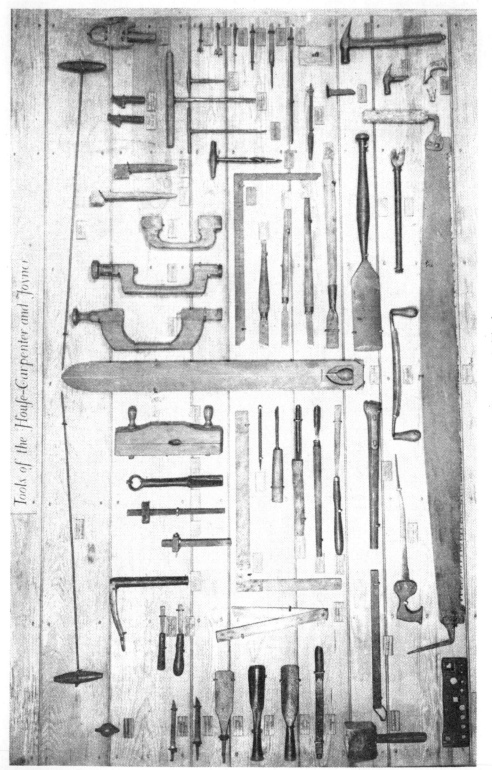

Tools of the House-Carpenter and Joyner

PLATE 29—Carpenter's Tools

his neighbors for services in a barn or in the open; when a meetinghouse had been erected, he and his family came, perhaps, a
score of miles through the woods or over creeks or muddy roads
to hear the sermon. A sermon, in fact, in the early days was a
rare treat, which stirred the countryside for miles around. It was
impossible for the little, scattered congregations to support a
minister, and months might elapse before an itinerant preacher
came by. Urgent were the appeals which poured in upon the
Synod of New York or the Synod of Philadelphia. "It grieves us
. . . to hear the melancholy representations of their destitute circumstances and their affectionate longings after the Bread of
Life," wrote one devout Presbyterian.[121]

But the supply of ministers was inadequate, for one could not
send to Ulster or Scotland for trained men, and there was in
America no Presbyterian college. Here and there academies sprang
up, patterned after the dissenting academies of England—at Fagg's
Manor, Nottingham, at Neshaminy—which sent forth a handful
of young preachers with a smattering of Latin and Greek and
a grounding in Calvinist theology. After the founding of Princeton in 1746, however, the stream of "circuit riders" grew until no
one from the Wyoming Valley to Georgia was beyond the reach
of the Gospel. In 1775 there were no less than eight youthful
ministers, recent Princeton graduates all of them, serving the Valley of Virginia alone.[122] A hearty welcome awaited them—the
leading member of the congregation entertained them, collections
paid their expenses, the best of everything was set before them,
they were urged to accept permanent calls to this church or that.

Thus it was that Princeton became the religious and educational capital of Scotch-Irish America. The graduate of Nassau
Hall invaded the South with the Bible in one hand and the Greek
or Latin textbook in the other. Having knit together his congregation and built a meetinghouse, he next busied himself with
founding an academy, modelled upon William Tennent's famous
Log College. It was an inspiring sight, these frontier schools,
where the youthful ministers gathered a group of boys to drill
them in Greek or Latin, or to expound moral philosophy from

---

[121]*Princeton Library MSS.,* AM 1424.      [122]*P. V. Fithian Journal,* p. 139.

a treasured copy of Witherspoon's lectures.[123] It was Samuel Stanhope Smith, Witherspoon's son-in-law, who founded Prince George Academy, which later became Hampden-Sydney College; John Brown, another Princeton graduate conducted a grammar school which was merged in Liberty Hall, the Washington and Lee of today. In Tennessee, when Samuel Doah founded the academy which grew into Washington College, he brought the books for the library over the mountains on horseback.[124]

Against the bulwarks of church and school the assaults of the established church proved vain. That some were fined or imprisoned for attending Presbyterian services, that others were obliged to pay taxes for the support of the Anglican minister, made them cling all the more resolutely to their own faith.[125] Even the Baptist and Methodist evangelists, who swept through the region, apparently carrying all before them, could not shake the Presbyterian congregations. In 1860 one third of the Valley of Virginia churches were Presbyterian, with twelve in Augusta and sixteen in Rockbridge. Decades after the Calvinism of New England had been weakened by Unitarianism and Princeton had lost much of its denominational character, the Scotch-Irish of the South clung tenaciously to the faith of Samuel Davies, John Witherspoon and Samuel Stanhope Smith.

Thus all along the line the Ulstermen held their own against the Tuckahoes, refused to adopt their agriculture, their customs, their religion, even resisted the slave system. "The western and eastern Virginian differ as absolutely from each other as either does from the New England Puritans," wrote a visitor to the Valley of Virginia in 1858. "Their lineage, their tastes, their habits are directly opposite. A valley farmer is a noble specimen of the yeoman. He has little Latin and less Greek, having derived his education in an 'old field school-house,' from a stern Scotch schoolmaster. . . . The Valley farmer is shrewd, sensible and refined, with just views of human affairs, generous to others, but frugal to himself; industrious and attentive to business, but full of fun

---

[123]William H. Foote, *Sketches of Virginia*, p. 444.
[124]Samuel Alexander, *Princeton College in the Eighteenth Century*, p. 185.
[125]J. G. Craighead, *Scotch and Irish Seeds in American Soil*, p. 320.

in his hours of leisure; a Democrat in politics, a Presbyterian in religion and a colonel in the militia."[126]

But though the Virginia and North Carolina Scotch-Irish never succumbed to Tuckahoe civilization, their dependence on slavery, limited though it was, placed a barrier between them and the Scotch-Irish of western Maryland. When the dark clouds of war settled over the nation in 1861, the former threw in their lot with the Confederacy, the latter usually with the Union. In fact, racial lines gave way entirely before sectional lines, so that for the Scotch-Irish the struggle was fratricidal in a double sense, a war of Ulsterman against Ulsterman, Presbyterian against Presbyterian. When Jackson's Valley veterans, many of them Scotch-Irish, came swinging through Frederick, they received no welcome, were held to be enemies, even perhaps by some who had blood ties with them as well as the ties of religion and racial origins.

Even while the Germans and Scotch-Irish were pressing southwest across the line of advance of the Tuckahoes, the latter, big and small planters alike, began to pour through the mountain passes. Western Maryland, Virginia and North Carolina were not, as some have contended, exclusively the land of the Cohee. If we examine the census, let us say, of Frederick County, Virginia for the year 1783, we find a very large proportion of English names. Granting that the Scholls, Gorses, Miers, Nisewangers, Steins, Brenners, Ringels, Sniders, Huffs, etc., were clearly German, we have every right to assume that the Pierces, Wingfields, Barnes, Gardiners, Bradleys, Bakers, Barrons, Jacksons, Harnells, Reynolds, Browns, Bushes, Nelsons, Dixons, Lemons, Taylors, Baileys and a host of others came from families in Albemarle, Orange, Fairfax or tidewater Virginia. Even Beverley Manor, the so-called Irish tract, had among its original settlers many persons of English names, some of which were common in Virginia. Side by side with the McLures, the McDonalls, the McCullochs, the Alexanders, the Kirkpatricks, we find the Davises, Lewises, Robinsons, Thompsons, Jennings, Bells, Russells, Andersons, Kings, Buchanons, Blacks, Lowrys, Palmers, Pages, Cunninghams,

[126]*Knickerbocker Magazine*, Vol. 52, p. 279.

Youngs, whose names smack more of Amherst or Stafford or Prince Edward than of Ulster.[127]

Had western Maryland, Virginia and North Carolina been overwhelmingly German and Scotch-Irish, the German language and the Scotch dialect would not have faded out so early. In the sections of Pennsylvania where the Germans were in the majority, Pennsylvania Dutch has survived to this day, but in Winston-Salem or Woodstock, it is a forgotten language. Reverend Harry Toulmin, in passing through Winchester, described the people as a "motley set of Germans, Irish, Scots and Anglo-Americans or Americans descended from Englishmen."[128] Out of this mass has developed a dialect of English which has more in common with that of West Virginia and the Ohio Valley than the speech of a Jefferson or a Byrd, yet it was the Tuckahoe who forced his tongue on the region, not the German nor the Scot.

Moreover, had a traveller along any main highway on a Sunday morning espied a church and stepped in to attend the services, the chances are that he would have heard a sermon, not by a Presbyterian nor a Lutheran, but a Methodist or a Baptist minister. No doubt, when the revivalists invaded the region, holding their camp meetings, exhorting, praying, threatening damnation to the unrepentant, a sprinkling of Scotch-Irish and Germans left their traditional faiths to join the growing movement. But in the main, it was the poor white from over the mountains, failing to find in the teachings of the Anglican ministers a satisfying solution for his religious problems, who fell in line with Bishop Asbury or with the Baptists. In the Valley of Virginia the Methodist and Baptist churches from an early date outnumbered those of the Germans and Scotch-Irish combined; in Washington County, Maryland, the Methodists, Episcopalians and Baptists in 1840 had twenty-five churches out of a total of sixty-three; in Frederick County the Methodists alone counted thirty-three, whereas the German Reformed had but eleven, the Lutherans seven, the Moravians five, the Presbyterians three. In Augusta

127*U. S. Bureau of Census*, 1790, Virginia; *Wm. Beverley Account Book*, N. Y. Public Library.
128*Toulmin Diary*, Huntington Library, p. 94.

County, a supposed stronghold of the Scotch-Irish and Germans, there were in 1860 twenty-one Methodist churches, while those of the Presbyterians numbered twelve, of the German sects seventeen.[129]

It has been pointed out that it was not unusual for German settlers to assume English names or to accept the English equivalent for German names, that Behringer became Barringer, Kohlman became Coleman, Berger became Barrier, Biber became Beaver, Zimmerman became Carpenter.[130] But it seems to have been overlooked that a fair number of German names and many Scotch and Scotch-Irish names in the Cohee region may be duplicated in the Piedmont. The Valley of Virginia had no monopoly of the Campbells, the Alexanders, the Pattersons, the Murphys, the McKennys, etc., and it is possible that some who are supposed to have come from Pennsylvania or directly from Europe, had in fact first settled in eastern Virginia and later moved west over the mountains.

The poor Tuckahoe, however, when he purchased land in Washington County, or the Shenandoah, or in Rowan, seems to have left behind him, not only his worn out fields and his tumbledown house, but his wasteful methods of farming. He kept more cattle and made better use of his supply of manure, he took precautions to preserve his soil by a rotation of crops, his fences were in better repair, his barn larger than before. This, no doubt, was partly the result of the excellent example set him by his German neighbor, but even more of his isolation and the necessity for self-sufficiency. He could not devote most of his time, as he had done in Middlesex or Albemarle, to producing two or three hogsheads of tobacco or ten barrels of flour a year to the neglect of everything else, because he could not get them to market. So he was forced to readjust his economy to bring it into line with that of his neighbors, to become in his farming a Cohee, not just a poor planter. Weld noted that poverty was almost unknown, for "every man owns the house he lives in and the land which he

---

[129] *U. S. Census,* 1860.

[130] G. D. Bernheim, *Hist. of German Settlements and the Lutheran Church in North and South Carolina,* p. 148.

cultivates, and every one appears to be in a happy state of mediocrity."[131]

But Weld was wrong when he said there were no large plantations in the Valley of Virginia, no persons distinguished by education or knowledge from the rest of the people. Had he visited what are now Clarke, Warren and Jefferson Counties, he would have seen wide fields of wheat, cultivated by slaves under the direction of overseers, many stately mansions, charming formal gardens (Plate 28). This region was a reproduction of eastern Virginia, a bit of Tuckahoe land west of the mountains. "The residences become better, the fields larger, . . . the countryside gives more the appearance of wealth . . . sometimes the appurtenances of the planters are richer," said La Rochefoucauld Liancourt as he approached Charlestown.[132] John Esten Cooke says that Millwood was the center of the Valley aristocracy, for numerous eastern planters settled there, "bringing with them the traits of the lowland, the cordial sentiments, the love of social intercourse and the attachment to the English Church."[133]

When George Washington visited the lower Valley, he must have felt perfectly at home, not only because of its associations with his early life, but because of the large numbers of relatives, friends and acquaintances whose estates were located there. Here was the plantation of John Augustin Washington, here that of Charles Washington, here lived Robert Carter Willis, here James Wormeley, here Ralph Wormeley on an estate of 3712 acres, here was Carter Hall, the princely home of the Burwells, there Saratoga, the estate of Powell Page. At Travellers' Rest, the residence of his former associate in the Revolutionary War, General Horatio Gates, his welcome would not have been very hearty; while he probably avoided the farm near Leesburg where the crabbed Charles Lee brooded over his disappointments and his treachery to the American cause.

Colonel Warner Washington led the van of the planter aristocracy invasion of the Valley, and as early as 1782 there were 134

[131]Isaac Weld, *Travels Through the States of North America and the Provinces of Upper and Lower Canada*, p. 232.
[132]La Rochefoucauld Liancourt, *Voyages*, pp. 76, 77.
[133]Quoted by J. Houston Harrison, *Settlers by the Long Gray Trail*, p. 111.

slaves on his Frederick County properties. Hugh Nelson with 64, Fielding Lewis with 47, Francis Willis with 36 and others followed behind. The story of Nathaniel Burwell is typical of the westward movement. Establishing first "quarters" near Millwood, he came each year to the village to inspect his land and buildings and give instructions to his overseers. Then he decided to convert the "quarters" into his home plantation and so erected stately Carter Hall, whose apartments and costly furniture excited the admiration of visitors. Burwell then widened his activities, clearing more land, bringing up additional groups of slaves, building mills.[134] Impressive also were the estates of the Pages, Randolphs, Nelsons, Allens and other Tuckahoe families. Robert Carter, of Nomini Hall, although he never lived in the Valley, owned six plantations in Frederick, named for various constellations, which he seems to have leased under the management of an agent.

In Maryland the plantation economy advanced northward and westward into Frederick, where it was halted by the Cohees along a line running up the Monocacy for a few miles and thence northeast to Pennsylvania. Isaac Weld on his way from the town of Frederick to Washington in 1795, noted the contrast of civilizations when he crossed this line. "Instead of well cultivated fields green with wheat, . . . large pieces of land which have been worn out with the culture of tobacco are here seen lying waste. . . . Instead of the furrows of the plow the marks of the hoe appear on the ground; the fields are overspread with little hillocks for the reception of tobacco plants and the eye is assailed in every direction with the unpleasant sight of gangs of male and female slaves. . . . The difference in the manners of the inhabitants is also great."[135]

But there were many instances when eastern planters acquired large estates west of the dividing line and established their slave economy in the midst of the Germans and Scotch-Irish. General Samuel Ringgold, who typified the landed gentry of Maryland,

---

[134] T. D. Gold, *History of Clarke County*, p. 43.

[135] Isaac Weld, *Travels Through the States of North America and the Provinces of Upper and Lower Canada*, p. 140.

owned an estate of 17,000 acres near Hagerstown, erected a fine mansion at "Fountain Rock," and brought in large gangs of slaves. The doors of the house were made of mahogany, the mantels were richly carved, the walls enriched with stucco-work, all under the direction of Latrobe. General Ringgold lived here in baronial style, entertaining lavishly, until his extravagance brought him to bankruptcy.[136] The Carrolls, the Fitzhughs, the Rochesters, the Sims, the Johnsons, the Lees and other families also upheld the Tuckahoe standard in the west. In the pages of Bartgis' *Republican Gazette* are numerous notices of sales of plantations operated under the slave system. We learn that Thomas Sprigg's estate comprised, in addition to furniture, utensils, carpenter's and blacksmith's tools, Helder and South Down sheep, mules, horses, cattle and hogs imported from England, and "a number of valuable slaves."[137] When George Scott and Robert T. Cary, of Washington County died in 1810, their estates were put on sale, including forty-five slaves, thirty horses, seventy cattle, sixty sheep, fifty hogs, wagons, stills, farm implements, etc.[138] (Plate 27).

In North Carolina the plantation economy invaded the west from two directions, the tobacco growers pushing out along the northern tier of counties—Vance, Person, Caswell, Rockingham, Stokes; the cotton planters invading Mecklenburg and other counties in the southwest. There seems, however, to have been no sharply defined line of division between the plantation and the farming sections, and very few large slaveholders. In Rowan County, a local historian states that there were overseers directing the work of groups of slaves "on a few plantations" only.[139] In Montgomery County in 1790 the largest slaveholder was Edmund Lilly with 28, the next James Turner with 25, the next James Tindle with 24. In Rockingham, Governor Alexander Martin owned 47, Valentine Allen 28, Richard Marr 23, and a number of other planters from 10 to 20; but the great mass held from one to five, or none at all.[140]

[136]J. T. Scharf, *History of Western Maryland*, II, p. 1023.
[137]April 21, 1810.                    [138]April 7, 1810.
[139]Jethro Rumple, *History of Rowan County*, p. 252.
[140]*U. S. Census for 1790*.

We gain an insight into the economy of the well-to-do planter from notices in the newspapers. Nicholas W. Gaither owned "twenty likely Negroes" which were offered for hire if the plantation were rented, together with horses, cows, corn, fodder, hay, wagons, farm implements, furniture, etc.[141] In Lincoln, the estate of Henry Connor embraced no less than fifty slaves, of whom some were "prime hands."[142] "The great mass of our population is composed of people who cultivate their own soil, owe no debt and live within their means," declared the *Fayetteville Observer* in 1837. "We have no overgrown fortunes." A resident of Moore County confirms this statement and adds, "We have surely more below than above mediocrity."[143]

Socially the Tuckahoe and the Cohee mixed no better than oil and water. The wealthy planter looked down upon the German farmer as a boorish peasant, close-fisted, ignorant, rude in his manners, outlandish in his dress. He smiled at his superstitions, had no appreciation of his folk-art, merely tolerated his religious beliefs, despised him for working in the fields, especially when he worked with Negroes. With the Scotch-Irish he had more in common, but he objected to the Scotch accent, disliked the Scotch canniness, resented the aggressiveness of the Presbyterian ministers. It was a strange fate which placed groups of people so different in religion, traditions, customs, education, sense of values, side by side in this southern West.

"Madam Grundy is sometimes apt to turn up her nose when she sees plain Mrs. Ashfield industriously mending a pair of breeches, the original color of which is lost in the obscurity of patches," remarked Paulding. "She wonders at her daughter pulling flax, or weaving, or turning a great spinning wheel . . . why Farmer Ashfield can think of making such a slave of his daughter, and why, as he can afford it, he do'nt send her to one of the great boarding schools in Philadelphia, to get a polish and learn to despise her vulgar old father and mother." But the Tuckahoe resented the Cohee no more than the Cohee resented him. "The farmer insists upon it at town meetings and elections," Paulding

---

[141]*Western Carolinian*, March 2, 1824.  [142]*Ibid.*, December 21, 1824.
[143]G. G. Johnson, *Ante-Bellum North Carolina*, p. 54.

continues, "that the Squire enjoys greater political privileges than he does . . . that the seat of government ought to be removed, that the poor enslaved Cohees may not be toted all the way to Richmond to hear orations and get justice, and that finally the Squire gives himself such airs of superiority that there is no such thing as getting along with him."[144]

Paulding spoke of the Tuckahoe as "a gallant, high-spirited, lofty, lazy sort of being, much more likely to spend money than to earn it."[145] Another visitor to the Shenandoah remarked that many of the "Virginians" spent all as fast as it came, "indulging in all manner of luxury and excess, giving their children most expensive educations which never turned to any account as they afterwards all sat down in small plantations."[146] The thrifty Cohees, despite their plain clothes and their willingness to work at hard labor were quick to resent patronizing airs. Paulding noted that "if a stranger is inclined to treat them as if their coats were as good as his, they will fight for him . . ., but it will sometimes go hard with him if he takes freedoms with them."[147]

Even in North Carolina, where the contrast between east and west was not so pronounced, the tobacco planters had little in common with the Cohees. "To tell you the plain truth," wrote a young lady of Franklin County of a Christmas party in Buncombe to which she had taken her visiting relatives, "there was only a few young ladies there that I thought proper to introduce them to, and I managed that admirably, as it was rather a mixed multitude, mountain boomers and backwoods folks in abundance. It reminded one of the 'poor man's dinner' and it was given for the purpose of encouraging that class."[148]

In the end the strange triangular battle of civilizations in the Blue Ridge region was won, not by the Germans, nor the Scotch-Irish, nor the slaveholding planters, but by the melting-pot. Each group lost something by its contact with the others, each contributed something. The Germans relinquished their language,

[144] J. K. Paulding, *Letters from the South*, pp. 111–114.
[145] *Ibid.*, p. 137.
[146] R. G. Thwaites, *Early Western Travels*, XI, p. 154.
[147] J. K. Paulding, *Letters from the South*, p. 164.
[148] G. G. Johnson, *Ante-Bellum North Carolina*, p. 62.

218

their folk art, their architecture; they retained their religious beliefs and not only kept their agricultural economy, but lent it to their neighbors. The Scotch-Irish, although they gradually gave up their dialect, their industry and to a large extent their agriculture, retained their loyalty to the Presbyterian Church and contributed to the South and the nation many leaders in political life. The Tuckahoes forced on their neighbors their language, their political system, their common law and to a limited extent slave labor. The poor-white easterner, when he took up his residence in the Cohee region, adopted the German system of farming and threw off his old slovenly way of life, but he would have none of the Presbyterian, or the German Reformed, or the Lutheran Churches, and left the ranks of the Episcopalians only to become a Methodist or perhaps a Baptist.

The clash of Cohee and Tuckahoe is of especial interest in the development of American civilization in that it was the first contact on a large scale of an established American culture with cultures recently transplanted from Europe. There were to be many such contacts in the years to come when the hordes of easterners, whose thought and economy had been moulded by two centuries of life in America, met in the great West the stream of immigrants from the Old World, or when this stream was diverted in part to the Atlantic seaboard itself. The Cohees did not stop the Tuckahoe advance, for the slaveholders leap-frogged their lines into the Ohio Valley, renewing their civilization in the blue-grass regions of Kentucky, in Tennessee and even in Missouri. But they demonstrated that the eastern Americans in their westward sweep would have to reckon, not only with new economic conditions, but with the influence of newcomers from Europe. It was already an old story when New Englanders and New Yorkers and Virginians rubbed elbows with Germans and Scotch-Irish and English and Scandinavians in the Mississippi Valley, or when Irish, Poles, Italians, Greeks settled in the great industrial centers of the East. In a very real sense, western Maryland, the Valley of Virginia and western North Carolina constituted a test laboratory of American civilization.

*Chapter VI*

# THE ARTISAN AT WORK

HAD WE visited London in 1686 we might have seen a brilliant and interesting spectacle—the grand procession of the Mercers' Company to celebrate the election of one of their number as Lord Mayor. Assembling at the Grocers' Hall they took their places in line—the Master, Wardens and Assistants, the liveried members in gowns faced with satin, the almsmen each bearing a banner, the gentlemen ushers resplendent in velvet coats set off by gold chains, the bachelors in gowns and scarlet satin hoods, the trumpeters, drummers, city marshals, the gentlemen of the Artillery Company led by Sir John Moore. The procession moved to the Guildhall and then to the Three-cranes wharf where all embarked on barges for Westminster. On their return they were met at St. Paul's churchyard by the pageants— Neptune on a coral rock attended by tritons, mermaids and other marine creatures, a gorgeous chariot adorned with paintings, jewels, gold and silver work, carrying a throne occupied by a beautiful maiden, and many others.[1]

The companies or guilds played a vital rôle in the life of the English city, town and village. Voluntary associations for the promotion of profession or trades, their functions were more varied and all-embracing than those of the modern trade-union. Their votes elected the mayor and other municipal officers; it was they who rushed to arms when an enemy threatened outside the city walls—they took over in part the matter of social security by caring for their own indigent, disabled and aged; they contributed liberally to religious and charitable institutions; they frequently lent large sums to the government in times of national peril; they fostered national commercial enterprises such as the London Com-

[1]P. H. Ditchfield, *The Story of the City Companies* (N. Y., 1926), pp. 20–21.

pany of Virginia by purchasing large blocks of stock. To the medieval worker his guild was a craft union, a social club, a political organization and a charitable institution, which influenced and regulated almost every move in his life.

In London alone there were scores of companies—the Mercers, Grocers, Drapers, Fishmongers, Goldsmiths, Skinners, Merchant Tailors, Haberdashers, Salters, Ironmongers, Vintners, Clothworkers, Armorers and Braziers, Bakers, Blacksmiths, Brewers, Carpenters, Coopers, Shoemakers, Curriers, Cutlers, Distillers, Glaziers, Glovers, Gunmakers, Pewterers, Shipwrights, Tallow Chandlers, Wax Chandlers, Weavers, Wheelwrights. Each company had its hall, large and beautifully decorated buildings, some of them, and the scene of many a brilliant banquet or exciting election. Here assembled the company in its livery of "red and white" with the emblems of their "mystery" or trade embroidered on their sleeves, or perhaps of scarlet and green, or dark red, or scarlet and black. Here the tables groaned with venison, swan, boar, sea-hog, while the music of the minstrels or the performances of players added to the gaiety.[2]

The guild was a self-governing body, electing its own officers and making regulations which had all the force of law. It inspected the wares of its members in order to uphold high standards of quality, and the cloth or pewter dish which proved defective was promptly thrown into the discard. It was careful to keep secret its "mysteries," or methods of manufacture. Since it usually possessed a monopoly under its charter, it took pains to drive all interlopers, foreigners as it called them, out of town. It often had important privileges and duties assigned to it by the government, the Grocers regulating the sale of drugs, the Goldsmiths being assayers of metals, the Vintners tasting and appraising wine. It regulated agreements between masters and apprentices, and did not hesitate to order a good lashing with birchen rods for the lad who was insubordinate or lazy.

In the guild there was little of the clashing of capital and labor which has characterized modern industry and has resulted in such bitterness, such huge losses and so much violence. The guild

[2]*Ibid.*, p. 20.

embraced masters, journeymen and apprentices. The employer usually had no more than a little shop, perhaps the front room of his residence, and employed two, three or in rare cases a dozen journeymen and an apprentice or two. He was himself a workman, taking his hand at the forge, or the potter's wheel, or the loom, or with the hammer and saw, or the needle. And every apprentice, if he showed intelligence and industry, had a chance of becoming a master in his own right.[3]

Mass production, through water, steam or electric power, labor-saving machinery and standardization, did not enter into the life of the artisan. His were the simple tools handed down to him by his father and his grandfather. He spun his wool or his cotton or his flax upon the foot-driven wheel; he hammered out his nails, his hinges, his knives and axes at the forge; he fashioned his chairs and tables with saws, chisels, gimlets, gouges, planes; his carriages were not turned off by the thousand in assembling plants, but created by hand from the axle-tree to the upholstery. His work was arduous and long, but it afforded endless interest and often an opportunity for the exercise of ingenuity and artistic taste. The craftsmen and tradesmen of England at the time when she was establishing her colonies in America, constituted a numerous, intelligent, powerful class, the very backbone of the nation.

It was inevitable that many should join the stream of emigrants to America. The lad who had finished his apprenticeship, but found employment uncertain, the journeyman who lacked the capital to open shop for himself, the interloper who had been driven out of town by the guild found opportunity beckoning across the Atlantic. Many left for religion's sake—Puritans dreaming of their wilderness Zion in New England; Quakers seeking escape from stern English judges and brutal English jailors; Presbyterians, Baptists, Roman Catholics. In America they were joined by the artisans of other lands, thousands of skilled workers from the Rhine Valley and Switzerland; Huguenots fleeing the persecutions of Louis XIV, among them some of the best weavers of Europe; hardworking, thrifty Scotchmen from the north of Ire-

[3]George Unwin, *The Gilds and Companies of London* (London 1909).

land, bringing with them their knowledge of the linen industry.

Some of the newcomers were established workers, men of moderate means, but able to pay their ocean fare and set up independent shops immediately upon their arrival. Over and over again one finds advertisements in the local gazettes of artisans from London or Dublin, bringing with them their tools and boasting of their skill, who began business at the Sign of the Dial, the Sign of the Pistol, or the Sign of the Wheel. "This is to give notice that Samuel Bowles, upholsterer from London at his shop in Queen Street, makes all sorts of upholstery wares," we read in the *South Carolina Gazette,* of December 1, 1737. In Williamsburg, Madam Bodie advertised in 1771 that she had just arrived from London and was ready "to make and trim in the newest taste sacks and coats, gowns and petticoats."[4]

These workers were tempted often to make the great venture to America because of reports of the scarcity of artisans and the very high returns for skilled work. As for the journeyman, he could expect rapid advancement and early independence. "At home . . . the laboring man must be a slave . . . or he will fall behind," wrote William Couper from Norfolk, Virginia, in 1802. "But that is not the case here, for if a man be only industrious but a short time here and takes care, he can soon be independent." Six years later he wrote: "Virginia is a very fine country for those that have a little money to begin business with for themselves."[5]

For the thousands of artisans who were not able to pay for their passage across the ocean, the indenture system opened the door of opportunity. It was better to work for a master in the New World for four or five years without wages, than to slave at home for a mere pittance and with poor chances of advancement. In America the indentured worker who had been trained at some craft always commanded a high price. "Just arrived, *The Searsdale,* Captain Reed, with one hundred and thirty-nine healthy servants," a dealer advertised in the *Virginia Gazette* in 1770, "among them many tradesmen—smiths, bricklayers, plasterers, shoemakers, house-carpenters and joiners, weavers, barbers and peruke-

[4]*Virginia Gazette* (Parks and Dixon), Oct. 24, 1771.
[5]*Letters of William Couper,* Apl. 12, 1802; Apl. 26, 1807.

makers, a clerk, a hatter, a rope-maker, a bookbinder, a painter, a mantua-maker, several seamstresses, etc. . . . The sale will commence, Wednesday, October 10, at Leedstown, on the Rappahannock."[6]

Many of these workers were purchased by planters, for there was need for trained artisans upon both the tobacco and rice plantations—carpenters to build barns, stables, tobacco houses, slave quarters and fences; blacksmiths for shoeing horses, repairing plows, making nails, hinges, locks, tires, chains, etc.; coopers to make tobacco hogsheads, or rice barrels or wine vats; tanners to convert hides, which would otherwise be wasted, into leather, and shoemakers to work it up into crude shoes for the slaves.[7]

Some of the trained artisans were purchased by established tradesmen. In 1759 we find Richard Ford advertising in the *Maryland Gazette* that gentlemen could depend upon having their tailor's work "done in the best and newest fashion," since he had "obtained several very good hands from England."[8] Cabinetmakers, silversmiths, goldsmiths, wigmakers, hatters, coachmakers and tailors especially sought the services of immigrant artisans, since they kept their work abreast of the times and were apt to be more skillful than American-trained workmen. In 1757 one of the Maryland stay-makers announced that he was planning to go himself to London "to supply himself with workmen and stay goods."[9]

Often bitter disappointment was in store, however, for indentured artisans had a habit of running away, perhaps taking with them their master's tools and other valuables, and when the worker was an imported convict, it was especially difficult to keep him at his work. In 1737 Peter Taylor, of Charleston, offered a large reward for the return of two "servants," one a carpenter and the other a saddler. "They stole a gun from me and the carpenter carried all his tools with him," he added feelingly.[10]

But the vast majority of the indentured artisans were honest,

[6]*Virginia Gazette* (Rind), Oct. 4, 1770.
[7]*Virginia Magazine of Hist. and Biog.*, I, p. 36; *South Carolina Gazette*, Apl. 7–14, 1733.
[8]*Maryland Gazette*, August 2, 1759.      [9]*Ibid.*, August 4, 1757.
[10]*South Carolina Gazette*, Apl. 2–9, 1737.

PLATE 30—Almodington, Somerset County, Maryland

PLATE 31—Marmion, King George County, Virginia

PLATE 33—Virginia sawmill

PLATE 32—Grist Mill, New Kent County, Virginia

hardworking men who sought to better their condition in the land of promise. Let us follow two of them, whom we shall call John and Ambrose Ratchford, from London, whose careers in Virginia will serve to illustrate the life, the opportunities, the disadvantages and the future of the immigrant craftsmen. They are joiners by trade, and have just completed their apprenticeships. Since they cannot secure work in London, they are persuaded to affix their signatures to indentures and sail for the Chesapeake Bay in the ship *Fortune*. A few weeks later they find themselves in the James River, looking out on the woods and plantations of Surry on one side and James City County on the other.

The ship ties up at a plantation wharf, and after the boxes of European goods have been taken off, the "servants" go ashore for inspection by prospective purchasers. Since their arrival has been advertised in the *Virginia Gazette* a number of planters and one or two master craftsmen are on hand. Long interviews follow in which the training, strength, character and price of each worker are discussed at length. In the end the two brothers are separated, John going to a large tobacco planter, Ambrose to a cabinetmaker in Williamsburg. So they bid each other good-bye, and promise that when they have completed their terms they will rejoin each other, perhaps to set up shop for themselves.

John finds his master kind, his food better than he had been accustomed to as an apprentice, his work hard but not beyond his strength. He makes chairs, tables and other simple furniture for the plantation, cuts out doors and windows for the slave quarters, reshingles barns and stables, aids the shipwright in building a new shallop, perhaps gives a hand to the cooper when the number of hogsheads falls short of the requirements of the tobacco crop. So the time passes quickly and not unpleasantly, and at the expiration of four years he is his own master, with two suits of clothes and his joiner's tools.

Since he has no capital it is necessary for him to work for wages. There is always work to be done, pay is high and before two years have passed he has saved enough to set himself up as master joiner and carpenter. Now he builds a residence, now he undertakes to mend the furniture of a wealthy planter, now he signs a contract to make pews for the parish church, and his income is far greater than he could have hoped for had he remained in England. But he finds that in Virginia as in England it is the possession of land which brings both wealth and prestige, so he lays out a part of his savings in a plantation of one hundred acres and plants part of it in tobacco. He continues for some years to spend part of his time on his trade, so that for the time being he is both planter and artisan. Gradually, however, he adds to his holdings, devotes more time to his crops and less to his trade, until after the expiration of a decade he lays aside the saw and the hammer entirely.

The experience of his brother is quite different. His master takes him to Williamsburg and puts him to work in his cabinet shop. He spends most of his time repairing furniture, replacing bits of veneer, mending a broken table leg, putting a new back on a chair. But his master has received an order from a neighboring planter for six mahogany chairs, a sideboard and a card table, and he is called upon to assist in the cruder part of the work. This is excellent experience and as the years pass he becomes less a joiner and more a skillful cabinetmaker. When his four years of service are completed, he continues with his master as a journeyman, receiving excellent wages, together with his food and lodging. Eventually, when his employer retires because of advanced age, he takes over his business, places his own name on the "Sign of the Chair and Table" which swings over the door of the shop, and becomes a prosperous, respected member of the colonial artisan class.

This class, while less numerous than in England and the northern colonies, played an important rôle in the life and economy of the South. The section had its carpenters, bricklayers, joiners, coopers, shipwrights, blacksmiths, gunsmiths, tailors, tanners, shoemakers, silversmiths, painters, glaziers, without whom the planters would have found it difficult to carry on their own activities. These men, scattered through the rural districts, or in such towns as Annapolis, Norfolk, Williamsburg and Charleston, lacked the sense of unity, the class consciousness which made their fellows a power to be reckoned with in the North. The carpenter of Westmoreland County, one of the men who aided in the reconstruction of Mt. Vernon, let us say, felt little kinship or common interest with the goldsmith of Norfolk or the cabinetmaker of far-off South Carolina. His world extended little beyond his own county, and there his group was vastly outnumbered by the planters. The artisan class was on a par with the small farmers in social rank, intelligence and prosperity, but unlike them they were not numerous and united enough to impress their will upon the County Court and the Assembly and force legislation favorable to their interests.

The Southern artisan labored under several serious handicaps, of which the greatest was competition from the artisans of England. The South was a region of great staple crops—tobacco, wheat, rice, indigo, the larger part of which went to England in exchange for manufactured products. The Board of Trade approved highly of this state of affairs, for it built up British industry and the merchant marine, gave England a surplus of goods for re-exportation and the treasury a steady revenue from the import duty. A tariff barrier against the mother country for the protection of American craftsmen was out of the question.

It was discouraging to the Norfolk artisan when he walked down to Water Street to see a ship come in from England. As he watched the sailors, aided by the Negro dockmen, unload crate after crate of manufactured wares—silverware and pewter; knives, scissors and screws; linen, cottons and woolens; saddles, bridles and harness; tables and chairs; perhaps a coach or a riding chair; all kinds of firearms; rugs, gloves, needles, thread, ribbon, buttons, combs, ink, locks, brushes, hats, nails, paper, wheels—he realized that the local merchants on Main or Church Streets would soon have these articles on sale at a price with which he found it hard to compete. He knew also that English ships made a practice of going directly to the wharves of the wealthy planters to bring them all kinds of goods needed for the plantation economy. None better than he realized that if a Byrd or a Carter or a Wormeley wished a silver porringer, or a shoe-buckle, or a dress for his wife, he ordered it through his agent in London; that the clothing on his back, the implements of his agriculture, the glass in his house, came from the mother country in exchange for Sweetscented or Orinoco.

The poor planter, although he had no direct business relations with England, secured what he wanted from the stores which were to be found on every river or large creek. Once or twice a year he would roll a hogshead of tobacco on board his shallop and head for the nearest of these stores, there to exchange it for axes, hoes, shoes, nails, cloth, pewter utensils, blankets, guns, iron pots. This he found to be less troublesome and expensive than to employ local blacksmiths or shoemakers or other artisans to make these articles for him.[11]

Had Robert Beverley, the historian, taken these conditions into consideration, he would not have been so harsh in his criticisms of his fellow Virginians for their failure to utilize their natural resources for the manufacture of useful goods. Although their country produced flax, hemp and wool, the people sent to England for every stitch of clothing, he complained; although they had furs in abundance, they never made hats; although they had vast forests of noble trees, their chairs, secretaries, tables, stools and chests were imported; despite the abundance of hides they made shoes only for their slaves; and the man who cut out for himself a pair of deerskin trousers was considered a most frugal manager.[12] Beverley's statement, greatly exaggerated as it is, shows not so much the poor economy of the planters as the difficulties under which the Southern artisan labored.

Almost as discouraging as the competition of English goods was the scarcity of towns in the South. In North Carolina, especially, this proved a serious handicap, for the sandbanks which hemmed in Albemarle and Pamlico Sounds prevented the development of large ports. Prior to the Revolution Wilmington was a mere village, while not until the end of the century could Edenton, Hillsboro, Fayetteville and Newbern boast of more than a few hundred inhabitants each.[13] Even though the pewterer, or cabinetmaker, or gunsmith established himself at some central

[11]*Middlesex (Virginia) County Will Book*, 1693–1713, pp. 55 *et seq.*
[12]Robert Beverley, *History of Virginia*, Ch. XVIII.
[13]Jas. Sprunt, *Historical Studies*, XX, No. 1.

228

spot—at a courthouse, or at the mouth of a large creek, or near a ferry—his clients found it difficult to reach him. When one had to go miles on horseback or by boat to have a watch repaired or purchase a pair of shoes, the game was hardly worth the candle. If the artisan, giving up his fixed abode, travelled from plantation to plantation, much of his time was wasted on the road and the equipment which he could take with him was inadequate. Moreover, since in the absence of coin tobacco or other agricultural products were the usual media of exchange, the artisan found it inconvenient and costly to carry his bulky pay around with him. Yet the itinerant workers—shoemakers, tailors, joiners, and even cabinetmakers—did play an important rôle in colonial life, and some of the most successful planters called them in to work up their raw materials.

An interesting itinerant cabinetmaker, who worked in a radius of fifty miles from Athens, Georgia, in the days when this region was sparsely settled, was "German" Davis. He seems to have gone from house to house in a cart with tools, hardware, veneers and inlays, trusting to the farmer to supply the walnut, pine and poplar woods cut in convenient lengths and properly dried. When he found work, he would put his horse in the stable, his travelling bag in the spare room and his tools and materials in an outer "office" or perhaps a corner of the barn. His work may be identified by the clean dovetailing, the use of mortise and tenon and the tendency to follow the Chippendale style. There can be no doubt that he was but one of many skilled itinerant artisans working at a distance from the centers of population.[14]

The Southern craftsman could have faced English competition with a sturdier heart, had he not been compelled to battle also against slave labor. Whether upon the plantation or in towns, whether in the cruder trades or the artistic crafts, the Negroes played an important rôle. We find them on the rice or the tobacco plantations, serving their masters as carpenters, coopers, blacksmiths, sawyers, wheelwrights, shoemakers, painters, etc. We may assume that they were, as a rule, not the most skilled or exact craftsmen, but they were capable of doing satisfactory work

[14] *Antiques,* XXXI, Jan. 1937, p. 19.

in shoeing horses and mules, making hogsheads, repairing barns and slave quarters, making wagons, cutting timber. The slave who had been trained to a craft always commanded a higher price than the ordinary field hand. "To be sold at public vendue," states an advertisement in the *South Carolina Gazette* in 1744, "a parcel of choice negroes, two of them good sawyers and one a good cooper."[15] Of another group offered for sale, one was a master shoemaker and well skilled in the carpenter's trade, and another "an extraordinary good cooper and very handy at the wheelwright's trade."[16] When Goose Creek Point plantation was sold in 1749, there were numbered among the slaves "several pairs of sawyers, two coopers, two or three indifferent house-carpenters and a ship-carpenter and caulker."[17] The use of slave artisans in the tobacco plantations of Virginia and Maryland, although less common than with the rice growers of South Carolina, was none the less frequent. Ralph Wormeley owned a Negro cooper and a Negro carpenter valued each at £35.[18]

"It was much the practice with gentlemen of landed and slave estates . . . so to organize them as to have considerable resources within themselves, to employ and pay few tradesmen and to buy little or none of the coarse stuffs and materials used by them," wrote General John Mason, son of George Mason. "Thus my father had among his slaves, carpenters, coopers, sawyers, blacksmiths, tanners, curriers, shoemakers, spinners, weavers and knitters and even a distiller. His woods furnished timber and plank for the carpenters and coopers and charcoal for the blacksmiths; his cattle . . . supplied skins for the tanners, curriers and shoemakers; and his sheep gave wool and his fields produced cotton and flax for the weavers and spinners, and his orchards fruit for the distiller. His carpenters and sawyers built and kept in repair all the dwelling houses, barns, stables, ploughs, harrows, gates, etc., on the plantations and the outhouses of the house. His coopers made the hogsheads the tobacco was prized in and the tight casks to hold the cider and other liquors. The tanners and curriers, with

[15]February 27, 1749, No. 518.
[16]*South Carolina Gazette*, Apl. 15, 1745, No. 577.
[17]*Ibid.*, January 2–19, 1749, No. 769.
[18]*Records of Middlesex*, 1698–1713, p. 130.

the proper vats, etc., tanned and dressed the skins as well for upper as for lower leather to the full amount of the consumption of the estate and the shoemakers made them into shoes for the Negroes. A professed shoemaker was hired for three or four months in the year to come and make up shoes for the white part of the family. The blacksmith did all the iron work . . . as making and repairing ploughs, harrows, teeth, chains, bolts, etc. The spinners, weavers and knitters made all the coarse cloths and stockings used by the negroes and some of finer texture worn by the white family. . . . The distiller made every fall a good deal of apple, peach and persimmon brandy."[19]

In the larger towns in all parts of the South, slaves were trained to various crafts and used in the shops of the larger shipwrights, cabinetmakers, shoemakers, wigmakers, etc. When John Dixon, of Williamsburg, left Virginia for England he offered for sale his Negro craftsmen, including blacksmiths, shoemakers, carpenters, barbers and plasterers.[20] In the same manner Abraham Knight, of Charleston, tallow chandler, when he left South Carolina, advertised for sale "three young negroes that work at the business."[21] One "young negro fellow" who "from his youth was brought up to weaving" not only could weave twelve yards a day, but actually was capable of constructing his own loom.[22] Despite innumerable cases of this kind one is inclined to doubt the statement that one Charleston cabinetmaker employed sixty slaves in his shop.[23]

The custom of hiring out Negro artisans was common in many parts of the South. When a master craftsman died, his widow often found that she could depend on a fair revenue from the work of his slave helpers. "This is to give notice that Mary Stevenson, widow to John Stevenson, glazier and painter . . . hath two negroes to hire out by the day who understand painting very well," we read in the *South Carolina Gazette*, in 1735.[24] Others seem to have made a business of purchasing trained artisans in

[19]Kate Mason Rowland, *Life of George Mason*, I, pp. 101, 102.
[20]*Virginia Gazette* (Hunter), Sept. 19, 1751.
[21]*South Carolina Gazette*, February 28, 1743, No. 466.
[22]*Ibid.*, September 22, 1746, No. 649.
[23]*Antiques*, August, 1931, XX, p. 83.    [24]October 4-11, No. 89.

order to hire them out to contractors or craftsmen, and the gazettes frequently carried advertisements of Negro blacksmiths, bricklayers, coopers, carpenters, wigmakers and barbers.

This use of Negro craftsmen tended to run white men out of the trades, since it not only lowered wages, but cast a stigma on skilled labor. Slave labor in the rice and tobacco fields had already struck a deadly blow at the yeomanry, now it began to undermine the small but important artisan class. "There is no laboring work done here but what is done by negroes," said William Couper of Norfolk, "and no white man would work with them, although he should be in want."[25] The planter who trained a slave to do his carpenter's work, was reducing by one the number of white carpenters, and perhaps was depriving the South of a white immigrant. Even today, more than seven decades after emancipation, in the North as well as the South, when Negroes enter an occupation, white men usually flee it. Negroes have practically a monopoly on the Pullman porter business, but they are excluded from certain unions and certain trades. In the old South, after the passing of wigs and elaborate hair dressing for men, the barber business fell largely into the hands of blacks. An old Southern gentleman once told me that on his first visit to the North he experienced a kind of shame for the white man who cut his hair and the white girls who waited on him at table. Thousands in the South were shocked when the first Negro postman delivered mail to their front doors. Thus, when the master craftsmen of the old South began to employ Negroes in large numbers, it tended to make carpentry, or bricklaying, or wheelmaking, or cooperage, or tanning the profession of slaves.

Slave workers not only degraded labor, but cheapened it. In 1740 carpenters and joiners received £2 a day in South Carolina money if white, £1 if black; bricklayers and plasterers £2 if white, £1.5 if black.[26] The large planters and the master artisans who owned or hired slave artisans regarded this situation with complacency, but it was bitterly discouraging to the craftsman who came to the province in search of work. In 1747 when a

[25]*Letters of William Couper,* Apl. 26, 1807.
[26]*South Carolina Gazette,* December 25, 1740.

German named Held planned to move to South Carolina in the hope that he could earn a good living as a weaver, a friend predicted that "his service in Carolina will last probably no longer than until the two negro slaves shall have learned the weaver's trade from him and can weave themselves. So it goes through all Carolina; the negroes are made to learn all the trades and are used for all kinds of businesses. For this reason white pepole have difficulty in earning their bread there, unless they become slave overseers or provide themselves with slaves."[27]

The white wage-earners in the crafts protested against this slave competition, but they lacked the numbers and the influence to enforce their wishes. The large users of slave artisans on the plantation and in the shop opposed restrictions and against this combination they were powerless. In 1750, however, they did secure a law putting certain restrictions on the use of hired slaves. No master was to permit his slave to "carry on any handicraft trade in a shop by himself," and each master was obliged to employ one white apprentice or journeyman to every two Negroes.[28] Unfortunately, this law, lacking the support of public opinion, was generally disregarded, and the craftsmen were left to face the full competition of slave labor.

It was in 1744 that a number of Charleston shipwrights petitioned the Council for relief: "That there being such a great number of negro men chiefly employed in mending, repairing and caulking of ships, vessels and boats, and working at the shipwright's trade and business in this town and harbor and other places near the same, that the petitioners who are white persons and have served their times to the trade of a shipwright can meet with little or no work to do, and they and their families are reduced to poverty and must be obliged to leave the province or run the risk of starving."[29]

Thereupon the Council summoned John Yarworth, John Daniell and other leading shipbuilders who at once answered the petition with a heated counterblast. They had used only their own

[27]*Urlsperger Nachrichten*, III, p. 216, quoted by Yates Snowden in *Notes on Labor Organizations in South Carolina*, p. 7.
[28]*South Carolina Gazette*, July 9, 1750, Supplement.
[29]*Journal of Council*, XI, p. 53.

233

slaves, they said; they had in no wise glutted the labor market; if the petitioners could not maintain themselves it was only from lack of industry; what they really wanted was a monopoly so they could demand exorbitant wages, and frequently they had refused work when it was offered them. "We are fully convinced that there is business in this place sufficient for three times the ship carpenters and that the complaint . . . is with no other view than to engross the whole trade into their own hands and thereby to have it in their power to make their own prices."[30]

Thus the English artisan who came to the South found conditions entirely different from those in London or Bristol. What struck him most of all was the absence of guilds. It seemed incredible that craftsmen could ply their trades without the guild to regulate hours and wages, watch over the quality of the output, present their wishes and grievances to the government. But the Southern artisans were too scattered, too few in numbers to organize unions modelled on the guilds. It would have been pointless for the two or three cabinetmakers of Williamsburg to form a guild, it would have been impracticable for them to unite with the cabinetmakers of Annapolis, or of Norfolk. Even in so large a place as Charleston there were not enough artisans in any one trade to make a respectable showing or wield appreciable influence. It is true that in 1794 the Charleston Mechanic Society was organized, with seventy-four members, but it partook more of the nature of a merchant guild than a craft guild.[31]

Yet that something of the old traditions remained is shown by the part taken by tradesmen in municipal parades to celebrate noteworthy events. Typical was the procession of July 4, 1788, at Norfolk, in joint celebration of the Declaration of Independence and Virginia's ratification of the Constitution. A band led the way, followed by groups of tradesmen of the town and vicinity, with standards held aloft bearing mottoes emblematic of their crafts. In the first division were fishermen, brewers and distillers, merchants, grocers, pilots, butchers, bakers, printers, shipwrights, blacksmiths, ropemakers. Behind them came the good ship *Con-*

[30]*Ibid.*
[31]Yates Snowden, *Labor Organizations in South Carolina* (Columbia, 1914), p. 11.

*stitution,* drawn by ten horses. The next division included carpenters, bricklayers, glaziers, seamen, cabinetmakers, hatters, coopers, shoemakers, saddlers, wigmakers, goldsmiths, chandlers, while the mayor, aldermen and councilmen drew up the rear. The crowds who lined the streets and peered down from upper windows were especially interested in two boys representing Adam and Eve attired in fig leaves, who accompanied the tailors to draw attention to the advances made in the art of making clothes.[32] Perhaps there were few in the crowd or the processsion itself who realized that this pageant in its origins went back to the Middle Ages, yet it was no more than a belated survival in America of the age-old tradition of the English guild.

Even more suggestive of the London Lord Mayor's pageant was the Fourth of July celebration at Norfolk in 1831. The military companies led the procession, followed by the tailors bearing a banner with Adam and Eve depicted and the motto, "Naked and ye clothed me." Next came other tradesmen on platforms mounted on wheels plying their vocations—blacksmiths working busily with forge, bellows, and anvil and distributing to the crowd simple articles as they were completed; carpenters sawing, hammering, planing in a workshop; stone-cutters, masons, bricklayers and plasterers slacking lime and laying bricks upon a miniature foundation. In like manner other pageants showed the work of tanners, curriers and morocco-dressers; shoemakers; painters; hatters; coppersmiths, brass-founders, and tin-plate workers; gunsmiths, watchmakers and silversmiths; ropemakers; shipwrights.[33]

Another survival of the English guild was the apprentice system. It was the ambition of most fathers that their sons should acquire land and enter the planter class, but there were some, men of humble fortune usually, who destined them to some one of the trades, and so apprenticed them to a carpenter, or tailor, or cabinetmaker, or silversmith. As in England, the master provided food, lodging, and clothing and promised to teach the apprentice his trade or "mystery" as it was often termed. For the lad it was an industrial school; the master secured a worker who

---

[32]T. J. Wertenbaker, *Norfolk—Historic Southern Port* (Durham, 1931), p. 88.
[33]*Norfolk Herald,* July 6, 1831.

became more and more helpful as the months passed. That the apprentice was considered a real asset is shown by the rewards offered for the return of those who ran away.[34]

The apprentice was protected from abuse by the terms of his contract, and if his father or his guardian was dissatisfied with his treatment, he might bring the matter into court. When a certain Francis Brown, of Lower Norfolk County, Virginia, subjected his apprentice to harsh treatment and failed to teach him his trade, the court took the lad away and apprenticed him to Thomas Nash, Jr., a cooper.[35] Not infrequently fathers left in their wills provisions for the apprenticing of their sons. "My son Marvill shall bring my son James in to school two years and then put him to prentice to some master of a ship till he comes of age to learn navigation," wrote William Blase, of Middlesex County, Virginia, in his will.[36]

In all parts of the South the trades prospered most which were protected in part or entirely from English competition, and which were most favored by local conditions. Of these the building trades were important. Not only was it impossible to import a house from Europe, but it was impracticable to import much of the material. It would have been worse than taking coals to Newcastle to bring timber across the ocean to Maryland, Virginia or the Carolinas. On the other hand, window glass and even sashes, mantels,[37] wallpaper, hardware, etc., were often imported since they could be had at a price which more than compensated for the cost of their transportation.

As persistent as the log-cabin myth is the tradition of houses built with English-made bricks. Yet for many a colonial mansion in the South, investigation has shown the contract with the local brickmaker for the bricks used in its construction, in others the brick itself by its size, color and texture reveals its American origin. The bricks used in the stately Georgian houses of Annapolis are as much a product of the Maryland soil as the tobacco of Calvert or St. Mary's. It paid to import many articles from Eng-

---

[34]*Virginia Gazette*, March 21, 1745; May 30, 1766; *South Carolina Gazette*, September 7–14, 1734, No. 33.

[35]*Lower Norfolk Deed Book*, No. 9.     [36]*Middlesex Order Book*, 1673–1700, p. 35.

[37]*Robert Beverley's Letter Book*, Apl. 15, 1771.

land because the cheapness of English labor more than offset the cost of transportation, but this could not have been true of so bulky and heavy a commodity as brick. Moreover, a large item in the cost of making brick was fuel, and fuel in England was far more expensive than in America where wood was to be had for the cutting.

We have evidence that brick occasionally was imported, possibly as ballast to offset an otherwise light cargo, but rarely indeed do we find an order for brick in the letters of merchants and planters to their factors in England, or stocks of brick in the inventories of importers.[38] In South Carolina, however, a vessel came in occasionally from Boston or London which listed brick as a part of her cargo. Thus the *Hannah* arrived in Charleston harbor in December, 1732, bringing a cargo of New England goods including 20,000 bricks.[39] Seven years later an Act of Assembly set the price of Carolina-made bricks at five pounds per 1000, of New England bricks at three pounds, and of English bricks at six pounds.[40]

But competition with local brickmakers was weak and every Southern town of any size and many rural communities had their brickyard. Typical, no doubt, was the yard at the landing near Gainby, South Carolina, which had two houses nearly 100 feet in length and a "good brick case" about forty feet by twenty and nine feet high. There were twelve arches and "a division in the middle." Wood was used for fuel.[41] The custom of piling the bricks with the headers facing the fire often vitrified one end giving it a dark-bluish tint, while leaving the other end and the sides red. It is this which made possible the checkerboard effect in so many Southern houses where the brick was laid in Flemish bond. The clay was forced into moulds to give the bricks the proper proportions before burning, and the presence of these moulds on many plantations shows that the planters themselves sometimes made their own brick.[42] A good brickmaker, who had

[38]The 99,315 bricks mentioned in the inventory of John Tucker, Norfolk merchant, were almost certainly imported. (*Lower Norfolk Deed Book*, H.)

[39]*South Carolina Gazette*, December 16, 1732.    [40]*Ibid.*, December 25, 1740.

[41]*Ibid.*, November 21–December 3, 1748, No. 763.

[42]*Will of Thomas Carter*, 1735, *William and Mary Quarterly*, XVIII, p. 51.

had experience in "setting and burning the kiln," always commanded good wages, or if a Negro a high price in the slave market.

As colonial New England was the land of frame houses and western Pennsylvania the land of stone houses, so the South was noted for its houses of brick. It is true that many of the small planters built their residences as well as their barns and tobacco houses of wood, but the scores of picturesque little cottages which have withstood the ravages of time testify to the popularity of brick construction. As for the stately mansions, churches and courthouses of Annapolis and Charleston and the tidewater regions of Maryland, Virginia and South Carolina, they were almost invariably of brick. Thus bricklayers constituted a numerous and important trade.

Wages were high. In Charleston, in 1761, bricklayers received six shillings a day in contrast to four shillings for coopers, five for tailors, and only two shillings sixpence for shoemakers.[43] Like tradesmen in the highly skilled crafts, bricklayers often advertised in the gazettes to secure work. "Patrick MacLein, master-bricklayer, just arrived from London, gives this notice to all gentlemen who are pleased to employ him, that he undertakes to finish any kind of building or other brickwork in the most workmanlike manner," we read in the *South Carolina Gazette*.[44] That some bricklayers, like many master carpenters, were also architects, is shown by a notice in *The Gazette* by Samuel Holmes, of Charleston, stating that "he draws draughts of houses and measures and values all sorts of workmanship."[45]

Even more numerous than the bricklayers were the carpenters. In a region where trees were abundant and timber cheap, there were many frame houses, and even when the walls of a residence, or church, or mill were of brick, the interior work called for the services of the carpenter and joiner. They were needed, also, to construct mills, barns, tobacco houses, bridges, fences, slave quarters. In the more thickly settled regions there was a large degree of specialization, so that one hears of joiners, forge carpenters,

[43]*Hist. Collections of South Carolina*, II, p. 260.
[44]May 11–16, 1748, No. 735.     [45]Feb. 2–9, 1734.

millwrights, clapboard carpenters, etc. But often, especially upon the plantations, the carpenter was called upon to do every kind of work, from the carving of moulding to the cutting and squaring of tree trunks with the whip-saw and the smoothing stick and the axe. Nor was it unusual for the same man to combine two or more trades, so that one finds carpenters who were also wheelwrights, or coopers, or shipwrights, or even working at such an unrelated task as making shoes.[46]

Like the bricklayers, carpenters received good wages. In Norfolk carpenters were earning no less than £5 a month, in 1785, with work guaranteed throughout the year, or eighty shillings a week for jobs of short standing.[47] It is true that this was at a time when the town was being rebuilt after its destruction during the Revolution, when every street and alley resounded to the sound of the hammer and the saw. But that wages were high even before the Revolution is shown by the fact that in 1776 no less than seven Norfolk carpenters owned their own houses, more than twice as many as any other group of artisans.[48] In South Carolina it was stated in 1732 that "a skilful carpenter is not ashamed to demand thirty shillings per day besides diet,"[49] which would seem excellent wages, indeed, despite the inflated condition of the currency.

Yet the carpenters and joiners, like other artisans, were plagued by the competition of slave labor. Not only did master carpenters or contractors often own one or more black workmen, but in case of need could hire others. Every large plantation had among its slaves at least one who was skilled with the saw and the hammer and was listed in the overseer's book as Carpenter Dick, or Carpenter Frank or Carpenter Pompey.[50] To Philip Fithian it seemed strange to see "a number of negroes very busy at framing together a small house,"[51] but for the Southerner it was an everyday occurrence.

[46]*South Carolina Gazette,* August 29, 1743.
[47]*Virginia Magazine of Hist. and Biog.,* XXIII, p. 408.
[48]W. H. Stewart, *History of Norfolk County,* pp. 363–367.
[49]Peter Force, *Tracts and Other Papers,* II, "A Description of the Province of South Carolina," p. 7.
[50]*South Carolina Magazine,* V, 8, pp. 214, 215.
[51]P. V. Fithian, *Journal and Letters,* p. 265.

The delicate nature of the joiner's work made him as closely akin to the cabinetmaker as to the carpenter, so that he often devoted part of his time to the fashioning of chairs, tables or cabinets. The sign swinging before the shop of William Brown, in Londontown, Maryland, which proclaimed him a "joiner and cabinet-maker" was by no means exceptional.[52] And we know by a glance at the surviving colonial houses that the joiners were artistic craftsmen of a high order, their cornices, panelling, doors, window sashes, mantels, with their skillful jointing and dovetailing, comparing favorably with those of the best European workmen.

The English carpenter or joiner who migrated to America brought his tools with him as a matter of course, and when they wore out purchased others which had been made in England. There were tool-makers in the South, but they were few in number and their workmanship was not of the best, so that the saw or the gimlet or the broadaxe which had been turned out from a Southern forge could be distinguished at a glance. When "a parcel of turning tools" were stolen from a store at Dorchester, South Carolina, the owner described them as "made in this country" and "very clumsy."[53] Consequently the carpenter of Maryland or Virginia or the Carolinas did his work with the same kind of tools as his fellow workers in the mother country. Apparently there was nothing in American conditions, in the nature of the wood or the requirements of house owners to call for any deviation from the traditional hammer, handsaw, smoothing plane, etc. No doubt the very high cost of labor was an inducement to place in the artisans' hands the finest tools that money could buy, but it seems not to have stimulated the invention and manufacture of new devices nor the improvement of those already in use.

So the Southern carpenter and joiner went his way, content to use the tools to which he had been accustomed from youth, and to which his father and grandfather had been accustomed. And despite the countless minor devices which today clutter up the records of the patent office, they are much the same as those used

[52]*Maryland Gazette*, October 18, 1753.    [53]*South Carolina Gazette*, July 1–8, 1732.

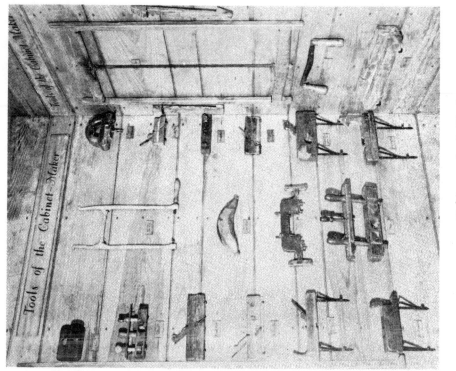

PLATE 35—Cabinetmaker's Tools

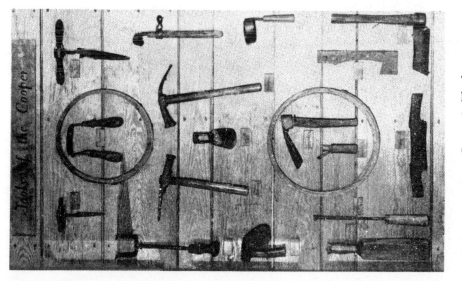

PLATE 34—Cooper's Tools

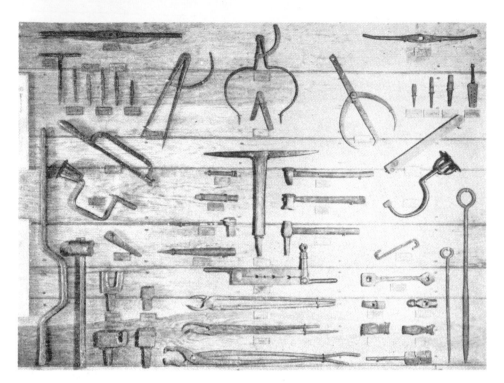

PLATE 36—Blacksmith's Tools

PLATE 37—Deane Shop and Forge, Williamsburg, Virginia

by the modern workmen. Had we stepped into the workshop of John Cumber, who lived in Henrico County, Virginia, two and a half centuries ago, his tools, however crude, would have been familiar to us. On his work bench, or hanging on the wall, we would see a smoothing plane, a jack plane, four "plow" planes, a "key-hole" saw, several gouges, two augurs, two joiners' heading chisels, a pair of compasses, a square, two pocket rules, two broadaxes, three adzes, two chisels, two handsaws, two hammers, a whipsaw, etc.[54] (Plate 29).

The task of Cumber and his fellow colonial carpenters was not lightened, as is that of his modern successors, by the complicated machinery of the mill. He did not receive his sashes, doors, mantels, moulding, shutters, flooring, cut out with precision and ready to be put into their proper places. With his crude tools he himself had to fashion these things. And though this tended to make construction costly, it added immeasurably to its charm. It is the modern mill with its tendency toward exactness and standardization which has covered the American countryside with boxlike, monotonous houses whose ugliness often stands out in contrast to the natural beauty of their surroundings. But the creation of the early builder was a thing of charm because he put into it his own handiwork, not the work of a machine. Every beam of an old Maryland or Virginia farmhouse, every door, every cornice, because of its very roughness is stamped with the character of the carpenter or joiner who hewed it into shape or gave it form with his saw, plane, chisel and gouge.

As the sawyers were the plebeians of the building trades, so the wood-carvers were the aristocrats. One has only to see the superb capitals from the interior pilasters of "Marmion," King George County, Virginia, exhibited in the Metropolitan Museum of Art (Plate 31), or the pediment of the front door of the Hammond House, Annapolis, or the staircase of Rosewell, to realize that the Southern wood-carver was a true artist. Like the joiner, the carver was allied with the cabinetmakers, and we might see him one day chisel in hand cutting out an intricate pattern for a mantel or a Palladian window and the next working on a Gothic or a Chinese

[54]*Henrico Records*, 1677–92, No. 1.

design for a table or a chair. Occasionally the carvers invaded still other fields of carving. William M. Gardner at his shop near the old Beef Market, Charleston, proclaimed himself a "house and ship carver and gilder,"[55] while Henry Hainsdorff, in Queen Street, worked as "gilder and house, ship and coach carver."[56] John Lord, of Charleston, set up his shop in Meeting Street, where he did "gilding and all the branches of house and furniture carving, in the Chinese, French and Gothic tastes." He carried a stock of "chimney glasses, girandoles, picture frames, console brackets . . . stair-case brackets, Ionic, Corinthian and composite capitals, trusses, mouldings . . . proper for decorating the inside of rooms."[57] Henry Crouch, an English house and ship carver who established himself at Annapolis, was "deemed by good judges to be as ingenious an artist at his business as any in the King's dominions."[58]

We do not know when the planters first began to paint their houses, and we may take for granted that their shingles and clapboards in the early days were left to weather. But the doors and windows and the interior woodwork were probably whitewashed or varnished. It was at the end of the seventeenth century that we find William Fitzhugh ordering from England "forty or fifty shillings worth of colors for painting, with pencils, walnut oil and linseed oil,"[59] while two decades later Hugh Jones says that it was the usual practice for the Virginians to paint weatherboarding with white lead and oil.[60] The professional house painter was frequently also a glazier, possibly because of the necessity of painting or priming the lead or the putty of the sashes and casements. He often allied himself, however, with the coachmaker, or the shipwright, or the cabinetmaker. John Haward, of Williamsburg, was a specialist in painting coaches and chariots,[61] while Richard Marten, of Charleston, proclaimed himself house-painter, sign-

[55]*South Carolina Gazette,* October 31, 1799.
[56]*South Carolina and American General Gazette,* October 2, 1776.
[57]Alfred C. Prime, *The Arts and Crafts,* etc. (Phila. 1929), p. 222.
[58]*Maryland Gazette,* January 7, 1762.
[59]*Virginia Magazine of Hist. and Biog.,* V, p. 160.
[60]Hugh Jones, *Present State of Virginia,* p. 32.
[61]*Virginia Gazette,* December 15, 1775.

painter and ship-painter.[62] Benjamin Hawes was even more versatile, not only painting coaches, but "undertaking all kinds of drawing, gilding, varnishing, painting coats-of-arms in water colors."

The workman purchased his colors from the local store, which imported them from England "ready prepared in bladders for house and ship painting," together with "dry colors, gold and metal leaf, brushes, etc."[63] In Charleston, Michael Jeancs, house-painter, ship-painter and glazier, rose to the status of a contractor, himself importing his white lead and other colors, linseed oil and "large crown glass for pictures and sash glass of all sizes for windows" and using skilled workmen "to do the labor."[64] Jeanes does not state whether his painters were white or black, but it is probable that he, like other Charleston contractors, trained slaves to do at least part of the work. We know that his townsman, John Stevenson, glazier and painter, owned two Negroes who "understood painting very well."[65]

The business of cutting down trees and sawing the trunks into beams, boards, lathes or shingles gave occupation to thousands of workmen, for there was a steady demand for building materials not only in the South itself but in the West Indies. Every large plantation had two or more sawyers, slaves usually, and the rasp of the pitsaw was almost as familiar as the song of the fieldhands. Sawmills were used for cutting out boards and framing timbers (Plate 33), but an examination of old houses shows that many of the heavy beams were fashioned either by the ripsaw or the axe. "I propose to keep eight pairs of sawyers constantly at work," said John Holmes, of Charleston. "I am ready and willing to furnish any persons any sort of boards, plank, timber, laths, poles or shingles of the best hard yellow pine . . . having an experienced person in my employ who understands both sawing and squaring to the greatest perfection."[66]

Shipbuilding and ship repairing, although less important in the South than in New England, gave employment to hundreds of

[62]South Carolina Gazette, Sept. 27, 1735.
[63]Ibid., February 13, 1742.
[64]Ibid., May 29, 1755.
[65]Ibid., October 4, 1735.
[66]South Carolina Gazette, January 2, 1742.

men. The fact that the region abounded in tall pines fit for masts, in oak for ship timbers, in pitch, tar and turpentine for caulking, in hemp for rope, offset to some extent the cheapness and skill of English labor. Had we visited the shipyards of Norfolk or Charleston at any time during the eighteenth century, we should have seen one or more brigantines or schooners and a half-dozen sloops on the ways or tied up at the wharves to receive the finishing touches. In Annapolis as early as 1698 there were under construction three ships for Maryland merchants and one of no less than 450 tons for an English owner.[67] And though the royal governors reported from time to time that shipbuilding in the South was inconsiderable, frequent notices in the gazettes of colonial-made vessels for sale tend to contradict them. In one number of the *Virginia Gazette,* two ships are advertised, one of about 236 tons, built in Gloucester County, the other of "about 350 hogsheads of tobacco," put together at Suffolk.[68]

In North Carolina there is little evidence of shipbuilding during the colonial period, despite the fact that masts, timbers, tar, pitch could be had in abundance from her forests. But it would have been useless to lay down the frame of a brig or a large schooner on the banks of the Chowan or the Pamlico, when she might stick fast on her first attempt to run through Hatteras Inlet. During the Revolution and after, however, shipbuilding became more active. "The subscriber has for sale at the town of Beaufort, . . . a new vessel on the stocks well calculated for a fast builder," it was stated in a local gazette in 1778, "55 feet keel, . . . 11 feet rake forward, 18½ feet beak and 7½ feet hold."[69]

More important than shipbuilding, however, was ship repairing and refitting. The arrival of the tobacco fleet from England, especially if it had encountered stormy weather, brought a burst of activity to the yards of Norfolk, Portsmouth, Annapolis and Baltimore. When a ship limped up the Elizabeth her cargo was unloaded, her sails and rigging stored in some nearby loft and her crew lodged at the various ordinaries. "She was then con-

[67]*Maryland Historical Magazine*, II, p. 169.
[68]*Virginia Gazette*, May 7, 1767.
[69]*James Sprunt Historical Studies*, XX, No. 1.

ducted to shallow water and careened by the aid of fall and blocks. Next a lighter, with steaming kettles of pitch or tar, was run up beside her bottom, so that the negro workers could caulk up every leaky seam. After this the various groups of artisans had their turn, for glaziers were needed to replace the broken glass, iron-workers to fit in new bolts, coopers to repair damaged hogsheads, sail makers to patch the torn canvas, carpenters to make new hatches, or replace masts or spars which had gone overboard."[70] When the ship *Phaeton,* bound to New York from Charleston, put in at Norfolk for refitting, the work required thirteen barrels of tar and four barrels of pitch, and gave employment to eight shipwrights of whom two were Negroes.[71] The cost of repairing, refitting and "victualling" the *Thomas and Sarah,* of London, was £586.1.9 3/9, including wages for ten ship-carpenters, one glazier, one sail-maker and one blacksmith.[72]

The unprecedented burst of activity in the ship-building industry during the French Revolution and the Napoleonic wars, brought constant employment at high wages to thousands of workers in the South. There was need for sawyers to cut down the trees and square the timbers; tar burners to tend the kilns which dotted the pine forests; shipwrights to shape the beams of the frame and fit into place planking, masts and spars; glaziers for the cabin windows; sailmakers, ship chandlers, anchor-makers, blacksmiths, ropemakers, blockmakers, ship carvers, caulkers.

The alternating periods of depression and activity in the ship-building and ship-refitting trades had no counterpart in the cooperage trade, for there was a constant demand for hogsheads and barrels. In Virginia, Maryland and North Carolina thousands of hogsheads were needed for the great tobacco crop; in South Carolina the planters made their own indigo vats, while the wharves of every Southern port were piled high with barrels packed with foodstuffs for shipment to the West Indies. To the West Indies went also vast numbers of "knock-down" hogsheads which the island planters put together for packing with sugar, while staves and heading for wine pipes went out to Madeira. Governor Gooch

[70]T. J. Wertenbaker, *Norfolk—Historic Southern Port* (Durham, 1931), p. 45.
[71]*Grenlees and Hardie Ledger,* p. 52a.    [72]*Ibid.,* p. 19.

estimated that Virginia alone required 100,000 hogsheads and barrels for her exports of tobacco, wheat and pitch and tar, while one vessel alone from North Carolina carried 4800 white-oak hogshead staves.[73]

The Southern cooper, moreover, unlike so many of his fellow artisans, had nothing to fear from English competition. Despite low wages in England it did not pay to send timber across the Atlantic from America to have it made up into hogsheads and barrels for shipment back to the planters. Thus it was that every town, every village, almost every plantation had its cooperage. Had we visited one of these establishments, in a plantation shed, or hidden in the woods, or in a back street of Norfolk or Charleston, the tools would have seemed primitive indeed. Today barrel staves, which must be properly curved with suitable increase of width in the middle and with bevelled edges to form tight joints, are turned out with great rapidity by complicated machinery. But the cooper of old had to depend upon his saw, his adze, his sunplane, his compass saw, his chamfering knife (Plate 34). The staves ready, he set them in an upright frame, bound the lower halves together with truss hoops, steamed them to make the wood pliable, planed the inside with his howel, cut out the heads and jointed them with dowel pins, prepared the grooves with his croze, fitted in the heads, drove down the hoops with his hammer. It was necessary that the wood be well seasoned and the joints fitted together with exactness, otherwise when the hogshead was rolled through the bed of a stream on its way to market, or was left out in the rain at a wharf, or was drenched with sea-water during a storm, the tobacco or sugar with which it was filled would be ruined. Despite the need of skilled workmanship, slaves were successfully trained to be coopers in all of the Southern colonies. No doubt the master picked the most intelligent of his young Negroes to train for this important work, who in turn gave to it his best efforts, for it brought certain valued privileges and a rank superior to that of the field hand.

Perhaps less numerous than the coopers, but indispensable to the economic life of the South, were the blacksmiths (Plate 36).

[73]*North Carolina Gazette* (Jas. Davis), May 15, 1778.

This was not the day when the smith confined his work to making horseshoes and fitting them on to the old family mare or the plough-horse. He was often a skilled artisan whose wide range of activities required long training and even talent. He might be toolmaker, lockmaker, nailmaker, cutler, hingemaker, screwmaker all in one; he might turn out such widely diversified objects as bells, plows, gutters, wheel-rims, jacks. John Purkis, of Charleston, was especially versatile, supplying "gentlemen, merchants, planters and artificers" with smith's work for "mills, engines or any machines, shipping or plantations; tools for goldsmiths, blacksmiths, as vices, hammers, beck irons, screws and tools to make most sorts of screws."[74] He was rivalled, however, by his fellow Charlestonian, Lustinu Stoll, whose shop was next to Granville's bastion on the bay, who made "broad and narrow axes, cooper's axes and adzes, drawing knives and all sorts of edged tools . . . also bells, spikes and small nails."[75]

These highly skilled smiths had to face the competition of English artisans, for no matter how heavy the product was it could be shipped across the Atlantic and sold at a profit. Every large importer had in his storehouse nails, hoes, axes, locks, saws, knives, plows, hinges, whose price and excellent workmanship the local smiths found it difficult to match.[76] But there was a constant call for repair work, not only upon visiting vessels in the larger ports, but upon pumps, tools, locks, wagons, etc. And in the country the local blacksmith, whether he were a white artisan who had set up his smithy at the county court, or a slave working for his master on the plantation, was an indispensable unit in Southern economic life. It was to him that the planter was forced to come when his horse needed shoeing, or his iron kettle developed a leak, or he wanted nails for a new barn, or the hinge of his garden gate broke. Nor did Longfellow's famous smith hold more interest for the children of old Cambridge than the brawny Negro smith of the South for the children of the rice and tobacco plantations.

[74]*South Carolina Gazette,* December 2, 1732.
[75]*Ibid.,* December 23, 1732.
[76]*Lower Norfolk Deed Book,* H, pp. 32–59.

Indeed, the blacksmith shop of old was a fascinating place. In one corner was the forge with its glowing fire which the smith urged on with the bellows; here was the anvil, here the tub of water for cooling the hot iron, here the heavy hammer, here the pick-up tongs or the side grip tongs[77] (Plate 37). Hanging on the wall beams one saw other tools, formerly in frequent use but almost unknown today—bending forks, bolt headers, punches, bird-cage bit stocks for making screws, square bore drills, screw taps, the compass.[78] On the earth floor, or propped against the wall were the products of the forge, mute witnesses of the smith's skill—wheel-rims, bolts, hinges, a shovel, iron pots, a spit, a small tub of nails, a pair of iron traces.

Much of the iron used by the smiths of Virginia and Maryland came from local forges. In Maryland the production of pig iron from the Principio Iron Works, Lawson's Iron Works, the Patapsco Iron Works, Onion's Iron Works, the Patuxent Iron Works, and others at one time assumed very large proportions. "I am erecting a furnace and forge in a back part near the mountains, though not so far from Patapsco as not to make carriage of bar iron commodious," wrote Doctor Charles Carroll, in 1752. To his agent in England he sent at one time thirty-five tons of pig iron, at another ten tons, at still another forty-five tons, at the same time complaining that the mother country by her low prices would "ruin her children of the plantations."[79]

The iron founder seems not to have entered into competition with the blacksmith until the Revolutionary period, when the need for casting firearms stimulated the erection of foundries. But the brass and copper founders were fairly numerous in the colonial period, and their harness buckles, coach knobs, hinges, fenders, fire dogs and bells were displayed in the shops of Annapolis, Norfolk, Williamsburg and Charleston.[80] James Haldane, of Williamsburg, advertised in March, 1772, that he made copper and brass stills, brewing coppers, sugar boilers, fullers' and hatters' coppers, capuchin plate warmers, tea kitchens, stew pans,

[77]Wolcott Collection of Handicraft Tools, Colonial Williamsburg, Inc.
[78]*Virginia Magazine of Hist. and Biog.,* XXXI, p. 370.
[79]"Letter Book of Charles Carroll," *Maryland Hist. Magazine,* XXIV, pp. 35, 192, 381.
[80]*Virginia Gazette,* August 8, 1751.

dutch ovens, etc.[81] Equally versatile was Philip Syng, of Annapolis, who made and repaired "all sorts of brass work such as candlesticks, heads or knobs of all sizes for shovels, dogs, etc., furniture for desks and chests of drawers, knockers for doors." He also cast "bells of all sizes" and gave "the best prices for old brass and copper."[82] In Charleston several skilled founders vied with each other for the patronage of the wealthy. John Robertson, "brass founder in King street," made "all sorts of brass candlesticks . . . also cabinet, desk, drawer, coach, chair and chaise mountings; brass tongs, shovels and fenders; bells, brass weights, candle moulds, sheet lead, sash and other weights."[83]

It is difficult to explain why the brass and copper founders were so much more numerous in the South than the pewterers. Even the humblest family had its quota of pewter utensils, while in the homes of the rich when silver expelled pewter dishes from the dining room, they merely retreated to the kitchen. The use of this cheap and convenient metal in basins, dishes, plates, spoons and porringers was almost universal, while pewter beakers, candlemoulds, candlesticks, ewers, flagons, salt-cellars and tankards were common. Yet the pages of the gazettes are strangely silent as to the existence of local pewterers and we have been able to identify a mere half dozen or so. One would imagine that the task of repairing old pewter utensils in itself would have been enough to keep a fairly large group of artisans employed. There is reason to believe that old pewter was occasionally melted down on the larger plantations and then recast into plates or basins or spoons. In 1774 William Smith and his brother, of Stafford County, Virginia, announced that they made "all sorts of moulds for casting pewter," and there are a few references to Virginia-made pewter utensils.[84] But the common practice seems to have been to send discarded pewter ware to England, there to be melted down and recast.

A few years ago archæologists at Jamestown were thrilled at the discovery of a pewter spoon-handle with a trifid termination bear-

[81]*Ibid.*, March 12, 1772.    [82]*Maryland Gazette*, March 15, 1759.
[83]*South Carolina Gazette*, December 16, 1760.
[84]*York County Deed Book*, 1773.

ing the "touch" of Joseph Copeland, of Chuckatuck, and the date 1675.[85] It is possible that this young man, a former apprentice of a London pewterer, may have worked steadily at his trade after coming to Virginia, but his career is lost in obscurity. Certainly very few followed in his footsteps, and Mungo Campbell of Annapolis; David Evans of Baltimore; William Willett of Upper-Marlborough, Maryland; Anthony Corne, William Linthwaite and Claudius Compaire, of Charleston; and a lone Norfolk worker, constitute almost the entire pewterers' fraternity of the South concerning whom we have any information. Nor have we any means of knowing whether these men were real artists comparable to the famous English or northern pewterers.

Far more numerous were the Southern silversmiths. Alexander Kerr, James Galt, William Waddell, James Craig and others catered to the growing demand in Williamsburg for silver porringers, punch bowls, ladles, salt-cellars, shoe-buckles, spoons, sugar dishes, tankards, thimbles, teapots, snuffers, basins, candlesticks, ewers, mugs, etc. It was the custom often for the silversmiths to import these articles from England and to offer them for sale in their shops, but some they fashioned themselves. James Craig announced in August 1772 that jewelry, gold and silver work was made in his shop, while Waddell took old gold or silver in exchange for new work or to be "worked up in any taste the owner chooses."[86] The Virginia silversmiths were usually also watchmakers and clockmakers, and might turn their attention one hour to making silver spoons or shoe buckles, the next to repairing "all sorts of plain, repeating, horizontal, stop and skeleton watches."[87]

In Charleston Moreau and Sarrozin made and repaired "all kinds of jewellers' and silversmiths' work, motto rings after the best and newest manner," and engraved coats of arms and sank seals "according to heraldry" and mended and cleaned clocks and watches.[88] Charles Harris called himself a "working silversmith" to indicate that he was more than a jeweller or repairer. He made

[85]*William and Mary Quarterly*, Second Series, XVIII, pp. 227 ff.
[86]*Virginia Gazette*, August 27, 1772; September 17, 1767.
[87]*Ibid.*, June 23, 1768.
[88]*South Carolina Gazette*, February 27, 1755.

and sold "new fashioned bottle stands, table-spoons feathered on the handle, dish stands, cruet frames after a new fashion, pepper casters, ink stands, tankards, fluted and plain turin ladles, punch ladles out of dollars, rings, buckles, buttons, etc."[89] Yet the silversmiths, like so many other Southern artisans, found it hard to compete with their English rivals, and but a fraction of the for-

FIGURE II. TANNING LEATHER

tunes which the planters invested in silverware ever came into their hands.

Quite different was the situation with all concerned with the tanning and currying of leather, and with converting it into shoes, saddles, harness and work-clothes. Every planter, great and small, was the owner of cattle, so that the supply of rawhides was abundant. When a cow or calf died, or was butchered for the winter's meat supply, the hide had either to be tanned in the colonies or go to waste. To pack it in the hold of a vessel for shipment to England meant that it would be spoiled before reaching London or Glasgow. "They have hides enough, and very cheap," it was reported in 1732, "they make good lime with oyster shells and the bark of oak trees is so plentiful that it costs nothing but the

[89]*Ibid.*, August 1, 1768.

trouble of gathering."[90] Yet only too often the planters did not take the trouble to remove the hide when a cow died. But gradually, upon the larger plantations, the owners began to import indentured workers trained as tanners, to set up small tanneries and to train slaves for the work. Here were brought, not only the hides produced on the plantation itself, but upon the small farms for miles around. In the seaport towns, where cattle were driven in for butchering and meat was exported to the West Indies in large quantities, tanning became an important occupation.

An arduous and complicated task it was, this tanning of hides on the Southern plantations (Fig. 11). The hide was first salted, then washed in large vats, then dried, then soaked in lime to remove the coagulated proteid matter, then worked over an inclined beam with a dull knife to stretch it and separate the fibers, then hung in a hot room to facilitate the "unhairing," then limed again, then gone over with the flesher's beam to remove fat, then washed again, then "pickled," then dipped in a solution of tannic acid made from the bark of oak trees. Finally came the successive stages of currying—scraping, cleaning, beating, smoothing and coloring.

The equipment required a considerable outlay, for the tanner could not begin work until he was provided with a mill for grinding the bark, with vats and pits, and with a set of tools—knives, scrapers, shears, etc. An Annapolis tanner announced in 1746 that in his yard "there is a good pump, a new millhouse, with a good mill and stone and several other convenient houses for following that business."[91] Another Marylander boasted that he employed an English tanner who had followed the business for twenty years and "would tan for any person by the hide, or for half," would purchase hides with good shoes, and would curry leather for those so desiring.[92] In South Carolina one tannery was put up for sale with "about 600 sides of leather in the vats, the greatest part of them tanned," and another with "five large, good, new vats, large troughs and other conveniences, with six cords of bark."[93]

[90]Peter Force, *Tracts*, etc., II, "A Description of the Province of South Carolina," p. 7.
[91]*Maryland Gazette*, January 21, 1746.    [92]*Ibid.*, October 13, 1730.
[93]*South Carolina Gazette*, July 14, 1733.

252

For the leather turned out by the local tanneries there were many uses. It might be made up into shoes or boots, might go into saddles, harness or work clothes, some was converted into bags, or bellows, or caps, or chair bottoms, or trunks or even moccasins. The plantation shoemakers, the Uncle Remuses of colonial days, usually confined their activities to making shoes

FIGURE 12. THE SHOEMAKER

for their fellow slaves. The planter often brought in a professional shoemaker to make up the shoes for his family, or perhaps purchased what was needed from London. Although the itinerant and the plantation shoemakers could not match the work of the famous Didsburys, there were shops in Charleston or Williamsburg which boasted of the latest styles for both women and men. John Lewis of Charleston made "buckskin boots of all sorts, spatterdashes, shoes, pumps and slippers, double channelled and turned after the best manner and newest fashion; likewise all sorts of the newest women's boots, shoes, pumps and slippers, inside and outside cork shoes, either silk or beaded, with hard clogs, toed clogs"[94] (Plates 38 and 39).

For the children of the plantation it was a delight to watch the

[94]*South Carolina Gazette,* June 1, 1748.

253

shoemaker at his work, his leather apron spread over his knees, his thread, twisted and waxed, stored in one drawer, and his pegs in another, his lasts, sewing vice, pincers, hammers, rasp, stitch bore, and other tools hanging on the wall or resting on the bench beside him. His work was often very crude and his clogs, or shoes with wooden soles, reminded one of the sabots of France. Beverley criticized the Virginians for permitting so many hides to go to waste. And when the planters do work up some of them into shoes for the slaves, he adds, the work is so badly done that the poorest white men would not wear them if they could find any others (Fig. 12).

A fair proportion of the local output of leather fell into the hands of the saddlers, to be made into saddles, bridles, harness, etc. Even in the pioneer period of the colonies, when the roads were mere paths in the woods and a lady's coach was unknown, travel by horseback was common. The planter, when he went to church or visited a neighbor, or attended court, led the mare out of his stable, fastened on the saddle and mounted for the journey. Bacon's Rebellion was fought largely on horseback, and at one time the youthful "rebel" had seven hundred cavalry under his command.[95] And as the early South was the land of saddles, so in the eighteenth century it became also the land of harnesses, for with better roads the use of coaches, chairs and chaises became widespread.

Typical of the professional saddlers was Richard Lewis, of Annapolis, who opened shop at the old prison, where he sold "men and women's saddles, bridles, pack-saddles, mail-pillions, etc., made in the best manner, at the most reasonable prices."[96] That saddlers sometimes used slave labor we know from a notice of the executors of Marmaduke Ash, a Charlestonian, when in addition to saddles, calf skins and saddlers' tools, a Negro man "from his infancy brought up to the saddler's business" was offered for sale.[97]

[95]T. J. Wertenbaker, *Torchbearer of the Revolution*, p. 126.

[96]*Maryland Gazette*, November 22, 1745.

[97]*South Carolina Gazette*, August 24, 1752. Ash also used indentured labor. *Ibid.*, Apl. 2, 1737. Among the Charleston saddlers were John Laurens and Thomas Nightingale.

Allied with the saddlers, yet constituting a distinct and important group, were the coachmakers. The wealthy planters vied with each other in the costliness and beauty of their coaches, as in their houses, gardens and lavish entertainments. Richly ornamented, drawn often by four or six horses, attended by liveried Negroes powdered and dignified, they made a splendid picture as they rolled along over the roads of Virginia or South Carolina. We gain an idea of what these vehicles were like from a bill for a post chaise of 1784. The chaise was to be very handsome, the body to be carved and run with raised beads and scrolls, the roof and upper panels to have plated mouldings and head plates; on the door panels were to be painted Prince of Wales ruffs with arms and crests in large handsome mantlings; the body was to be highly varnished, the inside lined with superfine light-colored cloth and trimmed with raised Casoy laces; the sides stuffed and quilted; there were to be polished plate-glass mahogany shutters, plated door handles, folding inside steps and a wainscoted trunk under the seat.[98]

These costly vehicles were usually made in England, the planters preferring to pay the heavy cost of transportation to trusting to the local makers. But when a wheel broke, or the upholstery wore out, or there was need for a fresh coat of paint, they found it impracticable to ship the coach back across the ocean. So there gradually developed in the larger towns a group of skilled artisans who in time became makers as well as repairers of coaches. In Williamsburg John Sheppard, Charles Talliaferro, Samuel Bowler, William Holliday, Eckanah Deane and others hung out their signs on the Duke of Gloucester Street or the Palace Green.

Deane, formerly an apprentice in Dublin, was very proud of the fact that he had made a coach, a phaeton and a chaise for no less a person than Lord Dunmore, the governor. In a notice in the *Virginia Gazette* he proclaimed his skill in making landaus, chariots, post chaises, carricles and chairs, steel springs and other metal work for vehicles, as well as in painting and gilding.[99] He then took occasion to warn the public against Peter Hardy, formerly

[98]*Virginia Magazine of Hist. and Biog.*, VIII, p. 334.
[99]*Virginia Gazette*, May 21, 1772.

his helper, but now his rival, "who resides near the madhouse and tells of his long experience in Europe, but never was one yard nearer it than he now is, nor in his life ever saw three four-wheel carriages made till within these two or three years."[100] The next week Hardy, nothing daunted, came back with a notice in which he called Deane the Palace Street Puffer, an Irish boaster, falsifier and victim of that "troublesome passion called envy." How lucky, even extraordinary, it had been for Deane, he added sarcastically, that he should have found a "greenhorn" who yet had completed one of the three coaches at the palace of which he made such a boast.[101] Whether the belligerent coachmakers contented themselves with hurling invectives at each other in the press, or whether their quarrel ended in a fisticuff when they met on the Duke of Gloucester Street or the Palace Green, we are not informed. Deane worked at his trade until his death in 1775, and Hardy moved to Botetourt Town, Gloucester, where he continued the "coach and chair making business."[102]

Prominent among the coachmakers of Charleston was Benjamin Hawes, who advertised that he had on hand "five riding chairs with iron axle-trees, neatly painted and gilt" with compartments large enough to hold two persons, "not one and a half"; as well as ten chairs and three sets of harnesses.[103] In the same city Benjamin Heope stated that he had been to the pains of getting timber peculiarly proper for riding chairs, and that any who employed him could depend upon prompt delivery at reasonable costs.[104]

Usually the coachmaker himself fashioned the wheels for his coaches, but he might turn to a wheelwright, if he so desired, for there were many in the South. To cut out rims, turn the spokes, forge the tires, bore the hub with the reamer required not only great skill but a special set of tools—gouges, round planes, hub lathes, travellers, draw knives, jacks, etc. Richard Webb, of Charleston, a newcomer from London, was typical of his group. He made "all sorts of carts and cart-wheels, waggons, coach and chair

[100]*Virginia Gazette* (Rind), November 11, 1773.
[101]*Ibid.*, November 18, 1773.     [103]*South Carolina Gazette*, Feb. 9, 1760.
[102]*Ibid.*, Sept. 22, 1774.     [104]*Ibid.*, March 14, 1748.

256

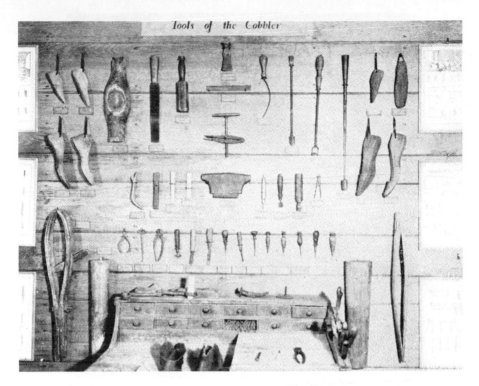

PLATE 38—Cobbler's Tools

PLATE 39—Shoemaker, Colonial Williamsburg

PLATE 40—Barber Shop, Williamsburg, Virginia

PLATE 41—Interior of Barber Shop, Williamsburg, Virginia

wheels, wheelbarrows and all other sorts of work belonging to the trade of wheelwright."[105] Although the wheel-maker was too much of a specialist to become commonly a part of plantation economy, we occasionally find either an indentured worker or a slave who was trained to do this trade. And to the country wheelwright came not only the broken wheels and carts of the plantation to which he belonged, but of the smaller farms for miles around.[106]

In the production of cloth and clothing the Southern workman was left almost unprotected from the killing competition of the mother country. Every English vessel which put into Charleston harbor or sailed up the James or the Potomac carried great boxes and bales filled with linen, calico, woolens, cotton cloth, caps, stockings, gloves, coats, vests, breeches, etc. Not only the planter and his family, but the overseer and even the slaves were usually clothed in English cloth, and less often in English-made garments. It was only when war or other disturbing factors sent up the price of English goods that they turned their attention to spinning, weaving and tailoring. Yet the South did have its spinners, weavers, fullers, tailors, its mantua-makers, hosiers, hatters and even furriers.

Spinning, of course, was the especial task of women, in humble homes, of the farmer's wife and daughters, on the larger plantations, of female slaves. A French traveller in Virginia wrote in 1686 that the importation of cloth was so universal that not a woman in the entire colony knew how to spin, but there is abundant evidence in inventories, wills and invoices, to contradict him. Nathaniel Harrison had three spinning wheels, Philip Ludwell three, Robert Dudley two, while Thomas Jefferson, ancestor of President Jefferson, owned a "hoop" spinning wheel. At Mt. Vernon, in one of the outhouses, buzzed a whole battery of spinning wheels and flax wheels, under the guidance of Negro girls, turning out yarn, flax thread for the loom.[107]

In fact Washington's own workmen seem to have made most of the cloth used upon his various farms. In one year, with the

---

[105]Ibid., Sept. 5, 1741.     [106]Ibid., April 11, 1740.
[107]E. E. Prussing, The Estate of George Washington (Boston, 1927), p. 445.

work of one man and four girls, he wove 815¾ yards of linen, 365¼ yards of woolen cloth, 144 yards of linsey and 40 yards of cotton for a total of 1365 yards. Later when he increased his force, his output included "striped woolen, woolen plaided, cotton striped, linen, wool-birdseye, cotton filled with wool, linsey, . . . cotton-India dimity, . . . broadcloth, counterpaid, etc."[108]

With the boycott of British goods following the Stamp Act and other repressive measures by the mother country in the decade preceding the Revolution, the production of colonial cloth was greatly stimulated. Wheelwrights turned their attention to making spinning wheels, looms were imported, hemp-mills were set up, people prided themselves on wearing only American-made clothes, and one man went all the way to England to learn how to prepare and use dyes.[109] At Williamsburg a manufacturing company was organized which gave employment to a number of spinning and weaving apprentices, and which announced that it was prepared to turn out as good cloth as could be had from England. To stimulate the good work the James City County Committee offered a reward of £40 for any person who should come to Virginia and make there 500 pairs of cotton cards and a like number of woolen cards.[110]

Robert Carter of Nomini, who for years prior to the Revolution had nourished hopes of establishing a cloth factory, in 1777 was elated when he discovered a group of six expert spinners and weavers equipped with spinning machines and looms, who knew how to make cottons, jeans, calicoes, muslins, velvets, corduroys and linens of "any fineness." Summoning these men to Nomini Hall, the Councillor worked out the details of his new venture, and in 1778 the factory was put into production at his Aries plantation in Westmoreland County. The workers, all of whom were white, agreed as a part of their duty, to teach certain selected slaves to spin, weave, shear, dye and full, so that eventually the blacks did most of the work. So long as the Revolution continued, the Aries plant prospered, not only supplying the needs of

---

[108]Paul Wilstach, *Mount Vernon*, p. 67.
[109]*Virginia Gazette*, September 15, 1775.
[110]*Ibid.*, (Dixon and Hunter), February 18, 1775.

Carter's plantations, but turning out a surplus for sale; but with the return of normal conditions, it ceased to prosper. None the less, it was still in operation when the Councillor died in 1804.[111]

The output of cloth would have been wasted had not fulling mills been erected to clean, shrink and thicken it by exposing it to moisture, heat and pressure. "The fulling mill at the mouth of Patuxent River is now provided with a good fuller and ready for work, such as fulling, dying and pressing," it was announced in October, 1769. "As this expensive undertaking was begun and prosecuted principally to encourage the manufacture of woollen country-cloth at a time when the apprehensive measures lately adopted . . . by the mother country render it indispensably necessary," the owners appealed to the public to support the work.[112] Fulling mills were set up also in Westmoreland County, Henrico and elsewhere in Virginia.

From the fulling mill the cloth passed into the hands of the tailors. On the plantations the easier tasks were performed by slaves, while a professional tailor was brought in under terms of indenture or hired by the day to make clothes for the owner and his family. William Ball, uncle of George Washington, directed that blankets of coarse cotton be cut out for his slaves, a good suit be made for each "not too leanly nor bobtailed," and that rolls of brown osnaburg be cut up into shifts or shirts. Bess, Winnie and other slaves were to be provided with thread and needles for this work, but he got a "tailor to make their woollen clothes."[113] In earlier days, when professional tailors were seldom available, the wealthy planters made a point of securing indentured tailors. "Pray if possible procure me a tailor for mine is almost free," wrote William Byrd I to his agents in England.[114]

In the golden days of the mid-eighteenth century, when the wealthy planters patterned their life upon that of the English country gentleman and so demanded the latest styles in clothes, tailors became quite numerous. Establishing their shops in Annapolis, Williamsburg, Norfolk, Charleston and other towns, they

[111]Louis Morton, *Robert Carter of Nomini Hall*, pp. 175–177.
[112]*Maryland Gazette*, October 12, 1769.
[113]Library of Congress, *Joseph Ball Letter Book*, February 18, 1744.
[114]*Virginia Magazine of Hist. and Biog.*, XXI, p. 130.

sought the patronage of the leading families for miles around. At Williamsburg, Madam Bodie announced in 1771 that she had just arrived from London, and was prepared to make or trim all sorts of ladies' sacks, coats, gowns and petticoats in the "newest taste." She also could make Brunswick dresses, Sultana robes and Robedecores, having served her time in the original shop in Pall Mall.[115] Ladies robed by this expert could find partners for the balls in the Palace not less gorgeously attired, for Robert Miller, or John Didip, or Jonathan Prosser all made men's apparel "after the best and newest fashions, laced or plain, full laced designs, figures to the waist."[116]

In the days when the ladies' wasplike waists contrasted strangely with their balloon skirts, it was important that their corsets should be made to order. Even in colonial days Paris had established its superiority to London in ladies' fashions, so that the colonial staymakers often boasted that they had received their training in the French capital. "Lately arrived from Paris, by way of London J. Quash, stay maker," states a notice in the *South Caroline Gazette,* "who makes and sells all sorts of stays, jumps or corsets, childrens' coats, slips and slip stays, all of the best and newest fashions."[117] Thomas Crawford, of Charleston, in 1737 made "a pair of stays" of which he was so proud that he offered to give them away to "any man or woman in the province" who could "make the like." Among the staymakers of Williamsburg were James Wilson, John Halpin, Robert Steele and James Douglas, the last appeal in style and skillful workmanship, all of them, if we may believe their advertisements. And woe to the unhappy lady who attended the theatre on the Green or a dance in the Palace or the Apollo room of the Raleigh Tavern if she wore stays which fitted poorly or were a season behind the times!

Nor were the Southern colonies destitute of hatters, despite the cheapness and fine workmanship of English-made hats and bonnets. William Prew, of Annapolis, "hatter from London," made "all sorts of beaver and castor hats for men, women and children." He also turned, cleaned and dyed hats.[118] The Southern

---

[115]*Virginia Gazette,* October 24, 1771.   [117]January 22, 1750.
[116]*Ibid.,* December 8, 1752.   [118]*Maryland Gazette,* September 11, 1751.

hatter, though handicapped by the scarcity of beavers in the region, was compensated by the presence of other fur-bearing animals. William Gren, of Charleston, who made "fine beavers and other hats very reasonably," offered 2s. 6d. to any "man or negro" who would bring in a "fox or raccoon" skin.[119] It is doubtful, however, whether any colonial hatter was capable of producing some of the awe-inspiring creations which towered over the heads of the ladies in certain periods of the eighteenth century.

The clothing fraternity did not end with the spinners, weavers, fullers, tailors and hatters, but included hosiers, mantua-makers, glovers and buckskin tailors. The abundance of skins and the rough life on the frontier created an especially large demand for buckskin coats and breeches, which, so it was claimed, were warm in winter and cool in summer. Some far-seeing planters not only themselves wore buckskin while at work, but had breeches made for their slaves.[120] Typical of the buckskin tailors was Thomas Robinson, of Charleston, who dressed skins, prepared "alom leather," washed and made buckskin breeches of several colors. The buckskin tailor retreated westward with the advance of the frontier, probably because the chief demand for his services was to be found in the west or because the supply of skins in the tidewater gave out.

The general use of wigs in the colonies and the necessity of making them fit the head produced a rather large group of barbers (Plates 40 and 41). Unlike his European fellow, the Southern barber wielded his razor only on the beards of his customers, not on their flesh, so that mention of barber-surgeons is rare. But he considered himself a skilled craftsman, almost an artist, since the making of wigs which would give dignity to the judge or grace to the gallant youth was not a task to be intrusted to a novice. Lawrence Withers, of Charleston, announced in the press in 1734 that he had received from England a quantity of fine gray hairs, of all sorts, "being the best for color and quality" that could be produced, which he was prepared to work up into wigs after the newest fashions.[121] The colonists had their own

[119]South Carolina Gazette, October 12, 1734.
[120]Peter Force, Tracts, etc., II, "Description of the Province of South Carolina," p. 7.
[121]South Carolina Gazette, January 18, 1734.

way of honoring gray hairs, for while a brown wig sold for from £8 to £10 in Charleston, a gray wig cost from £10 to £25.[122] The old barber-shop was the predecessor of the modern beauty parlor, for there the ladies could secure the strange creations with which they decked their heads—"towers, locks, têtes, etc."[123] With the passing of wigs and the simplifying of feminine headdress, the barber became a mere cutter of hair and the trade fell largely into the hands of slaves.

In brewing and distilling, as in so many other industries in the South, the chief stimulus was the abundance and cheapness of raw materials. The planter set up a cider press when he saw hundreds of apples in his orchard rotting on the ground, or turned to brewing to utilize his crop of barley or the fruit from his persimmon trees, or wrote his agent in England to send him a copper still so that he could convert his corn or rye or wheat into whiskey. So, in the cellar of the mansion house, one found not only imported liquors—Madeira, Bordeaux, Burgundy, West Indian rum—but casks of plantation beer and ale, or bottles of home-distilled spirits. That brewing and distilling as a by-industry on the plantation was sometimes attended by vexatious difficulties, we gather from the letter of Peter Lyons to his London factors, complaining that the still which they had sent him leaked in many places and everything put into it tasted strong of copper and was "cankered and poisonous."[124]

Perhaps it was such experiences as this which persuaded many of the planters that it would be wise to sell their grain and fruit to professional distillers and brewers and in return purchase from them their rum and beer. Yet so late as 1759, when a distillery was offered for sale, the owner dilated upon the opportunity it presented for large profits as it was the "only distillery in Maryland, if not also Virginia."[125] At the time of the Revolution there was a distillery near Norfolk which the American forces burned to keep it from falling into the hands of the enemy.[126] There was a distillery in Charleston so early as 1756, while in 1759 a planta-

[122]*Ibid.*, November 27, 1752.     [123]*Virginia Gazette*, December 1, 1752.
[124]Frances N. Mason, *John Norton & Sons*, p. 67.
[125]*Maryland Gazette*, September 6, 1759.
[126]T. J. Wertenbaker, *Norfolk—Historic Southern Port*, p. 69.

tion known as the Distillery was put on sale with its "buildings, stills, vats and every other utensil."[127]

The professional brewers were far more numerous than the distillers. In Charleston one Egan ran a brewery which, he boasted, rivalled those of the northern colonies and kept in South Carolina "near £20,000 a year."[128] It was in 1752 that another brewer announced that he desired to secure his barley and hops from local planters rather than "procure his materials from England," and would pay fifteen shillings a bushel for good barley and twenty pounds a hundredweight for good well-cured hops. This would enable him not only to sell beer cheaper, but to make it better and stronger.[129] In Virginia there were breweries in Williamsburg, Fredericksburg, Norfolk, Gloucester County, and elsewhere. The professors and students of William and Mary, at the long table of the common hall, washed down their food with ale made in the college brewery;[130] while the governor regaled his friends with beer from the Palace brew-house.[131]

In the making of candles the professional had to compete not only with the English chandlers, but with plantation manufacture. So simple and inexpensive were moulds and so plentiful the supply of tallow, that even the smaller planters often made their own candles. And upon the great estates the preparing of the tallow, the stretching of the flax and cotton wicks in the moulds, the pouring of hot tallow, were routine activities. The inventory of Robert Carter listed nine "old pewter candle moulds," Lord Fairfax, the genial old friend of George Washington, had twenty-four, while Philip Ludwell had no less than one hundred.[132]

Yet as early as 1737 we find a professional chandler established in Charleston, where he sold "good winter candles" at forty shillings a dozen pounds, soap at from two to three shillings a pound, and "bee or wax chandles" at 7s. 6d. per pound.[133] In time the industry attained a degree of prosperity, partly because of the

[127] *South Carolina Gazette*, December 1, 1759.
[128] *South Carolina History & Gen. Mag.*, XXI, p. 66, 667n.
[129] *South Carolina Gazette*, March 2, 1752.
[130] *Virginia Magazine of Hist. and Biog.*, V, p. 170.
[131] *Ibid.*, XVII, p. 37.
[132] *Ibid.*, VI, p. 263; VII, p. 13; XXI, p. 413.
[133] *South Carolina Gazette*, March 12, 1737.

increasing demand for ship candles and of growing exports to the West Indies.[134] Among the Virginia chandlers were Morto Brien, of Williamsburg, who made soap as well as candles and offered to buy "tallow, myrtle wax, wood ashes and tobacco ashes";[135] and Freer Armston, Lewis E. Durant and Co., and Murphy and Carnick, all of Norfolk. That slaves were used in soap and candle shops we gather from a notice from Abraham Knight, of Charleston, upon leaving South Carolina, that he would offer for sale "three young negroes that work at the business."[136]

Of the millions of pounds of tobacco shipped to Great Britain from Virginia and Maryland, a small part came back in the form of snuff. With the stimulus of the double saving in freight, the local makers might have monopolized the snuff industry had it not been for the costliness of the bottles in which snuff was packed. William Couper declared that snuff "is the scarcest thing we have here," selling at nine shillings a pound in Virginia, despite the fact that tobacco could be had for four and a half pence per pound. Yet, in 1779, a certain Monsieur Dubois was making Rappee, Scotch and Macauba snuff in Williamsburg,[137] while four years later George Mason's son was engaged in erecting a snuff manufactory in Fairfax County. Across the Potomac at Bladensburg, Richard Thompson made snuff which he packed in Weston's or Kippen's bottles and in "country-made" pots, and sold at from $3.00 to $5.00 a dozen bottles. The boycott of English imports proved a great simulus to the local producers for years, and no sneeze was truly patriotic unless induced by a pinch of local snuff.[138]

In a country where every man owned his gun, both for hunting and for protection, the gunsmith was indispensable. He did not compete with the famous Pennsylvania-German smiths in making the deadly frontier rifle, however, but confined his activities largely to repair work. If the planter needed a new stock for his

[134]Gov. Gooch to Lords of Trade, May 24, 1734.
[135]Virginia Gazette (Parks), July 26, 1776.
[136]South Carolina Gazette, Feb. 28, 1743.
[137]Virginia Gazette (D. & N.), July 10, 1779.
[138]Ibid. (Rind), October 8, 1772.

gun, or if the cock broke, or if the barrel had to be blued, bored or rifled, he brought it to James Geddy, in Williamsburg; or to James Lowry, at the Sign of the Pistol, in Charleston; or to Ephraim Goosley, at Yorktown, "whose materials and workmen were from the best shops in London."[139]

A larger fraternity were the watchmakers and clockmakers and in every town of any size one would find swinging in the wind the Sign of the Dial, or the Sign of the Watch, or the Sign of the Crown and Dial. These men not only did repairing and cleaning, but claimed that they could make "all sorts of plain, repeating, horizontal and skeleton watches, and also repeating and musical clocks."[140] But they did not attempt to compete with the makers of the elaborate English eight-day clocks, which recorded not only the hours, minutes, seconds and days of the month, but the "moon's age in the arch." One of these importations was decorated with a hunting scene "where the buck, dogs and sportsmen" were to be seen in full chase "as natural as the thing itself." In the arch was a slave at work in the fields, and the motto: "Success to the planters." "The last is his own invention," the local dealer explained, "and he hopes will please his friends."[141]

The South was slow to develop potteries. "There is not one potter in all the province [of South Carolina] and no earthenware but what comes from England," declared one observer in 1732. In the same year Governor Gooch assured the Board of Trade that Virginia had one small pottery only, situated at Yorktown, whose output was quite insignificant.[142] Yet fourteen years later we find Edward Rumney establishing a pottery at Annapolis, "having furnished himself with persons exceedingly well skilled in the business of making earthenware." In St. Mary's County, Thomas Baker made at his pothouse "earthenware of the same kind as imported from Liverpool or made in Philadelphia, such as milk-pans, butter-pots, jugs, pitchers, dishes, plates, etc." He employed good workmen from Liverpool and Philadelphia, who were provided with all the necessary equipment.[143]

[139]*Tyler's Magazine*, III. p. 299.     [140]*Virginia Gazette* (Rind), June 23, 1768.
[141]*South Carolina Gazette*, March 2, 1761.
[142]*Gooch Papers*, II, p. 431.     [143]*Maryland Gazette*, September 2, 1756.

It would be a matter of great interest could some of the work of the Southern potters be identified. At Jamestown excavators have discovered many earthenware utensils, a baking dish, a deep plate, bowls, etc., made of red clay unglazed on the outside, but with a greenish glaze within. Other utensils, decorated with tulips in sgraffito, were probably imported from England, and it is doubtful whether the South, save in the regions settled by the Germans, ever produced slipware and sgraffito. Yet we can make no positive statements on this point until excavations at the site of Baker's or of Rumney's pothouses disclose fragments of their work.

That the South was capable of producing artistic craftsmen of high merit is shown by the long list of cabinetmakers. While Duncan Phyfe, Benjamin Randolph, William Savery, Thomas Affleck and other northern artists in wood have been lauded and honored, their Southern fellow workers are left in obscurity. Yet there is reason to believe that with the identification of more of the furniture of Benjamin Bucktrout, or John Shaw, or Josiah Claypoole, the cabinetmakers of Williamsburg, Annapolis and Charleston will be recognized as skilled workmen and real artists. Although these men were subjected to a competition from England from which the cabinetmakers of Boston, New York, and Philadelphia were almost free, they were able to turn out hundreds of secretaries, tables, chairs and sofas in keeping with the elaborate interiors of the great plantation residences. Robert Carter, of Nomini Hall, would not have ordered from Bucktrout eight mahogany chairs stuffed with black leather and eight mahogany elbow chairs,[144] had they contrasted unfavorably with his imported furniture (Plate 42).

The colonial cabinetmaker enjoyed the advantage of abundant and cheap wood proper for his work. It was a costly matter, on the other hand, to send Virginia walnut to England, work it up into tables or secretaries for shipment back across the Atlantic. Not only were the freight costs heavy, but there was risk of injury to fine furniture in the holds of the tiny vessels of the day. The Maryland and Virginia cabinetmakers used pine for the seats of

[144]*Robert Carter Account Books*, June 14, 1774.

chairs and the frames of tables, beds and desks, but only for the hidden parts. In Norfolk and Maryland poplar was also put into framework, while elsewhere in the South yellow pine predominated. The main surfaces were of walnut or mahogany, or more rarely of cherry, and for inlaying and occasionally for veneer the cabinetmakers used boxwood, holly and satinwood.[145]

Cabinetmaking in the South followed very closely the changing styles in England, since the local craftsmen had an opportunity to view the very latest work from London. The Chippendale chair displayed in the shop of an importer one month, might be copied by the local craftsmen the next; while the planter who brought in a table or secretary of a new design might set the fashion for an entire province. There can be no doubt, also, that the cabinetmakers bought English books of designs and used them in their work. The newly arrived craftsman gave impulse to the spirit of imitation, since he took pride in his ability to make furniture in the most "admired fashion in London." A part of the output of the Philadelphia shops found its way into plantation houses and so left its imprint on Southern work, while not infrequently workers from the Quaker city migrated to Maryland or South Carolina.

Josiah Claypoole, one of these migrants, took up his work in Charleston just where he left off in Philadelphia. In March, 1740, he announced that he made "desks and book cases, with arched pediments and O.G. heads, common desks of all sorts, chests of drawers of all fashions, fluted and plain, all sorts of tea tables, side boards and waiters, rule joint skeleton tables, frames for marble tables, all after the newest and best fashions and with the greatest neatness and accuracy."[146] Gerrard Hopkins, at the Sign of the Tea Table, Gay Street, Baltimore, made chests of drawers, desks, bookcases, servitors, tables, chairs, settees, clockcases, couches, candle-stands, etc., from mahogany, walnut, cherry and maple.[147]

John Shaw, of Annapolis, is outstanding among Southern cabi-

[145]*Maryland Historical Magazine*, XXV, p. 1.
[146]*South Carolina Gazette*, March 22, 1740.
[147]A. C. Prime, *The Arts and Crafts*, etc., p. 172.

netmakers because some of his work has been identified. A secretary bearing his label shows his taste and skill at inlaying, the oval figure on the door which incloses a design of acorns and leaves being especially well done. Another secretary, with broken pediment and scroll work and with beautiful inlaying, would do credit to the best of the Philadelphia craftsmen.[148] Lieutenant Commander P. W. Yeatman, Ret., of Princeton, New Jersey, owns a corner cupboard and a table in the Hepplewhite style, made for his family in 1790 by one of the early cabinetmakers of Norfolk, Virginia, which reveal the excellence of the work done in that bustling mercantile city (Plate 43).

Had we visited the shop of the early cabinetmaker we should have witnessed an interesting scene. Now the workman selects a piece of seasoned wood for his frame, now he cuts it into the proper lengths, now he shapes it with his draw knife, now he does the dovetailing, now he fits on the legs or backs or sides of mahogany or walnut, now he busies himself with the carving, now with gluing, now with varnishing. If he carries on a large business he may have one or two slaves to help him, with perhaps a white specialist or two to do the carving, or the turning, or the upholstering. Hung on the walls or scattered on the workbench are an interesting assortment of tools—routers, chair shaves, jointer planes, skew rabbit planes, grooving planes, smoothing planes, screw clamps, compass saws, an ogee, a brace with bits, gouges, chisels, dovetail saws, etc. (Plate 35).

With the cutting off of imports of paper with the Revolution, attempts were made in both Virginia and North Carolina to establish paper mills, and one finds urgent appeals in the gazettes of both colonies for old linen cloth. We "request the favor of the public and most particularly the mistresses of families and the ladies in general . . . to save all their rags and scraps of linen of all sorts," stated one Hillsboro manufacturer in 1777, "old thread stockings, thrums from their linen looms and every kind of linen is useful." In this way they would aid a necessary manufacture. "When the young ladies are assured that by sending to the paper mill an old handkerchief no longer fit to cover their snowy breasts,

[148]*International Studio*, March, 1931, pp. 44–47.

there is a possibility of its returning to them again in the more pleasing form of a *billet doux* from their lovers, the proprietors flatter themselves with great success."[149]

The list of Southern artisans could be extended even further would space admit. There were upholsterers who made Venetian blinds, hung wallpaper and stuffed chairs and sofas, made feather beds and cut out window hangings; cutlers who turned out everything from an axe to a surgeon's lancet; bakers who were kept busy supplying bread for departing ships or packing biscuits for the West Indies; tar, pitch and turpentine makers, pot-ash makers, book-binders, glass workers, dyers, tinners, and the large and important group of workers in the gristmills and sawmills, ropemakers, blockmakers, masons, turners, etc.

The artisan class of the old South in its size, character and development was shaped by three of the four great forces underlying American civilization. All-important was inheritance. The workmen who opened their little shops on the Palace Green at Williamsburg, or on Church Street in Norfolk, or on Tradd Street, Charleston, came usually from England, bringing with them English tools, traditions, styles and methods of work. Occasionally one finds among them an Irish cabinetmaker, or a Huguenot silversmith, but the proudest boast of the artisan was that he had served his apprenticeship in a London shop. And the fact that the stream of migration continued throughout the colonial period and even later, prevented the gradual weakening of this bond. The cabinetmaker imitated the latest English styles in tables and chairs; the tailor cut his suits to conform to those worn at Court; if the English coopers or blacksmiths used a new tool, it was not long in finding its way across to South Carolina or Maryland.

But inheritance and continued contact with the mother country could not offset the powerful influence of local conditions. The artisan class in the South was transformed by the South itself. The paucity of towns, the competition of England, the use of slave labor, the system of plantation industry, all tended to decrease the number of artisans and to weaken their position in the society of the region. On the other hand they had the advantage

[149]*North Carolina Gazette* (Jas. Davis), November 14, 1778.

in many fields of an abundance of raw materials. The forests of the South alone were a godsend to the workers, supplying wood for sawyers, coopers, carpenters, shipbuilders, cabinetmakers and fuel for brickmakers, blacksmiths, founders, potters, tar-burners, etc.

On the whole, the artisan class was an important factor in the structure of Southern society. Its slow retreat before the advance of the factory system and its final almost complete disappearance was a major misfortune, a misfortune more acutely felt than in the North, since this sturdy, intelligent, prosperous group constituted a sorely needed element of strength and democracy in a society economically unsound and basically aristocratic.

## Chapter VII

# MANSIONS ON THE ASHLEY

TO VISITORS from the North, Charleston seems a foreign city, quite unlike Boston or Philadelphia, or even Richmond or Atlanta. The quaint old streets lined with stuccoed houses whose second-story balconies and hipped roofs covered with pink or purple tiles remind one of southern France or perhaps of the West Indies; the pre-Georgian residences of .the wealthy merchants and planters, their two- or three-decked verandas overlooking luxuriant gardens protected by high walls but visible through the beautifully wrought iron of the gates; stately Georgian mansions with classic doors and pedimented fronts—all these speak of a life and of traditions as unique as they are interesting.

They bring to mind the medley of peoples who laid the foundations of the city in the seventeenth century—Barbadians, driven from their island by the encroachment of the sugar plantations upon their farms; settlers directly from England, some of them men of good connections, others land-hungry peasants and bondsmen seeking to start life over again in the New World; Huguenots, determined to make for England the wine and oil she so badly needed in return for a refuge from persecution; English dissenters, fearful of what was to come when the Roman Catholic James became king.

The old buildings tell stories as interesting as any gleaned from manuscripts or tradition. In this stuccoed house set off by quoins, tiled hip roof and classical door dwelt one of Charleston's early merchants, who grew rich by exporting timber, cattle and foodstuffs to the West Indies, or by sending out long pack trains to the Cherokees to barter off knives and blankets for deerskins and beaver. A few blocks away down on the water front Negro slaves toiled in his warehouse storing barrels of rice or unloading cargoes of manufactured goods from an English merchantman.

This mansion, with its three stories, its pedimented roof, its three tiers of porticoes looking out on the garden, belonged to a wealthy planter who was driven to Charleston by the malaria of the rice fields or drawn there by the gaiety and interest of its social life. In fancy we see the dances in the great drawing-room on the second floor, or sumptuous meals in the dining room below, or the planter receiving his friends in the reception room or walking with them through the garden. We surmise that he had visited England or perhaps had been educated at Oxford or Cambridge, for many details of the house bear the stamp of the mother country—the Doric pilasters of the classic front door, the quoins which climb up the corners of the walls, the carving of mantels and cornices, the graceful curves of the staircase.

One often hears it said that if old houses could speak they would tell many interesting stories of people and of life in past years. But do they not speak? Do they not tell interesting stories to those who have the art of listening? The visitor to Charleston, even though he knows nothing of the history of the city, is greeted on all sides with evidence of its origins; he sees the influence of France in a tiled roof or a street balcony; suspects that there is a smattering of Dutch in the colonial amalgam because of the curving lines of a gable-end. A quaint doorway and a basement arcade suggest the influence of the West Indies; the many old Georgian houses speak of the continued dominance of English culture; the great porticoes, the large windows, the shutters, the height of the ceilings, the elevated basements reveal much of the heat of the Charleston summer and the value placed upon shade and the harbor breeze; the size of the mansions, the costliness of their ornamentation, the plan for domestic economy, bring back a life of ease and culture, based on wealth and the attendance of slaves.

The story of Charleston is one of alternating periods of great prosperity and of disaster. At one time the conversion of the river marshes into rice fields pours wealth into the city, then a disastrous fire leaps from one building to another and leaves whole sections a heap of bleak chimneys and blackened walls; now it is the cultivation of indigo which brings back the golden days,

PLATE 42—Cabinet Making, Williamsburg, Virginia

PLATE 43—*Right:* China Press, Charlottesville, Virginia.
*Left:* Corner Cupboard, Norfolk, Virginia

PLATE 44—*Left:* Old view of Tradd Street, Charleston.
*Right:* Mathews House, 43 East Battery, Charleston

PLATE 45—*Left:* Miles Brewton House, 27 King Street. *Right:* Drayton Hall

now the Revolution with its interruption of trade, its sieges and its devastation lays its baleful hand over the city and the surrounding country; now new hope comes with the gin and the cultivation of sea-island cotton, now an earthquake brings terror to the people and ruin to many of its houses. The Charleston of today is built in part upon the ashes of the Charleston of other ages.

But Charleston has escaped the devastation of "progress" more than many other American cities. After all the most destructive agency is the hand of the house-wrecker. New York has been destroyed and rebuilt every few decades for the past two centuries, as the Georgian houses of the eighteenth century gave way to those of the early national period, these in turn to the brown-stone front, and the brown-stone front houses to the skyscrapers. The towers of Manhattan are not built on the ruins of New Amsterdam, for their foundations, sunk as they are many feet below the street level, have obliterated almost the last trace of the old Dutch buildings. But Charleston, despite fires and wars and earthquakes, still has many relics of colonial days.

It was in 1669 that the first contingent of settlers set sail from the Downs for South Carolina under the patronage of that strange genius, Anthony Ashley-Cooper, later Earl of Shaftesbury. The settlers were representative of what was to come, for they were a mixed company—English, Irish and Welsh, some of them younger sons of country squires, others laborers and artisans, still others servants. The storms which they encountered were also emblematic of the history of the colony they founded; while their devious route, which took them by way of Barbados, and other Caribbean Islands, where they took on additional settlers, including three Negroes, foreshadowed the close connection of South Carolina with the West Indies.

The stream of migration from the Antilles, thus started, soon grew to such proportions that Charleston was often regarded as a West Indian city and Barbados as the parent of Carolina. The planters from the island laid out their plantations on Goose Creek, north of the town, and because of their numbers, their numerous slaves, their farming experience, soon made themselves the dominating factor in the colony. They were largely responsible, also, for the beginning of the West Indian trade which later became of first importance, for they shipped out to the islands the staves so urgently needed for sugar hogsheads, and timber for all kinds of building, together with salt meat and corn, bringing back sugar and molasses.

In 1680 began two new streams of immigration to add to the complexity of an already heterodox society—the Huguenot stream and the stream of English dissenters. Of the French Calvinists who fled at the intimation that Louis XIV was going to revoke the Edict of Nantes, a fair sprinkling were induced by English agents to make their homes in Carolina, and for two decades they continued to come, some bringing a small remnant of their belongings, but most armed only with courage, intelligence and skill in agriculture or the trades.[1]

The English dissenters fled from the expected wrath of Heaven when the Catholic Duke of York should ascend the English throne. Through the exertions of Daniel Axtell and Joseph Morton, both of whom were later made landgraves, no less than 500 English Calvinists arrived within the space of a month. At the same period came Scotch Covenanters, who sought to make a separate settlement at Port Royal; Dutchmen from New Amsterdam and Dutchmen direct from Holland; Baptists escaping from the heavy hand of the Massachusetts authorities; a few Quakers, a few Irish Catholics, here and there a Spanish or Portuguese Jew. Out of this complex mass slowly evolved the South Carolinian of Charleston and the coastal region.

Prosperity came with the introduction of rice culture. It is said that in 1686 a ship's captain brought a package of seed rice from far-off Madagascar to Doctor Henry Woodward, whose experiments proved so successful that the planters turned eagerly to the new staple and every bit of land where flooding was possible was pressed into service. By 1696 the crop had become so great that it was with difficulty that ships could be found to move it, and wealth, undreamed of before, began to flow into the Carolina low country.

[1]Samuel G. Stoney, *Plantations of the Carolina Low Country*, pp. 17, 18.

Rice culture tended to make society aristocratic. To secure a crop it was necessary to flood the fields two or three times a season, and this in turn could be done only by raising a levee, damming a stream and erecting a reservoir. Water was admitted through an upper gate in the levee and later drained off through a lower gate. All this required capital far beyond the means of the poorer planters, so that the number of families who could participate in the rich rice profits was comparatively small. What tobacco was to eastern Maryland and Virginia, rice was for South Carolina. It built up an aristocracy of planters and merchants, fastened the slave system upon the region, studded the country-side and the streets of Charleston with fine residences, made possible for the leading families a life of refinement and even elegance.

A few old houses which have escaped the destructive forces of the past two centuries and a few others which have been rebuilt apparently upon their original lines, give us the clue to the architecture of pre-Georgian Charleston. When we stroll along the quaint old streets, lined by stucco houses, some with hipped roofs, others presenting a Dutch gable-end to the roadway, some covered with pantiles, here and there a second-story iron balcony, we are carried back to the days of the Carolina proprietors (Plate 44). Typical was the so-called single house, the narrow end fronting directly on the street in the manner of Amsterdam or Delft, the main door in the center of the long side, leading into an entrance hall. Since the house was but one room deep, the apartments of each floor were strung out one behind the other. In the early days in the residences of the merchants, the front room of the ground floor was often used as a shop. In 1734 a "good dwelling house" was advertised for sale, "consisting of a shop and three other rooms on the first floor, a dining room and two bed chambers on the second floor and two very good garrets on the third, with a kitchen, store room and other conveniencies backwards."[2] A house "at the Point, near Col. Pinckney's" was three stories high, "with two rooms on a floor," the "brick kitchen, chaise-house and stable for three horses" apart from the main structure.[3]

[2] *South Carolina Gazette*, June 22–29, 1734.    [3] *Ibid.*, July 31–August 7, 1749.

In the early decades of the city many houses were built of wood, since it was generally held that frame houses were cooler than those made of brick. But after the great fire of 1740 the General Assembly passed an act that all building should be of brick or stone, that all "tall" wooden houses must be pulled down by 1745,[4] and that the use of wood was to be confined to window frames, shutters and to interior work. That this law was often disregarded we learn from an article in *The London Magazine* of 1762, which states that of the Charleston houses some were of brick "but more of timber." When in time the inflammable frame buildings gave way to row after row of somber brick fronts, the Charlestonians added a touch of softness and color by covering them with stucco, often in shades of pink, green, yellow and blue, in some cases tooled to simulate cut stone. Nothing more than this differentiates old Charleston from the cities to the north, or more clearly links it with the West Indies and with southern Europe.

Equally picturesque, equally foreign to American architecture, are the pink or deep purple tiles which in former days seem to have been almost universal and which still linger on many an old residence or office or stable. The law of 1740 made obligatory the use of tile, slate or stone for roof coverings, and ordered the removal of all wooden shingles by 1745.[5] The Charlestonians use pantiles, whose graceful curves give a wavy appearance to the roofs, which is in marked contrast to the almost flat surface of the German tiled roofs of Winston-Salem. The convex pantiles may well have been introduced by the Huguenots, since they are typical of southern France, especially of the Bordeaux region from which so many of them came. The concave pantile, which is also common in Charleston, is almost unknown in this part of France.

We have another suggestion of southern France in the many balconies which hung over the street, where one could catch the cooling breezes after sundown, or watch parades or other spectacles below.[6] In the nineteenth century balconies were made of iron often beautifully wrought, but in colonial days wood seems

4*Ibid.*, December 25, 1740.    5*Ibid.*, December 25, 1740.
6See view of Charleston, 1761, *London Magazine*, 1762, p. 296.

to have been the usual material. And since even the hardest of woods were liable to decay, there was always the danger that an unsound timber might give way with fatal consequences. One owner was frank enough to state, when advertising his house for sale, that "as the balconies were not at first made of lasting wood and by being constantly in the weather are going to decay," he would make a due allowance in the price and the purchaser could either remove them or "refit to his taste."[7]

It seems clear that the Huguenots left an imprint upon Charleston architecture out of proportion to their numbers, and even today some of the older streets remind us strongly of Bordeaux. The stuccoed walls, the window balconies, the hipped roofs covered with convex pantiles, features which were all common in the Huguenot centers in France, could not have found their way to South Carolina by chance. When a merchant made the trip to Martinique or Guadeloupe, he could hardly have been so fascinated with the houses of Port-de-France or Basse Terre as to imitate them in constructing his own residence on Tradd Street or South Battery. Nor can the French influence be ascribed to the influx of refugees from Santo Domingo fleeing the horrors of the Negro Insurrection, since it antedates that event by many decades.

The Huguenots, in conjunction with a few Dutch settlers, may also have been responsible for the Flemish and Dutch influence in Charleston, for some of them had resided for a considerable time in Holland before sailing for South Carolina. As we look out over the water to the mass of buildings between Granville and Craven's bastions shown in the "Prospect of Charleston" in 1761, we are struck by the frequent recurrence of the Dutch gable end. Even today one finds on some of the narrow old streets, or tucked away behind a garden or up an entrance driveway, old houses set off by the graceful curves of the Flemish gable or the more rigid lines of the Dutch gable. In the newspaper notices of the day are frequent references to Dutch roofs, but these refer, apparently, to the gambrel rather than to the character of the gable end. But the custom of pinning the house together by means of exterior beam

[7]*Ibid.*, August 11, 1733, No. 82; see also November 25–December 2, 1756.

anchors, which was so common in old Charleston, was certainly an importation from Holland.[8]

Typical of the pre-Georgian period, and probably one of the oldest houses in Charleston, is the Mathews house at 43 East Battery, which is still owned by the Mathews family (Plate 44). The narrow end rising directly from the sidewalk, the stuccoed walls, the hip roof, the absence of an elevated cellar, the entrance on the long side facing the garden, the simplicity of doors and windows all lead to the conclusion that this old building goes back to the early decades of the eighteenth century. The two-story portico, with its plain round columns and its doorway opening upon the street, while almost certainly a later addition, may well antedate the Revolution. The slave quarters are in the rear. Similar to the Mathews house are some of the Tradd Street houses, whose convex pantiled roofs flaring sharply at the eaves give an even greater impression of age, lend an even stronger French flavor. No. 25 Meeting Street is in the same style, save that the side portico is lacking, while the sharp street gable end with its curving elbows is more reminiscent of Amsterdam than of Bordeaux.

When we leave Charleston to visit the estates of the rice planters we find that some of the earliest, as well as most interesting, houses remain as witnesses not only of the architectural trends of the day, but of the life, tastes and wealth of the planters. There have been fires in the Carolina low country, the Revolution and the Civil War left many mansions mere heaps of blackened ruins, but there has been no such wholesale destruction as in the city. Medway goes back to 1686, in the very infancy of the colony, Middleburg to 1699, Mulberry to 1714, Brick House, Edisto, to 1725.

The rice plantations spread themselves over the river bottoms of the Ashley and Cooper, and to the banks of the Santee on one side and the Edisto on another, all within a fifty-mile radius of Charleston, which was the commercial as well as political and social center of the colony. The entire region, like eastern Virginia and Maryland, was intersected with natural waterways, so that the planters found communication with the capital both convenient

[8]Several examples are to be found on Tradd Street.

278

and cheap. Nothing was more common than to see their "pet-tiaugers," or glorified canoes hollowed out of cypress trees, taking on their cargoes of rice at the plantation wharf, or gliding down one of the rivers to the songs of the Negro crews, or unloading at the warehouses of the Charleston waterfront (Plate 47).

There was an intimacy of plantation and city, unknown in the tobacco-growing regions, in which merchants often became rice growers, and rice growers dabbled in trade. The time had not arrived when agriculture was considered the ideal pursuit of the gentleman and the trader relegated to an inferior class. When the planter found that his sons exceeded the number of plantations with which he could endow them, he saw no disgrace in sending the younger ones to sit behind a counting desk in the houses along the Bay. Thus Charleston life was intimately affected by life on the rice farms, and in turn affected it.

One would expect, therefore, a close relationship between rural and urban architecture. In fact such a relationship existed, but conditions in the open spaces of the country were so different from those on crowded Church Street or Tradd Street or South Battery, that a distinctive rural architecture developed. There was no need for the narrow single house, there was greater opportunity for through drafts, the builder could determine the proportions of his house without regard to space or the location of houses to right or left. He could place his entrance in front, please his fancy with front staircases, make use of timber construction without breaking the law.

The oldest surviving plantation mansion, Medway, shows how quickly prosperity came to the low country, for it was built but sixteen years after the founding of the colony. It shows, also, in a striking way the persistence of European traditions and the eagerness of each colonist to build in the manner of his homeland, for Medway is as Dutch in its lines as its owner, the Dutchman Jan Van Arrsens, could make it. The house has since been enlarged by the addition of wings and a second story, but it takes only a cursory examination to visualize the original one-and-a-half-story cottage, with the tell-tale stepped gable ends, with badly burned brick stuccoed over and with entrances both in front and in rear.

279

How wide was the influence of Dutch architecture in the rice country we do not know, but it is noteworthy that in the three most interesting survivals of the early period—Medway, Mulberry and Brick House, it strikes the predominant note. Mulberry, with its so-called Dutch gambrel, its S-shaped beam anchors and its four pagoda flankers crowned by bell-shaped roofs shows unmistakably the influence of the Netherlands (Plate 46). If we may believe family tradition, Thomas Broughton, the planter, Indian trader, soldier and politician, who built the old mansion, modelled it upon Seaton, the ancestral house in England. Since Seaton was designed by Sir John Vanbrough, the Dutch-English architect, it is not difficult to trace this flavor back to Holland. Certainly Mulberry is unlike any other house in the Carolina low country.[9]

Middleburg, the house built by Benjamin Simons on the east branch of the Cooper, on the other hand, has a strong resemblance to the Charleston single house, and save for the fact that it is built of wood would not be out of place on Tradd Street itself. The single-room depth with through draft, the hip roof, the use of vertical boarding for the partitions, the exposed corner posts all proclaim Middleburg as perhaps the oldest frame house in South Carolina.

In studying the transit of culture from Europe to the American colonies, we find that one individual in building his residence is swayed by tradition, or his love for the homeland, another yields to the force of local conditions, or to the influence of surrounding populations. Whereas Jan Van Arrsens, the Dutchman, erected a Dutch house for his Back River plantation, the Huguenot, Paul de St. Julien, living in a neighborhood predominated by Huguenot families, put up a residence that was far more English than French, more Virginian than Carolinian. Hanover is a one-and-a-half-story frame cottage, with exterior chimneys and gambrel roof very much in the style of the famous Moore house at Yorktown. If it were not for the words PEU A PEU, the abbreviation of *Peu à peu l'oiseau fait son nid,* in the stucco band at the top of one of the chimneys, one would never suspect that this was the house of a Frenchman[10] (Plate 7).

[9]S. G. Stoney, *Plantations of the Carolina Low Country,* pp. 50, 51.
[10]*Ibid.,* pp. 51, 108, 109.

A second great era of building, which gave to South Carolina some of its most beautiful structures and coincided with the introduction of Georgian architecture, was based upon the wave of prosperity which followed the introduction of indigo as a supplementary crop to rice. England was in .sore need of indigo, since the recurrent wars with France made the supply uncertain and subjected the great woolen industry to serious inconvenience. At the same time many of the older Carolina rice plantations were wearing out, so that Goose Creek and other communities were already on the road to ruin. Thus when an intelligent and determined woman, Eliza Lucas, the mother of Thomas and Charles Cotesworth Pinckney, began experimenting with indigo, she had the blessings both of the English government and her fellow planters. By. 1742 all doubts had been dispelled, and many a planter who had watched with growing concern the decline of his annual rice crop, turned eagerly to this new staple.[11]

When England, alarmed at the inadequacy of the West Indian output of indigo, placed a bounty of 6d. a pound on the Carolina product, the profits became very large. The price in England was often as high as 6s. a pound, and the returns to the planters 33 to 50 per cent. In the excited conversations in the drawing rooms of Charleston or in the churchyards of St. Andrew's or St. James's after services, it was said that a man with care and good luck might double his capital every five or six years. Moreover, since it was not a "marsh crop" like rice, it spread the plantations to the uplands and brought thousands of acres within the economic sphere of Charleston. It was the introduction of Georgian architecture which gave dignity and charm to the South Carolina buildings of the pre-Revolutionary period, but it was indigo wealth in large part which made them possible.[12]

In Charleston and throughout the low country the foreign tinge to architecture, whether French, Dutch or West Indian, became fainter as the Georgian gained ground. None of the colonists, not even the Virginians, were more directly under the cultural dominance of the mother country, none more frankly imitated English fashions, whether in clothing, furniture, gardens, reading or

[11]Harriot H. Ravenel, *Eliza Pinckney.*
[12]Ulrich B. Phillips, *Life and Labor in the Old South,* pp. 50–52.

architecture, than the Carolinians. The young men who went to Oxford or Cambridge for their education, no doubt thought the houses of Charleston or the rice plantations ridiculously out of date. The merchant or planter who visited England on pleasure or business and was received in some of the Georgian houses of London, had visions of a similarly stately residence on his Cooper River plantation or his lot on Church Street.

When the time came to build, the owner might call in a professional architect, explain what he wanted and trust to him for the plans and the supervision of the work. Or he might take down from his shelves the most recent book on architecture, thumb over its pages until he found a design to his fancy, himself modify it to conform to distinctive conditions in South Carolina, and then employ a master "carpenter" to do the actual construction. If his library had no copy of James Gibb's *A Book of Architecture,* or Batty Langley's *City and Country Builder's and Workman's Treasury of Designs,* he could stop into Jacob Viart's bookshop to purchase them.[13] There can be no doubt that the South Carolina gentleman put his own tastes, sense of proportion, his personality into his country mansion or his Charleston house not less than the wealthy planters of Virginia or Maryland.

But there were able architects at hand if he desired to use them—Samuel Holmes, who made "draughts of houses" and measured and valued "all sorts of workmanship in houses";[14] John Ward; Dudley Innan, who designed houses "according to the modern taste";[15] the "ingenious Mr. William Rigley Naylor, architect and surveyor,"[16] and many others. Innan, who was careful to announce that he had "lately arrived from London," promised to produce buildings of "more conveniency, strength and beauty, than those commonly erected in this province." Good taste in building, he thought, was a talent "brought into the world with a man," but a talent which must be cultivated and improved. Innan gives clear evidence that the modification of Georgian architecture to suit the distinctive needs of the Carolina climate

[13]*South Carolina Gazette,* March 16, 1752.
[14]*Ibid.,* February 2–9, 1734.     [15]*Ibid.,* April 29–May 6, 1751.
[16]*South Carolina Hist. and Gen. Mag.,* X, p. 170.

and other local conditions was a matter of careful planning. "A structure though ever so beautiful cannot yet be perfect," he points out, "unless supplied with all the conveniencies necessary to remove the disadvantages proceeding from great heat and cold," of which he thought there were "but few in or near this town."[17]

Among the newcomers were specialists, such as Ezra Waite, "civil architect, house-builder in general and carver from London." Waite came to South Carolina fortified with "twenty-seven years' experience, both in theory and practice, in noblemen and gentlemen's seats." That this long training stood him in good stead is obvious from a glance at his superb work on the Miles Brewton house, where he carved all work in the four main rooms and "calculated, adjusted and draw'd at large for the work by the Ionich entabliture and carved the same in the front and round the eaves."[18] There is nothing more delicate, more beautiful in American carving than the pilasters, the capitals, the broken pediments, the mantels, the interior and exterior cornices of this exquisite house.[19]

In short the Georgian architecture conquered Charleston and the rice country just as it conquered all the other colonies, in large part replacing the styles which had developed through tradition and the force of local conditions. But South Carolina Georgian at once took on characteristics of its own. The elevation of the main floor to catch the breeze, the general use of porticoes, the richness of the carvings, the occasional use of stucco on the outer walls, differentiate it from the New England Georgian, or the New York Georgian, or the Annapolis Georgian, or the Virginia Georgian.

To the architects of the new style the old type of narrow Charleston house, with the entrance on the long side, perhaps half hidden by neighboring buildings, presented a perplexing problem. Fundamental to Georgian architecture are proportion and balance. It is at its best only when there is space for a main pavilion, square or nearly square, set back from the street, with em-

[17]*South Carolina Gazette,* April 29–May 6, 1751.
[18]*South Carolina Hist. and Gen. Mag.,* XV, p. 144.
[19]*Charleston, South Carolina,* A. Simons and S. Lapham, Jr., pp. 13–26.

phasis upon a central doorway approached by stairs, the whole set off, if possible, by flanking subsidiary buildings. But to attain this ideal the architects had to break sharply with Charleston traditions, and this, in many cases, was impossible because of the limitations of building space. It was impossible, also, where the owner desired to remodel his house by adding to it "modern" features.

Thus there developed the single type Charleston Georgian house (Plate 49). Since the street end was the most conspicuous part of the house, the architect did what lay within his power to render it ornate by quoins on the corners, flat arches over the windows, marble bands between stories and carved cornices. On the long side, towering over the portico, a pediment, supported by ornate brackets and enclosing a semi-circular fan window, gave an additional approach to the Georgian. Yet the architect must have considered his work a failure so long as the classical door with its columns, its pediment, its carved capitals was lacking. He could not make this door an entrance from the street directly into the end reception room, for it was too narrow and in many cases elevated five or even more feet above the sidewalk. So he hit upon the unique, though not entirely satisfying, expedient of placing the street door outside the main building as an entrance to the lower piazza.

The door itself is often a thing of beauty, but it is far too elaborate for the function it performs, and seems merely a bit of stage setting where the actors step through a door in the scenery leading nowhere. Transfer one of these sham doors to an English, or a Maryland or a Philadelphia Georgian house, and it would harmonize perfectly. But when one views the porch door of the Henry Manigault house, let us say, with its fluted columns, its Corinthian capitals, its fan light, its rich moulding, one has a sense of incongruity, of beauty misplaced, of emphasis put upon the wrong spot (Plate 49).

The double and triple portico, running along the side of the house and overlooking the garden, quite as much as the tiled roofs and stuccoed walls, gives Charleston its West Indian or southern European flavor. Whatever its origin its utility is clear.

PLATE 46—Mulberry Castle, near Charleston

PLATE 47—South Carolina Plantation Boat

PLATE 48—*Left:* Fireproof Building. *Right:* Nathaniel Russell House

PLATE 49—Henry Manigault House, Charleston

The observant La Rochefoucauld Liancourt states that the architects designed it in order to "keep the sun from the sides of the houses and permit the admission of fresh air from the north or east."[20] He might have added that it afforded also a place for the family to gather after sundown to enjoy the cool air and to look out over the garden beneath. The portico ran the full length of the house, elevated in some cases over a brick arcade, its delicate round columns, its cornices, its shallow arches, adding a touch of the ornate to an otherwise disfiguring feature. That the portico was common by the middle of the eighteenth century we know from advertisements in *The Gazette,* for the owner when he wanted to sell his property invariably dwelt upon the coolness and size of the "piazza."[21]

In the so-called double house, in which the architect had a free scope for his talents, the Georgian reached its nearest approach to perfection. Selecting a lot of sufficient frontage he discarded the old narrow form for the wide Georgian façade, with its central door, its evenly distributed windows, its highly ornate cornice, its front portico approached by double stairs. The doorway, when partly obscured by the portico above, he usually capped with a low arch enclosing a fanlight, but when the porch was in the rear or at the side, he set it off with a pediment supported by columns or pilasters. The high basement, which perhaps was half hidden behind a brick arcade, raised the main floor high above the street level and added to the charm of the proportions. The dignity lent to Westover or the Palace at Williamsburg by the height of the roof, in Charleston is attained by the elevated basement.

What Mt. Pleasant is to Philadelphia, what the Hammond house is to Annapolis (Plate 18), the Miles Brewton home is to Charleston, and like Mt. Pleasant and the Hammond house a shroud of tragedy hangs over the place (Plate 45). The owner, who had entertained Josiah Quincy in its beautiful rooms in 1773 and Sir William Campbell two years later, turned his back upon it forever rather than give his assent to the declaration of inde-

[20]*Voyages,* IV, p. 8.
[21]*South Carolina Gazette,* December 13, 1751; May 3, 1754.

pendence against England.[22] Embarking with his wife and children he was never heard of again and the estate passed to his
sisters, Mrs. Charles Pinckney and Mrs. Jacob Motte. During the
Revolution the mansion was used as headquarters by Sir Henry
Clinton, and one may still see his profile, faintly scratched by a
young officer upon a marble mantel.[23]

As we step through the wrought-iron front gate with its two
ornate lanterns, we come directly to the marble stairs which lead
in easy stages to either side of the porch. The porch itself is a
thing of beauty, with its stone pillars, its Ionic capitals, its fine
pediment enclosing a circular window, and Ezra Waite's exquisite
cornices. Entering through the wide door with its carved frame
and fanlight, we find ourselves in a flagged hall which widens
in the rear to give room for the mahogany staircase lighted by a
Palladian window (Fig. 5). The fluted pilasters, the arch of the
upper hallway resting on Ionic columns, the elaborate cornices,
the broken pediments of the doors, the heavy frieze, the marble
mantels combine to give an impression of lavish ornateness. Even
had we not known the owner, there could be no doubt that this
was the house of one of Charleston's great, to whom beauty meant
much and costs meant little.[24]

Similar to the Miles Brewton house in architecture, and not less
interesting in its history, is the John Edwards house, built about
1770. But Edwards, in contrast to Brewton, was an ardent Revo-
lutionist, and with the capture of Charleston in 1780, was imprisoned and sent in exile to St. Augustine, while his beautiful
residence was occupied by Admiral Arbuthnot. Restored to its
rightful owner upon the departure of the British, the house again
became a center of interest in 1793, when Mr. Edwards' son-in-
law, John B. Holmes, opened its doors to the family of the Comte
de Grasse, who were fleeing the horrors of the Santo Domingo
slave insurrection.[25]

As in so many other Charleston Georgian houses the front

[22]Edward McCrady, *The History of South Carolina in the Revolution*, pp. 183, 184.
[23]A. R. H. Smith and D. E. H. Smith, *The Dwelling Houses of Charleston*, p. 100.
[24]*The White Pine Series*, XIV, pp. 219, 220; *The Octagon Library*, I; A. R. H. Smith
and D. E. H. Smith, *The Dwelling Houses of Charleston*, pp. 93–100.
[25]A. R. H. Smith and D. E. H. Smith, *The Dwelling Houses of Charleston*, p. 199.

portico is approached by double stone stairs, broken by landings and set off by wrought-iron balustrades. The portico itself is supported by columns and pilasters with Ionic capitals. The weatherboarding, which is of cypress, like that of Mt. Vernon is cut to resemble blocks of stone, so that one has to view the house closely to realize that it is built of wood. The hallway, broken by an arch, runs through to the stairway in the rear. The mantels, the friezes, the broken pediments of the doors, while less elaborate than those of the Miles Brewton house, are fully in keeping with the dignity and charm of this stately old residence.

On the plantations of the low country, where there were no limitations of space, the new architecture blossomed forth at its best. A few miles to the west of Charleston, on the Stono River, is one of the earliest and most charming examples of South Carolina Georgian—Fenwick Hall. A two-story brick structure, with classical front door and hipped roof flaring at the eaves and capped by a balustrade, it is not unlike Westover or Carter's Grove. In former days, when balanced by two brick flankers, its proportions must have been as correct as those of the Hammond house or of Mt. Pleasant. Unfortunately, a disfiguring wing with octagonal ends was added late in the eighteenth century, which is not only out of keeping with the original building, but throws it out of balance.

John Fenwick, brother of Robert Fenwick, one of the famous "Red Sea Men," prospered in business, became prominent in politics and contracted a fortunate marriage. He is supposed to have built Fenwick in 1730. His son Edward won distinction in a different field, for his thoroughbred horses, some of them imported from England, were famous throughout the colonies. For the lavish entertainments of father and son, and at a later date of John Gibbes, who purchased the place, the beautiful drawing room, dining room and chambers were eminently suited. The panels, the carvings and mouldings, all of Carolina cypress, have a simplicity and with it a heaviness, typical of the early Georgian. The interior woodwork of the wing, done in pine, shows the more delicate touch of the age of the Adam brothers.[26]

[26]Samuel G. Stoney, *Plantations of the Carolina Low Country*, pp. 55, 56, 122–133.

The glory of the Carolina low country is stately Drayton Hall (Plate 45). Built by Councillor John Drayton, and escaping the devastation of the Revolution and the fury of Sherman's troops in 1865, it has stood for two centuries as a monument to the magnificence of the Ashley River aristocracy. After the War between the States it fell upon evil days, its beautiful garden disappeared, weeds grew in the front lawn, and to the chance visitor it seemed a ghostly mansion, nourishing its memories of passed events and almost forgotten men and women. The two supporting flankers, which once added to the dignity of the place, have long since gone.

The house is elevated upon a high basement, so that the excellent proportions are preserved despite the wide expanse of the brick walls and the low pitch of the roof. In true Carolina style one mounts to a front platform by twin stone steps, adorned with wrought-iron balustrades. Rising above and partly over this platform is a two-story portico, supported by Doric columns and surmounted by a pediment. Entering the front door, we find ourselves in the great entrance hall, 29½ feet by 23½ feet, set off by an elaborate though somewhat heavy mantel, by a beautiful frieze and panelling, and by a shallow arch over the entrance to the stair hall in the rear. The stairs themselves, which rise from either side in three stages to a platform above, are in keeping with the richness of the great drawing room above to which they lead. The entrance hall below opens into a chamber to the left, the library to the right, the dining room on one side of the stair hall and the small drawing room on the other; while above are four chambers, two on each side of the great drawing room. In the basement, or ground floor, are the servants' hall, kitchen, office and storage rooms.[27]

Some of the Georgian houses of the Carolina low country have recently been restored to their original beauty, but many others have been obliterated or fallen into a state of decay beyond reclamation. The Glover mansion, near Dorchester, advertised for sale in 1733, must have rivalled Fenwick or even Drayton Hall. It was described as "a beautiful dwelling house 45 foot long and

[27]Samuel G. Stoney, *Plantations of the Carolina Low Country*, pp. 58, 59, 142–161.

35 foot wide, two floors, four rooms on a floor; with buffets, closets, etc., a dry cellar underneath, with several convenient rooms pleasantly situated, a good pasture, barn, negro houses, etc."[28]

In South Carolina, as in Maryland and Virginia, the planter's residence was in the center of a cluster of buildings which gave the appearance of a little village. A plantation near Goose Creek bridge comprised "a good brick dwelling house, two brick storehouses, a brick kitchen and wash house, . . . a barn with a large brick chimney, with several rice mills, mortars, etc., a winnowing house, an oven, a large stable and coach-house, a cooper's shop, a house built for a smith's shop."[29]

An Englishman visiting the Charleston region in the mid-eighteenth century would have been perfectly at home in one of the handsome drawing rooms or bed chambers of the Georgian houses. Here he would have recognized an English marble mantel, here ornate hearth tiles from the mother country, here an English grate, here an English window frame, there English wallpaper.[30] With the advent of sash windows, glass panes and sheet glass were imported in large quantities, so that the stately apartments of the new mansions were far better lighted than the rooms of the earlier houses. The wallpaper, where wallpaper was used in lieu of panelling, was also brought over from England. "Lately imported from London, several sets of fine figured paper hangings for rooms, ceilings and screens," Thomas Boaden, "upholsterer from London," announced in 1756.[31] Later in the same year he got in a fresh supply of "mock India paper," for "hanging of rooms, ceilings, staircases, etc.," which he promised to put up in the best manner.[32]

To the wealthy families of South Carolina the Revolution brought heavy losses in both personal wealth and in young blood. In 1779 a British force, striking from Florida, carried off thousands of slaves, helped themselves to costly silver plate, converted thoroughbred studs into cavalry horses and left many plantation

[28]*South Carolina Gazette*, Feb. 10–17, 1733.    [29]*Ibid.*, Aug. 11, 1733.
[30]*Ibid.*, July 19–25, 1735; June 23, 1757; Dec. 3, 1748; Aug. 28, 1749.
[31]*South Carolina Gazette*, Oct. 28, 1756.    [32]*Ibid.*, Dec. 16, 1756.

houses in flames. The next year Charleston itself fell to the enemy. In the surrounding country brother fought against brother, son against father, enraged partisans plundered and burned and their property was plundered and burned in reprisal. When at last the British sailed away, they took with them many Loyalists, some of them persons of wealth and ability, leaving the Revolutionists to the contemplation of their victory, but also of their ruined estates, the loss of the English market and the bounty on their indigo.

Yet prosperity was quick to return. As early as 1758 a certain McKewn Johnstone had proved by experiment that the river tides could be made to do the work of flooding the rice fields, but it was only after the Revolution that the planters reaped the full benefit of his discovery. Johnstone supplied his plantation with a system of dikes, ditches and flood gates, which protected the crops from the tides when he wanted them to be dry and opened them to the rising water when he wished to drown them. This method, of course, could not be used below the "salt-points," but higher up where the water ceased to be brackish, it brought enormous profits. These profits were for the rich man only, however, for the poor planter could not afford the outlay necessary for clearing the swamps, building dikes, cutting ditches and keeping the complicated system in working order. The rice crop of the post-Revolutionary period, even more than in colonial days, was the basis, not for a sturdy yeomanry, but for a planter aristocracy.

The prosperity which came from rice culture would have been less pronounced, had not a chance visitor to South Carolina solved the problem of husking the grain. Jonathan Lucas, an English millwright, was a gift from the sea, as he was shipwrecked at the mouth of the Santee and there on a rice plantation perfected the first successful rice mill. Prior to this invention the task of separating the chaff from the grain had been difficult and costly, so that what Whitney's cotton gin did for the culture of cotton, Lucas' mill did for rice growing.

Under the impulse of returning good times Charleston took on new life and new residences arose on all sides, some of them even more costly than those of the colonial period. More than ever, also, the city became the mecca of the wealthy planter seeking safety from the malaria of his rice fields. Men who were content with simple though usually comfortable houses on their plantations, lavished money upon big town residences, where they could entertain their friends with stately hospitality. It was the rice-millionaires, more than the merchants, who were responsible for the architectural beauty of post-Revolutionary Charleston.

It soon became obvious that with political independence the city was not to attain architectural independence. The habit of relying upon the mother country for guidance in cultural matters could not be entirely broken even by the resentment created by the war with its cruelties and its hardships. It is true that the ties of friendship and commerce with France which grew out of the treaties of 1778 made the local builders conversant with French practice, but it was the English books of architecture now as formerly which chiefly fixed the styles. The most noteworthy figure of the period, Gabriel Manigault, a native Charlestonian of Huguenot descent, received his education in England and Geneva, and brought back a library of architectural books and a mind stored with new ideas.

Yet there was no sudden transformation of Charleston architecture. Many of the houses which arose on Meeting Street, East Bay, Bull Street and elsewhere in the last decade of the old century and the first decade of the new, must have seemed quite familiar to the oldest Charlestonian. He recognized the traditional single house, with the narrow end on the street, its ornate door opening upon the piazza and the real entrance on the long side. When he strolled down to Bull Street, he would have compared William Blacklock's new house, with its high basement, double front stairs protected by wrought-iron rails leading to the ornate front door, and its well-balanced façade with pediment, to the Miles Brewton house or to Drayton Hall.

On the other hand, he found many evidences that the times were changing, that some of the new houses broke sharply with the old traditions, that in others differences in detail brought them in line with the new style. The dictators of style, of course, were the Adam brothers (Plate 51). One has only to step inside the

Nathaniel Russell house, or the Daniel Ravenel house, or the George Edwards house, to be greeted on all sides by the influence of these masters (Plates 48 and 50). Here one sees a mantel with delicate columns, graceful garlands, urns and classical figures; here a frieze enriched with foliate designs; here a door with pilasters and entablature; here a charming ceiling centerpiece. In older houses the heavy, ornate mantels of the Georgian period, now quite out of style, were often ripped out to make room for the simpler mantels of the day, with their delicate, classical ornamentation.[33]

The architects who went over wholeheartedly to the "new taste," had no scruples in breaking all the former rules of proportion. They built houses, such as the Nathaniel Russell residence, whose height, according to the old ideals, was far too great for its width. The severe dignity of the façade was often broken by a four-sided bay; winding stairs replaced the single or double straight flight of former days; the oval drawing room became popular; panelling gave way to wallpaper; windows increased in height, were set off by flat arches and at times sunk in arched recesses; doors discarded the classical pediment in favor of the low arch fitted with fan light; the wrought-iron balcony became more common; marble bands appeared between stories to break the monotony of the brickwork.

Typical of the new style is the Middleton-Pinckney house, built in 1796–97, now used by the city Water Department. The house was begun by the widow of John Middleton, and completed at a total cost of $53,800 by Thomas Pinckney, whom she married in 1797. The acquisition of a bride and a new mansion came as consolations to Pinckney for his defeat in the presidential election of 1796. The house itself, which towers four stories above the street level, comprises a rectangle about sixty-eight feet by thirty-one, with large bays jutting out on either side and carried through to the roof. The poor proportions, the absence of porch or piazza, the rather low roof would make this building dull and unattractive were it not for the white flat arches of the windows and the ornate stone band between the first and second stories. Inside, the

[33]*The Octagon Library,* I, *The Dwelling Houses of Charleston,* pp. 102–144.

great oval drawing room, the marble staircase in the rear bay, the delicate entablature of the doors give dignity and charm to the building and proclaim it as a pioneer in the post-Revolutionary architecture of Charleston.[34]

Similar is the Judge King house on George Street (Plate 51). Born in Scotland, King came to Charleston in 1805, where he at once joined the bar. Both he and his wife won distinction, he for his ability as a jurist, she for her lavish entertainments, especially for her annual Race Week ball. The house is three stories high and is in the form of a Greek cross, with large bays projecting from the front and rear façades, somewhat in the manner of Bacon's Castle. We enter through a pedimented classic door in the front bay approached by double stairs, to find ourselves in a wide hallway leading to curving stairs in the rear bay. To the left is the dining room, to the right the reception room. Even the recent conversion of the house into a high school with the consequent additions and changes has not obscured its dignity and the beauty of its interior decorations.[35]

The Nathaniel Russell house, also typical of the post-Revolutionary style, is noted for its elliptical staircase which springs unsupported from floor to floor in graceful curves (Plate 48). In the four-sided bay which projects on the south side are three large oval rooms, one on each floor, which open upon the staircase landings through curved doors. The front door leads, not into the hallway, but into the lower east room fronting the street, its ornate arch enclosing a graceful fan light. Over this door the letters N. R. are woven into the wrought-iron balcony. In 1811, when a tornado swept Charleston, the house was seriously damaged, the windows broken in, the furniture ruined, the "extensive back buildings entirely unroofed."[36]

Charleston, with its traditional conservatism, was slow to accept the classic revival. When Jefferson was patterning his beautiful university group at Charlottesville after Roman temples and William Thornton and Benjamin H. Latrobe were planning the

[34]*Ibid.*, pp. 100–102.
[35]A. R. H. and D. E. H. Smith, *The Dwelling Houses of Charleston*, pp. 141, 142.
[36]*Ibid.*, pp. 142–155; *The Octagon Library*, I, *The Dwelling Houses of Charleston*, pp. 96–99.

national capitol, it continued placidly under the influence of Manigault and other architects of the Adam brothers school. Not until a native Charlestonian, who had studied under Hoban, had fallen under the spell of Jefferson and Latrobe, and had won fame as the designer of the Washington Monument, set up his office in the city, did Greek and Roman porticoes make their appearance amid the old Georgian and the post-Revolutionary houses. Robert Mills, although but little of his work in Charleston remains, seems to have been the leader in turning architectural taste to the neoclassic.

His Fireproof Building, built in 1826, as a repository of local records, is said to be the first building of fireproof construction in the United States (Plate 48). Mills had been greatly shocked by the loss of life in the burning of the Richmond Theatre, in which seventy-one persons lost their lives including the governor of Virginia, and was determined to prove that such disasters could be prevented. He described the building as having "entrances at two fronts under the familiar portico with its four Doric columns, each column three and a half feet in diameter, and placed on an arcade, rising two floors to height of building, surmounted by entablature and pediment." There is a double flight of stone steps from the street. "The basement, cornices and portico are all of stone, the walls of brick, the roof covered with copper; and further, all sashes, frames and shutters are of iron."[37]

Inspired by this example Charlestonians now began to build private residences in the classic style, their porticoes usually patterned after the monument of Lysikrates or the Tower of the Winds.[38] Unlike Jefferson's houses, where an effort was usually made to conceal height, these Charleston classic residences tower above the street, keeping the proportions of their porticoes by elevating them upon arched basements. But a touch of the old style reappears in the wrought-iron balconies over the front door, half hidden in the shadow of the projecting roof. The windows are tall and narrow, the ceilings lofty, the moulded baseboards unusually wide, the stairs in a great circle at the end of the hall,

[37]H. M. Pierce Gallagher, *Robert Mills*, p. 52.
[38]*The Octagon Library*, I, *Charleston*, p. 152.

the mantels of black-and-gold-veined marble. In place of the furniture of Chippendale, or Sheraton or Hepplewhite design, are the stiffer and more ornate Empire chairs and tables.

It was in 1830 that James Nicholson built the mansion on Rutledge Avenue, later used as a girl's school and known as Ashley Hall. Rising high above an arched basement, the porch, with its Ionic capitals, its pediment cut with three windows of pointed arches, its curved recession containing the front door and over it a wrought-iron balcony, it announced that for Charleston the period of classic residences had arrived. At one time this interesting house was occupied by George A. Trenholm, Secretary of the Treasury of the Confederate States, and at another by Charles Otto Witte, Consul of the German Empire.[39]

Similar was the house of William Ravenel, built about fifteen years later. Facing the old problem of putting a large house on a narrow lot, and wishing to conform to the current mode, he built what was essentially a single-type Charleston house with a classic portico on the street front. The main door, however, is in the narrow end, opening into a long hall which leads past two narrow rooms on one side and the carriage entrance on the other, to the main staircase. The drawing room, one of the largest in the city, runs the full width of the house. The earthquake of 1886 wrought havoc with this mansion, toppling over the fine Corinthian columns, and even wrecking the stone arches on which they stood.[40]

Strangely enough, the handsome classic residence of William Roper, next door, escaped serious injury. In this house the architect combined much that was typical of the old Charleston with the new style. The wide classic front portico resting on an arcaded base, with its five Ionic capitals and flat balustraded roof, link it with the work of Mills and other classicists; the side piazza, rising in three tiers, harks back to colonial days; the long narrow windows opening upon wrought-iron balconies remind us of the post-Revolutionary work of the Middleton-Pinckney house or the Nathaniel Russell house.

[39]A. R. H. and D. E. H. Smith, *The Dwelling Houses of Charleston*, p. 333.
[40]*Ibid.*, pp. 182, 183.

The taste for the classic found expression, also, in public build-ings. Market Hall, built in 1841, with its Doric portico, its ornate frieze, its double front steps with elaborate wrought-iron balus-trade, its arched basement, would not be greatly out of place in Rome itself. Charleston College, after the addition of its beau-tiful Ionic portico in 1850, was brought over to the prevailing style. The Planters and Mechanics Bank, with its fluted Doric col-umns, its elaborate frieze and its correct proportions, is one of the most beautiful buildings in the city. The Charleston Hotel, built in the decade before the War between the States, is note-worthy for its elevated porch adorned by fourteen Corinthian columns. It is the embodiment, not only of the spirit of southern classicism, but of the wealth and power of South Carolina during the sway of King Cotton.

"There are between five and six hundred houses in Charles Town," wrote a visitor in 1732, "besides five handsome churches, viz. one for those of the Church of England, one for the Pres-byterians, one for the Anabaptists, one for the Quakers and one for the French."[41] Some years later, when William Gerard De-Brahm was in the city he noted two Anglican churches, St. Michael's and St. Philip's, "and six meeting houses, viz. an Inde-pendent, a Presbyterian, a French, a German and two Baptist." As an afterthought he mentioned "an assembly for Quakers and an other for Jews."[42] Although evidence is lacking as to the architecture of some of these structures, there can be no doubt that it was as diverse as the beliefs of the congregations who wor-shipped in them. There could be no similarity between St. Philip's with its three porticoes and octagonal tower, and the Baptist meet-inghouses or the Quaker "assembly."

Time has dealt so heavily with the churches of Charleston that one must turn to the country parishes to study the architecture of the Anglican Church in South Carolina in the first decades of the eighteenth century. Fortunately three of the most interesting buildings remain, St. Andrew's, on the Ashley River, St. James's,

41"A Description of the Province of South Carolina," p. 6, *Tracts and Other Papers,* Peter Force, Vol. II.

42P. C. J. Weston, *Philosophies, Historico, etc.,* W. G. DeBrahm.

PLATE 50—George Edwards House

PLATE 51—*Left:* Judge King House. *Right:* Doorway, showing influence of
Adam Brothers

PLATE 52—St. Andrew's Church

PLATE 53—St. James', Goose Creek

on Goose Creek, and Strawberry Chapel, on the West Branch of the Cooper River. These charming little buildings, despite their affiliation with the Anglican Church, have little in common with the rural churches of England. In fact, had St. James's been pulled apart, transported to Dorset or Middlesex, and put together in a village green, few would have recognized it as a church. The low roof, the rounded windows, the absence of tower or steeple, the stuccoed walls would have made it seem out of place, a kind of curiosity. But in the lowlands of South Carolina, surrounded by rice plantations and overhung by moss-covered trees, it fitted perfectly into the landscape.

St. Andrew's, the oldest standing church in South Carolina, was built in 1706 (Plate 52). Its Dutch gable ends, its flaring roof, the arched windows and doors, the quoins, the stuccoed walls, the absence of tower or steeple, the rounded ceilings, the tiled floor give this little church a flavor suggestive of the West Indies. The transept and choir were added in 1723. The building was burned in 1764, but was at once restored within the old walls.

Not less charming and even more interesting is St. James's (Plate 53). This was the house of worship for the settlement of Barbadians on Goose Creek, and one still sees in fancy the planters as they gather in the churchyard among the tombstones to exchange news of friends and relatives in the far-off island. We watch them file in through the west door with its Doric pilasters and pediment enclosing the image of a pelican tearing its own breast to feed its young, to take their seats in the boxlike pews and listen to the sermon delivered from the wine-glass pulpit. Before them is the highly ornate reredos, or decoration behind the minister, with its Corinthian pilasters, its carved and broken pediment framing the royal arms, done in colored plaster. Outwardly the stuccoed walls, the quoins, the lack of tower or cupola, the arched windows proclaim the kinship of this church with St. Andrew's. Only the low jerkin-head roof and the absence of transepts give it an individuality of its own.

Of like kind is Strawberry Chapel. In South Carolina, as in Virginia, the parishes were often so large that it was impossible for all the people to gather for services at one church, no matter how centrally located. So it became the practice to erect chapels of ease for the more remote members of the congregation, where services were held at lengthy intervals by the rector and more frequently by lay readers. Strawberry, on the West Branch of Cooper River, has survived to the present day to show us what these chapels were like. Its low jerkin-head roof with flaring eaves, its stuccoed walls, its arched windows mark it as a typical example of the early low country church.

We do not know what the first St. Philip's Church in Charleston was like, save that it had a brick foundation and a superstructure of black cypress. Built in 1682 on the present site of St. Michael's it was described as large and stately. By 1722 it had become so decayed and unsafe that it was necessary to construct a new building. The proprietors contributed £500, private subscriptions came in and the vestry were able to put up what was called at the time the handsomest church in America. Turning their backs upon the architecture of the rural districts, the builders went directly to Wren and his disciples for their ideas. The new St. Philip's, with its classic porticoes, its octagonal tower, its restrained dignity was a far cry indeed from St. Andrew's or St. James's.

"It has three aisles, an organ and a gallery all round," said a visitor. "The steeple rises octagonal, with windows in each face of the second course ornamented with Ionic pilasters, whose entablature supports a balustrade, from this the tower still rises octagonal, with sashed windows on every other face, till it is terminated by a dome, upon which stands a lantern for the bells, from which rises a vane in the form of a cock."[43] The church was opened for service in 1723, but the congregation had to take their chairs with them, for it was only in 1727 that pews were installed. No doubt there were some who wished that the former arrangement could have continued, for the pews were granted only to those who made a substantial "benevolence," varying apparently from £60 to £100. The church had a narrow escape in the great fire of 1796, when it was saved by the courage of a Negro sailor, who climbed to the top of the tower and tore off

[43]Mrs. St. Julien Ravenel, *Charleston, the Place and the People,* pp. 97–99.

298

the blazing shingles. His reward was a gift of his freedom, a sum of money and a completely equipped fishing boat.

Unfortunately, there was no one to save the building when in 1835 another destructive fire swept Charleston. "St. Philip's! the least exertion would have saved it," a looker-on wrote. "Nothing was done, however, they stood and saw it burn to ashes. The steeple caught first, one wet blanket would have extinguished it. . . . That one spot spread, wreathed slowly round and finally burnt the church to the ground."[44] So a third St. Philip's arose, which has lasted to the present day despite fires, war and earthquakes (Plate 54). Taken singly or as a group, its three Doric porticoes are well proportioned and beautiful, but they are dwarfed by the great tower which rises in successive stages out of the front roof. This tower, itself, with its pilasters, its circular windows, its Ionic and Corinthian capitals, its slender spire would adorn such a building as Christ Church, Philadelphia, but in its present setting, when viewed from the front, it looks like a tall monument of which the church is the base.

One wonders why the South Carolina clergy did not share the prejudice of the Virginia Anglicans against Renaissance church buildings. Apparently they thought it just as appropriate to worship God in a building adorned with Greek porticoes as in a Gothic chapel. When in 1752 Governor Glenn laid the cornerstone for a new church in Charleston, to be known as St. Michael's, the design selected resembled closely that of St. Martin's-in-the-Fields, London (Plate 55). "This church will be built on the plan of one of Mr. Gibson's designs," stated the *South Carolina Gazette,* "and 'tis thought will exhibit a fine piece of architecture when completed."[45] The Mr. Gibson here referred to may well have been James Gibbs and the plan taken from his *Book of Architecture,* with modifications to suit the taste of the builder and the vestry.

The building is of brick, 130 feet by 60, the tower rising through the roof high above the Doric portico to an open belfry. Here were hung in 1764 a set of eight bells which for a century and a half have rung out tidings of joy or sorrow for thousands

---

[44] *Ibid.,* pp. 482, 483.      [45] *South Carolina Gazette,* Feb. 22, 1752.

of Charlestonians. A clock made by Aynsworth Thwayts, London, was installed in the tower and its four faces appear between the Corinthian pilasters of the second octagonal stage. The interior is as clearly a product of the Renaissance as the exterior, and its recessed choir with its richly decorated vaulted ceiling supported by Corinthian pilasters, its ornate cornice, its arched windows, might have been the work of Sir Christopher Wren himself. The church is a visible evidence of the ascendency of English culture in Charleston in the eighteenth century, and ignores the medley of traditions—early English, West Indian, French, Dutch—which had formerly shaped the architecture of the city. St. Michael's would have been more in place on one of the narrow streets of the City of London, than amid the tiled roofs and stuccoed walls of Charleston.[46]

The new church architecture in the rural districts, if we may judge from one interesting chapel which has survived, is far more American, less English than the two famous Charleston churches. Pompion Hill chapel, on the East Branch of the Cooper, is merely an early low country church reclothed in the Georgian style. It is more closely related to Gloria Dei, in Philadelphia, than to the Wren churches of London. The brick walls, the heavy cornice, the Palladian window in the chancel, the high-backed benches differentiate this building from St. Andrew's and St. James's, while the jerkin-headed roof, the absence of a tower, the plainness of the interior differentiate it from St. Michael's or St. Philip's. It would be interesting to know what its predecessor was like, since a comparison of the present building with the cypress structure of 1703 would no doubt illustrate the changing styles in the church architecture of this region. For the building of the chapel of 1763 the government gave £200 and £370 more was raised by subscription, of which Gabriel Manigault gave £50.[47]

In the first half of the nineteenth century, the South Carolina congregations—Baptists, Methodists, Presbyterians, and others—abandoning their former architectural styles, went over heart and

---

[46]Geo. S. Holmes, *Historic Sketch of St. Michael's;* Mrs. St. J. Ravenel, *Charleston, the Place and the People,* pp. 154, 155.

[47]S. G. Stoney, *Plantations of the Carolina Low Country,* pp. 64, 65, 177–181; *S. C. Hist. and Gen. Mag.,* XIV, p. 112.

PLATE 54—St. Philip's, Charleston

PLATE 55—St. Michael's, Charleston

PLATE 56—*Upper left:* Wrought-Iron Work, Market Hall. *Lower left:* Gate, Sussa House. *Upper right:* Gateway, St. John's Lutheran Church. *Lower right:* Nathaniel Russell House, Charleston

soul to the classic. The rectangular body with roof extended to cover a Doric or a Corinthian portico of six columns, the rows of windows high enough to light both the body of the church and the gallery, the great front door with its flat arch became almost mandatory for every new church structure. The synagogue, built in 1838, the Wentworth Street Baptist Church, the Westminster Street Presbyterian Church, the Bethel Methodist Church, all of Charleston, conform strictly to this model. They are Greek temples pure and simple, diverted from the worship of Zeus or Apollo to the worship of God.

It was Robert Mills who led the way with his First Baptist Church, built in 1822. "This church is purely Greek in style, simply grand in proportions and beautiful in its details," Mills wrote enthusiastically. "The plan is of the temple form, divided into four parts, the portico, the vestibule, the nave and the vestry room. The length of the building is a hundred and ten feet, and the breadth sixty feet. The facade presents a portico of four massy columns of the lightest proportions of the Doric, surmounted by a pediment. Behind this portico rises an attic story squared up the height of the roof and crowned by a cupola or belfry. You enter the vestibule by three doors, on each side of which the gallery stairs ascend. . . . At the extreme end of the nave of the church are the baptismal font and the pulpit, lighted by a large vaulted window. Above three sides of the nave a double colonnade extends, rises up to the roof and supports the gallery. The lower arch of the columns is Doric, the upper Ionic."[48]

Nothing more than the wrought-iron work of Charleston gives charm and individuality to this unique city. Here is a garden gate, a graceful tangle of rosettes and spirals topped by a quaint old lantern; here an iron balcony beneath high shuttered windows, its delicate urns and interlocking circles hardly visible against the brick walls; there a railing to the winding front steps of some old mansion, the severity of its balusters relieved by the figure of a harp or an inverted heart. Blacksmiths, the earlier of the workers in wrought iron called themselves, but they were as much artists as the architects who designed the houses, the cabi-

[48]H. M. Pierce Gallagher, *Robert Mills*, p. 83.

netmakers who made the Chippendale or Sheraton chairs with which they were furnished, or the carvers who fashioned the graceful cornices or friezes (Plate 56).

Tunis Tebaut, descended no doubt from the Tebauts of the Huguenot settlement on the Santee, was the first of these wrought-iron workers of whom we have record. In his shop on Beal Wharf, he and his partner, William Johnson, hammered out many a gate and balustrade. Most of the workers of later times were Germans. On the gates of St. Michael's, amid the urns and rosettes and the labyrinth of graceful curves, one finds the words "Justi Fecit." This Justi came to Charleston from Germany in 1820. Even more important is his fellow Teuton, Werner, who came over in 1828 and for four decades worked steadily at his trade. Among his many helpers was "Uncle Toby Richardson," a Negro, who is said to have developed great skill. Still another German, Frederick Julius Ortmann, arrived in 1847, and after serving in the Confederacy, continued his work for many years (Plate 56).

The history of the architecture of Charleston and the surrounding country illustrates admirably all four of the fundamental forces which created American civilization. The settlers, like settlers in other colonies, brought with them their architectural traditions and tried to build houses on the banks of the Ashley and Cooper like those they had been accustomed to in their native lands. Sturdy Jan Van Arrsens made his Medway in the Dutch tradition, the Huguenots gave Charleston a flavor of southwest France which lingers to the present day, the Barbadians introduced the building practices of the West Indies, while the inheritance of England was always obvious. With this complex background it was inevitable that early South Carolina architecture, when a distinctive architecture emerged, should be a product of the melting-pot. Charleston in the eighteenth century was outwardly very different from Boston or New York or Annapolis, because the component parts which went into its make-up were very different.

But it was different, also, because local conditions were different. The Charleston builders, or the architect for a plantation house, had to take into consideration the heat of summer, the prevailing winds, the available building materials, the social life of the owners, the domestic service of Negro slaves. The tiers of piazzas, the very large windows with blinds or shutters, the height of the ceilings, the elevation of the basement and the location of drawing rooms on the second floor were all concessions to the climate. The great size of the residences, the richness of the decorations, the costliness of the furnishings were a part of the sumptuous life of the planter-merchant aristocracy. The building materials depended, of course, upon what was available in the immediate neighborhood, so that lower South Carolina became a region of brick and frame houses, and not, save in rare cases, of houses of stone.

And South Carolina, even more than some of the other colonies was subject to the cultural dominance of England. By the middle of the eighteenth century she had developed an architecture of her own, distinguishable at a glance. Yet this architecture was brushed aside, or at best profoundly altered, to make room for the English Georgian. The wealthy Charlestonian would have thought himself far behind the times had he not built in the "modern taste," or perhaps modified his old residence by putting in mantels and ceiling moulding from designs in the English books on architecture. Yet the South Carolina Georgian, like the New England Georgian, the Pennsylvania Georgian, the Annapolis Georgian, took on characteristics peculiar to itself, had its own marked individuality. The new styles, like the old, could not escape the moulding influence of climate, building materials, labor, the habits and life of the people.

Yet the Charleston region, more than New England or Virginia or Maryland, clung to many of its own traditions in the face of invading styles. The Georgian architects were forced in many cases to reshape their plans to make them conform to the old Charleston single house; they scratched their heads in perplexity when they found they could not discard the old double- or triple-decked piazzas. When Gabriel Manigault came back from Europe imbued with the ideas of the Adam brothers, his houses went up side by side with others built in the old pre-Revolutionary style. But the fact that Charleston did accept, even

303

though reluctantly, the architectural ideas then popular in England, shows that it was still subject to the cultural influence of London. But for the next great change, the change to the neoclassic, the prevailing influence was national, not foreign. It was her own great son, Robert Mills, who was chiefly responsible for dotting, not only Charleston, but Columbia and other places in South Carolina, with Greek and Roman temples, and Mills' inspirations came chiefly from Thomas Jefferson. True, Mills studied under Hoban and Latrobe, but his chief influence upon South Carolina was to bring to it the architectural style already accepted in Virginia and elsewhere. Mills made the architecture of his native State less interesting, less distinctive, brought it more into line with national architecture, but he marks at least a temporary and partial declaration of independence of European ideas.

*Chapter VIII*

# THE GOOD EARTH

THE DAY laborer, or cotter, or tenant farmer, who affixed his signature to an indenture guaranteeing his passage to one of the southern colonies, had before him a pleasing vision—a vision of a farm with ample acres and rich soil to be his own without restrictions, a vision of a comfortable cottage, of cattle grazing in green meadows, of orchards and gardens and woods. He was leaving behind him forever such vexatious things as rents, tithes, socage, manorial court dues, tolls, services. He was willing to bid good-bye to friends and neighbors, turn his back upon the country of his birth, risk his health, even his life on one of the tiny ocean-going vessels of the day, spend four or five years as a bonded laborer, only because of the hope that was held out that some day he would have land of his own and elevate himself into the envied yeoman class.

But there were others who came to the colonies, men who had accumulated a little store of capital which they hoped to invest to good advantage in America, whose interests and plans were very different. They knew that they could purchase land in large quantities—a thousand acres, perhaps five thousand acres—but their problem was how to secure the labor necessary to put it under cultivation. What would it profit them to own an estate half the size of Shropshire, if it must remain covered by forests for lack of hands to clear it, plant corn or tobacco, build houses and barns and fences? Perhaps they eyed hopefully their fellow passenger on the immigrant vessel, the would-be yeoman, with the thought that here might be a future tenant. If in England thousands of poor men were glad to pay rentals to the lords of manors, why not in America? So they laid their plans to buy a tract of the most desirable land, or perhaps secure a grant from the English or the provincial governments.

It is unlikely that either the poor laborer or the small capitalist understood the forces which were at work in America favorable or unfavorable to their hopes. They could not foresee the part to be played by the cheapness and abundance of land, by the scarcity of labor, by the character of the soil, by the climate, by the force of English tradition, by the ambitions of royal favorites, by the needs of the English government. Of these forces the most important was the almost unlimited amount of land. Even though the King, or the Governor, or the Council of State put restrictions upon the granting of land to poor settlers, even though vast acres were purchased or secured by fraud by wealthy or influential men, even though proprietors tried to impose feudal institutions on the people, in the end holdings were apt to be democratic in character, because there were usually places where the poor man could secure a farm ample for his needs.

In England itself landholding, despite important changes produced by the Black Death and the Peasants' Revolt, was still aristocratic in character. Serfdom had almost disappeared, the number of villains had been gradually diminishing for centuries, the percentage of tenants and yeomen had become larger and larger; yet it was the squire, the lord of the manor, who owned most of the countryside. Even though the poor man seldom labored on the demesne or delivered two chickens and a goat at Michaelmas, as formerly, he had to pay a heavy rental for his land. And with the enclosure movement which crept slowly over England, turning agricultural lands into sheepfolds, he was fortunate if he could find a bit of ground to lease. In fact, thousands of men had been turned out of work, sturdy beggars wandered over the countryside and the almshouses were filled to overflowing. England's undemocratic land system was costing her dear in the waste of human resources.

The size and character of the landholdings in the seventeenth century varied greatly. But the estate of Thomas Bacon of Suffolk, father of the American patriot, Nathaniel Bacon, serves well as an example of the agricultural economy of the times. His seat at Friston Hall, with its barns, chapel, stables, outhouses, gardens and orchards comprised five acres; the demesne, including woodland, arable and pasture brought £50 a year; from his copyhold tenants, manorial court fees, fairs, fishing rights and tolls he received £30; the rental of Friston Hall farm was £135; a farm called England brought £70; another, known as Smarts, rented for £100; Little Borrough Marsh farm for £32; the decoy pool was let for £20; the Shepherd's farm for £60, and a large sheep walk for £50. If landholding in England's colonies was to be patterned upon this model, the New World would be as undemocratic as the Old.[1] No doubt Thomas Bacon was a lenient, kind lord of the manor, but there were many who hoped that there would be no Thomas Bacons in America to monopolize the land, turn the freeholders into tenants and fence off great sheepfolds.

Of great importance in determining whether the vast American lands were ultimately to belong to the poor man or the rich was the cost of the ocean fare across the Atlantic. It was futile for a farm laborer, or a blacksmith's apprentice, or even a small tenant to think of purchasing land in Maryland or South Carolina, unless he had the means to migrate to America. Only too often he found he could span the great ocean barrier only by selling his one valuable asset, the thing above all others which was needed there—the labor of his two hands. And since he must sell this in advance, buy his passage with it on credit, as it were, he had to bind himself to work four or five years after his arrival for the London Company or a group of investors or for an individual master. Servant they called him, although he rarely occupied the position of a domestic.

The saving feature of this arrangement was the fact that it was temporary. Had the poor immigrant bartered off his liberty for a lifetime, the plantations of the Chesapeake Bay region and the Carolinas would indeed have rivalled the baronies of England. The South would have been a region of great estates, its people divided between powerful landholders comparable to the English nobility, on the one hand, and bonded workmen who were feudal serfs in all save name, on the other. As it was, the indentured workers were constantly graduating into the freeman class, thus depleting the number of hands on the large plantations, and

[1]British Museum, *Additional MSS.* 22249.

opening an active market for farm land in small quantities. So long as the stream of indentured workers remained constant, the number at any one time who had not completed their terms would be constant, while the number of freedmen would continue to mount from year to year.[2]

When Sir Thomas Dale reached Jamestown in May, 1611, he found the people playing bowls in the streets.[3] The London Company had brought to Virginia a number of tenants, or more properly indentured workers, whom they had employed in raising crops, building houses, erecting storehouses, etc., but since all they produced went into the public store, out of which all were fed and clothed, it was impossible to keep them from loafing on the job. The stern but keen governor at once put his finger upon the cause of the trouble, and assigned to the more industrious three acres each, for which he was to pay an annual rent of two and a half barrels of grain for himself and a similar amount if he had a servant. This step toward individual enterprise not only acted as a tonic to the colony, but it was a first step toward the ideal of a small farmer class.

From the first the London Company had held out to each "tenant" the prospect of eventual freedom and a "dividend" of land. In addition it transported him to Virginia, supplied him with clothes, weapons, tools and farm implements, and gave him

---

[2]This becomes obvious if we examine the following table in which it is assumed that the same number came over each year, the same proportion died in service, and that each man or woman served for four years.

| | Number of indentured workers imported | Number in service at End of Year | Number Gaining Freedom | Total Number of Freedmen |
|---|---|---|---|---|
| First year | 1800 | 1500 | | |
| Second year | 1800 | 3000 | | |
| Third year | 1800 | 4500 | | |
| Fourth year | 1800 | 6000 | 1500 | 1500 |
| Fifth year | 1800 | 6000 | 1500 | 3000 |
| Sixth year | 1800 | 6000 | 1500 | 4500 |
| Seventh year | 1800 | 6000 | 1500 | 6000 |
| Eighth year | 1800 | 6000 | 1500 | 7500 |
| Ninth year | 1800 | 6000 | 1500 | 9000 |
| Tenth year | 1800 | 6000 | 1500 | 10,500 |

[3]A. Brown, *Genesis of U. S.*, pp. 490, 491.

a year's store of provisions. The tenant served for seven years, paying to the Company one half his annual crop, and at the expiration of his contract he was at liberty to move to his "dividend" to start life as a yeoman. It was on December, 1617, that a certain Captain Robert Smallay proudly wrote in his will: "I give to my wife Elizabeth my house and grounds at Bermuda Hundred."[4] So far as is known this is the first bequest of land in all English-speaking America.

To the former Company tenant, the little holding of 100 acres seemed a princely estate. He had faced the perils of the ocean, the Indian, the Virginia sickness, had labored long and hard for it; and now he was a member of the yeoman class, a holder of land almost without restriction. So he set to work to erect his simple cottage, lay out his orchard and his garden, clear away trees, plant wheat or Indian corn or tobacco, build fences, put up his barn, set aside a pasture for his cows. By the time King James revoked the charter of the London Company and converted Virginia into a royal colony, that province had already become the land of the small farmer. The visitor who sailed up the James saw at intervals on both banks, half hidden in the forests, little clearings of a few acres, owned by freemen who tilled their soil with their own hands or the hands of their sons.

Thus from the very early years the land system of Virginia differed radically from that of England. The manor, with its landlord, its demesne, its three-field system, its servile population, its leet court, was entirely unknown on the banks of the James and the York. Had Thomas Bacon duplicated in Virginia his Suffolk holdings, bringing over his tenants, cotters and other workers, the whole thing would have dissolved within a decade. The men who had labored so faithfully for him in England, in this new land of opportunity would have deserted to secure land unburdened with rents and tithes and feudal dues.

In Maryland, on the other hand, early landholding was less democratic, for certain features of the feudal system were transplanted, and despite the uncongenial soil of the New World, survived for decades. Had Thomas Bacon migrated to St. Mary's

[4]*Virginia Magazine of Hist. and Biog.*, XII, pp. 175, 176.

County in the middle of the seventeenth century, he would have been quite at home amid the manors with their courts leet and their courts baron, their bailiffs, constables, tenants and freeholders. At St. Gabriel's Manor he might have seen the steward break a twig in two, and retaining one part for the lord of the manor, deliver the other to a tenant as evidence of the transfer.[5] This ·was the seizin by the rod, a custom having its origin in feudal days. He might have been present when a tenant swore fealty to the lord of the manor, promising to be true and faithful, as though he were ready at any moment to buckle on his armor and follow him into battle or in an assault on a castle.

The records of the court leet and court baron of St. Clement's Manor, St. Mary's County, make interesting reading. At the session of 1659 John Ryve, "gentleman," was steward; Richard Hoster, constable; Arthur Delahay and eight others "resiants";[6] Thomas Jackson, Rowland Mace, and nine others leaseholders; and Robert Sly,[7] "gentleman," William Barton, "gentleman," Robert Cole, Luke Gardiner, Bartholomew Phillips, Christopher Carnall, John Norman and John Goldsmith, freeholders. When the jury was sworn they proceeded to present one Samuel Horns for breaking "the peace with a stick" and committing bloodshed on the body of John Mansell, and Robert Cole for marking a hog belonging to the lord of the manor; ordered every man to have his land "bounded, marked and laid out," and fined those freeholders who had absented themselves from court.[8]

Living on the Maryland manor were leaseholders, the title to whose land resided in the lord of the manor, leaseholders who held title under certain restrictions, and "resiants," or residents, who were subject to the jurisdiction of the manorial court. Leases were made out for twenty-one years, at the termination of which period the tenant had to make renewals, but the rent was low and was usually paid in tobacco or grain. The freeholder, for his part, could not transfer his holdings without paying relief. Yet the

[5]Clayton C. Hall, *The Lords Baltimore and the Maryland Palatinate*, p. 186.
[6]Residents.
[7]Robert Sly was speaker of the Lower House of Assembly in 1658. His residence on the manor survived until 1934.
[8]John Johnson, "Old Maryland Manors," *Johns Hopkins Studies*.

freeholders of a Maryland manor had a status in no sense inferior to that of freeholders in Virginia, and many of them occupied positions of prominence. Robert Sly of St. Clement's possessed a stately residence 132 feet long, large enough to accommodate the Maryland Council for their meeting in 1659, was speaker of the Lower House of Assembly, and a man of more note than Thomas Gerard, to whom he swore fealty as lord of the manor.

The introduction of slaves in large numbers and the opening of new land to the west led to the disintegration of the Maryland manorial system. On St. Clement's the number of leaseholders dwindled, the freeholders increased, while the "resiants" doubled and quadrupled. By 1670 the manor had become little more than a judicial district. Although the custom of granting manors continued far into the eighteenth century, they were merely large tracts in the hands of wealthy men, without feudal features, which might be divided into leaseholds but usually were sold outright to small freeholders. Thus the early Maryland manor was but a passing phase in the life of the colony, a phase, however, which might have proved stifling to democracy, had it persisted.

But though those who came to Virginia and Maryland with capital to invest and those who had accumulated it in the colony could not establish a lasting manorial system, they could and did try to secure title to the richest and most convenient lands and so preclude the poor man from settling upon it. It was their hope that in time, as land became scarcer, many newcomers would be forced, either to purchase from them at advanced prices, or take leaseholds on long tenure. Even in Sir William Berkeley's administration the monopolizing of great tracts was a matter of serious complaint,[9] and the evil grew steadily worse as the settlements advanced westward and north across the deep-water region to the Fall Line.

With the vast wilderness to the west of the falls of the James inviting the settlers, at first sight it would seem impossible to practice any form of land monopoly. If the governor's favorites had seized on every acre of tidewater Virginia, there would still be room for thousands of farms. Unfortunately, the Piedmont

[9]*British Public Record Office*, CO5–1371, pp. 292–297.

region was not open to settlers at this time because of Lord Howard of Effingham's treaty of 1784 which reserved it as a hunting ground for the Iroquois. The freedman who dared lay out a farm on the Rivanna or the North Anna was inviting the tomahawk and the scalping knife.

The disappointment of the poor immigrant when he found that all the best and most convenient sites were held by wealthy and influential men, was all the more bitter because in many cases they had obtained title by fraud. The Kings of England, in order to encourage emigration to Virginia, pledged the government to grant fifty acres to any person who would pay the passage of a new settler. If one brought over twenty indentured workers he was entitled to 1000 acres; if he himself were a newcomer he could claim fifty acres for his own passage and fifty more for each member of his family who accompanied him.

This arrangement opened a rich field for land-grabbing. An examination of the books of the secretary of the colony revealed that often both the person brought in and the person who paid his passage secured fifty acres, that many certificates for transporting settlers were used several times, that persons who had lived in Virginia for years were set down as immigrants, that false names were inserted in the lists and sworn to.[10]

"The first abuse of this design was by the ignorance and knavery of surveyors," it was stated, "who gave out draughts of surveys without ever actually surveying it or even coming on the land; only they gave the description by some natural bounds and were sure to allow large measure, so that the persons for whom they survey'd might enjoy larger tracts of land than they were to pay quit rents for. . . . Then great liberty was used in issuing out certificates for rights by the county clerks and especially by the clerks of the Secretary's office which was and is still a constant mint of these rights, where they may be purchased at very easy rates, of the clerks, from five shillings to one shilling per right." Thus the real settlers for whom the land was intended "had the least share" of it.[11]

[10]*Ibid.*, CO5–1406, *Council Minutes*, Dec. 9, 1712.
[11]Hartwell, Blair and Chilton, *The Present State of Virginia*, H. D. Farish, Ed., p. 17.

Colonel Philip Ludwell, one of the most influential men in the colony, was guilty of a fraud which would have shamed some of the "land barons" of the West in the nineteenth century. Having brought in 40 immigrants and received his patent for 2000 acres, he changed the record with his own hand by adding a cipher to the 40 and another to the 2000, making them 400 and 20,000 respectively. Although the fact was notorious at the time, so great was his power that the matter was hushed up and his rights were not disputed.[12]

When the wealthy planter had received his patent for ten or twenty thousand acres and deposited it safely in the strong box of his "great hall," he usually made a pretense of "seating" his land in conformity with law. Every grant was made with the proviso that the land be "planted and seated" within three years, and in 1666 the Assembly passed an act to explain what this meant. "Building an house and keeping a stock one whole year upon the land shall be accounted seating," they declared, "and clearing, tending and planting an acre of ground shall be accounted planting."[13] Edward Randolph reported that this provision was habitually avoided. "They cut down a few trees and make therewith a little hut, covering it with bark, and turn two or three hogs into the woods by it. Or else they . . . fell twenty or thirty trees and put a little Indian corn in the ground . . . and sometimes make a beginning to fence it, but take no care of their crop."[14] Robert Beverley, in his *History of Virginia,* denies this charge, but it was reiterated by so many witnesses that we are obliged to accept it. In fact, the law of 1666 was so badly drawn as to be almost useless. It did not specify the kind of house to be erected, nor how many cattle the owner must keep on his land, nor how many acres he could hold by clearing and seating one acre.

More serious for the large landholders were the King's quit-rents. This tax, or land rental, paid into the royal treasury, amounted to two shillings a hundred acres, or £50 a year on

[12]Sainsbury, *Cal. of State Papers,* V, pp. 360–362.
[13]Hening, *Statutes,* II, p. 244.
[14]*British Public Record Office,* CO5–1359, pp. 20–22.

50,000 acres. Obviously, to hold an extensive tract for a decade or two would drain the resources of even the wealthiest and turn land speculation into a losing game. But the fertile brains of the so-called "great men" of the colony were not long in finding ways to avoid this tax. The King had consented to remission of quitrents in newly opened regions in order to encourage the settling there of poor men unable to make payments until they had conquered the first difficulties and hardships of the frontier. How far it was from furthering this end is shown by a clause in Sir William Berkeley's instructions in 1662. Hearing that the order of our father "to exempt the planters from paying quit rents for the first seven years hath turned to the great prejudice of that our coloney," wrote Charles II, "and that many have abused that grace and taken occasion thereby to take and create a title to themselves of such quantities of land which they never intend to or in truth can occupy or cultivate, but thereby only keep out others who would plant and manure the same, we do therefore revoke all such grants as contrary to the intention of our royal father."[15]

But the holders of large tracts were not discouraged. When rent rolls were drawn up to list all landholders and the number of acres they possessed, the surveyors knew full well that if they included the unoccupied lands of members of the Council or other influential men, they were putting their jobs in jeopardy. And it was a bold sheriff who dared go beyond the rolls in collecting the rents of a Ludwell or a Beverley, or to distrain for non-payment. "There is great concealment of quit rents," reported Henry Hartwell, "chiefly by the granting vast quantities of land to the richer sort of inhabitants, some holding forty, fifty or sixty thousand acres, by whom the sheriffs are so overawed that they take their accounts as they themselves would have it."[16]

Even the governors were not long in discovering that it was prudent to wink at these irregularities, since the very men upon whom they relied for the support of their administrations were concerned in them. Any attempt to ferret out frauds in the grant-

[15]*Virginia Magazine of Hist. and Biog.*, III, p. 19.
[16]*British Public Record Office*, CO5–1359, pp. 91, 92.

ing or surveying of land, any suggestion that it might be for the King's service to collect quitrents on unoccupied land was greeted with frowns not only around the Council board, but in the House of Burgesses. So it is not at all surprising that none of the governors prior to Sir Francis Nicholson, who had a genius for getting into trouble wherever he went, dared to make an issue of the matter.

Nicholson made a tour of inspection in which he uncarthed so many frauds that he determined to sue some of the largest landholders in the General Court for arrears of quitrents in order to make them disgorge. This was like asking the Court to pass sentence on itself, for it is probable that every member held considerable tracts for which he paid no rents, and there were many dark hints to the governor that he was treading on dangerous ground. But Nicholson was never a man to be intimidated. Singling out Major Lawrence Smith, Mr. Richard Whitehead and several others in partnership with them in holding title to many thousands of acres in various counties, he ordered the attorney-general to sue them for £80. It was generally understood that this was to be a test case, and if Smith and his associates lost, other offenders would have to pay great "sums of money" to the Crown or else give up title to lands estimated at "some hundred thousand acres."[17] No doubt the small planters and freedmen wished the governor every success in his suit, but this availed him nothing against the opposition of the "great men," who could and did make life for him almost intolerable. In the end he sought a way to withdraw without "losing face," so that "when the court was ripe for judgment," he consented to the compounding of the case for less than half the amount due.[18] Thus, the incident, so far from serving as a deterrent to landgrabbing, proved a practical demonstration of the helplessness of the government, and an invitation for renewed frauds on a larger scale than ever.

A few years later Edward Randolph came to Virginia and at once began prying into the conduct of government to see what irregularities he could report to the King. Nor was he long in

[17]*British Public Record Office*, CO5–1359, p. 23.       [18]*Ibid.*

putting his finger on the land evil. It might be well to enquire how it came to pass that the colony was not better inhabited, he wrote, "considering what vast numbers of servants and others have yearly been transported thither. . . . The chief and only reason is the inhabitants and planters have been and at this time are discouraged and hindered from planting tobacco . . . and servants are not willing to go there as formerly, because the members of the Council and others, who make an interest in the government, have from time to time procured grants of very large tracts of land, so that there has not for many years been any waste land to be taken up by those who bring with them servants, or by such servants who have served their time faithfully with their masters, but it is taken up and ingrossed beforehand, whereby they are forced to hire and pay a yearly rent for some of those lands, or go to the utmost bounds of the colony for land." This it was, he added, which forced newcomers, who are "brought up only to planting, to seek their fortunes in Carolina or other places."[19]

Randolph suggested that the King insist upon the payment of arrears of quitrents to recover the monopolized lands and in the future limit all grants to 500 acres. This he thought would increase the population and with it the revenue from tobacco, by "inviting home those who for want of land left Virginia." The Board of Trade was so impressed with these revelations that they put the matter before Governor Andros and asked him what he thought should be done. But Nicholson's failure in the Lawrence Smith case was fresh in Andros' memory, and he had no desire to involve himself in the matter. He knew of no frauds in granting patents to land, he replied, and could suggest no remedy for what had already been done, it "being a matter of property." He agreed, however, that to limit the size of future grants would hasten the filling up of the frontier region.[20]

In the meanwhile the Board of Trade had been working out a new plan which they inserted in their instructions to Nicholson when he returned to Virginia in 1698. To prevent the taking up of land by persons who make no use of it to the exclusion of real

[19]*Ibid.*       [20]*British Public Record Office*, CO5–1359, p. 113.

settlers, they said, they suggested that in the future "whoever will sit down and plant on any vacant piece of land, shall have 100 acres granted himself, and the like quantity for each laboring person that he shall carry over . . . within three years from the date of the patent, under the yearly quit rent of two shillings for 100 acres."[21] But they doomed the plan to failure from the start by instructing Nicholson to advise with the Council and Assembly how "the method now proposed may be put into operation." If the governor ever laid the scheme before them it is certain that the Council, so far from telling him how to put it into force, advised him to report back that it was unwise and impracticable. Yet Nicholson, despite his former failure, acted with considerable vigor to prevent the usual frauds in a tract of land south of the James known as Blackwater, which had just been opened for settlement. Upon examining the entries for this region he found them so vague and irregular that some could have been stretched to include almost any amount of land, 10,000 acres, 20,000 acres or even more. In this way the holders of patents could have grabbed all that was worth having, "by which means they would have kept other people from seating it or else have made them pay for it."[22] Thereupon Nicholson forbade the secretary to issue further patents until proper surveys had been made. But he paid dearly for his boldness, for he was once more treading on the toes of some of the leading men of the colony. Before long the ugly looks and sarcastic remarks of his official advisors, whenever they met around the Council table, warned him that he had incurred their bitter hostility. A few years later they preferred charges against him before the Board of Trade, many of them apparently trumped up for the occasion, which eventually brought about his removal from office.[23]

Nicholson was not so conscientious in carrying out the Board's direction to draw up a correct rent roll, showing every landholder and the number of acres he owned. It is true that he ordered the various counties to make the rolls, but apparently did not protest when the sheriffs, intimidated by the wealthy landholders, deliber-

[21]*Ibid.*, pp. 288, 289.   [22]*Ibid.*, CO5–1360, pp. 440, 441.
[23]*Virginia Magazine of Hist. and Biog.*, III, p. 376.

ately omitted their great unoccupied tracts.[24] When the governor left the colony in 1705, with Ludwell, Byrd, Blair and the others baying at his heels, the opportunities for frauds were as great as ever.

In fact, with the opening of the eighteenth century, when the settlements were advancing into the Piedmont, new and vast possibilities for graft presented themselves. Alexander Spotswood's Knights of the Golden Horseshoe, when they reached the summits of the Blue Ridge and looked out to east and west over hundreds of square miles of verdant country, no doubt had pleasant visions of great holdings for themselves and their posterity. The aristocrats were all the more angered, then, that two laws had been passed, one in 1710 and the other in 1713, designed to prevent the old frauds in granting patents, and in the payment of quitrents and the seating of new lands. One clause, especially, which made holdings liable to forfeiture for non-payment of quitrents, aroused their bitter protests.

The meetings in the Council Chamber of the beautiful new capitol at Williamsburg became tense with excitement, and Spotswood was the object of frowns and rebuffs. Councillors, Burgesses and other large landholders gathered in knots on the Duke of Gloucester Street or in Bruton churchyard after services, to denounce the law and the governor. If Spotswood had not meddled in the land question, they whispered, one might easily have secured title to great tracts on the headwaters of the Pamunkey and the Mattaponi to the west, or on the Nottoway and Meherrin to the south, lying directly in the path of new settlement. Already many smaller landholders were coming in with arrears of quitrents to prevent the forfeiture of their lands and if this kept up the larger might have to follow suit. So several influential men deliberately let their payments run in arrears as a demonstration of the powerlessness of the governor, while the Auditor-General, John Grymes, upon whom the enforcement of the law was largely dependent, led the way in defying it.[25]

In the end Spotswood wearied of his rôle of champion against

[24]The entire rent roll is printed in: T. J. Wertenbaker, *The Planters of Colonial Virginia*, Appendix.
[25]*British Public Record Office*, CO5–1318, Art. I; *Ibid.*, CO5–1318, Spotswood to Board of Trade, Dec. 22, 1718.

the land-grabbing dragon and not only came to terms, but joined forces with it. In 1720 he gave his approval to two acts, one taking the teeth out of the laws of 1710 and 1713, and the other erecting the counties of Spotsylvania and Brunswick and freeing them from quitrents for seven years.[26] In the meanwhile word came to him that certain forces working against him in England had brought about his downfall and that he was soon to be replaced as governor. Deciding to reap a rich harvest while the sun shone, he made out a patent for 40,000 acres in Spotsylvania County to three men named Jones, Clayton and Hickman, putting them under bond to reconvey the land to him as soon as he left the executive office.[27] In the same way he obtained another tract for 20,000. Governor Drysdale exposed the fraud before the Board of Trade, but Spotswood's influence at court was great enough to secure a confirmation of the patents.[28]

The agents of the proprietors of the Northern Neck took their cue from the office of the Secretary of Virginia, for they were not one whit behind in the matter of land-grabbing. In fact they boldly helped themselves or their families to tens of thousands of acres of the vast tract between the Rappahannock and the Potomac. Their methods and their rather warped sense of moral obligation are shown in a very frank letter from George W. Fairfax to Bryan Fairfax, in 1783. "I hope you'l second my intention of deputing you to act as the present Lord's agent . . . I make no scruple in saying . . . I would undoubtedly avail myself in making the best provision I could for our family. . . . Don't suppose, sir, that I mean by any unjustifiable ways . . . but I should now acquit my conscience in looking over all the surveyors returns in the office and when I found any vacant lands would make out the deeds to your eldest son or a friend you can trust, that would reconvey to him or any of them, for you know that you cannot make the deeds to yourself."[29] This was the principle on which the agents acted from Nicholas Spencer to George William Fairfax.

The most unblushing of all in carving out for his family lands

[26]Ibid., CO5-1319, Spotswood to Board of Trade, Jan. 16, 1721.
[27]Calendar of State Papers, Am. and W. I., IX, pp. 131-32.
[28]Virginia Magazine of Hist. and Biog., XIII, p. 10.
[29]Quoted by H. C. Groome, Fauquier during the Proprietorship, pp. 87, 88.

which in extent matched many a European principality, was Robert Carter, dubbed "King Carter" because of his great power and haughtiness. In the year 1724 alone he took over for himself, his sons and grandsons, 86,978 acres in the present counties of Fauquier and Prince William. A tract of 10,000 acres which Carter called "The Lodge" he made out in the name of George Turberville; another 10,000 went to his son-in-law, Mann Page; 6000 on Kettle Run he granted his son Charles; 12,000 to his sons John and Charles; 41,660 to Mann Page, Lewis Burwell and Carter Page; and 6030 acres to his son Robert.[30] In 1730 Carter's grasping hand reached over the Blue Ridge when he gave his sons, Landon and George, 50,212 acres on the banks of the Shenandoah.[31] When he died in 1732 Carter had possession of 300,000 acres.

The proprietors of the Northern Neck would probably not have permitted this appropriation of such vast tracts of their land had they not stood in need of Carter's influence in the Council of State. The Fairfax proprietorship lay between the Potomac and the Rappahannock as far as "their head springs," and with the opening of the Shenandoah Valley to settlement it became necessary to determine what these sources were, and draw the line to connect them. Since the tributaries to both streams spread out fanwise, the proprietors could gain or lose hundreds of square miles according to the "head spring" selected. Carter seems to have done yeoman work in securing a final settlement which conceded most of Fairfax's claims and turned over to him not only all the lower Valley, but Hardy, Hampshire and Morgan Counties as well. So the proprietors could afford to close their eyes while their agent took a "rake-off" of a mere hundred thousand acres or two.[32]

While this was going on, across the Potomac influential Marylanders were demonstrating that they were not less adept than the Virginians in helping themselves to the public lands. But they had to be somewhat more careful, since they dealt, not with the Crown, but the Proprietor. The Baltimore family were not

[30]*Ibid.*, p. 94.    [31]*Virginia Magazine of Hist. and Biog.*, XIII, p. 117 n.
[32]*Ibid.*, XXVIII, pp. 297–318.

greatly concerned with who held the land or whether it was divided into large or small estates, but they were insistent in demanding the payment of quitrents and this made it difficult for speculators to withhold large areas from the market. So a Dulaney or a Carroll, once his deed was made out and recorded, had to divide the tract up for lease or sale or put it under cultivation himself without undue delay.

So they instituted the custom of taking out warrants for land and waiting until all arrangements had been made for disposing of it before securing actual title. Obviously this was a mere subterfuge to avoid paying quitrents, but a fat fee to the two judges who issued deeds, another to the Surveyor General and still another to the Examiner General were enough to put the matter through. If all went well, there might actually be a kind of gerrymander, in which the bounds of the proposed grant took devious turns in order to embrace the most fertile soil. And they embraced often, also, far more land than the warrant itself specified—two, three, perhaps ten times as much.

The author of *Sot-Weed Redivivus* was quite right in holding that for

> ". . . one man to monopolize
> More land than yet he occupies
> And foreigners the quit-rents pay
> In sterling coin, is not fair play."

We gain an idea of the vastness of the holdings from the fact that the average grant for which warrants were taken out in the years from 1728 to 1733 was for no less than 28,535 acres. Among the great Maryland landholders were Benjamin Tasker, Daniel Carroll, Thomas Johnson, Edward Lloyd, William Paca, Daniel Dulaney, Thomas Lee Sims and others who occupied important offices or boasted of great influence with the government. The gay group which surrounded the governor at Annapolis, attended productions of Shakespeare in the old theatre, danced the minuet with beautifully gowned women, and read original poems and essays at the meetings of the Tuesday Club, received a goodly part of their income from the sale or lease of wilderness lands in far-off Frederick and Washington.

Though the rich succeeded thus, by fair means or foul, in getting title to land, they found it more difficult to induce poor immigrants or freed indentured workers to settle on it as tenants. No matter how fertile the soil, how convenient the location, how liberal the terms, the settler would pass it by if he could find some little bit of land which he could call his own. So many had had bitter experiences with the landlords of England or Ulster or the Palatinate, that they were distrustful of even the most liberal offers of a Byrd or a Beverley or a Dulaney. The traveller Schöpf, as he passed through Virginia, was surprised to see great expanses of uncleared land. This was explained, he said, by the fact that individuals owned tracts which they would not sell. And though they were willing enough to grant leases for long terms, tenants were "not easily to be had so long as it is anywhere possible to buy land. . . . The smallest possession has for every man more charm than the most imposing leasehold."[33]

One of the first Virginia landholders to discover this fact was William Fitzhugh, of Stafford County. Coming to Virginia in 1670, this keen business man built up a fortune by tobacco-planting, trading, speculating in land and by various other activities. As agent, with his son-in-law, George Brent, for the proprietor of the Northern Neck, he made use of the familiar methods to take possession of some of the richest tracts in Virginia. As one thumbs over the old records, one finds entry after entry in which Fitzhugh grants lands to Brent and Brent confirms lands to Fitzhugh.[34] At his death in 1701, Fitzhugh willed to his six sons 54,000 acres in a score or more different tracts.[35]

When Fitzhugh heard in 1686 that a group of Huguenots were seeking lands in America, he made strenuous efforts to secure them as tenants for a tract of 21,996 acres which he owned in upper Stafford. His proposal to the exiles, proposals which were

[33] J. D. Schöpf, *Travels,* etc., Ed. A. J. Morrison, p. 31.
[34] *William and Mary Quarterly,* VI, p. 225.
[35] *Virginia Magazine of Hist. and Biog.,* I, p. 17.

repeated over and over by wealthy Virginia landowners, would have been considered liberal in the extreme in any European country. He would lease the land "to them for three lives," he wrote, "paying twenty shillings per annum for every hundred acres, and they may have the liberty of renewing two or three lives at any time, paying for each life to be renewed one year's rent."[36] He was in a position to save the Huguenots many of the hardships and hazards of making a new settlement, he pointed out, together with the losses and troubles they must sustain before it was brought to any "maturity or perfection," and he hinted that he had been induced to make such favorable terms only because of the mounting costs of the quitrents. Yet, if the Frenchmen would not be satisfied with a leasehold, he was ready to sell them the land at £7 a hundred acres. Apparently, the Huguenots were not impressed by these arguments, for they passed Fitzhugh by, but had they accepted his terms, the Stafford County tract would have become a typical Virginia manor.

The Virginia manor and the eighteenth-century Maryland manor had little in common with the English manor—there were no courts baron and leet, no services in kind, no demesne. It entailed merely the dividing of a tract of land into lots or farms, which were leased for three lives, renewable by the payment of a year's rent. Thus the tenant at his death could pass the farm on to any other two persons in succession he chose to name, possibly to his wife and son, possibly a son and grandson. He had to pay a rental at Christmas or Michaelmas, usually of 20 shillings a hundred acres,[37] meet all taxes, build a house and plant an orchard of at least 150 apple trees. Among the tracts in Virginia specifically called manors were the Brent Town Manor, Cedar Creek Manor, the Manor of Cleve, South Branch Manor, Fairfax Manor, Manor of Belvoir, Manor of Greenway Court, Great Falls Manor and the Manor of Leeds;[38] and in Maryland Monocacy Manor, Carroll's Manor and many others.

Of these the most important was the Manor of Leeds, estab-

[36]*Virginia Magazine of Hist. and Biog.*, I, pp. 408–10.
[37]H. C. Groome, *Fauquier during the Proprietorship*, pp. 74, 75.
[38]*Virginia Magazine of Hist. and Biog.*, XXXII, p. 189.

lished by Lord Fairfax upon a vast tract which straddled the Blue Ridge and spread out to the Shenandoah River on one side and the branches of the Rappahannock on the other. The proprietors succeeded in settling a large number of tenants here, apparently because they offered especially liberal terms, in some cases making the rental only one shilling for twenty-one years on condition that the lessee survey the land at his own expense and erect a house twenty feet by sixteen. The list of tenants on that part of the manor in the limits of Fauquier County in 1777, preserved in the Huntington Library, contains 107 names, and shows leaseholds varying in size from 100 to 250 acres. If we may judge from the names, the settlers were chiefly English in origin, with here and there a McQuin, or a Flinn, or a Sullivan to testify to an infusion of Irish. The Manor of Leeds remained in the hands of the heirs of Lord Fairfax until 1806, when it was sold to Chief Justice John Marshall, J. Markham Marshall and Rawleigh Colston.[39]

The famous Beverley Manor in the Valley of Virginia seems not to have been a manor at all, for Beverley's Account Book shows that the land was not leased but sold. Among the purchasers was George Washington, who paid £10 for a tract of 400 acres and £35.6.4½ for another of 1177 acres. The usual price was fifty shillings a hundred acres. To many of the poor Scotch-Irish who bought fifty or more acres and tried to establish themselves as small farmers, Beverley extended credit, trusting that in time they would have a sufficient margin to pay off their mortgages. Only when a tenant failed to meet his payments for a number of years did he take the matter into the courts.[40]

Across the Blue Ridge in Caroline Beverley had large holdings which he did succeed in leasing in small parcels and which brought him in nearly £150 a year. Some of his tenants paid a rental of one hogshead of tobacco, which they rolled down to Roy's Warehouse on the Rappahannock, others paid only 500 or 600 pounds of tobacco. In case the crop was good and the farmer

[39]H. C. Groome, *Fauquier under the Proprietorship*, pp. 232, 233.
[40]*Wm. Beverley Account Book, Records of Lands in Beverley Manor*, New York Public Library.

industrious he might make an extra hogshead for the support of his family or even to put into his savings for the eventual purchase of a slave or a small plantation; if the yield was poor Beverley would have to carry him over into the next year with the word "arrears" written against his name in the Account Book.[41]

That the leasing of land was a troublesome and not always a profitable business we know from a letter of Daniel Dulaney in 1764. "Every gentleman who lets out land in this country knows how difficult it is, with the utmost care, to make any considerable profit . . . and how impracticable it is to get an annual rent equal to half the interest which would arise from the money for which the land would sell, or to prevent the abuses of tenants in the commission of waste."[42] Robert Carter, of Nomini, often called Councillor Carter, was constantly harassed by complaints that a dwelling house was in bad repair, or that a tobacco house was tumbling down, or a barn leaking. Some of his tenants seem to have raised large families and small crops of tobacco, but others gave indications of a fair degree of prosperity. On his Brents Tract, Charles Sanford, in Farm No. 1, worked the land with seven slaves; Thomas Blundel, on No. 2, with eight; Gerard McKenney, on No. 3, with nine; Thomas Randal, on No. 4, with seven. Ann Barbara Tidewell, on No. 6, divided the 683 acres into six parts and let them to subtenants. The good lady complained to Carter that her dwelling was old, the kitchen old, the dairy old, the cornhouse old, and the overseer's house ruinous.[43]

Like Beverley, Carter found it difficult to collect his rentals. "The failure of their crops of tobacco last year has I believe rendered it impossible for them to pay their rents, most of them being very poor and intirely dependent on the crops they make," one of his agents wrote him in 1793. In such cases the Councillor gave the tenants one, two or perhaps ten years to make payments, or even lowered the rental. He was angered, however, at a certain Abraham Vaughn, who complained that Carter was very rich and he a poor man. "It is said that you have been living on my

[41] *William Beverley Accounts,* New York Public Library.
[42] *Johns Hopkins Studies,* 31st Series, No. 1, p. 70—"The Land System in Maryland, 1720–1765," C. P. Gould.
[43] Journal of Nomini Hall, 1784, Library of Congress.

land many years, making crops thereon," Carter replied. "Did you ever contribute to make me rich?" Clearly he had the better of this argument, especially since the law was on his side, but had Vaughn come back by asking how the Carter family got possession of such vast tracts of land he would have struck him in his Achilles heel.

In time the Councillor laid out more and more of his property in leaseholds, until finally he counted his tenants by the hundreds. On his Goose Creek tract there were 105 tenants in 1793, paying aggregate yearly rentals of 5300 pounds of tobacco and £325 in Virginia currency; at Piney Ridge, Bull Run and Chappawamsie 112 tenants paying 20,508 pounds of tobacco and £340 in currency. The management of these numerous leases he entrusted to agents, who made yearly reports and received 8 per cent of the income for their trouble. Carter took good care that his tenants should not exhaust his soil and his woodlands, and set down exactly the number of acres to be used as a garden, or for pasture, or for arable, and insisted upon a rotation of crops.[44]

Some of the other Virginia and Maryland landholders were not so successful as Beverley, Carter and Lord Fairfax in securing leaseholders. The more enterprising, rather than permit their estates to lie idle while quitrents were piling up, corresponded with agents in Switzerland, or Ulster, or Pennsylvania, in an effort to bring in groups of fifty or more families, to whom they proposed to sell parcels of ten or twenty thousand acres. William Byrd II, who owned a tract of 105,000 acres on the upper Roanoke River, partly in North Carolina and partly in Virginia, was negotiating with a Mr. Ochs in 1735 to bring over a colony of Swiss. "I had much rather have to do with honest industrious Switzers than the mixt people of Pennsylvania," he wrote. Disappointed that this group settled elsewhere and anxious to establish the upper Roanoke as a partly settled region, he offered to present 10,000 acres in fee simple and to appeal for exemption from quitrents for several years, to any group of 100 families who would settle upon them.[45] "If your Swiss do not come," he

[44]Louis Morton, *Robert Carter of Nomini Hall*, pp. 72–79.
[45]*Correspondence of William Byrd, II*, July 15, 1736, Huntington Library.

added, "I must dispose of my land to the Scotch-Irish who crowd over to Pennsylvania."

Two years later Byrd agreed with a Mr. Tscheffely that if he would bring in 100 families from Pennsylvania, he would sell them "for ready money" a tract of 24,000 acres. But ready money was just what both Mr. Tscheffely and his prospective settlers lacked, and when four or five men appeared on the spot and offered to take small parcels on several years' credit, he turned them away.[46] The terms on which Byrd hoped to sell are set forth in a letter to a Mr. Leaberger in November, 1740. "I told you that if a number of people would come before the end of October last and purchase 30,000 acres together, I would sell it for £3 current money the 100 acres. But when that time was expired . . . I have been obliged to pay to the King £525 sterling on account of that land, and therefore cannot afford to sell it so cheap. . . . To sell it out in small parcels will occasion a great deal of trouble, and then it can't be sold under £5 the 100 acres."[47]

Despite the cheapness of land, despite the many failures of the landlords to secure tenants, it is obvious that leaseholding was far more common in colonial Virginia and Maryland than has been supposed. But it was a tenantry very different from that of England, since the owner had to offer the most liberal terms to tempt poor men to settle on his land and to prevent their moving away. Nor was there danger that it would fasten itself upon the two colonies, growing with the years and choking out the small independent farmers. With the opening of the vast West following the Revolution, there was no need for foreign immigrants or for poor planters whose farms were worn out, to become tenants. A journey over the mountains would assure them fertile land of their own in the Kentucky blue-grass region, or in Tennessee, or in the old Northwest or even in Missouri. Tenantry was the child of land monopoly, and land monopoly in the United States could last only so long as temporary barriers remained—the Indian barrier, or the barrier of poor transportation. When these were swept away the flood of humanity would drain off from the so-

---

[46] *Ibid.*, March 15, 1740.
[47] *Ibid.*, November 12, 1740.

called manors of the East to the great region beyond the mountains.

Some of the great landowners, when they were unable to lease or to sell on advantageous terms, kept their holdings and passed them on to their heirs. When a Carter or a Page drew up his will, it was the oldest son who was apt to receive the home plantation, while the younger sons had to content themselves with "quarters" or perhaps uncleared land in the Piedmont. There they often not only carved out a fortune for themselves, but had great areas of "fresh" land to divide in turn with their own numerous progeny. "King" Carter left a fortune in land to his sons John, Robert, Charles and Landon, besides large estates to his daughters Elizabeth, Judith, Anne and Lucy, who spread the Carter power and wealth from one end of Virginia to the other.[48] Charles Carter, of King George, in his will of 1762, left to his son John his Manor of Cleve, and large tracts in Fauquier, Prince William, King George and Culpeper; to his son Landon, Ludwell Park, Norman's Ford, Red Oak and other tracts in Fauquier and Prince William. Both sons were to hold their lands in tail, with the privilege of leaving a third, which also was to be entailed, to a second son.[49]

This practice of entailing land was one of the most serious deterrents to democratic landholding in the colony, for without it the great estates in a few generations would have been divided and subdivided into comparatively small tracts. On the other hand, entailing by itself would not have been sufficient to hold together great estates, had there not been some way of deriving a profit from the land. If a Byrd or a Carter could not people his acres with tenants, he had to cultivate them himself or sell; he could not let them remain idle indefinitely. The size of his permanent holding would be limited, therefore, to the number of acres he could convert into tobacco fields.

The planters discovered even in the seventeenth century that slave labor could be made profitable only by the constant supervision of the owner or of an overseer. Left to themselves the blacks

---

[48]*Virginia Magazine of Hist. and Biog.*, 408–28.
[49]*Ibid.*, XXXI, pp. 53–67.

loitered or made mistakes which ruined the crop. The number of slaves under the direction of one overseer differed according to the character of the plantation and the slaves and the ability of the overseer himself, but the most efficient unit seems to have been from 12 to 25. Robert Carter, of Westmoreland, in 1791 had 509 slaves distributed in 19 plantations or quarters, varying from 114 slaves at Nomini Hall to 3 each at "John Peck's" and "Robert Michel's." But the numbers in the regular quarters, which Colonel Carter named after the constellations, were far more uniform— 42 at Aries, 40 at Leo, 29 at Virgo, 26 at Scorpio, 25 at Libra, 24 at Capricorn, 23 at Cancer, 21 at Taurus, 18 at Sagittarius, 14 at Aquarius, 14 at Gemini. Since there was a large sprinkling of children at each quarter, the number of slave workers to each overseer was probably about 15. Colonel Carter employed a steward to make tours of inspection, report on the work of the overseers and to knit together the far-flung system of plantations and quarters.[50]

Peter Jefferson, father of Thomas Jefferson, has left us the account book which he kept for several years for Colonel William Randolph, showing the operation of the home plantation, Tuckahoe, and the various scattered quarters. In 1746, Crafford Ready, overseer at Tuckahoe, produced 15,780 pounds of tobacco, or 15 hogsheads, receiving 1434 pounds as his share and 1097 pounds in wages. Charles Jordan at the Lower Quarters produced 22 hogsheads, Thomas Tilman at Dover 14 hogsheads, Timothy Mooney at Hatt Creek 7 hogsheads and Henry Wain, at Rappahannock 21 hogsheads.[51] The conditions under which John Bowe engaged John Gilman as overseer were no doubt typical. Bowe agreed to give Gilman one tenth of all the crops, furnish him 400 pounds of pork, a cow to milk and corn for the use of his family, a girl to stay in the house with Mrs. Gilman to help her wash and cook, and to provide at least ten hands with five plow horses or mules.[52]

But there were limitations upon the system of large scattered

[50]*Robert Carter of Nomini Hall*, by Louis Morton (Princeton University Press).
[51]*Peter Jefferson Account Book*, Huntington Library.
[52]Agreement between John Bowe and John Gilman, July 28, 1808, Huntington Library.

holdings run by slave labor directed by overseers. The prodigal use of the soil brought about the decay of many large plantations in the older regions; the overseers were often wasteful and inefficient, interested more in producing a large crop than conserving their employer's property; the wealthy planters habitually lived beyond their means, so that many had to sell part of their lands and slaves to keep out of debt. It was a strange balancing of economic and social forces which made it possible for the poor planter with his 200 acres, one or more sturdy sons, a horse, a plow and 5 or 6 cows, to live side by side with the proud owner of 30,000 acres and 300 slaves. It was slavery which was chiefly responsible for the Randolphs, the Carters, the Beverleys, the Byrds, the Cockes; it was cheap land which made possible the sturdy Virginia yeomanry.

That this yeomanry outnumbered the aristocracy twenty-five or more to one becomes obvious when we examine the rent rolls, not only of the deep water region, but of the Piedmont and Valley, where the original grants were often so huge in size. In Prince William in 1777, for instance, Colonel Cocke, with his 3744 acres, Landon Carter with 5027 acres, William Ellzey with 3977, Cuthbert Harrison with 1317, Colonel Henry Lee with 1600, Thomas Thornton with 1427, Walter Talliafero with 1120 acres, Colonel Thomas Blackburn with 11,300, and several others represent the large holders. But all around them were the small farmers, some owning 300 acres, some 200, some no more than 25 or 50 acres. Side by side with Cuthbert Harrison, with his 1317 acres, we find Leonard Heart with 120, William Hughes with 368, James Hamrich with 130, James Hazlebrig with 26, Richard Hazlebrig with 210, James Homes with 144.[53]

The Culpeper rent roll of 1764 shows much the same condition, save that Robert Beverley held a tract of 19,835 acres. The Armistead estate had 5393 acres, George Buckner 1700, James Barber 1800, Humphrey and Richard Brooks 1768 each, Henry Field 1835, John Fry 2400, Colonel William Greene 5561, John Hoffman 3525, Joseph James 2373, Tackaria Lewis 3888, the Rooles estate 3347, Colonel Philip Roote 9300, Reverend John

[53]A Rental for Prince William County, Huntington Library.

330

Thomson 7563, Colonel Richard Tutt 3358, the Thornton estate 3210. But even though Culpeper was just emerging from the frontier stage, most of the holdings were small—farms of 400 acres, 300 acres, even 100 acres.[54]

In the Shenandoah Valley large holdings were even rarer. The rent roll of Berkeley County in 1776 begins with Thomas Adams with 316 acres, John Abril with 150, George Ashbridge with 224, Thomas Aikin with 216, Jacob Alimong with 370, Cuthbert Amdersan with 180, Henry Ambrose with 400, James Abril with 226.[55] The German and Scotch-Irish immigrants seem to have passed this county by, for the names are predominantly English. Farther up the Valley, in Dunmore, the present Shenandoah County, there was a mixture of English and Germans in which Weavers, Whites, Woods and Watsons rubbed elbows with Witzels, Woolfs, Westerbergers, Zwiglers and Warthmillers. But there were the same uniformly small holdings which seldom included more than 500 acres.[56]

In North Carolina the struggle between large landholders and poor settlers was even more bitter than in Virginia and Maryland, and at times led to actual violence. On the whole the Proprietors and the Crown tried to pursue a just and wise land policy. They wanted to settle the Piedmont region with sturdy farmers, whether from England, Germany, Switzerland or Ulster, as a protection against the Indians or the Spaniards, increase the quitrents and build up British commerce. They had no interest in keeping the structure of society democratic, but they were opposed to the acquisition of huge tracts of land by influential men by fraudulent means, for which no quitrents were paid and from which poor settlers were excluded.

On the other hand, the Crown did not hesitate to issue rights to enormous tracts to responsible business men in return for a guarantee to bring over European settlers, and in one instance actually granted over a million acres to a single group of associates. It seemed legitimate and wise to encourage those who were

---

[54]Rental for Culpeper County, 1764, Huntington Library.
[55]Berkeley Rental, 1776, Huntington Library.
[56]Rental for Dunmore County, 1776, Huntington Library.

willing to advance money to groups of indigent Swiss or Scotch-Irish for their passage to America, since settlers were so urgently needed. They could not foresee that the conditions would frequently be violated and that so far from encouraging settlement, many families were discouraged from coming to North Carolina and others forced to settle upon fertile spots without deeds or other legal sanction.

Thus the scene was set for injustice, bitter resentment, clashing interests, rioting and defiance of law. Influential men in the provincial government disregarded the instructions of the King in order to line their own pockets, the Assembly clashed with the governor and Council, Lord Granville with English land speculators, the land speculators with squatters. Matters were complicated by the indefiniteness of the boundary with South Carolina, so that a farm in Mecklenburg might have three rival claimants —one under a South Carolina patent, one under a North Carolina patent, and the other by virtue of actual possession and the building of a residence, barns and the planting of orchards, gardens and fields.

Amid the confusion, the clash of conflicting interests, the frauds and the defiance of the English government, men almost lost sight of the fact that the social structure of the province was at stake, that out of this struggle might come a democratic society or an aristocratic society depending upon which side won the victory. Were the hardy settlers who were peopling central and western North Carolina to be owners of their little plantations, free of debt, unincumbered by heavy taxes, or were they to be tenants, or, if owners, shackled by debts to speculators or to influential politicians? Did the land belong to those who settled on it, improved it, defended it against the Indians, or to absentee landlords who had secured their titles in some cases by bribing an official or by winning the governor's favor, or perhaps by altering a patent?

It was the policy of the proprietors to grant to every settler, rich or poor, as much land as he could reasonably be expected to put under cultivation. In 1667 they promised that each head of a family should have sixty acres, with another sixty acres for every man servant capable of bearing arms, and fifty acres for other servants. In addition the servant himself, at the expiration of his term, was to have fifty acres. Every landowner was to pay to the proprietors a quitrent of a half penny an acre.[57] Changes were made from time to time in these terms, but the basic policy remained the same. In 1691 the government gave power to Governor Philip Ludwell to sell land at one shilling per one hundred acres. This, however, opened the door to so many abuses that the proprietors were forced to give instructions that no land be disposed of save by themselves in London.

In 1721 the situation was complicated by the purchase by the Crown of the rights of seven of the eight proprietors and the confining of the rights of Lord Granville, who refused to sell, to the northern half of North Carolina. Thereafter the people of one part of the colony looked to the King for land, of the other part to this sole remaining proprietor. There followed a period, not only of confusion and conflicting claims, but of such frauds in making grants as to arouse the ire of the people and to retard the settlement of the province. Governor Richard Everard issued patents for 400,000 acres in which the amount of land, the description of the boundaries, the sums paid, and even the name of the patentees were left blank.[58] "This irregularity gave rise to such endless and exorbitant frauds," wrote one official in 1754, "that it has not been possible at this day to come to any exact knowledge of the state of these grants." Some of the patents which were intended to be for 500 acres were expanded when the holders filled in the blanks to ten times that amount.[59]

If we may believe Edmond Porter, Sir Richard not only winked at these frauds, but actually joined in the general scramble. Filling up an old obsolete blank warrant for 10,000 acres, which had long "lain about" as wastepaper, his son gave a bribe of £300 to the Receiver General and so got a patent to 10,000 acres of rich land on the northwest branch of the Cape Fear River.[60] Porter accused Governor George Burrington of a fraud even more glar-

[57]*Colonial Records of North Carolina*, V, p. 93.
[58]*Colonial Records of North Carolina*, V, p. 93.
[59]*Ibid.*, III, p. 497.        [60]*Ibid.*, p. 599.

ing, declaring that he got his Stagg-park and Burgar lands by altering an old warrant for 640 acres, by erasing the "640" and substituting 5000. It seems to have been a policy of "I nudge you and you nudge me." The land officers fattened on great fees and bribes, the governor, members of the Council and others prominent in the government came off with large tracts of fertile land. But the King suffered in his revenue, the province suffered because of the discouragement of settlers, the settlers themselves suffered because they found the best lands pre-empted. "Immense sums have been collected," it was pointed out, "and numerous patents granted for much of the most fertile lands . . . yet uninhabited and uncultivated, environed by great numbers of poor people who are necessitated to toil in the cultivation of bad lands whereon they hardly can subsist."[61]

From time to time the Crown officials sought to make the large landholders disgorge, by demanding the enforcement of the laws which required them to put their estates under cultivation. "Let them clear and cultivate at least five acres a year of every hundred acres," it was demanded, "or let their patents revert to the Crown, so that the land can be granted to real settlers." Yet when a new law was passed by the Assembly it was so loosely drawn and evasion so easy, that the King was advised to disallow it.[62] The clause in land patents requiring actual cultivation was habitually disregarded, for the Council, who alone could enforce compliance, were among the chief owners of large unoccupied tracts. Had it been possible to enforce the payment of quitrents, thousands of acres would have been abandoned to the Crown, but rents also were habitually evaded. There was no justice in disposing of land to persons who showed not the least disposition to comply with the conditions nor pay the quitrents, one observer[63] wrote in 1743. Governor Gabriel Johnston had already granted 104,700 acres upon which the rents, which should have yielded £2094 a year, had totalled an average less than £500, and this kind of thing should be ended at once.

The granting of huge tracts by the Crown itself on condition

[61]*Ibid.*, III, p. 195.    [62]*Ibid.*, V, p. 100.
[63]Probably Henry McCulloh, *Ibid.*, IV, p. 1134.

that the recipients people them with settlers, though less conducive to fraud, led to many abuses and even to violence. In 1736 warrants were issued for no less than 1,200,000 acres to Henry McCulloh and a group of associates upon condition that they bring in 6000 European Protestants within ten years, after which they were to pay quitrents at the rate of 4 shillings a hundred acres. Eight years later the warrants were translated into 12 grants of 100,000 acres each, laid out on the Yadkin, Catawba and the headwaters of the Neuse and Cape Fear Rivers, and the grantees exempted from quitrents until 1756.[64] Since a large part of the land was situated in Lord Granville's part of the province, the associates agreed to pay an annual rent to him of £400 until 1760 and after that date 4 shillings for every 100 acres.

McCulloh bestirred himself to bring in immigrants, but with scant success, so that by 1754 he had settled on the lands only 854 persons.[65] In the meanwhile the Creeks and Cherokees went on the warpath and bands of warriors, passing through the mountain defiles, fell upon the outlying Carolina settlements. Soon terrified refugees began to pour into Salisbury and Bethabara with stories of attacks on isolated farms, of slaughtered men, women and children, of burned houses and devastated fields, of the torturing of prisoners, of gallant defenses of fortified posts, of daring escapes. Twice Bethabara itself was in deadly peril, but the hidden foe withdrew once at the ringing of a bell, thinking themselves discovered, and a second time at the blowing of a trumpet.[66] One victim, though pierced by several arrows, eluded his pursuers, forded the Yadkin, and wandered all night in a pelting rain, but at last reached Bethabara, where good Brother Bonn attended him and saved his life.

These terrible events put a complete stop to all plans for bringing in new settlers, so that McCulloh was twice granted extensions of time to fulfill the conditions of the grant, first until 1760 and later until 1762. Finally, it was agreed that he and his associates were to retain as much land as they had settled, on the basis of 200 acres for each settler. So commissioners were appointed

[64]*Ibid.*, V, xxxii.  [65]*Ibid.*, V, p. 104.
[66]S. A. Ashe, *History of North Carolina*, I, p. 300.

to take the count, prevent fraud and make due returns to the governor and Council. Thereupon McCulloh's son, Henry Eustace McCulloh, who had come to the colony to look after the interests of the associates, made ready to ascertain the lines of the grants and subdivide them into parcels to suit the needs of the settlers.[67]

To his surprise he found this almost impossible. With the ending of the Indian menace scores of poor families had moved into western North Carolina—Scotch-Irish and Germans from Pennsylvania, small planters from eastern Carolina, recent immigrants who had worked out their terms of indenture—and finding the best lands had been pre-empted by the McCulloh associates and that they were still vacant, settled down upon them. "Sufficient to the day is the evil thereof," expressed their attitude to the McCulloh patents. Perhaps they hoped that actual possession would give them valid titles, perhaps they hoped McCulloh would sell on nominal terms, perhaps they were determined to defy both him and the provincial government.

Those settlers whom the patentees had brought over from Europe, paying their ocean fare and other expenses, were morally as well as legally bound to pay for their holdings. For the squatters the case was quite different. The government had made these enormous grants with the sole purpose of encouraging settlement and the McCulloh associates were to receive land only for service performed. Was it right, after they had fallen far short of what they had promised, that they should take advantage of families who had moved in of their own volition and at their own expense? In equity and in accordance with old custom, it was the settler who should have had title, not the associates.

None the less, when the younger McCulloh appeared in Rowan County with his patents and his surveyors, he was able to come to terms with the squatters. Calling them together, he promised to charge them only for the land itself, and not for the houses, barns, fences they had built on it, nor for the accrued interest and quitrents. So the settlers, fearing lengthy lawsuits with the possibility of evictions, bowed to the inevitable and agreed to pay on the average £8.10.0 per 100 acres.

[67]*Colonial Records of North Carolina*, V, p. xxxii.

But when McCulloh moved on to Mecklenburg County, he met with a very different reception. Here the farmers were faced with the possibility that if they purchased title to their land from him, they might still face eviction from the South Carolina authorities if the dividing line, when eventually settled, should place them in that province. It was in March, 1765, that McCulloh found 150 men assembled on Sugar Creek, determined to prevent his making any surveys. In vain he argued with them, denounced them and produced copies of the patents. They told him "the best usage he should expect to meet with would be to be tied neck and heels and be carried over the Yadkin." None the less, he proceeded to the farm of James Norris, who had agreed to have it surveyed, while the crowd of armed men trailed along behind, taunting him and asking him whether he expected to have so large an attendance at his funeral. When the surveyor tried to "fix his compass" they swarmed around him, snatched it from the staff and seized and broke the chain in several places. Finding that to persist would be to "risk losing his life," McCulloh gave up the attempt for the moment and returned to New Bern to lay his complaints before the government.[68]

With the passage of time, the squatters became more determined than ever to uphold their rights, even with arms in their hands. When the officers of the law, even Governor Dobbs himself, came to Mecklenburg to force obedience, they were openly defied, threatened and treated with great indignity. In 1762 the sheriff of Anson County raised a posse to apprehend some of the rioters, but he found a mob awaiting them. The sheriff commanded them, in the King's name, to lay down their arms and restore peace. But they "damned the King and his peace" and beat and wounded several of the posse. When indictments were found against the ringleaders, they could not be executed "by reason of the threats and frequent abuse committed upon the officers of justice."[69]

But this was mild compared with the treatment accorded a group of surveyors in 1765, which McCulloh not inaptly terms "The War of Sugar Creek." "Thy poor friend John Frohock . . .

[68]*Colonial Records of North Carolina*, VII, p. 24.  [69]*Ibid.*, V, p. xxxiv.

has undergone the bastinado," he wrote Edmund Fanning. "It made my heart quite full when I first saw poor John, he got a damnable wipe across the nose and mouth. Abraham, they say, is striped from the nape of his neck to the waistband of his breeches, like a drafting board. Poor Jimmy Alexander had very near had daylight let into his skull. . . . Providentially detained by particular business I was not there. Had I been present I most assuredly and without any ceremony had been murdered. . . . John Frohock says I can hardly form an idea equal to the horror of their behavior. . . . Shall not my soul see its revenge! By the eternal God, it shall not be for want of my utmost exertions."[70]

Apparently McCulloh never secured his revenge. In 1772 he returned to England to be with his father, who was advanced in age and very infirm, and was still there when hostilities broke out between the colonies and the mother country. In 1777 the Assembly passed an act penalizing all North Carolinians who were living beyond the limits of the United States in 1776 and had failed to return, and two years later all the McCulloh land was confiscated. In the meanwhile, McCulloh had reached New York, avowedly on his way to North Carolina, but was either persuaded or forced to remain there. He wrote imploringly to his friend James Iredell to draw up a memorial to the Assembly, making his excuses for his absence and requesting the restoration of his property, but though Iredell did his best, the legislators were obdurate.[71] At this time, when the wheel of fortune had thrown so many new men into places of authority and when democracy was making substantial gains, there was little hope of a sympathetic hearing for an absentee landlord and owner of great unoccupied tracts of land who was suspected of Tory sympathies. The land from the first should have belonged to the people, and the absence of McCulloh was no more than a plausible pretext for righting an old wrong.

Thus in North Carolina, as in Virginia and Maryland, the battle was fought out for possession of the soil between the forces of aristocracy and democracy. On the one side we see the un-

<hr>

[70]*Ibid.*, Vol. VII, pp. 32, 33.
[71]Griffith J. McRee, *James Iredell*, I, pp. 411, 412, 438–41.

scrupulous use of wealth or influence, through bribery, or false warrants, or favoritism, in getting title to large tracts; on the other, the refusal of the common man to become a dependent or even a tenant so long as there was available land on which to settle. In North Carolina the squatter played a more important rôle than in Virginia and Maryland, defended his rights more vigorously, proved a greater obstacle to an undemocratic distribution of land. In many cases he defied the law, refused to pay quitrents, threatened the landlord with violence and during the Revolution made good his title to his farm.

In South Carolina matters were complicated by Locke's Fundamental Constitutions. It is difficult to understand why the proprietors thought it would be desirable and practicable to establish in the forests of America this feudal scheme. They should have foreseen that they could not create a real nobility by bestowing such meaningless titles as landgrave and cacique, that they could not hold men in serfdom in a land where labor was dear and natural resources abundant. Yet they went ahead with their plans, dividing the colony in counties, the counties into seignories, baronies and "colonies." The seignories were retained by the proprietors themselves, the baronies were granted to landgraves and caciques, while the colonies were reserved for freemen, who might establish manors and people them with leet men. Their provincial society envisaged overlords, nobles, lords of the manor, small freeholders and serfs, as undemocratic a setup as one could devise, ignoring not only all social trends in England for the preceding two centuries, but the lessons taught by the settlement of Virginia, Maryland and New England.

The Fundamental Constitutions were never fully established, and with the purchase of the proprietary rights by the Crown were thrown into the discard. But the proprietors clung to them long enough to create certain evils in land distribution which remained to plague the colony for years. In fact, the passing of the old regime was marked by a scramble for land by influential men which for its selfishness and disregard of justice and the public welfare outdid the worst scandals of other colonies. The proprietors had granted about 800,000 acres to the sham nobles, most of it before 1700, very little of which had been surveyed, or ascertained, or occupied during their lives. In 1721, with the passing of the proprietors, some of the heirs and assignees unearthed the old patents and so got hold of vast tracts of land. And though the Attorney General decided that their claims were absolutely void in point of law, they clung to them with the utmost determination.[72]

Since the grants were in most cases quite vague, the patent-holders made their own selections, usually along the banks of the navigable rivers or wherever the most fertile land was to be found. In some cases they seized pine lands, and when they had burned off the "lightwood" to make pitch and tar, shifted their claims to "planting land." Since the grants were not recorded, the claimants took up far more than they were entitled to even had the patents been valid. "Proper inquiry would show some have sold double the quantity of acres granted by their patents, besides what they hold themselves," stated the Attorney General. Several of the patentees held from 12,000 acres to 48,000 acres, he added, which they expected to sell at extravagant rates. The whole number of these landholders did not exceed thirty, whose personal interests were being preferred "to the welfare and prosperity of the whole province,"[73] and newcomers were compelled either to purchase from them at exorbitant rates or take up poor and remote lands.

At this juncture the Assembly, which was completely in the control of the large landholders, passed an act guaranteeing the validity of all grants made by the proprietors provided they were sworn to by a surveyor, irrespective of defects in describing the land. Governor Robert Johnson, who worked hand in glove with the aristocratic landgrabbers, signed this bill and sent it to England for approval. In the meanwhile, he not only threatened actual settlers who tried to secure title to any lands claimed by his friends or himself, but even tracts to which they might want to expand their elastic patents. In fact, many poor families who had laid out farms on the southern frontier and had been driven out by recent Indian raids, now hesitated to return because of the revival of the old proprietary grants.

[72]*Calendar of State Papers, America and W. I.,* 1732, p. 205.  [73]*Ibid.,* p. 206.

Thereupon, a Doctor Thomas Cooper, together with several deputy surveyors, went to the region and began making surveys with a view to bringing the matter into the royal courts. But this was just what the patentees wished to avoid. So the lower house of Assembly sent their messenger to arrest Cooper and put him in jail. Throughout the colonial period there were many clashes between the provincial assemblies and the representatives of the Crown, in which these local bodies defended the people against infringements on their rights and their interests. It was an unusual, almost unprecedented, occurrence, then, when the South Carolina Assembly, with the ardent support of the governor, tried to thwart the King's efforts to protect the true interests of the colony and its people. Stranger still was it for a group of colonials to repudiate that bulwark of English liberty, the *habeas corpus.*

Yet, when Doctor Cooper secured a writ of *habeas corpus,* the messenger, with the full backing of the Assembly, refused to recognize it. Later two merchants waited upon Governor Johnson with a request from Cooper that he himself issue a *habeas corpus,* but were arrested for their pains, forced to pay large fees and to make an humble apology. In the meanwhile the people, regarding Cooper as a martyr to their cause, elected him to the Assembly which had done him such cruel injustice, but it was only some time later that he got out of jail, after paying enormous fees. "The laws of our mother country are set at naught and termed 'Old Ballads,'" wrote William Frewin. "The King's offices are ransacked and his officers insulted, ridiculed and affronted."[74]

Since even the most prominent men in the colony laid themselves open to persecution if they attempted to thwart the influential patentholders, there was little chance for a poor cattle hunter, like a certain Edward North, once he had aroused their suspicions. North had turned his knowledge of the woods to account by pointing out vacant lands to newcomers. Thereupon the governor "in very boisterous and threatening language told him he would lay him in jail."

In the meanwhile James St. John, appointed Surveyor-General

[74]*Calendar of State Papers,* 1733, pp. 122–125.

341

by the King, arrived in South Carolina, with Horatio Walpole, his deputy. They were not long in sizing up the situation, and in 1732 St. John wrote at length to the Board of Trade, denouncing the illegal grabbing of huge tracts and advising that the act of the Assembly validating the old patents be disallowed. Thereupon the clique in power, including the governor, opened their guns on him. He had delayed to produce his commission and take the oath of office, they said, he had extorted exorbitant fees, he had treated the Council and Assembly with contempt. In the end he was arrested on some "slight and frivolous pretense" and held prisoner until released by the express order of the Board of Trade. When the people elected the friends of Cooper and St. John to the Assembly, the dominant faction refused to seat them.

Robert Wright, the chief justice, chided the Assembly for attempting to undermine the *habeas corpus*. But so far were they from heeding this warning, that they passed an act to protect their messenger and in so doing asserted their independence of all judicial review. No public officer should be liable to suit or penalty, it declared, for refusing obedience to a writ of *habeas corpus* for any person imprisoned by order of either house for violating its privileges. Wright, himself, they did not venture to arrest, but they struck at him by refusing to provide for his salary. Never did a colonial legislature display such boldness and determination in such a bad cause. Had the King been the oppressor and had they been defenders of the rights of the province and the people, their rôle would have been almost heroic. But to defend their exorbitant and often fraudulent claims to land which should have gone to real settlers, by defying his Majesty, persecuting his officers, even attacking the *habeas corpus,* was a travesty on justice and a prostitution of representative government.[75]

From this uninspiring spectacle one turns with relief to the efforts of the British Government, seconded by Governor Johnson and the Assembly, to encourage immigration by the creation of 11 townships of 20,000 acres each at a distance of about sixty miles from Charleston. There were to be 2 on the Altamaha, 2 on the Savannah, 1 on the Edisto, 2 on the Santee, 1 on the Wa-

[75]H. L. Osgood, *The American Colonies in the 18th Century,* IV, p. 123.

teree, 1 on the Black, 1 on the Pedee and 1 on the Waccamaw. These townships were avowedly modelled upon the towns of Massachusetts and New Hampshire, which, the Government thought, had proved successful in "civil concerns" and in gaining security for the people "against the insults and incursions of the neighboring Indians." There were to be central villages located on the waterways, with home lots laid out for each head of a family; agricultural lands in the surrounding region of which each settler was to have 50 acres for every member of his family, including servants and slaves; and commons of not over 300 acres for woodland and pasturage.[76]

The governor and Assembly were enthusiastically in favor of this scheme, since it not only offered no threat to their holdings, but actually enhanced their value by giving them a back-country and a protection against the Spaniards and the Indians. So they passed an act appropriating part of the receipts from a duty on the importation of slaves to the expenses of laying off the townships, paying the ocean fare of Protestant immigrants and providing them with tools and provisions.[77] As a result, there began a migration to South Carolina of hard-working, intelligent Swiss, Germans, Welsh, Scotch-Irish, who added a new element of democracy and greatly aided in the upbuilding of the colony.

We become a witness of the hardships and sufferings of these new American pilgrims through the account written by Robert Witherspoon of the migration of his grandfather and his family. The giving up of her home in Ireland seems to have broken the heart of his wife Janet, for she died at sea the day after they set sail from Belfast, to the grief and despair of the children. But she was thus spared the terrors and hardships that were to follow. The voyagers encountered such terrific storms at sea that the *Good Intent* sprang a leak, and only the incessant work of the sailors at the pumps kept her afloat until she arrived at Charleston. Here they remained several weeks, and then, in the dead of winter, set sail for the back country in an open boat, with their tools and one year's provisions of corn, rice, flour, beef, pork, rum

[76]*Calendar of State Papers, Amer. and W. I.,* 1730, p. 140–142.
[77]*Statutes,* III, pp. 334–341.

and salt. This inland journey proved almost as distressing to the pious immigrants as the ocean voyage, not only because of the cold and rain, but the "blasphemous oaths" of the boatmen.

When at last they reached their future home, their spirits sank, for before them lay not a farm as they had expected, but a wilderness; in place of a comfortable house, only a temporary hut of clay. The first day the fire went out and one of the party had to go many miles through the woods and swamps to secure a few glowing embers. But even with a cheery blaze the night was filled with anxiety, for there was no door to their hovel, and they had neither dog nor firearms to drive off the wild beasts whose howlings filled the woods.

Then followed the task of building a house, clearing away the trees, planting crops, putting up fences and barns. The newcomers were in terror of the Indians, they feared that they might be "bit by snakes, or torn by wild beasts," or lost in the woods. But the most pressing danger was illness, for some were soon "taken sick with ague and fever, some died and some became dropsical and also died." Yet the Witherspoons proceeded with their arduous task of home building and community building, so that within a few years Williamsburg, where they had settled, was passing out of the frontier stage and had become an established and promising settlement.[78]

One would suppose that the South Carolina government, in recognition of the hardships endured by these brave people and the services they rendered the colony by opening the back country, would have been scrupulous in carrying out all the promises made them. Yet the landed aristocracy, not satisfied with the holdings they had already obtained, reached out for some of the most fertile spots reserved for the Williamsburg settlers. The Ulstermen had come over with the express stipulation that lands in the townships should be granted only to *bona fide* settlers, and now, to their intense indignation, they found that influential Charlestonians had secured title to thousands of acres which they held for purposes of speculation.

"To our great concern," the settlers wrote, "we have found the

[78]William W. Baddie, *History of Williamsburg,* pp. 10–15.

land in this township a common unrestrained range to all persons and the best land therein taken up by persons who have not at this time settled the same nor, in all probability, will at any time reside thereon. Some of us have been sued for trespass on land pointed out to us by the Deputy Surveyor and have been caused considerable damage and others have become tenants rather than remove their families. Some time past, we presented our humble petition to the Governor's Council setting forth our said grievances and praying, but we could obtain no answer."[79] Surely greed and injustice could go no farther!

One must beware of a sweeping condemnation of the Southern aristocracy for its self-seeking land policy. Some of the largest holders no doubt persuaded themselves that they were doing their full duty to the people who settled on their property by getting surveys and titles and by advancing credit for provisions, clothes and tools, or actually paying their fare across the ocean. They played the rôle in a large scale of the real-estate agent of today. In some cases they had to pay heavy sums in quitrents, so that they were in actual danger of losing money on their ventures. Many were exceedingly lenient with those who had purchased farms on credit, and permitted their mortgages to run on for years before resorting to eviction.

On the other hand, only too often we have the uninspiring spectacle of land-grabbing by the wholesale, by men who were unscrupulous enough to resort to fraud and influential enough to escape punishment. The soil should have gone to the people who settled upon it, the men who made the great venture of crossing the Atlantic, who braved the dangers and hardships of the frontier, who converted the wilderness into prosperous, civilized communities. But many of them had to pay tribute in the form of the purchase price or of rentals to some prominent man at Annapolis, or Williamsburg, or Charleston, who lived in luxury, in part at least, upon the revenues from his "western" lands.

There can be no doubt that the land policy of the Southern colonies was second only to the slave system in building up the aristocratic type of society. It was the vast landholdings of "King"

[79] *Ibid.*, p. 64.

Carter, rather than the culture of tobacco or his mercantile ventures, which made his descendants a power in Virginia for over a century. And it was this policy which went hand in hand with slavery to threaten the existence of the small farmers.

My friend, the late Lyon Gardiner Tyler, once remarked to me: "It is easy enough to kick a dead lion, but after all the Old South produced a splendid aristocracy, which gave the nation men of the stamp of Washington and Jefferson." There is much truth in this statement. Even though the aristocracy was based on an unsound economy and in some cases on actual fraud, there was much in it that was admirable as it reached its full development at the time of the Revolution. We know the planter aristocrats for what they were—for the most part kindly men whose chief delight was in their family circle, feeling deeply the weight of responsibility which their command of human beings imposed upon them, agriculturalists upon whose shoulders rested the burden of several large plantations, business men who must dispose of their crops to the best advantage and purchase supplies in large quantities, accomplished gentlemen who must be able to dance the latest steps and converse upon all topics of interest, men of education who could quote a passage from Ovid and who read Shakespeare and Milton, political leaders realizing their responsibility not only to their own group but to the small farmer and to the colony as well.

But there were many among them, of whom Jefferson was a notable example, who realized that this aristocracy was but the glittering apex of an unsound society. It was the small farmer, working hard upon his little farm for a meager living, competing with slave labor, enjoying few privileges of education and culture, looking to the upper class for political leadership; it was the poor white trash, ignorant, degraded, undernourished, taking refuge in the infertile uplands or the mountains; it was the artisan, the merchant, the professional man, relegated to a secondary if respected class by the landed aristocrats; it was the millions of black slaves upon whose shoulders rested the economic structure of the South; it was the total of these groups which outnumbered the privileged few fifty to one.

Perhaps the South would have been what it was even had it adopted an essentially democratic system of land distribution. In the end the vast Carter holdings were cut up into smaller and smaller plantations, and small freeholders followed the plow where formerly gangs of slaves worked at the command of the overseer. Yet it is obvious that Samuel Kercheval was right when he condemned in vigorous language "the profligate manner of granting away lands in immense bodies" as unwise and unjust. "Instead of promoting the speedy settlement and improvement of the country," he added, "instead of holding out to the bulk of society every possible encouragement to make the most speedy settlement and improvement in the new country, monopolies in several instances were given, or pretended to be sold, to a few favorites of the governing powers, whereby these favorites were enabled to amass vast estates, and to lord it over the great majority of their fellow men. Such are the blessings of kingly government. But the people of this free and happy republic have abundant cause to rejoice and bless their God that this wretched kind of policy and high-handed injustice is done away, in the freedom and wisdom of our institutions, and that we have no longer our ears assailed, nor our understanding outraged, with the disgusting, high-sounding title of 'My Lord' applied to poor frail human beings."[80]

[80]Samuel Kercheval, *History of the Valley of Virginia*, p. 158.

# CONCLUSION

THE average American thinks of the Old South as a unit. To him the region below the Mason and Dixon Line was a land of wealthy planters, who built stately mansions, tilled their broad acres with the labor of scores of slaves, lived luxuriously, took their religion lightly and looked down on their neighbors of the North as sanctimonious and hard-fisted. He gives the South full credit for the able group of men who contributed so much to winning independence and drawing up the Constitution, but blames the section for its unwillingness to abolish slavery and for secession and war.

Yet one cannot delve far into the history of the South without discovering that no part of the country was more complex, had a larger number of conflicting groups and interests. As we have seen, the region prior to the Revolution comprised at least five sections rather than one. To cross the border from the tobacco region to the back country on the one hand or to the pine belt on the other, brought changes not less startling than to pass from Maryland into Pennsylvania. The rice planter, the tar-burner, the tobacco planter, the Norfolk merchant, the German settler in the Valley of Virginia or western North Carolina, together constitute about as ill-assorted a group as one can find anywhere.

Nor was the South homogeneous in nationality. The tobacco and rice planters were English save for an occasional Huguenot or Scotch family, but the back country was a melting pot, where Germans, Scotch-Irish, English, Swiss, Scotch Highlanders and other racial groups rubbed elbows and slowly yielded their cultures and languages. Today one often speaks loosely of the Southern accent, but there are many different dialects in the South. At the University of Virginia, where the students came from all parts of the South in ante-bellum days, it was easy to identify the Charlestonian accent, the up-country South Carolina accent, the Alabama accent, the North Carolina accent.

348

In religion there was as great variety as in race and language. In Virginia, Maryland and South Carolina the Church of England was established by law, but it had to contend with Puritan, Roman Catholic, Presbyterian and other groups who protested against taxation by the vestries and sought complete freedom of worship. In the back country Lutherans, German Reformed, Dunkards and Quakers set up their meetinghouses side by side with Presbyterian and Episcopal churches, while all were shaken to their very foundations by the Baptist and Methodist revivals.

Even in agriculture there was little uniformity. The economy of the small tobacco planter differed from that of a Carter or a Byrd, for without a gang of slaves he himself was forced to work, hoe or plow in hand, in the fields; he lacked the advantage of plantation manufacture, his methods of marketing his crop were different. Agriculture in the back country, based as it was on German traditions, was more intensive, more efficient than in the tobacco region. The rice and indigo planters of eastern South Carolina had little in common with the farmers of the Piedmont. When we speak of the Southern planter we should specify the large tobacco planter, or the small tobacco planter, or the rice and indigo planter, or the back-country farmer.

The South is often regarded as a non-commercial section in which the occupation of the trader was avoided by the sons of real "gentlemen." Yet it would be hard to find abler or more successful merchants than Niel Jamieson, John Goodrich, or scores of others. We hear much of Westover, or Carter's Grove, or Drayton Hall and similar mansions, but the interesting Moravian buildings at Winston-Salem, the cottages of the Piedmont, the stone residences of the Valley of Virginia are usually ignored.

Why, then, if there were such wide divergencies in the South, is it proper to speak of it as a section, distinct from New England or the Middle Colonies? What did Southerners have in common to differentiate them from other Americans? Why did they unite in secession, in creating the Confederacy and in resisting the invasion of Union troops?

The chief unifying forces were agriculture and slavery. Despite the activities of the merchants of Charleston, Norfolk, Alexandria and Annapolis, the Carolinas, Virginia and Maryland were over-whelmingly agricultural. There was no fishing industry, no great shipbuilding interest, the artisan class was weakened by slave labor and English competition, the fur trade was of minor im-portance. The Southern countryside was one vast expanse of woods and plantations and farms with not a town worthy of the name, save for a few small mercantile cities hugging the coast or the shores of the great inland waters. Whatever differences there were between big and little planters, between wheat growers and rice growers, they were agriculturalists, jealous to protect their estates and their crops from hostile legislation either by the Brit-ish Parliament, or later by the United States Congress.

Southern agriculture differed from Northern agriculture, not only in its great staple crops such as tobacco, rice and cotton, for which its soil was especially suited, but in its farm economy, in which labor costs were kept down at the expense of the soil. South-ern agriculture in most regions was extensive, Northern agricul-ture intensive. Travellers in crossing the Mason and Dixon Line were struck with the contrast between the farms of the Quakers and Germans of Pennsylvania and the tobacco plantations of eastern Maryland. On the one side were huge barns, expanses of ripening wheat, fat horses and cattle, blooming orchards, excel-lent fences; on the other they saw fields reverting to forest, dilapi-dated fences and barns, gangs of slaves at work. It was as though there were two strangely contrasting worlds on either side of this imaginary line.

Even more than the soil, it was slavery which bound the South together and created a sense of brotherhood between South Caro-linians and Marylanders, or Virginians and Georgians. Slavery was stronger in some regions than in others, some planters owned scores of Negroes while some had but one or two, hundreds of thousands of white families had none at all. Yet the presence of the blacks influenced profoundly the life of every man, woman and child in the South, created a race aristocracy and a sense of the unity of all whites. When the North freed its slaves during or after the Revolution, slavery became a distinguishing mark of the South.

With the wearing out of the tobacco fields of eastern and Piedmont Virginia, Maryland and North Carolina, and the spread of intensive agriculture in the back country, it is possible that slavery might have lost its grip on the South had it not been for its extension into new territory and the discovery of new uses for it. But with the opening of the West for settlement, thousands of planters crossed the mountains to establish their slave economy in the fertile plains of Kentucky and Tennessee. Farther south the invention of the cotton gin, together with the cheapening of cloth manufacture in England, brought about a vast expansion of cotton growing and a new demand for slave labor. Soon the roads were dotted with groups of slaves making their way westward and southward to work in the newly opened fields, and slavery became fastened on the region so firmly that only a bloody war could uproot it.

But we must beware of interpreting the South of colonial and early national times in terms of the South of Calhoun and Jefferson Davis. True, the later South was the outgrowth of the earlier; its civilization was the development and expansion of the civilization which produced Washington, Jefferson, Madison and the Pinckneys. But had the wheel of fortune made a different turn, had there been no cotton gin, had Jefferson succeeded in keeping slavery out of the Ohio Valley, there probably would have been no "conflict irrepressible," no united South. The upper tier of Southern States might have thrown off slavery, expanded the intensive agriculture of the Valley of Virginia and western Maryland until the whole region was covered with little farms, and had opened mines, built factories and wiped out Mason and Dixon Line in so far as it separated two contrasting civilizations. The foundations of the New South of today, with its great industries, its rich fruit and trucking areas, its important mineral output, its growing middle class, were laid in colonial, not postwar days. That the structure was not completed a century ago is explained by the diversion of the builders to the enlargement of the structure of slave civilization, and with the collapse of that civilization in 1865, they had only to begin where their ancestors had left off.

The giant shipbuilding plants of Newport News and elsewhere are the legitimate heirs of makers of Baltimore clippers;
the Birmingham steel mills had their forerunners in Spotswood's
iron works and the furnaces of the Patapsco; the great apple and
peach orchards of Virginia and Georgia hark back to the private
orchards of a Byrd or Wormeley; the great Southern middle class
is but an outgrowth of the colonial yeoman and artisan; the men
who represent them in the State and national governments had
their forerunners in the colonial assemblies. The winning over
of hundreds of thousands of Southerners by the Methodist and
Baptist Churches, the giving of Southern society its Puritanical
tinge, occurred in the days of Asbury, not of Bishop Cannon.

If then we are to understand, not only the ante-bellum South,
with its aristocratic social structure, its wasteful agriculture, its
courtly gentlemen, its ignorant yeomen, its fine mansions, and crude
huts, but the New South of today, we must turn back to colonial
days. We must study the origins of the people who came to the
Southern colonies, the character of the civilizations they brought
with them, the influence of the South itself upon them, the way
one culture affected another, the emergence of new civilizations
in the fertile plains of Maryland, Virginia and the Carolinas and
in the great Appalachian region.

# INDEX

# INDEX

Adam brothers, influence of in South Carolina, 287, 291–292

Adam Thoroughgood House, typical Virginia cottage, 82

Agriculture, in tobacco region, 41–43; experiments in, 42–43; books on, 41, 45; in Piedmont, 125, 146–153; introduction of scientific, 150–152; of Scotch-Irish, 200; contrasts in, 349; chief occupation of South, 349–350

Albemarle County, Virginia, 14; transportation from costly, 135–136; peddling in, 139–140; artisans in, 140–141; religion in, 155

Allason, William, trade of, 145

Allen, Arthur, residence of, 85

Anburey, Thomas, criticizes Virginia roads, 134; describes home industry, 183; describes destruction of forests, 146; on migration to West, 148

Andros, Sir Edmund, policy on land frauds, 316

Anglican Church, established, 1; apathy in, 153–154; westward move weakens, 153–154; Great Awakening assails, 155–162

Annapolis, Md., 7; a center of culture, 46; the drama at, 60–62; influence of, 69; architecture of, 105; wood carving, 242; tanners, 252; saddlers, 254; hatters, 260; pottery at, 265; cabinetmaking in, 267–268

Apprentices, in South, 236

Architects, introduce Georgian architecture, 92–93; John Arris, 92; David Minitree, 92; William Buckland, 92; Henry Cary, 93; Henry Cary, Jr., 93; use English books, 104–105; James Wren, 108–110; Thomas Jefferson, 111–115; in South Carolina, 282–283

Architecture, in Back Country, German, 174–180; the log cabin, 174–175; Georgian influence on, 176; Swiss barns, 176–177; Wachovia, 177–180; of Scotch-Irish, 206–208; Michael Brown house, 208; Fort Defiance church, 208

Architecture, in Carolina Low Country, origins of, 271–274; riches from rice, 274–275; of pre-Georgian period, 275–280; use of wood, 276; tiles, 276; balconies, 276–277; Huguenot influence, 276–278; the Mathews house, 278; Medway, 279–280; Dutch influence, 280; Mulberry, 280; Middleburg, 280; Hanover, 280; Georgian period, 280–289; English architectural books, 282; Ezra Waite, 283; single type Georgian, 284–285; the double type Georgian, 285–289; Miles Brewton house, 285–286; John Edwards house, 286–287; Fenwick Hall, 287; Drayton Hall, 288; imported materials, 289; the Revolution, 289–290; new rice prosperity, 290–291; post-Revolutionary period, 290–293; Middleton-Pinckney house, 292–293; Judge King house, 293; Nathaniel Russell house, 293; classical period, 293–296; Robert Mills, 294; Fireproof building, 294; Ashley Hall, 295; William Ravenel house, 295; Roper house, 295; Market Hall, 296; early churches, 296–298; St. Andrew's, 297; St. James', 297; Strawberry Chapel, 297–298; Wren period, 298–300; St. Philip's, 298–299; St. Michael's, 299–300; classical churches, 300–301; wrought-iron work, 301–302

Architecture, in Tobacco Region, origins of, 71–72; 90, 116; early frame houses, 73–75; early houses of brick, 75; use of tile, 75; shingles, 76; first Virginia cottage, 76–80; early porches, 76; interior of Virginia cottage, 78; chimneys, 78–79; windows, 80–82; second type Virginia cottage, 80–82, 100; third Virginia cottage, 82–83; the Maryland cottage, 82–84; early manor houses, 84–86; early churches, 86–89; public buildings, 89–90; the Georgian period, 91–105; influence of books on, 92–93; the Wren Building, 93–94; the Capitol, 95–96; the Palace, 96–97; Raleigh Tavern, 99; Carter's Grove, 100, 102; Westover, 103–104; Georgian churches, 105–111; the classic period, 111–115; Capitol at Richmond, 112–113; Monticello, 114; University of Virginia, 114–115; Berry Hill, 115; forces molding, 116–117; invades back country, 215–216

Aristocracy, in Rice Region, forces creating, 275; influence of indigo on, 281–282; interest in architecture, 282; the second rice period, 290; influence of land policy on, 345–346

Aristocracy, of Tobacco Region, influences

355

which molded, 6, 29, 68–70; power of, 10, 22; intellectual life of, 19–70; origins of, 19–22; education of, 22–39; schools, 29–31; golden age of, 27–28; slavery, 28; interest in law, 34–35, 38–39; daily life of, 40–41; agriculture of, 41–43; reading of, 43–47; interest in architecture, 47–50, 93; gardens, 50–53; art, 53–57; music, 57–60; interest in theater, 60–62; religion, 62–64; medicine, 64–65; scientists among, 65–68; local conditions mold, 69–70; statescraft, 70; soil exhaustion, 119–120; extravagance of, 120; expansion westward, 119–121, 123–125; land policy, 345–346; description of, 346; unsoundness of, 346–347

Arris, John, Virginia architect, 92

Art, in planter region, 53–57; of Germans in South, 182–185

Artisans, 21; in Piedmont, 140–142; in Valley of Virginia, 171, 202–203; of tobacco and rice regions, 222–270; migration to America, 222–224; as indentured workers, 223–226; competition with England, 227–228; itinerant, 229; slave competition, 229–234, 239; rural life, 228–229; unorganized, 234–235; parades, 234–235; apprentices, 235–236; brickmaking and bricklaying, 236–238; carpenters, 238–241; woodcarvers, 241–242; sawyers, 243; house-painters, 242–243; shipwrights, 243–246; coopers, 246; blacksmiths, 246–248; founders, 248–249; pewterers, 249–250; silversmiths, 250–251; tanners, 251–252; shoemakers, 253–254; saddlers, 254; coachmakers, 255–256; wheelwrights, 256–257; spinners, 257–258; weavers, 258–259; fullers, 259; tailors, 259–260; hatters, 260–261; buckskin tailors, 261; barbers, 261–262; brewers and distillers, 262–263; chandlers, 263–264; snuff-makers, 264; gunsmiths, 264–265; watchmakers, 265; potters, 265–266; cabinetmakers, 266–268; papermakers, 268–269; importance of, 269–270; foreigners among, 269; factory system injures, 270

Ashley Hall, history and description of, 295

Aust, Gottfried, pottery of, 182–183

Back Country, 9, 14–15; political history of, 15; advance of Tuckahoes to, 164–168; settlement of by Cohees, 168–173; German civilization in, 174; German architecture in, 174–180; log cabins, 175; Swiss barns, 176–177; Wachovia, 177–180; German music, 180–181; German art, 182–185; German customs, 185–187; Pennsylvania German in, 188–191; slavery, 193–194; artisans of, 194–195;

Scotch-Irish in, 196–211; plantations, 214–217; land policy in Virginia and Maryland, 312–331; land policy in North Carolina, 331–339; land policy in South Carolina, 339–345.

Bacon, Nathaniel, Sr., 22; residence of, 84

Bacon, Thomas, landholdings of, 306–307

Bacon's Castle, 76; typical early Virginia manor house, 85

Baecher, A. W., pottery of, 184

Bagby, G. W., describes bateau navigation, 131–132; describes soil exhaustion, 148

Balconies, in Charleston, 276–277

Ball, Joseph, medical ideas of, 64; clothing of his slaves, 258

Baltimore, 11; cabinetmaking in, 267

Bannister, John, scientific work of, 67–68

Baptists, persecution of, 160–161; in back country, 210, 212–213

Barbadians, at Charleston, 2, 273–274

Barbecues, in Piedmont, 143

Barbers, in South, 261–262

Barns, Swiss, in back country, 176–177

Bassett, Burwell, residence of, 102

Bateau, on upper rivers, 131–132

Bell, Peter, Jr., pottery of, 183–184

Bell, Peter, Sr., pottery of, 183

Belvoir, probable model for Mt. Vernon, 50

Berkeley, Sir William, on education in Virginia, 25; experiments in silk, 43

Berry Hill, description of, 115, 124

Beverley, Robert, on Virginia schools, 25; interest in science, 68

Beverley, William, tract of in Valley, 166, 324; tenantry under, 324–325

Beverley Manor, 166; description of, 324

Binns, J. A., introduces gypsum, 150–151

Black Water Tract, land frauds in, 317

Blacksmiths, in Piedmont, 140–142; in back country, 194–195; of plantations, 230; work and tools of, 246–248

Blair, Rev. James, founds William and Mary, 26

Bond Castle, typical Maryland house, 83; description of, 86

Bookstores, in Annapolis and Williamsburg, 46; religious books in, 62–63

Brewers, in South, 262–263

Brewton House, description and history of, 285–286

Brick, used at Jamestown, 75; chimneys of, 78–79; in Flemish bond, 81; diaper work in Maryland, 84; made in South, 237–238; imported, 236–237; use of in Charleston, 276

Bricklayers, in South, 238–239

Brickmakers, in Piedmont, 141; in South, 236–238

Bridges, Charles, paints Virginians, 54–55

Brown, Michael, House, description of, 208

Bruce, J. M. C., builds Berry Hill, 124

Bruce, P. A., on origins of Virginia aristocracy, 19
Buckland, William, Annapolis architect, 104–105
Bucktrout, Benjamin, Williamsburg cabinetmaker, 266
Bullitschek, Joseph, Wachovia organmaker, 180–181
Burrington, Governor George, land frauds of, 333–334
Burwell, Lewis, 22; manor house of, 86
Burwell, Nathaniel, plantation of, 214
Bruton Church, Michel describes, 88–89; the second building, 106–107; history of, 107
Buckskin tailors, need for, 261
Byrd, William I, uses pantiles, 75; writes for tailor, 259
Byrd, William II, educated in Europe, 26; imitates English gentry, 28–29; love of classics, 36–37; library of, 39, 44, 48; garden of, 51–52; paintings of, 54–55; interest in science, 66–67; river transportation, 118; land policy of, 326–327

Cabell, M. F., on wasteful farming, 147
Cabinetmakers, in Piedmont, 141; in back country, 194–195; work of, 225–226, 266, 268; Benjamin Bucktrout, 266; John Shaw, 266–268; Josiah Claypoole, 266–267; tools of, 268
Callister, Henry, on origins of Maryland aristocracy, 19; criticizes music in Maryland, 57; musical interest of, 60; as a scientist, 68
Canal boats, use of in South, 132–133
Canoe (see Pettiauger), tobacco carried in, 128–131; use of in Revolution, 131
Capitol, Richmond, description of, 112–113
Capitol, Williamsburg, 35; description of, 95–96; historic events in, 95–96
Carpenters, in Piedmont, 141; in back country, 195; plantation, 230; in South, 238–241; slaves as, 239; tools of, 240–241
Carter, Robert (King Carter), 22; builds Christ Church, Lancaster, 108; acquires vast holdings, 319–320
Carter, Robert, of Nomini, 22; intellectual interests of, 40; library of, 44–47; garden, 52; devoted to music, 59; medical books of, 64–65; cloth factory of, 258–259; tenants, 325–326
Carter Hall, description of, 215
Carter's Grove, 48; a Renaissance building, 100; description of, 100–102
Cary, Henry, Virginia architect, 93; builds Capitol at Williamsburg, 95
Cary, Henry, Jr., Virginia architect, 93
Castle, The, description of, 77

Catholics, Roman, in back country, 196–197, 199
Chandlers, slaves as, 231; numerous in South, 263–264
Charleston, South Carolina, 1, 4, 8, 11, 14; immigrants, 2; use of bricks in, 236–238; wages in, 238; wood carvers, 242; house painters, 242–243; sawyers, 243; shipbuilding, 243–244; founders, 249; silversmiths, 250–251; shoemakers, 253; saddlers, 254; coachmakers, 256; wheelwrights, 256; tailors, 260; hatters, 260–261; barbers, 261–262; brewers, 263; distillery, 262–263; chandlers, 263–264; gunsmiths, 265; cabinetmaking, 267; origins of people, 271–274; history of, 272–273; riches from rice, 274–275; early architecture, 275–280; wooden houses, 276; tiles, 276; balconies, 276–277; Huguenot influence, 276–278; Mathews house, 278; Georgian architecture, 280–289; indigo, 281; architectural books, 282; Ezra Waite, 283; single type Georgian, 284–285; Miles Brewton house, 285–286; John Edwards house, 286–287; the Revolution, 289–290; post-Revolutionary architecture, 290–293; Middleton-Pinckney house, 292–293; Judge King house, 293; Nathaniel Russell house, 293; classic architecture, 293–296; Robert Mills, 294; Fireproof building, 294; Ashley Hall, 295; William Ravenel house, 295; Roper house, 295; Market Hall, 296; St. Philip's, 298–299; St. Michael's, 299–300; classic churches, 300–301; wrought-iron work, 301–302; forces shaping architecture, 302–304
Charlottesville, Virginia, artisans in, 141
Chimneys, in tobacco region, 78–79; in early Maryland, 83–84
Christ Church, Alexandria, described, 110–111
Christ Church, Lancaster County, Virginia, described, 108
Christ's Cross, a typical Virginia cottage, 78
Churches, early in tobacco region, 86–89; at Jamestown, 87–88; St. Luke's, 88; early Bruton, 88–89; Yeocomico, 89; later in tobacco region, 105–111; Wren ignored in tobacco region, 106; Bruton, 106–107; the Virginia Georgian, 107–111; Christ Church, Lancaster County, 108; Pohick, 108–110; Christ Church, Alexandria, 110–111; stone used in, 111; in Wachovia, 178, 180; in Charleston region, 296–301
Classic Architecture, in Virginia, 111–115; Capitol at Richmond, 112–113; Monticello, 114; University of Virginia, 114–115; Berry Hill, 115; precedes revival in Europe, 117

Classics, in English schools, 23; in tobacco region, 24–25, 30–31, 33, 35–38, 44–45
Claypoole, Josiah, Charleston cabinetmaker, 267
Clayton, John, scientific work of, 66
Clockmakers (see Watchmakers)
Coachmakers, in Piedmont, 140–142; in back country, 195; in tobacco and rice regions, 255–256
Cohees, settle back country, 168–173; clash of with Tuckahoes, 168–169, 210–211; Paulding describes, 210–211; dislike Tuckahoes, 217–218; influence of back country on, 218–219
Collinson, Peter, sends seed to Virginia, 42; praises Westover garden, 52
Cooper, Dr. Thomas, landgrabbers persecute, 341
Coopers, in Piedmont, 141; of plantations, 230; in South, 245–246; tools of, 246
Costumes, of Germans, 186–187; of Scotch-Irish, 206
Couper, William, on opportunities of artisans, 223; on price of snuff, 264
Crouch, Henry, Annapolis wood carver, 242
Custis, Daniel Parke, library of, 41; medical books of, 65

Dancing, in Piedmont, 142–143
Davies, Samuel, leads Great Awakening in Piedmont, 158–159
Davis, "German," itinerant cabinetmaker, 229
Digges, Edward, experiments with silkworm, 43
Distilling, of Scotch-Irish, 202; plantation, 231; in Southern cities, 262–263
Dobbs, Governor Arthur, squatters defy, 337
Drayton Hall, history and description of, 288
Dulaney, Daniel, at Cambridge, 32; land policy of, 325
Dulaney, Lloyd, scientific interests of, 68
Dutch, at Charleston, 2, 274; influence on architecture, 275; 277–278, 280

East Anglia, influences Virginia architecture, 80
Eaton, Thomas, school of, 25
Eaton Hall, 29; garden of, 51; influence on Palace, 96–97
Eddis, William, praises colonial stage, 62
Education, of tobacco planters, 22–39; difficulties of, 24–27; schools, 24–25, 29–31; tutors, 24, 31–32; classics, 24–25, 30–31; colleges, 26–27; law, at William and Mary, 34–35; planters grounded in law, 38–39; in back country, 209–210
Edwards House, history and description of, 286, 287

Eltham, description of, 102
England, cultural influence on colonists, 9; diverseness of architecture, 71; "palisaded" houses in, 71–72; competition of with Southern artisans, 227–228; building materials from, 289; land holding in, 306–307
English Literature, in tobacco region, 43–47
Engravings, in tobacco region, 56–57
Everard, Governor Richard, land policy of, 333

Fauquier, Francis, influence on Jefferson, 34; musical interests of, 59; will of, 65; has copy of Palladio, 112
Feilde, F., scientific work of, 68
Fenwick Hall, description and history of, 287
Fireproof Building, Mills describes, 294
First Baptist Church, Charleston, Mills describes, 301
Fithian, Philip V., describes planter life, 40; on planters' libraries, 45, 47; on music at Nomini Hall, 59; criticizes worship in Virginia, 63–64; on Sunday observance, 154; log houses, 175; visits Scotch-Irish communities, 198–199; on Scotch-Irish weaving, 201; on Scotch-Irish music, 205; Scotch-Irish food, 205–206; Scotch-Irish costumes, 206
Fitzhugh, William, employs tutor, 24; buys books, 44; building methods of, 86; land policy, 322–323
Fontaine, Rev. James, describes double canoe, 130
Foote, W. H., on Piedmont independence, 163
Forests, wantonly destroyed, 5, 146
Fort Defiance Church, description of, 208
Founders, Brass and Copper, in South, 249
Founders, Iron, work of in South, 248–249
Fountain Rock, described, 216
Frauds, in land grants, 312–322, 332–334, 340–342
Frederick, Maryland, 14; German newspapers at, 188–189
Frederick County, Maryland, Tuckahoes in, 167; Germans in, 170–171
Fristoe, Daniel, on Baptist revivals, 160–161
Frontier, influence of, 6–7; slow advance of, 118–119; expansion into Piedmont, 119–123; life on, 123–125; effect on religion, 153–155
Fry, Joshua, plantation of, 122
Fulling, in South, 259
Funk, Joseph, founds Singers' Glen, 181

Gambrel, the, in Virginia and Maryland, 82–83; in early Maryland, 83
Gardens, of tobacco region, 50–53; of Gov-

ernor's Palace, 51; at Westover, 51–52; at Mt. Vernon, 53

Gavin, Rev. Anthony, Anglican frontier minister, 154

Gentry, of England, planters claim descent from, 19–20; education of, 22–23; golden age of, 28; influence on planters, 28–29

Georgian Architecture, Dutch influence, 91; in tobacco region, 91–105; in Virginia and Maryland, 104–105; the Annapolis school, 105; in South Carolina, 280–289; single type house, 283–285; Charleston double house, 285–289

Germans, resist melting pot, 3; introduce log houses, 73; settle Southern back country, 168–173; in Maryland, 170–171; in Virginia, 171–172; in North Carolina, 172–173; architecture of in South, 174–180; music of, 180–181; art of, 182–185; customs of, 185–187; costumes, 186–187; thrift of, 187, 192–193; weddings of, 187; ignore politics, 187–188; household economy of, 192; few use slaves, 193–194; artisans, 194–195; names Anglicized, 213

Glaziers, in South, 243

Glover House, description of, 288–289

Graceham, founding of, 170; music in, 180–181; artisans of, 195

Granville, Lord, proprietary rights of, 333

Great Awakening, in Virginia, 155–162

Guilds, importance of in England, 220–221; organization of, 221–222; none in South, 234–235

Gunsmiths, in Piedmont, 142; in back country, 194–195; repairing by, 264–265

Habeas Corpus, suspended in South Carolina, 341–342

Hagerstown, Maryland, a log-house town, 175; Catholic Church at, 199

Half-timbering, in tobacco region, 73–75; in Wachovia, 178

Hallam, Lewis, in Virginia and Maryland, 61–62

Hallam, Sarah, a favorite at Williamsburg, 61

Hammond, John, on early Virginia cottage, 80

Hammond House, described, 105

Hanna, C. A., on origins of Scotch-Irish, 196

Hanover, description of, 280

Hanover County, Virginia, religious revival in, 156–159

Hatters, in Piedmont, 141; handicapped in South, 260–261

Henkel, Paul, deplores disuse of German, 190

Henrico, Virginia, houses of, 73, 75

Henry, Rev. Patrick, derides revivalists, 157

Highlanders, defeated at King's Mountain, 2

Hill, Colonel Edward, building methods of, 48

Hite, Jorst, brings settlers to Valley, 171

Hodge, Charles, describes Valley Germans, 171

Hogsheads, rolling of, 126–128; canoe transport of, 128–131

Hook, John, Piedmont trade of, 145–146

Huguenots, at Charleston, 2, 274; influence on architecture, 276–278, 280; Fitzhugh desires as tenants, 322–323

Hunter, Robert, describes life in Virginia, 47

Indentured workers, inadequate, 5, 22; artisans among, 223–226, 259; and land system, 307–309

Indigo, restores prosperity in South Carolina, 281

Inns of Court, Americans at, 38–39

Irish, in back country, 196–197, 199

Itinerant artisans, work of, 229

James River, navigation of, 7–8, 146, 165; double canoe on, 128–131; the bateau on, 131–132; channel improved, 131; the canal boat, 132–133

Jamestown, first Assembly, 1; no log houses in, 71–72; first houses, 73; frame houses, 72–73; brick houses, 75; first churches, 87–88; State House at, 89–90; pewterer of, 249–250; pottery at, 266

Jamieson, Neil, mercantile interests of, 16, 145

Jarratt, Rev. Devereux, evangelical work of, 161–162; his congregation turns Methodist, 162

Jefferson, Peter, plantation management of, 329

Jefferson, Thomas, on school education, 30; at William and Mary, 34; love of classics, 37–38; musical interests of, 59; religious views, 63; at Carter's Grove, 102; architectural work, 111–115; dislikes the Georgian, 111–112; designs Capitol at Richmond, 112–113; designs various residences, 113–114; Monticello, 114; University of Virginia, 114–115; at launching of first bateau, 131; on Virginia roads, 134; blacksmith shop of, 137; describes Piedmont farming, 147; on soil erosion, 148; contour plowing, 150; crop rotation, 151–152; champions religious freedom, 162–163

Johnson, Governor Robert, land policy of, 340; establishes townships, 342–343

Johnston, Governor Gabriel, land grants of, 334

Joiners, in South, 238–241; work and tools of, 240–241

Jones, Hugh, on Virginia dialect, 68, 69;

on Virginia cottage, 81, 91; says Wren designed College, 93–94
Justi, wrought iron work of, 302

Kemp, Richard, house of, 75
Kentucky, tobacco civilization in, 17–18; migration to, 148–149
Kercheval, Samuel, describes German stoves, 185
King House, history and description of, 293
King's Mountain, battle of, 2
Kneller, Sir Godfrey, paints Americans, 54

Land, as motive for immigration, 305; system in England, 306–307; freedmen acquire, 307–309; in Virginia and Maryland, 312–331; an American feudal system, 309–311; abuses in Virginia, 311–322; seating laws abused, 319; quit rents, 313–318; Sir Francis Nicholson, 315–318; Edward Randolph reports on, 315–316; Alexander Spotswood, 318–319; the Northern Neck, 319–320; "King Carter," 319–320; Maryland warrants, 320–322; William Fitzhugh, 322–323; backwoods manors, 323–328; Manor of Leeds, 323–324; William Beverley, 324–325; Councillor Carter, 325–326, 328–329; William Byrd II, 326–327; in the West, 327–328; the multiple plantation system, 328–330; small freeholders, 330–331; in North Carolina, 331–339; frauds, 332–334; Lord Granville, 333; the McCulloh grant, 334–338; disorders, 337–338; in South Carolina, 339–345; Locke's Constitutions, 339–340; fraudulent grants, 340–342; Habeas Corpus suspended, 341–342; townships, 342–345; creates aristocracy, 345–347
Land Warrants, abuses of in Maryland, 320–322
Languages, Modern, merchants use, 23; in tobacco region, 30
La Rochefoucauld-Liancourt, on Valley Germans, 171–172; describes Valley plantations, 214
Laurens, Henry, mercantile interests of, 16
Lee, Governor T. S., plantation of, 167
Leeds, Manor of, description of, 323–324
Lely, Sir Peter, paints Americans, 54
Levingston, William, builds first American theater, 60
Libraries, law books in, 38–39; books on agriculture, 41; of tobacco region, 43–47; classics in, 44; Councillor Carter's, 44–46; Robert Beverley's, 45; "King" Carter's, 45; circulating, 46; English literature in, 45–47
Lineman, J. C., on origins of Scotch-Irish, 196
Littleton, Southey, residence of, 85

Locke's Constitutions, influence on land-holding, 339–340
Log cabin, not known in early Virginia, 72; introduced by Germans, 73; in back country, 174–175; in Wachovia, 177–178; Scotch-Irish build, 207–208
Log College, influence on back country, 209–210
London Company, sends seeds to Virginia, 43; guilds help finance, 220–221; land system of, 307–309
Looms, in Piedmont, 138–139; in back country, 194–195, 200–201; slaves use, 231, 233; of Councillor Carter, 258–259
Lossing, Benson J., complains of Virginia roads, 134
Loudoun County, scientific farming in, 150–151
Lucas, Jonathan, rice mill of, 290
Ludwell, Philip, secures land by fraud, 313
Lynchburg, river trade of, 131–132
Lynnhaven Church, plan of, 89

McCulloh, H. E., squatters use violence against, 336–338; lands of confiscated, 338
McCulloh, Henry, huge land grant to, 335–336
Madison, Bishop James, career of, 33–34, 36
Madison, President James, blacksmith shop of, 139; dance at house of, 143
Manigault, Gabriel, Charleston architect, 291, 303
Manors, in England, 306–307, 309; early feudal in Maryland, 309–311; later in Virginia and Maryland, 323–328
Mason, George, pew of in Pohick, 110; plantation industry of, 230–231
Mathews House, Charleston, description of, 278
Mecklenburg County, North Carolina, Scotch-Highlanders in, 2
Medicine, in tobacco region, 64–65
Medway, description of, 279
Melting pot, active in South, 3; in back country, 14–15, 218–219; in West, 17
Mennonites, 16; forbid slavery, 193
Mercantile region, 9; character of, 11–12; political history of, 12
Merchants, education of, 23; use of roads by, 134; in Piedmont, 144–146; in back country, 202–204; of Charleston, 279; able in South, 349
Middleburg, description of, 280
Middleton-Pinckney House, history and description of, 292–293
Middletown, Virginia, clockmakers of, 195
Methodist Church, 161–162; in back country, 210, 212–213
Michel, Francis Louis, describes Virginia churches, 87–89

Mills, grist, in Piedmont, 140; at Richmond, 152

Mills, Robert, influences Charleston architecture, 294, 301

Minitree, David, designs Carter's Grove, 92

Mitchell, John, scientific work of, 67

Monticello, 48, 114; blacksmith's shop at, 137

Moravians, journey of to North Carolina, 169–170; found Graceham, 170; found Wachovia, 172; forbid slavery, 193; artisans, 195

Mt. Airy, garden of, 52; paintings at, 54

Mt. Vernon, Washington reconstructs, 49–50; garden, 53

Music, in tobacco region, 57–60; for dances, 58; in Anglican churches, 59; of Southern Germans, 180–181; of Scotch-Irish, 205

Naval Stores, output of in South, 12–13

New South, outgrowth of Old South, 16; 351–352

Newspapers, German, influence of, 188–189

Nicholson, Sir Francis, founds Williamsburg, 94; prosecutes for land frauds, 315–318

Nomini Hall, life at, 40; music at, 59

Norfolk, Scotch in, 1; artisans parade, 234–235; shipwrights in, 244–245; distillery at, 262; chandlers of, 264

Northern Neck, land policy in, 319–320

Ogle, Cuthbert, musical library of, 57; gives music lessons, 58

Orange Courthouse, barbecue at, 143

Page, Governor John, on Virginia schools, 31; criticizes English universities, 32; interest in science, 66, 68

Painters, house, in South, 242–243

Palace, Governor's, Williamsburg, description of, 96–97; history of, 97

Paper-making, Revolution stimulates, 268–269

Parks, William, sells religious books, 62–63

Patuxent River, fulling mill on, 259

Paulding, J. K., describes German farmers, 186; contrasts Tuckahoes and Cohees, 217–218

Peale, C. W., career of, 55–56; paints Sarah Hallam, 61

Peddlers, in Piedmont, 139–140

Pelham, Peter, organist at Williamsburg, 58–59

Pennsylvania-German dialect, persistence of, 3; in Maryland, 170–171, 173; in back country, 188–191; newspapers, 188–189; preaching in, 189–190; succumbs to English, 189–191

Pennsylvania Germans, in South Carolina, 2; settle in back country, 168–173; in Maryland, 170–171; in Virginia, 171–172; in North Carolina, 172–173; civilization of, 173–174

Persecution, of Baptists, 160–161

Pettiaugers, use of in rice region, 278–279

Pewterers, scarcity of in South, 249; Joseph Copeland, 250

Philosophical Society, at Williamsburg, 66

Piedmont, transportation in, 6–8, 126–136; development of, 118–163; isolation of, 136–137; duplicates tidewater, 136; home industry in, 137–139; peddlers, 139–140; artisans, 140–142; social life, 142–144; hunting, 143; merchants, 144–146; agriculture, 146–153; soil exhaustion, 146–148; religion, 153–163; the Great Awakening, 153–163

Pinckney, Thomas, house of, 292–293

Pine Belt, character of, 12–13

Plantations, shape planter's life, 6, 39; manufacture on, 21; "quarters," 122–123; in Piedmont, 121–123; home industry in Piedmont, 137–139; in back country, 214–217; slave artisans on, 230–231; carpenters, 239; sawyers, 243; coopers, 296; blacksmiths, 247–248; tanners, 251–252; shoemakers, 253–254; wheelwrights, 257; spinners, 257–258; weavers, 258–259; clothing, 259; brewers, 202; distillers, 262–263; chandlers, 263; buildings on in South Carolina, 289; multiple system of, 328–329; of Councillor Carter, 328–329; Peter Jefferson's management of, 329; limitations of, 329–330

Pohick Church, description of, 108–110

Pompion Hill Chapel, description of, 300

Porches, in early Virginia and Maryland, 76, 80; reasons for discarding, 81; in Maryland, 83; of Bacon's Castle, 85

Portico, in Charleston, 284–285

Porter, Edmund, exposes land frauds, 333–334

Potomac River, navigation of, 204

Potters, Germans in South, 180–185; few in tidewater region, 265–266

Presbyterian Church, in Piedmont, 156–159; in back country, 197, 208, 210, 212–213; in Ulster, 198

Princeton College, influence on back country, 209–210

Quitrents, frauds in, 313–318

Raleigh Tavern, description and history of, 99–100

Randolph, Edward, exposes land frauds, 313, 315–316

Ravenel House, description and history of, 295

Revolution, The, brings ruin to Charleston region, 289–290

Rice, creates Carolina aristocracy, 274–275; the rice region, 278–279; tides in cultivation of, 290

Richmond, port of upper James, 128, 130, 135; grist mills, 152

Rind, William, circulating library of, 46

Ringgold, General Samuel, mansion of, 215–216

Rivanna River, navigation of, 135; mills on, 140

Rivers, transportation on, 7–8, 203–204; aid settlement, 7–8; influence life in South, 8; highways of commerce, 118; rafts on, 128; navigation of with canoes, 128–131; the bateau on, 131–132; the canal boat, 132–133; of Valley of Virginia, 165

Roads, rolling, 126–128; for wagons, 133–134; in back country, 203–204

Roanoke River, navigation of, 132, 135

Robinson, John, career of, 201–202

Robinson, Reverend William, preaches at Hanover, 156–157

Rocky Ridge, port of upper James, 128, 130

Rolling Roads, use of, 126–128

Roper House, description of, 295

Rose, John, influences Virginia gardens, 51

Rose, Reverend Robert, migrates to Piedmont, 121–123; originates the double canoe, 128–130, wilderness circuit of, 154–155

Rosegill, description of, 84–85

Rucker, Anthony, designs river bateau, 131

Russell House, description of, 292–293

Russworm, Francis, gives music lessons, 58


Saddlers, in Piedmont, 140–142; in back country, 194–195; work of in South, 254–255

St. Andrew's, description of, 296–297

St. Clement's Manor, feudal customs in, 310–311

St. James's, Goose Creek, description of, 297

St. John, James, landgrabbers assail, 341–342

St. Luke's, Smithfield, Virginia, a survival of the Gothic, 88

St. Mary's County, Maryland, architecture of, 83–84

St. Michael's, Charleston, description of, 299–300

St. Philip's, Charleston, description and history of, 298–299

Salem, North Carolina, German architecture in, 177–178, 349; pottery of, 182–183

Sawmills, in early Virginia, 74–75

Sawyers, many in South, 243

Schools, in tobacco region, 24–25, 29–31;

English, 24, 26–27; American imitate English, 29–30; subjects taught, 30–31

Schöpf, J. D., describes home industries, 139

Science, books on, 43; in tobacco region, 65–68

Scotch, at Charleston, 2, 274; many become Southern merchants, 11–12; tutors in tobacco region, 31–32

Scotch-Irish, 4, 14; at King's Mountain, 2; in South Carolina, 2; resist melting pot, 3; move west, 17–18; settle back country, 168–169; origins of, 196–198; migration to America, 197–198; agriculture of, 200; weaving, 200–201; slavery, 201; distilling, 202; merchants, 202–204; customs, 204–206; dialect, 204–205; music, 205; food, 205–206; clothing, 206; architecture, 206–208; religion, 208–210; education, 209–210; Civil War divides, 210–211; settle Beverley Manor, 324

Scotch-Irish Dialect, 17; in back country, 204–205

Shaw, John, Annapolis cabinetmaker, 267–268

Shenandoah River, transportation on, 165, 204

Shenandoah Valley (see Valley of Virginia)

Shingles, in tobacco region, 76; German, 176

Shipbuilding, in South, 244–245

Shipwrights, slaves as, 233–234; in South, 243–246

Shoemakers, in Piedmont, 140–142; in back country, 194–195; on plantations, 231, 253–254; tools, 254

Silversmiths, work of in South, 250–251

Slavery, importance of in South, 5, 21–22; evils recognized, 28; accelerates westward move, 120–121, 165; expands to Piedmont, 122–123; Southern Germans oppose, 193–194; Scotch-Irish adopt, 201; of back country Tuckahoes, 215–217; competition of with artisans, 229–230, 239; undermines feudal manors, 311; unifies whites, 350; extension of, 351

Slaves, as artisans, 138, 229–234, 239; artisans hired out, 231–232; competition with white artisans, 229–234, 239; as shipwrights, 233–234; carpenters, 239; painters, 243; coopers, 246; saddlers, 254; wheelwrights, 256–257; spinners and weavers, 257–259; clothing of, 259; chandlers, 264

Small, Dr. William, influence on Jefferson, 34; interest in science, 68

Smyth, J. F. D., arrested in Maryland, 171

Snuff, made in South, 264

Social life, of tobacco aristocracy, 40–41; in Piedmont, 142–144; of Germans, 185–187; of Scotch-Irish, 204–206

Soil Erosion, in Piedmont, 148

# INDEX

Soil Exhaustion, 330; causes of, 5; and settlement of west, 18, 119–121; in Piedmont, 146–148

Spinners, on plantations, 253, 258

Spotswood, Alexander, designs Bruton Church, 106; expedition to Valley of Virginia, 164; tries to stop landgrabbing, 318; becomes landgrabber, 318–319

Spotsylvania County, slavery in, 124–125

State House, at Jamestown described, 89–90; burns, 94

Stegg, Charles, and Williamsburg's theater, 60

Stephensburg, Virginia, wagon-makers of, 195

Stoves, German, in back country, 185

Strasburg, potteries of, 195

Stratford, garden restored, 52–53

Strawberry Chapel, description of, 297–298

"Sugar Creek War," described, 337–338

Swiss, 1, 4, 14; in South Carolina, 2; resist melting pot, 3; settle Southern back country, 169–173

Symes, Benjamin, school of, 25

Tailors, in Piedmont, 140–142; in back country, 195; numerous in South, 259–260

Tanners, in Piedmont, 140–142; in back country, 195; on plantation, 230; work of in South, 251–252

Tatham, William, describes hogshead rolling, 127; on canoes, 128–131; on the bateau, 131–132

Taylor, Colonel Francis, building methods of, 49; home industries of, 138–139; takes dancing lessons, 142–143

Tenantry, in Virginia and Maryland, 320–328

Tennent, John, medical researches of, 65

Tiles, in tobacco region, 75; use of by Germans, 178–179; use of in Charleston, 276

Tobacco, becomes staple crop, 3; cultivation of, 10; culture of in Piedmont, 121–123, 146–149; transportation of in Piedmont, 126–136; hogshead rolling, 126–128; transportation in canoes, 128–131; the bateau, 131–132; canal boats, 132–133; decline of cultivation, 149; in back country, 215–216

Tobacco Region, character of, 9–10; intellectual life, 19–70; aristocracy in, 19–70; education, 22–39; schools, 24–25, 29–31; golden age of, 27–28; slavery, 28; molding influences, 6, 29, 68; interest in law, 34–35, 38–39; daily life, 40–41; agriculture, 41–43; reading, 43–47; gardens, 50–53; art, 53–57; music, 57–60; theater, 60–62; interest in religion, 62–64; medicine, 64–65; science, 65–68; influence of Williamsburg and Annapolis on,

69; local conditions, 69–70; statescraft, 70; architecture, 47–50, 71–117; log cabin myth in, 72–73

Toulmin, Reverend Harry, on Valley artisans, 194–195

Townships, in South Carolina, failure of, 4; land policy in, 342, 345; hardships in, 343–344

Transportation, in Piedmont, 6, 118–119, 126–136; waterways aid, 7; hogshead rolling, 126–128; the double canoe, 128–131; the bateau, 131–132; the canal boat, 132–133; on frontier, 169–170; in back country, 203–204

Tuckahoes, westward advance of, 164–168; 211–212; clash of with Cohees, 168–169, 210–211; in back country, 211–218; dialect of, 212; despise Cohees, 217–218

Tutors, in tobacco region, 24, 31–32

Tye River, Rose's plantation at, 121–123

Ulster, Scotch-Irish, 196–198; industries of, 197–198

Universities, English, Americans at, 26–27, 32

Valley of Virginia, log houses in, 73; Spotswood explores, 164; settlement in by Tuckahoes, 165–168; rivers in, 165; rich soil of, 165–166; German houses in, 174–179; German music, 181; Singers' Glen, a center of German music, 181; potters of, 183–185; German customs, 185–188; German newspapers, 188; slavery, 193–194; German artisans, 194–195; Scotch-Irish, 198–211; plantations in, 214–215

Virginia, University of, Jefferson designs, 114–115

Virginia Cottages, origin of, 3, 80; first type of, 73–80; second type of, 80–82

Virginia Dialect, origin of, 3

Wachovia, Moravians found, 172; architecture of, 177–180; music in, 180–181; pottery in, 182–183; decline of German at, 189–190; artisans of, 182–183, 195

Wages, of bricklayers, 238; of carpenters, 239

Waite, Ezra, artistic carving of, 283

Warner, Augustine, son in English school, 24

Washington, George, library of, 44, 48; reconstructs Mt. Vernon, 49–50; creates his garden, 53; Peale's portraits of, 56; engravings of, 56–57; attends theater, 61; visits Eltham, 102; vestryman of Pohick, 108–109; pew of in Pohick, 110; on richness of Valley soil, 166; in Valley, 214; spinners and weavers of, 257–258

Watchmakers, work of in South, 265

Waterways, influence on South, 7

363

Wayland, J. W., on German aversion to politics, 188; on German economy, 192

Weavers, in Piedmont, 138–139; in back country, 194–195, 200–201; Scotch-Irish, 200–201; slaves as, 231, 233; Revolution favors, 258; of Councillor Carter, 258–259

Webber, William, persecution of, 160

Weld, Isaac, contrasts Tuckahoe and Cohee agriculture, 215

West, influence of Old South upon, 17–18

West Indies, influence on Charleston, 2, 273–274, 277

Westover, paintings at, 54; description and history of, 103–104

Wheat, culture of in Piedmont, 148–153

Wheelwrights, in Piedmont, 141–142; on plantations, 256–257; make spinning wheels, 258

Whitefield, George, preaches at Williamsburg, 155–156; at Hanover, 157

Wig-makers (see Barbers)

William and Mary College, founding of, 26–27, 32; educational system, 32–36; Jefferson at, 34; law school, 34–35; skepticism at, 35–36; Wren Building, 94

Williamsburg, South Carolina, settlement of, 2

Williamsburg, Virginia, a center of culture, 46; music, 57–60; the drama, 60–61; philosophical society at, 66; influence of, 69; sash windows, 79; founding, 94; the Capitol, 95–96; the Palace, 96–97; restoration, 97–98; Raleigh Tavern, 99; cottages, 100; Bruton Church, 106–107; Whitefield at, 155; silversmiths, 250–251; shoemakers, 253; coachmakers, 255–256; weavers, 258; tailors, 260; breweries, 263; chandlers, 264; snuff made in, 264; gunsmith, 265; cabinetmaking, 266

Winchester, Virginia, pottery at, 183–184; artisans, 194–195; Catholic Church at, 199

Winston-Salem, German architecture in, 177–180

Wollaston, John, itinerant painter, 55

Woodcarvers, in South, 241–242; Henry Crouch, 242; Ezra Waite, 283

Woodstock, Virginia, Germans in, 171

Woodward, Henry, introduces rice culture, 274

Wormeley, Ralph, at Cambridge, 32; residence of, 84–85

Wren, Sir Christopher, perfects Renaissance architecture, 91; designs William and Mary, 26, 93–94; influence of in Charleston, 298–300

Wren, James, designs Pohick, 108–109; designs Christ Church, Alexandria, 110

Wright, Robert, landgrabbers assail, 342

Wrought Iron Work, in Charleston, 301–302

Wythe, George, opens law school, 34–35, 36

Yeocomico Church, description of, 89

Yeomanry, history of, 10–11; fear aristocracy, 21; westward expansion of, 121–123, 166–167; influence of back country on, 213–214; immigration and, 305; recruited from freedmen, 307–309; avoid manors, 322–323; extent of, 330–331; in Valley, 331; defy landgrabbers in North Carolina, 337–339

Young, Arthur, visits Ulster, 197